尾田栄一郎

Would you believe it?! This T-shirt has the yellowness of 300 lemons!! Volume 84 is about to begin!!

–Eiichiro Oda, 2017

iichiro Oda began his manga career at the age of 17, when his one-shot cowboy manga **Wanted!** won second place in the coveted Tezuka manga awards. Oda went on to work as an assistant to some of the biggest manga artists in the industry, including Nobuhiro Watsuki, before winning the Hop Step Award for new artists. His pirate adventure **One Piece**, which debuted in **Weekly Shonen Jump** in 1997, quickly became one of the most popular manga in Japan.

ONE PIECE VOL. 84
NEW WORLD PART 24

SHONEN JUMP Manga Edition

STORY AND ART BY EIICHIRO ODA

Translation/Stephen Paul
Touch-up Art & Lettering/Vanessa Satone
Design/Yukiko Whitley
Editor/Alexis Kirsch

Printed in the U.S.A.

Published by VIZ Media, LLC
P.O. Box 77010
San Francisco, CA 94107

10 9 8 7 6 5 4 3 2 1
First printing, November 2017

www.viz.com

RATED T FOR TEEN

PARENTAL ADVISORY
ONE PIECE is rated T for Teen and is recommended for ages 13 and up. This volume contains fantasy violence and tobacco usage.

ratings.viz.com

SHONEN JUMP MANGA

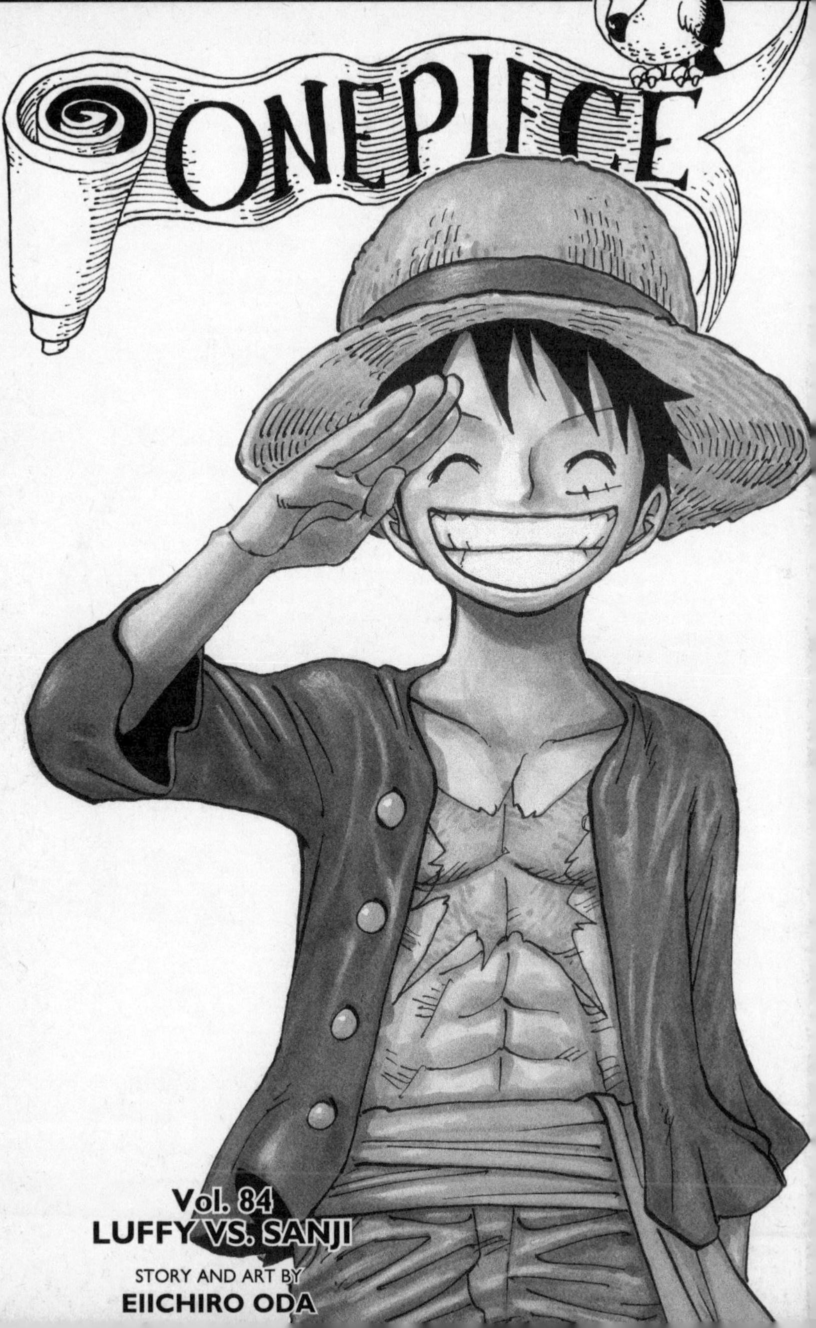
ONE PIECE

Vol. 84

LUFFY VS. SANJI

STORY AND ART BY

EIICHIRO ODA

The Straw Hat Crew

Tony Tony Chopper

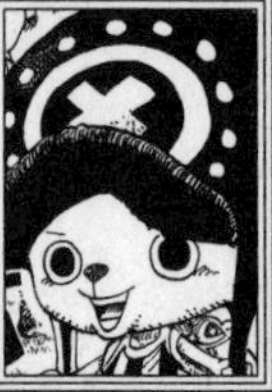

After researching powerful medicine in Birdie Kingdom, he reunited with the rest of the crew.

Ship's Doctor, Bounty: 100 berries

Monkey D. Luffy

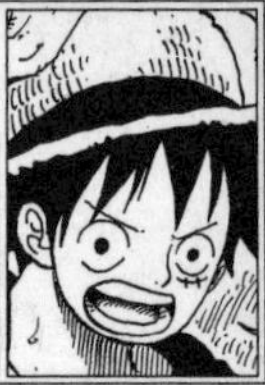

A young man who dreams of becoming the Pirate King. After training with Rayleigh, he and his crew head for the New World!

Captain, Bounty: 500 million berries

Nico Robin

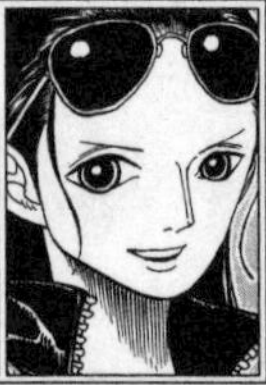

She spent her time in Baltigo with the leader of the Revolutionary Army: Luffy's father, Dragon.

Archeologist, Bounty: 130 million berries

Roronoa Zolo

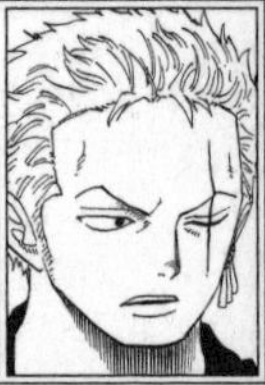

He swallowed his pride and asked to be trained by Mihawk on Gloom Island before reuniting with the rest of the crew.

Fighter, Bounty: 320 million berries

Franky

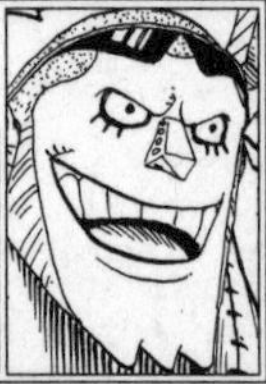

He modified himself in Future Land Baldimore and turned himself into Armored Franky before reuniting with the rest of the crew.

Shipwright, Bounty: 94 million berries

Nami

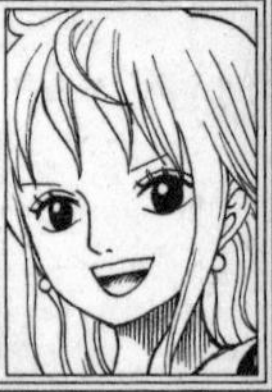

She studied the weather of the New World on the small Sky Island Weatheria, a place where weather is studied as a science.

Navigator, Bounty: 66 million berries

Brook

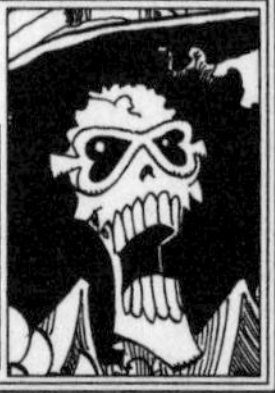

After being captured and used as a freak show by the Longarm Tribe, he became a famous rock star called "Soul King" Brook.

Musician, Bounty: 83 million berries

Usopp

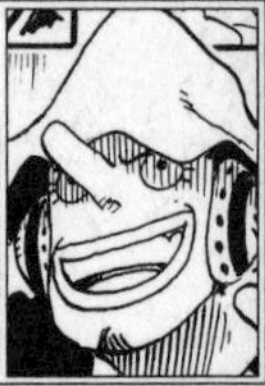

He trained under Heracles at the Bowin Islands to become the King of Snipers.

Sniper, Bounty: 200 million berries

Shanks

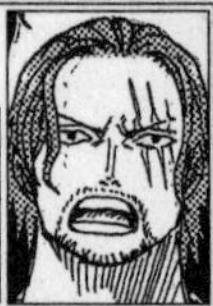

One of the Four Emperors. Waits for Luffy in the "New World," the second half of the Grand Line.

Captain of the Red-Haired Pirates

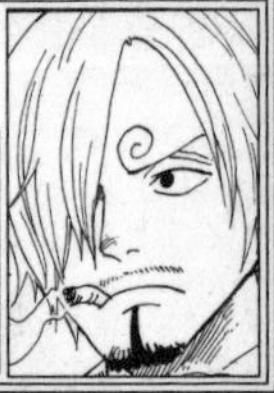

After fighting the New Kama Karate masters in the Kamabakka Kingdom, he returned to the crew.

Cook, Bounty: 177 million berries

Wano Kingdom from his grasp. Meanwhile, Sanji is in terrible danger! His true father has arranged a political marriage for him with Big Mom's daughter. Sanji agrees to meet Big Mom in order to refuse the marriage. When the crew hears about that, they send a retrieval team to Whole Cake Island to get their cook back, and wind up in a fight with some of Big Mom's officers. Meanwhile, Sanji's birth family arrives at Big Mom's lair, ready to celebrate the wedding they helped orchestrate...

The story of ONE PIECE 1»84

Big Mom Pirates

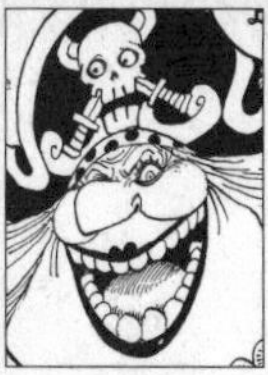

Charlotte Linlin

Captain, Big Mom Pirates

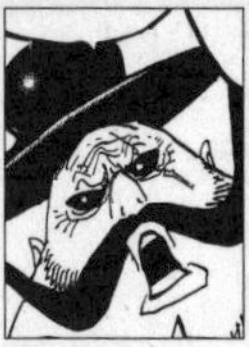

Baron Tamago

Fighter, Big Mom Pirates

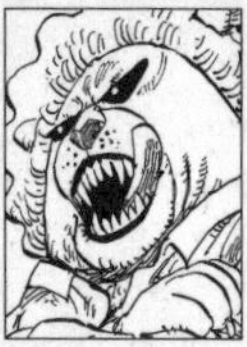

Pekoms

Fighter, Big Mom Pirates

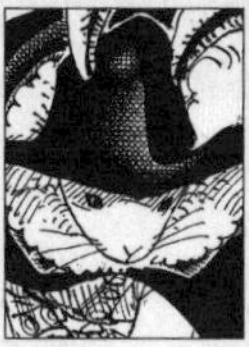

Randolph

Cranerider, Big Mom Pirates

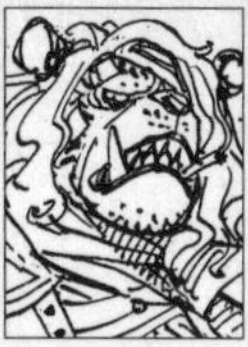

Treetop Pedro (Jaguar Mink)

Leader of the Guardians

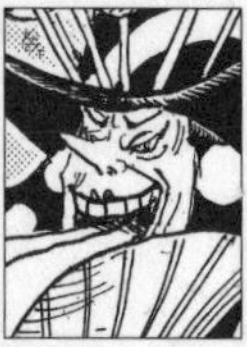

C. Perospero

1st Son of Charlotte

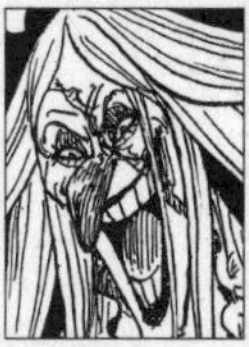

C. Brulee

8th Daughter of Charlotte

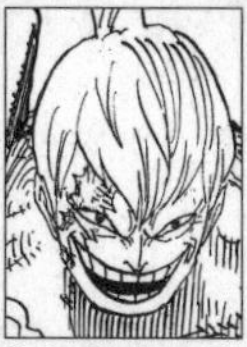

C. Cracker (Sweet 3)

10th Son of Charlotte

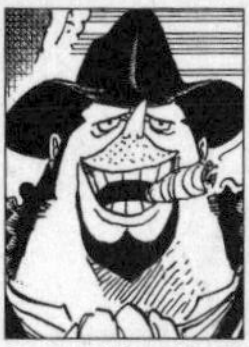

Capone "Gang" Bege

Captain of the Firetank Pirates

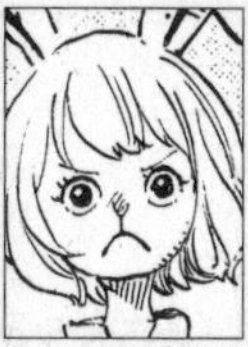

Carrot (Bunny Mink)

Battlebeast Tribe

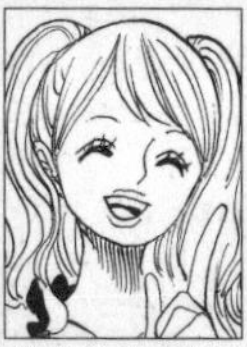

Charlotte Pudding

35th Daughter of Charlotte

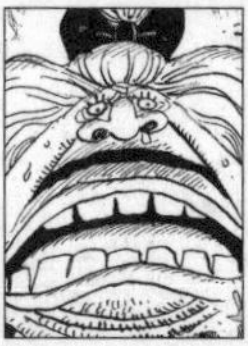

Pound

Lola's Father

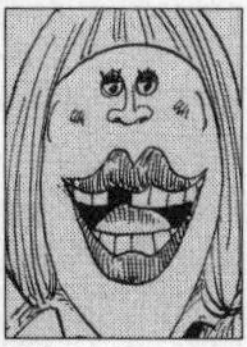

Lola

?th Daughter of Charlotte

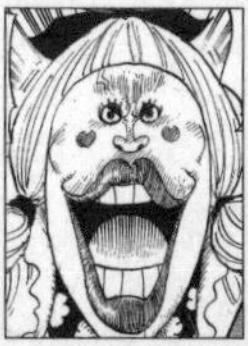

C. Chiffon (Bege's Wife)

22nd Daughter of Charlotte

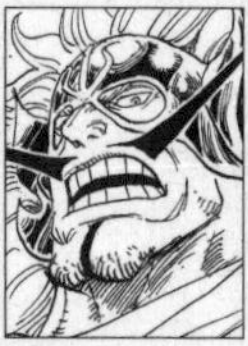

Vinsmoke Judge

King of Germa Kingdom

Germa 66

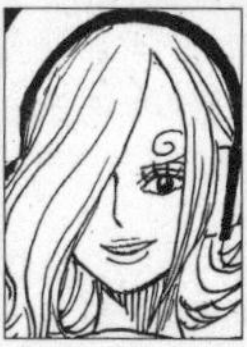

Vinsmoke Reiju

Eldest Daughter of Vinsmoke

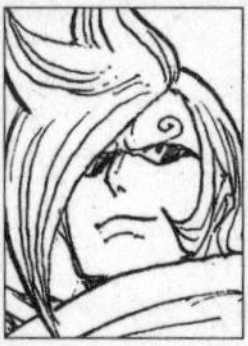

Vinsmoke Ichiju

Eldest Son of Vinsmoke

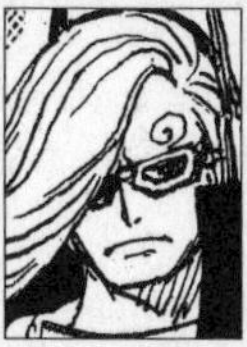

Vinsmoke Niji

Second Son of Vinsmoke

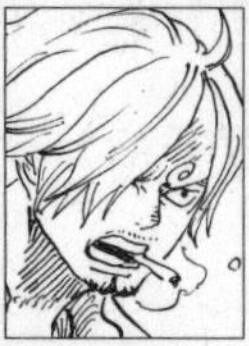

Vinsmoke Sanji

Third Son of Vinsmoke

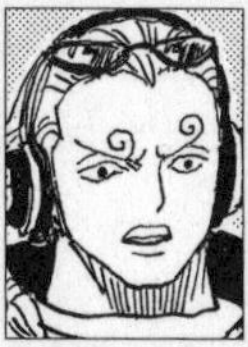

Vinsmoke Yonji

Fourth Son of Vinsmoke

Story

After two years of hard training, the Straw Hat pirates are back together, first at the Sabaody Archipelago and then through Fish-Man Island to their next stage: the New World!!

The crew happens across Law on the island of Punk Hazard, and they travel to Dressrosa to defeat Doflamingo. Next, the crew forms an alliance with the samurai and minks to topple Kaido, an Emperor of the Sea, and rescue

Vol. 84
LUFFY VS. SANJI

CONTENTS

Chapter 839: I OWE YOU MY LIFE!

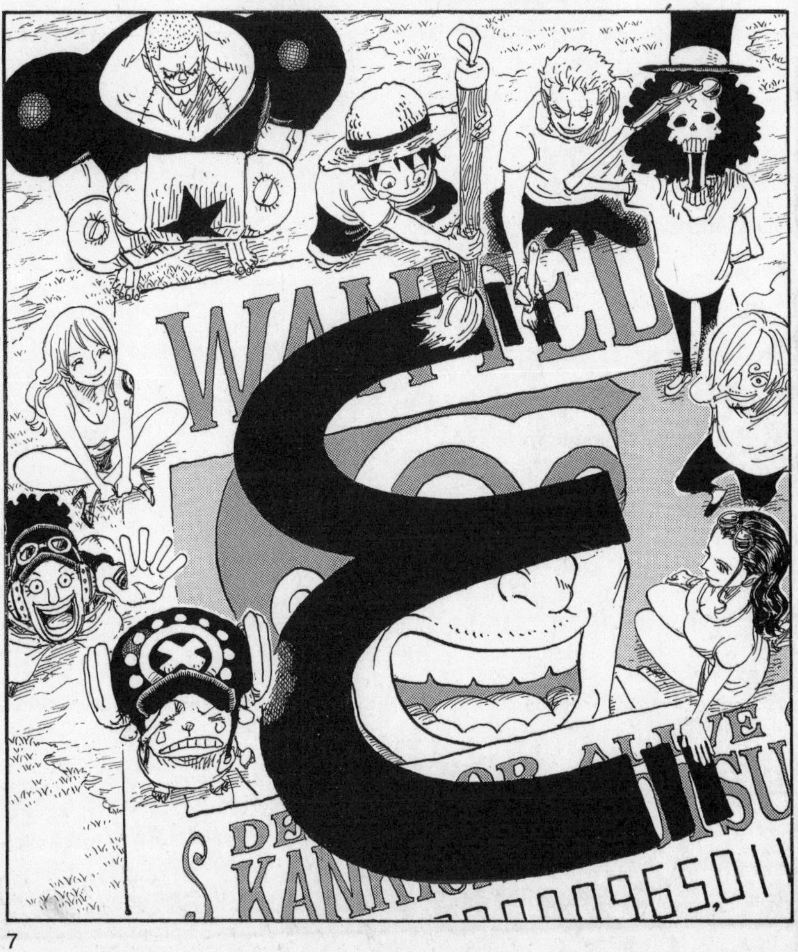

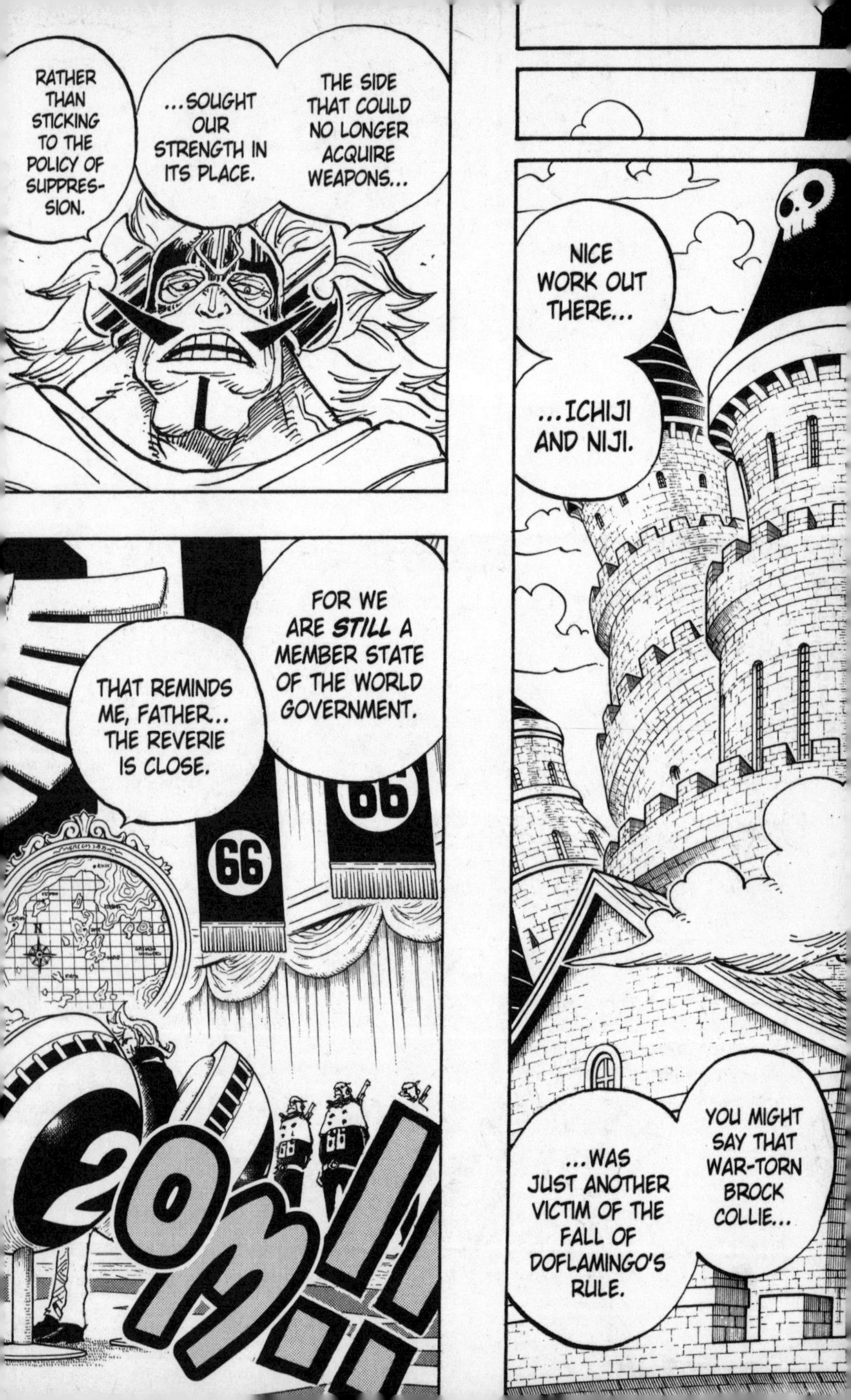
NICE WORK OUT THERE...
...ICHIJI AND NIJI.
YOU MIGHT SAY THAT WAR-TORN BROCK COLLIE...
...WAS JUST ANOTHER VICTIM OF THE FALL OF DOFLAMINGO'S RULE.
THE SIDE THAT COULD NO LONGER ACQUIRE WEAPONS...
...SOUGHT OUR STRENGTH IN ITS PLACE.
RATHER THAN STICKING TO THE POLICY OF SUPPRES-SION.
FOR WE ARE STILL A MEMBER STATE OF THE WORLD GOVERNMENT.
THAT REMINDS ME, FATHER... THE REVERIE IS CLOSE.
66
66

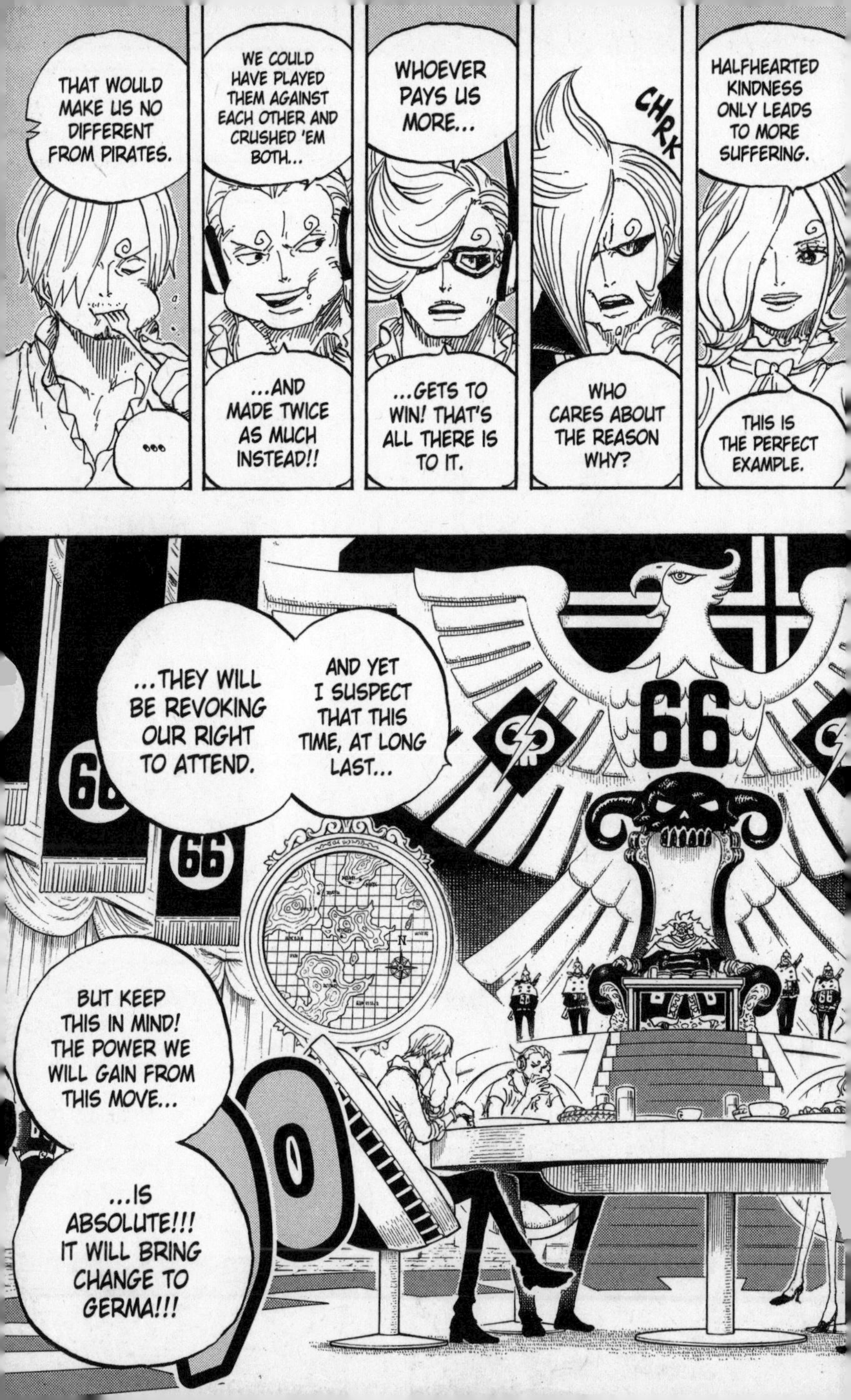
HALFHEARTED KINDNESS ONLY LEADS TO MORE SUFFERING.
THIS IS THE PERFECT EXAMPLE.
CHRK
WHO CARES ABOUT THE REASON WHY?
WHOEVER PAYS US MORE...
...GETS TO WIN! THAT'S ALL THERE IS TO IT.
WE COULD HAVE PLAYED THEM AGAINST EACH OTHER AND CRUSHED 'EM BOTH...
...AND MADE TWICE AS MUCH INSTEAD!!
THAT WOULD MAKE US NO DIFFERENT FROM PIRATES.
...
66
AND YET I SUSPECT THAT THIS TIME, AT LONG LAST...
...THEY WILL BE REVOKING OUR RIGHT TO ATTEND.
66
66
BUT KEEP THIS IN MIND! THE POWER WE WILL GAIN FROM THIS MOVE...
...IS ABSOLUTE!!! IT WILL BRING CHANGE TO GERMA!!!

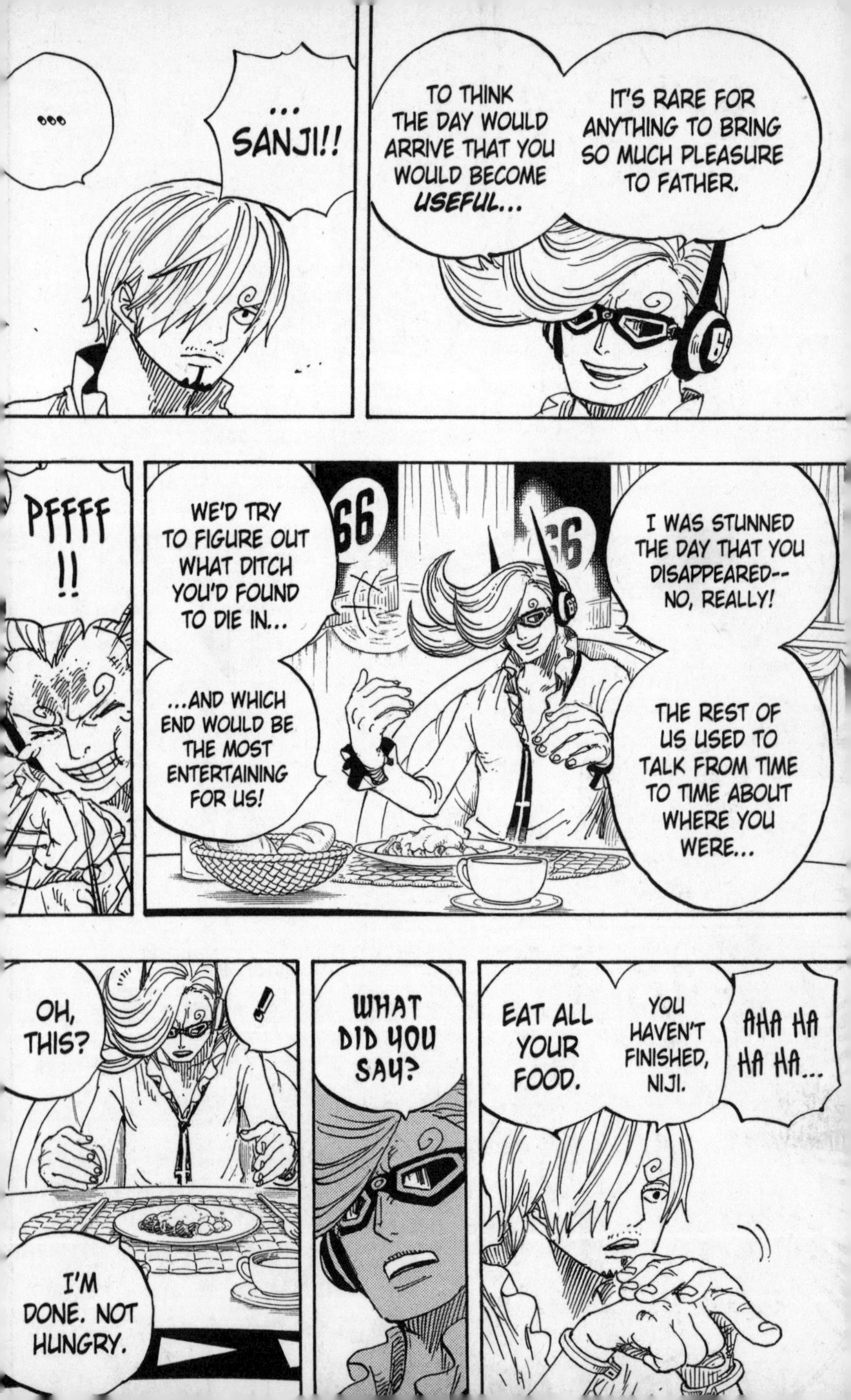
IT'S RARE FOR ANYTHING TO BRING SO MUCH PLEASURE TO FATHER.
TO THINK THE DAY WOULD ARRIVE THAT YOU WOULD BECOME *USEFUL*...
...SANJI!!
...
I WAS STUNNED THE DAY THAT YOU DISAPPEARED-- NO, REALLY!
THE REST OF US USED TO TALK FROM TIME TO TIME ABOUT WHERE YOU WERE...
WE'D TRY TO FIGURE OUT WHAT DITCH YOU'D FOUND TO DIE IN...
...AND WHICH END WOULD BE THE MOST ENTERTAINING FOR US!
PFFFF !!
AHA HA HA HA...
YOU HAVEN'T FINISHED, NIJI.
EAT ALL YOUR FOOD.
WHAT DID YOU SAY?
!
OH, THIS?
I'M DONE. NOT HUNGRY.

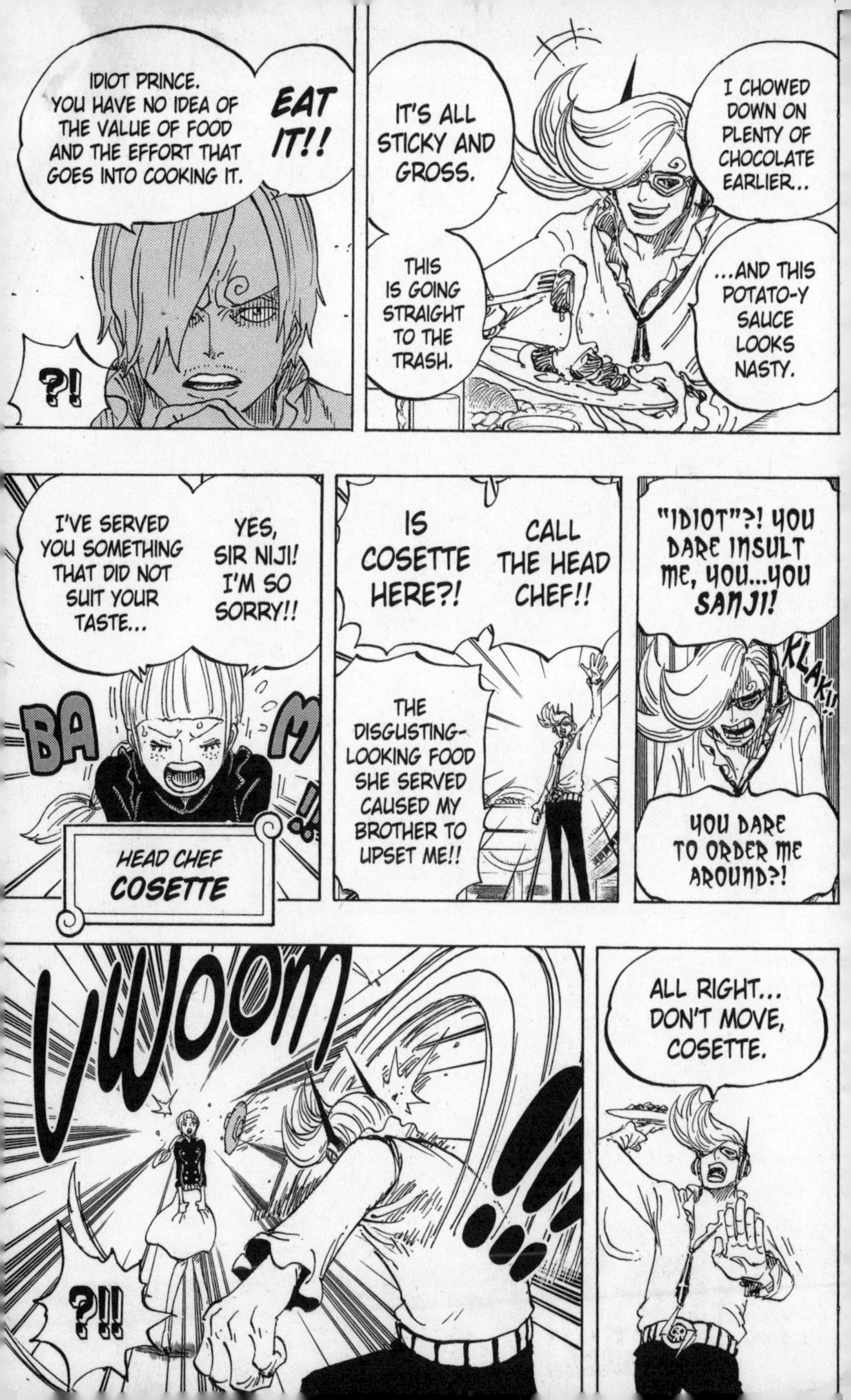
I CHOWED DOWN ON PLENTY OF CHOCOLATE EARLIER...
...AND THIS POTATO-Y SAUCE LOOKS NASTY.
IT'S ALL STICKY AND GROSS.
THIS IS GOING STRAIGHT TO THE TRASH.
IDIOT PRINCE. YOU HAVE NO IDEA OF THE VALUE OF FOOD AND THE EFFORT THAT GOES INTO COOKING IT.
EAT IT!!
?!
"IDIOT"?! YOU DARE INSULT ME, YOU...YOU SANJI!
KLAK!!
YOU DARE TO ORDER ME AROUND?!
CALL THE HEAD CHEF!!
IS COSETTE HERE?!
THE DISGUSTING-LOOKING FOOD SHE SERVED CAUSED MY BROTHER TO UPSET ME!!
YES, SIR NIJI! I'M SO SORRY!!
I'VE SERVED YOU SOMETHING THAT DID NOT SUIT YOUR TASTE...
BAM!!
HEAD CHEF COSETTE
ALL RIGHT... DON'T MOVE, COSETTE.
VWOOM
?!!

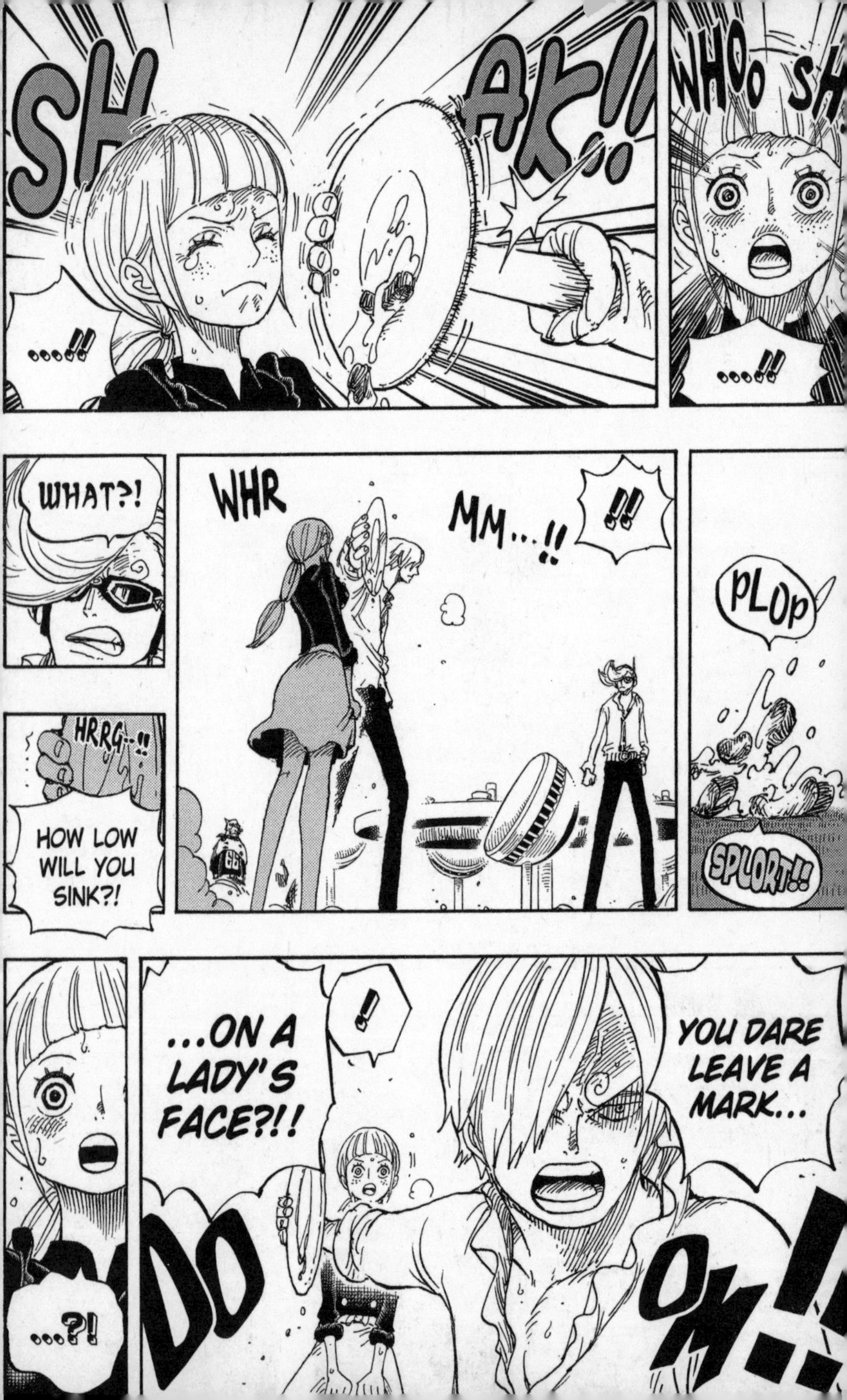
WHOO SH
...!!
SH
AK!!
...!!
PLOP
SPLORT!!
!!
MM...!!
WHR
WHAT?!
HRRG..!!
HOW LOW WILL YOU SINK?!
YOU DARE LEAVE A MARK...
!
...ON A LADY'S FACE?!!
DO
OK!!
...?!

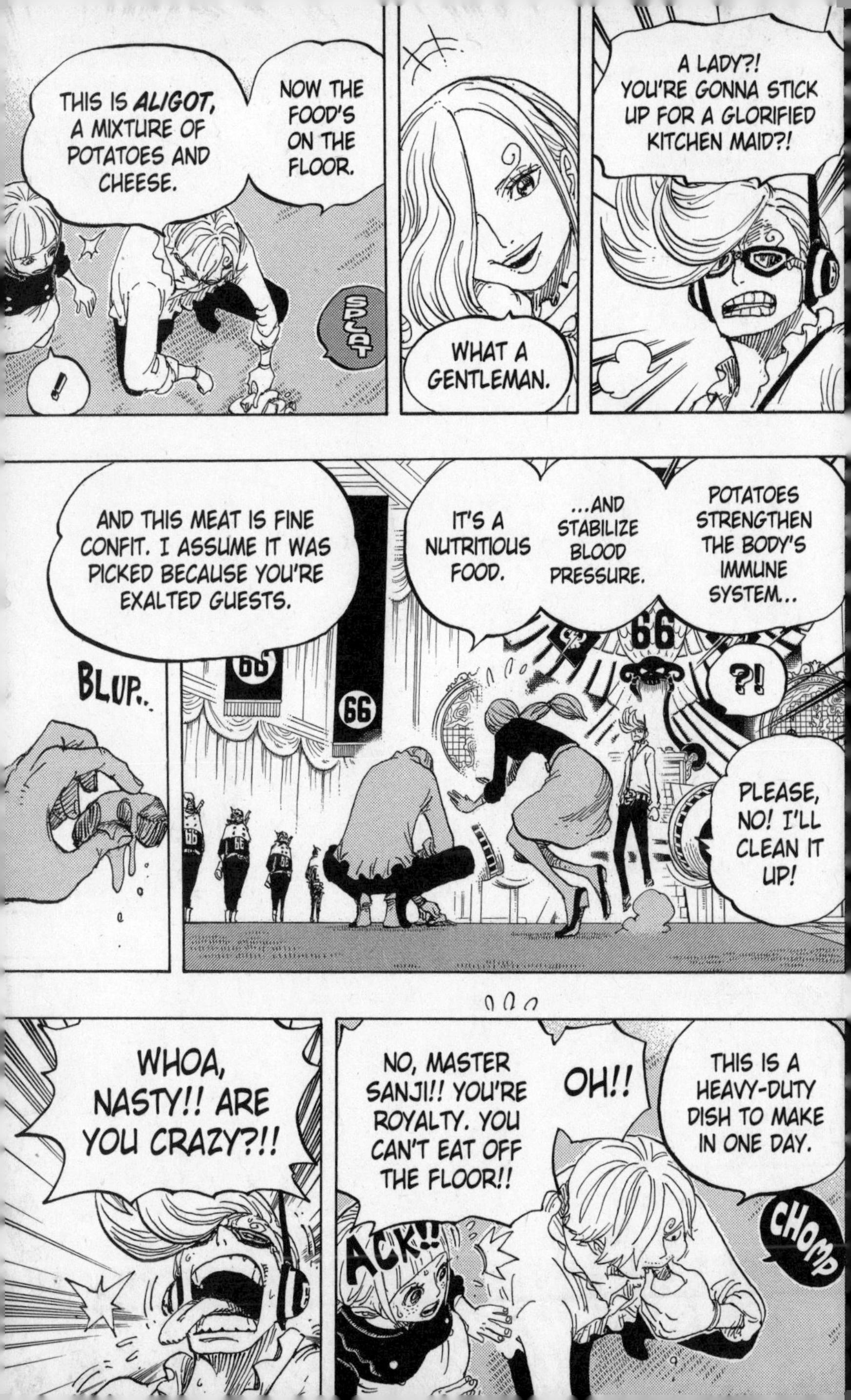
A LADY?! YOU'RE GONNA STICK UP FOR A GLORIFIED KITCHEN MAID?!
WHAT A GENTLEMAN.
NOW THE FOOD'S ON THE FLOOR.
THIS IS *ALIGOT*, A MIXTURE OF POTATOES AND CHEESE.
SPLAT
!
POTATOES STRENGTHEN THE BODY'S IMMUNE SYSTEM...
...AND STABILIZE BLOOD PRESSURE.
IT'S A NUTRITIOUS FOOD.
AND THIS MEAT IS FINE CONFIT. I ASSUME IT WAS PICKED BECAUSE YOU'RE EXALTED GUESTS.
?!
PLEASE, NO! I'LL CLEAN IT UP!
BLUP..
THIS IS A HEAVY-DUTY DISH TO MAKE IN ONE DAY.
CHOMP
OH!!
NO, MASTER SANJI!! YOU'RE ROYALTY. YOU CAN'T EAT OFF THE FLOOR!!
ACK!!
WHOA, NASTY!! ARE YOU CRAZY?!!

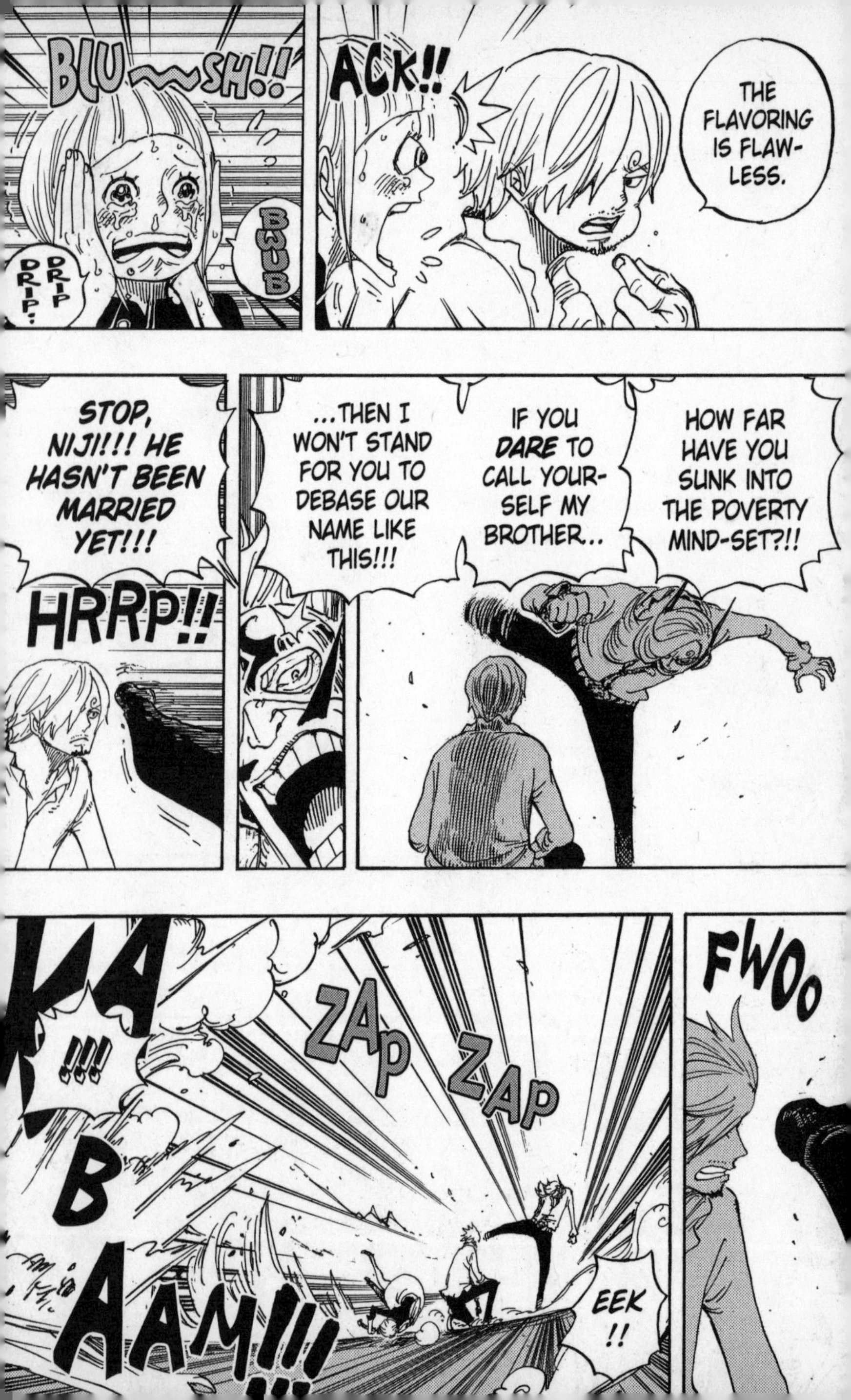
THE FLAVORING IS FLAW-LESS.
ACK!!
BLU~~SH!!
BWUB
DRIP DRIP
HOW FAR HAVE YOU SUNK INTO THE POVERTY MIND-SET?!!
IF YOU DARE TO CALL YOUR-SELF MY BROTHER...
...THEN I WON'T STAND FOR YOU TO DEBASE OUR NAME LIKE THIS!!!
STOP, NIJI!!! HE HASN'T BEEN MARRIED YET!!!
HRRP!!
FWOo
EEK!!
ZAP ZAP
KA!!!
BAAM!!!

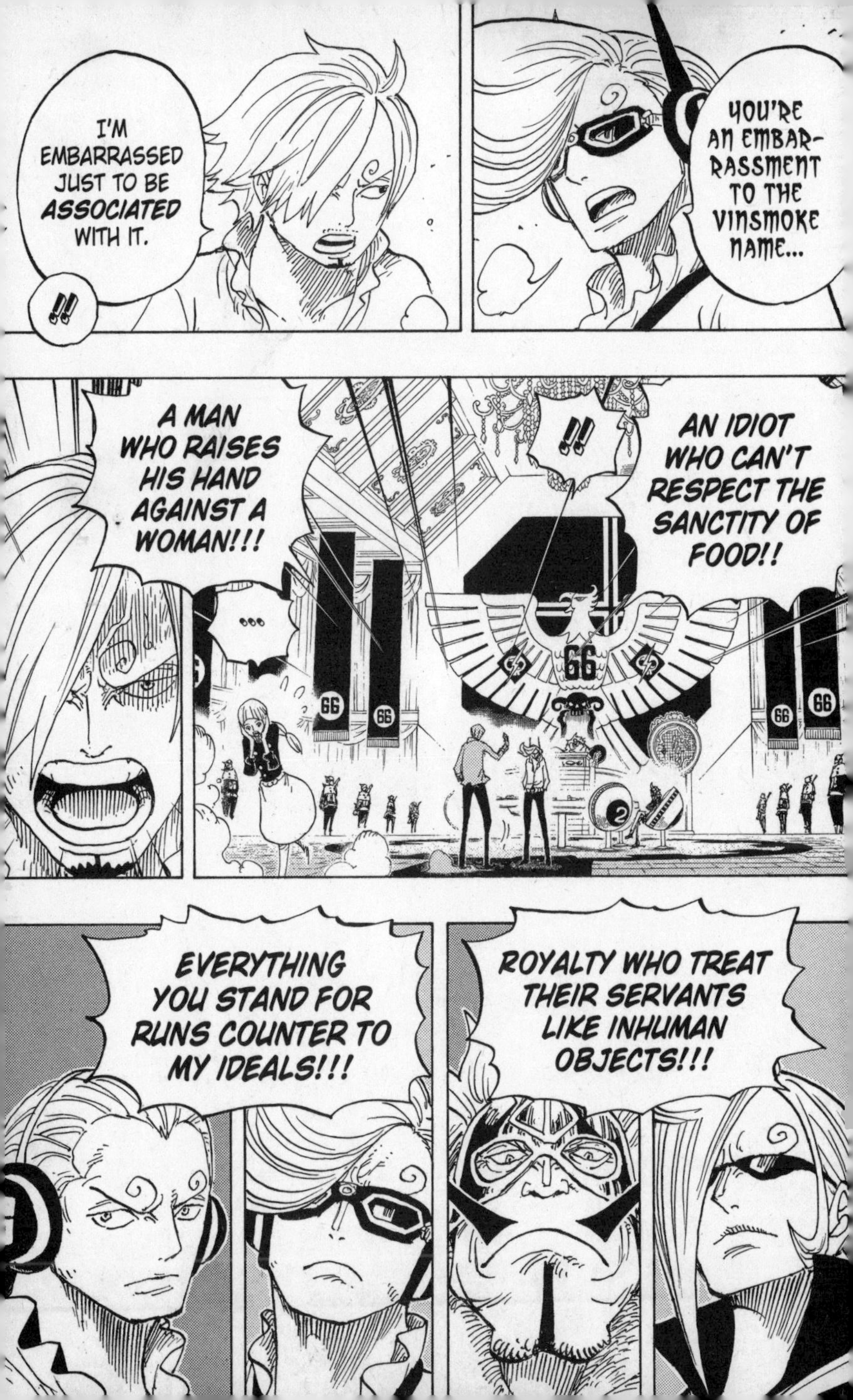
YOU'RE AN EMBARRASSMENT TO THE VINSMOKE NAME...
I'M EMBARRASSED JUST TO BE ASSOCIATED WITH IT.
!!
AN IDIOT WHO CAN'T RESPECT THE SANCTITY OF FOOD!!
!!
...
A MAN WHO RAISES HIS HAND AGAINST A WOMAN!!!
ROYALTY WHO TREAT THEIR SERVANTS LIKE INHUMAN OBJECTS!!!
EVERYTHING YOU STAND FOR RUNS COUNTER TO MY IDEALS!!!

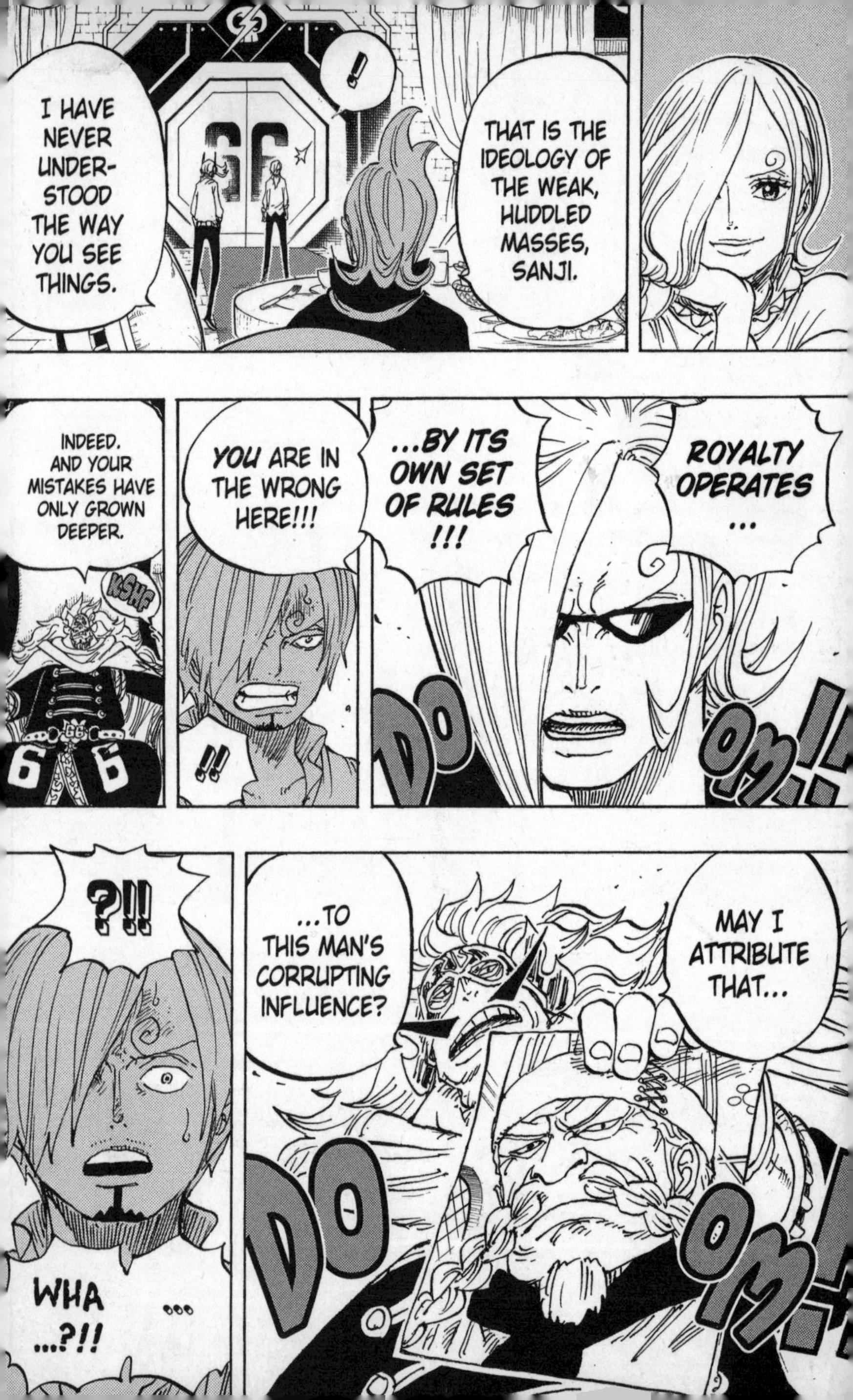

THAT IS THE IDEOLOGY OF THE WEAK, HUDDLED MASSES, SANJI.
!
I HAVE NEVER UNDER-STOOD THE WAY YOU SEE THINGS.
ROYALTY OPERATES ...
...BY ITS OWN SET OF RULES !!!
DOOM!!
YOU ARE IN THE WRONG HERE!!!
!!
INDEED. AND YOUR MISTAKES HAVE ONLY GROWN DEEPER.
WSHF
MAY I ATTRIBUTE THAT...
...TO THIS MAN'S CORRUPTING INFLUENCE?
DOOM!!
?!!
...
WHA ...?!!

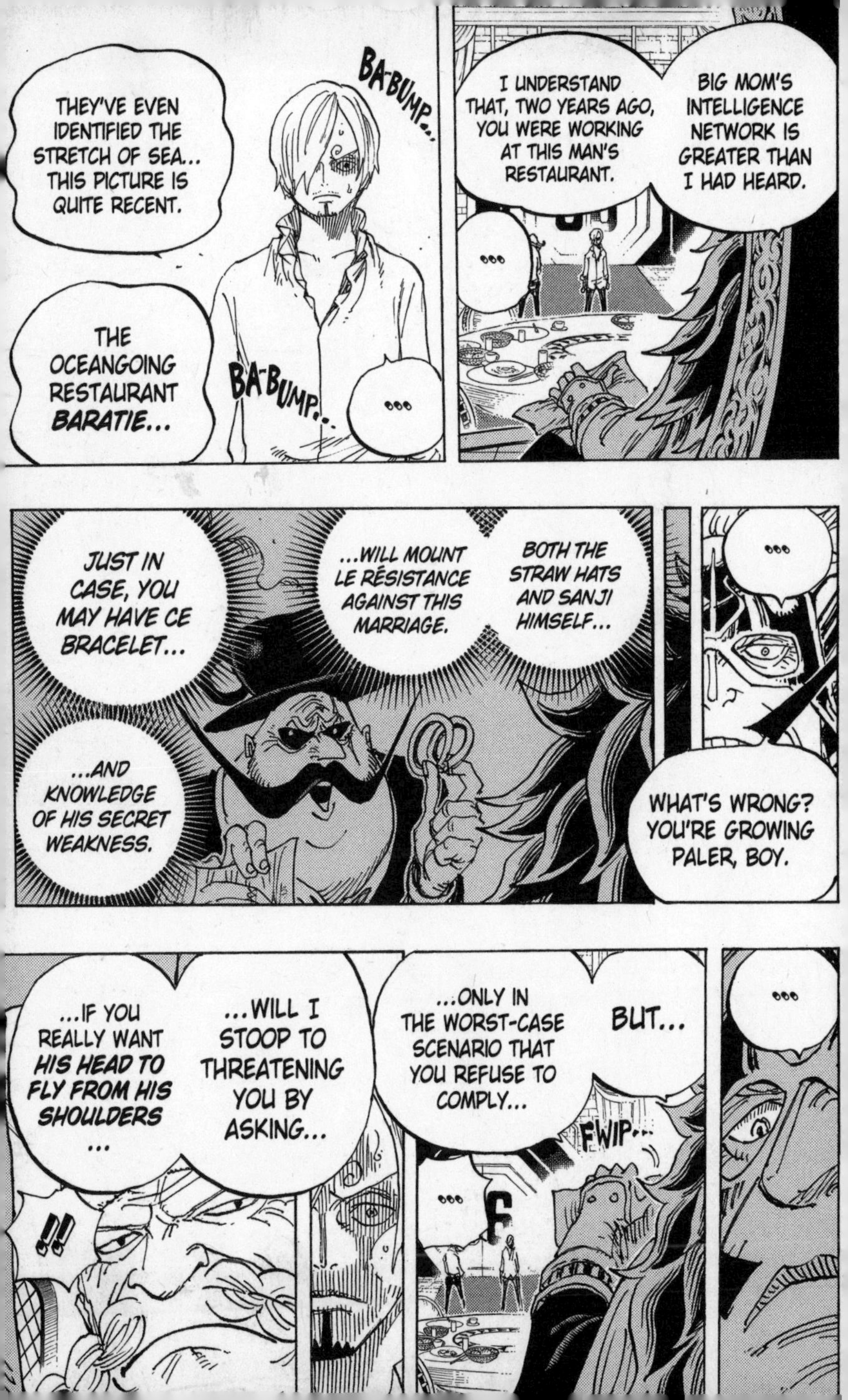
BIG MOM'S INTELLIGENCE NETWORK IS GREATER THAN I HAD HEARD.
I UNDERSTAND THAT, TWO YEARS AGO, YOU WERE WORKING AT THIS MAN'S RESTAURANT.
...
BA-BUMP...
THEY'VE EVEN IDENTIFIED THE STRETCH OF SEA... THIS PICTURE IS QUITE RECENT.
BA-BUMP...
...
THE OCEANGOING RESTAURANT ***BARATIE...***
...
WHAT'S WRONG? YOU'RE GROWING PALER, BOY.
BOTH THE STRAW HATS AND SANJI HIMSELF...
...WILL MOUNT LE RÉSISTANCE AGAINST THIS MARRIAGE.
JUST IN CASE, YOU MAY HAVE CE BRACELET...
...AND KNOWLEDGE OF HIS SECRET WEAKNESS.
...
BUT...
...ONLY IN THE WORST-CASE SCENARIO THAT YOU REFUSE TO COMPLY...
FWIP...
...
...WILL I STOOP TO THREATENING YOU BY ASKING...
...IF YOU REALLY WANT ***HIS HEAD TO FLY FROM HIS SHOULDERS*** ...
!!

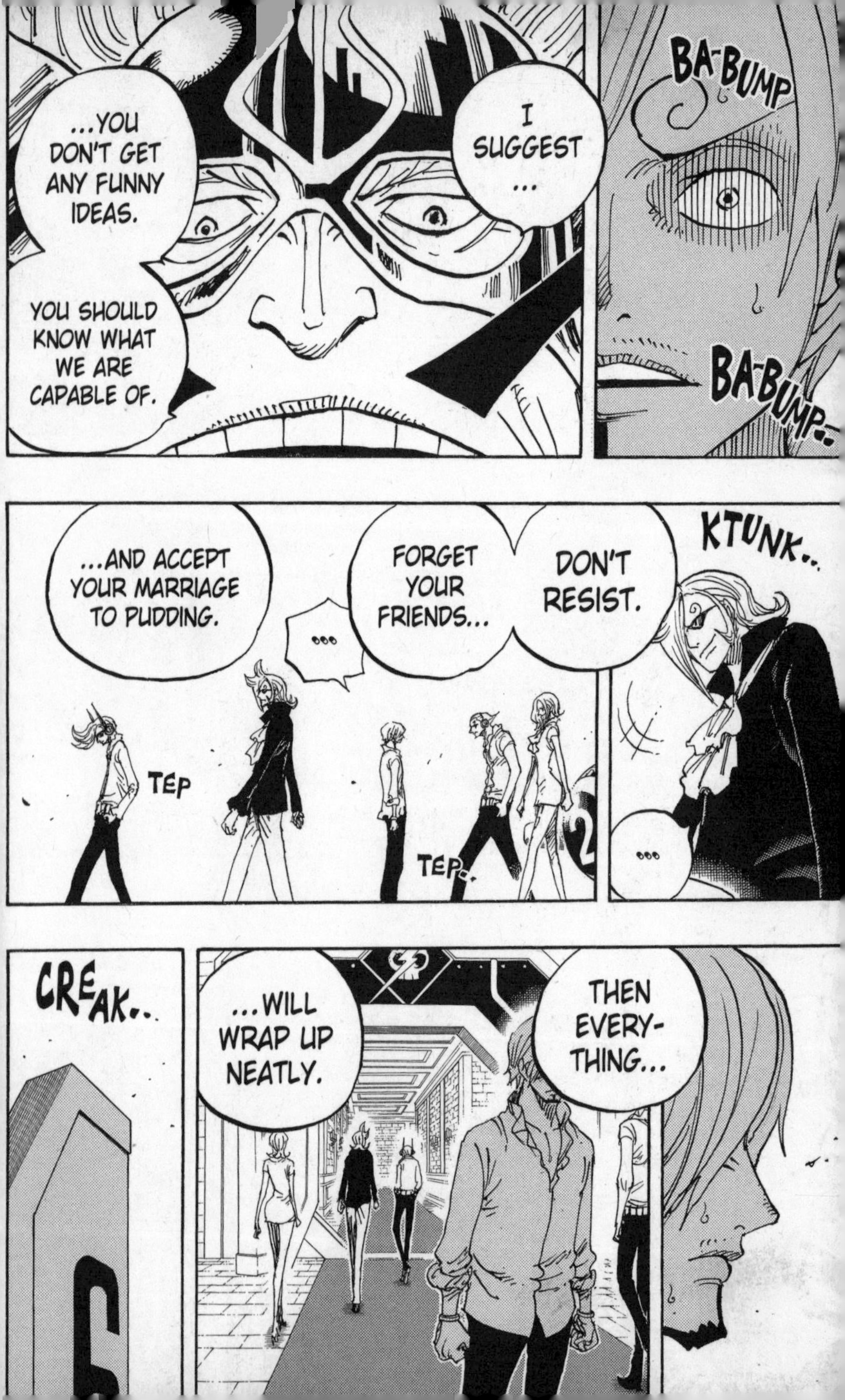
BA-BUMP
BA-BUMP...
I SUGGEST...
...YOU DON'T GET ANY FUNNY IDEAS.
YOU SHOULD KNOW WHAT WE ARE CAPABLE OF.
KTUNK...
...
DON'T RESIST.
FORGET YOUR FRIENDS...
...
...AND ACCEPT YOUR MARRIAGE TO PUDDING.
TEP
TEP...
THEN EVERY-THING...
...WILL WRAP UP NEATLY.
CREAK...

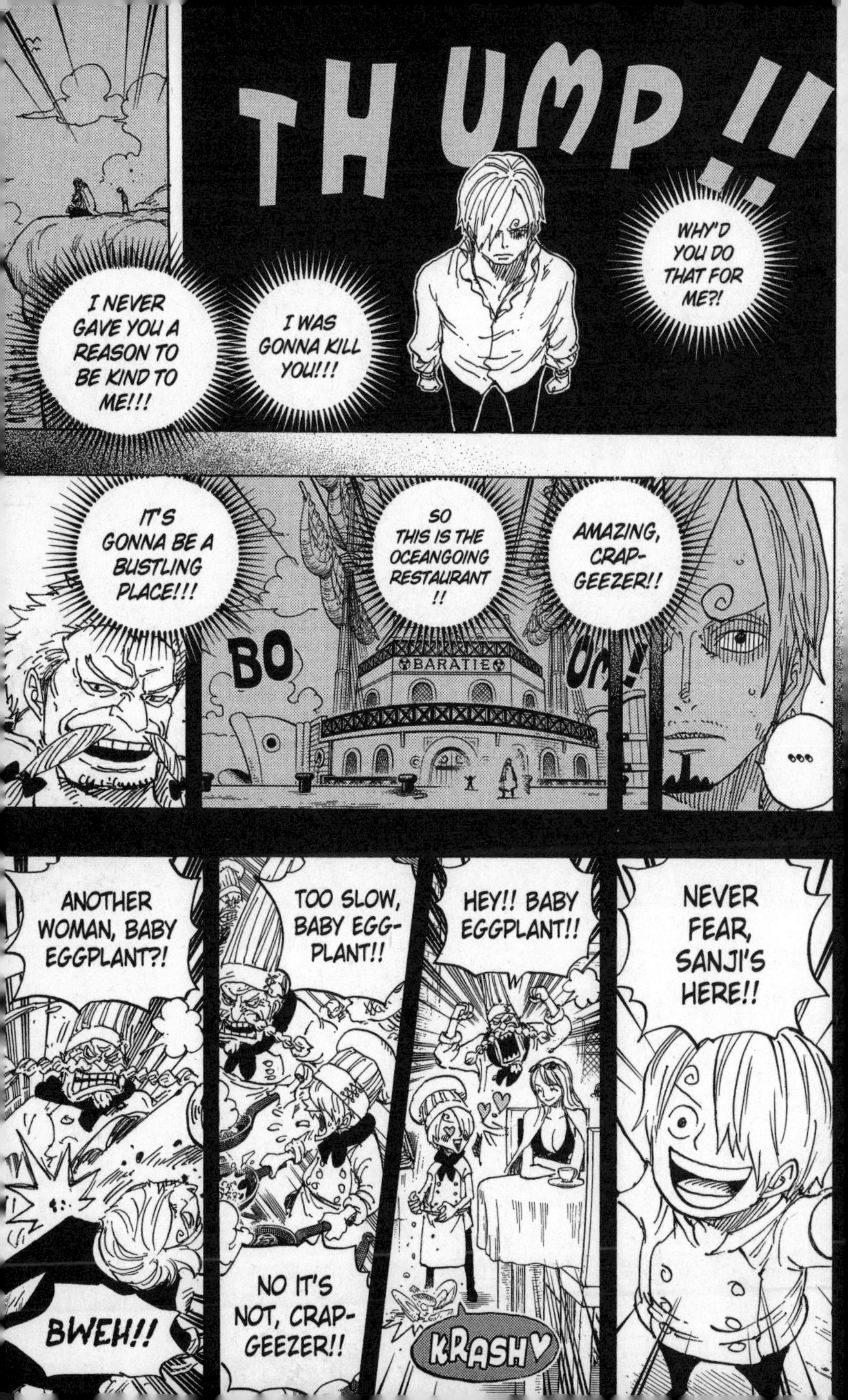
THUMP!!
WHY'D YOU DO THAT FOR ME?!
I WAS GONNA KILL YOU!!!
I NEVER GAVE YOU A REASON TO BE KIND TO ME!!!
AMAZING, CRAP-GEEZER!!
...
SO THIS IS THE OCEANGOING RESTAURANT !!
BARATIE
BOOM!!
IT'S GONNA BE A BUSTLING PLACE!!!
NEVER FEAR, SANJI'S HERE!!
HEY!! BABY EGGPLANT!!
KRASH♥
TOO SLOW, BABY EGG-PLANT!!
NO IT'S NOT, CRAP-GEEZER!!
ANOTHER WOMAN, BABY EGGPLANT?!
BWEH!!

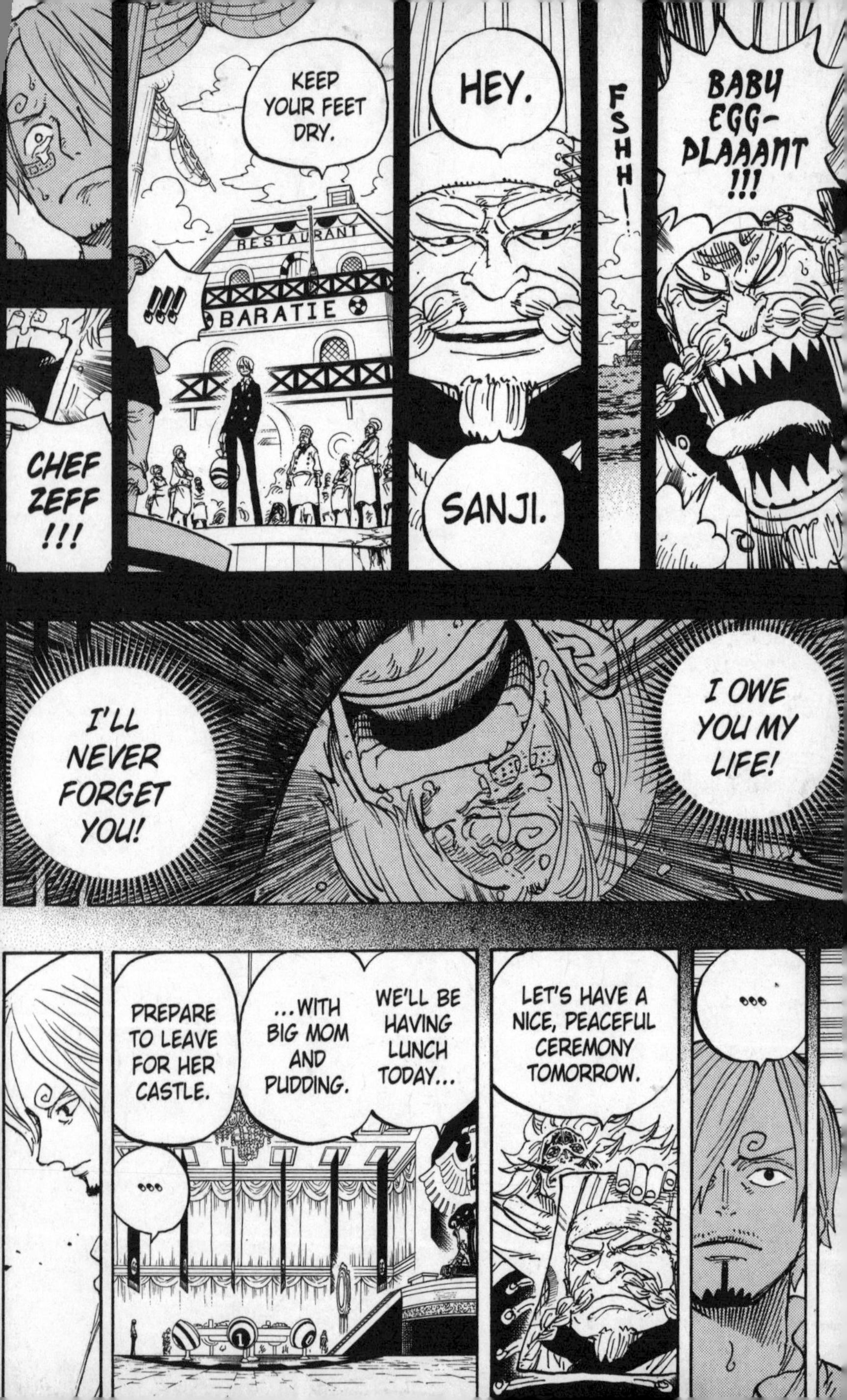

BABY EGG-PLAAANT!!!
FSHH!!
HEY.
SANJI.
KEEP YOUR FEET DRY.
!!!
RESTAURANT
BARATIE
CHEF ZEFF!!!
I OWE YOU MY LIFE!
I'LL NEVER FORGET YOU!
...
LET'S HAVE A NICE, PEACEFUL CEREMONY TOMORROW.
WE'LL BE HAVING LUNCH TODAY...
...WITH BIG MOM AND PUDDING.
PREPARE TO LEAVE FOR HER CASTLE.
...

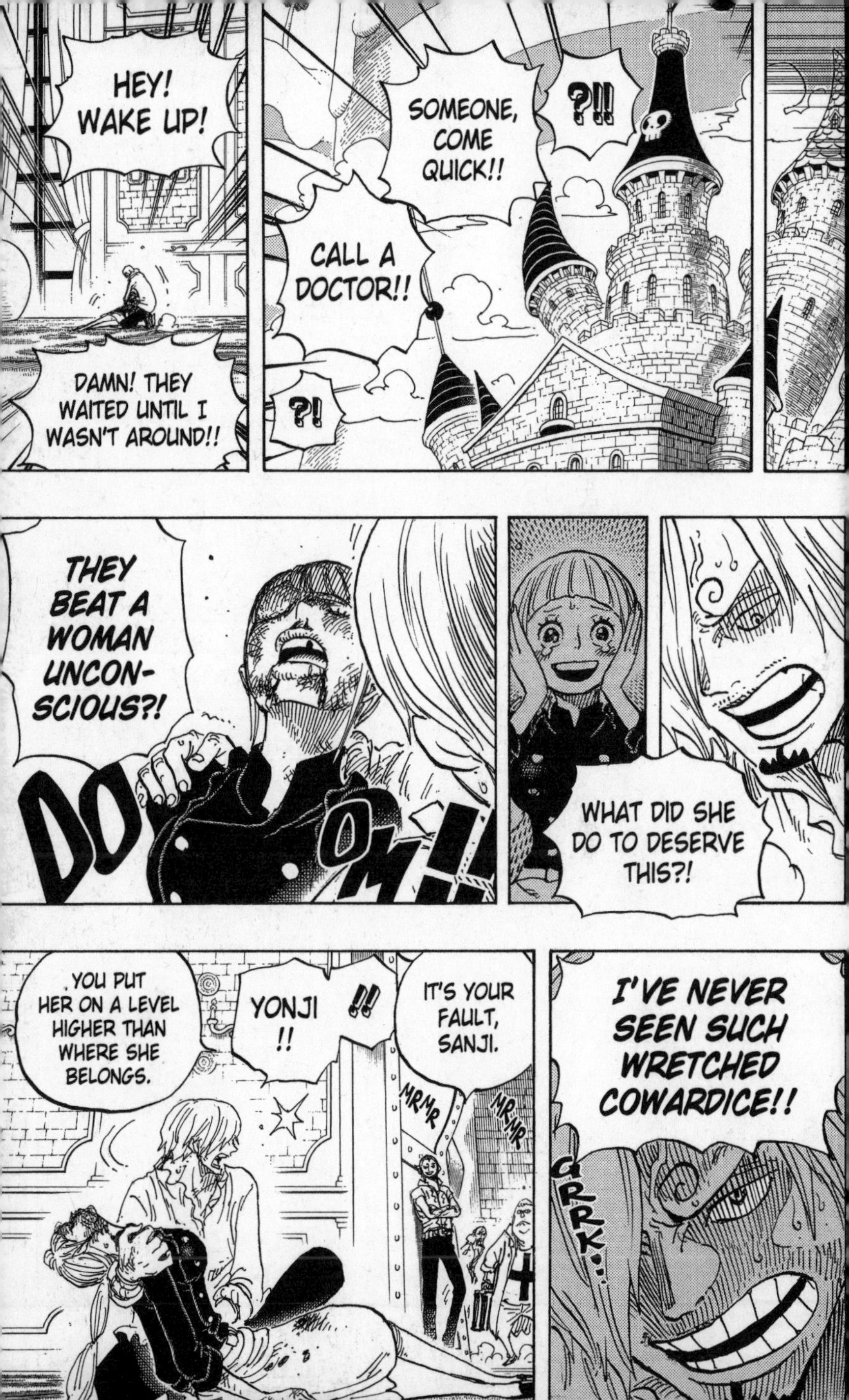
?!!
SOMEONE, COME QUICK!!
CALL A DOCTOR!!
?!
HEY! WAKE UP!
DAMN! THEY WAITED UNTIL I WASN'T AROUND!!
WHAT DID SHE DO TO DESERVE THIS?!
THEY BEAT A WOMAN UNCON-SCIOUS?!
DOOM!!
I'VE NEVER SEEN SUCH WRETCHED COWARDICE!!
GRRK...
IT'S YOUR FAULT, SANJI.
MRMR
MRMR
!!
YONJI !!
YOU PUT HER ON A LEVEL HIGHER THAN WHERE SHE BELONGS.

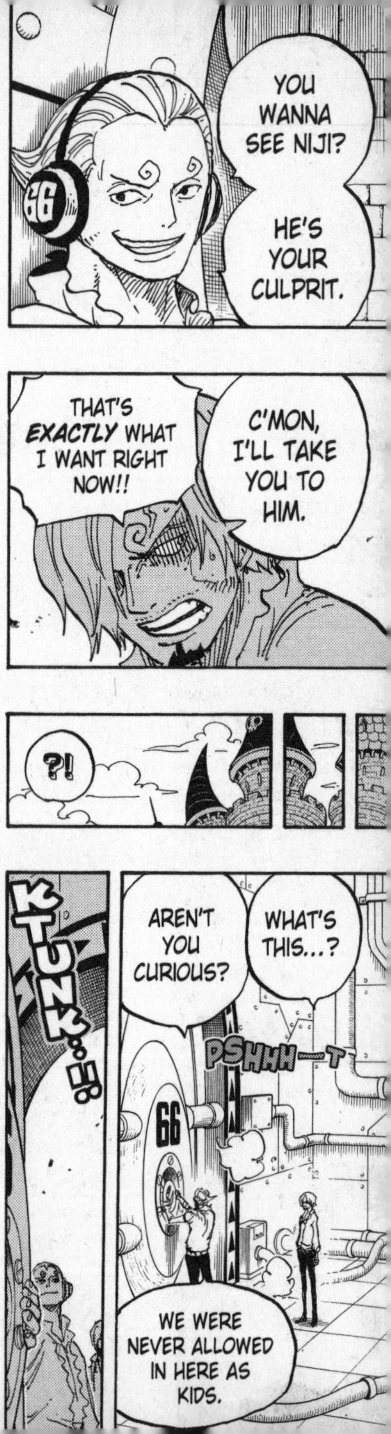
YOU WANNA SEE NIJI?
HE'S YOUR CULPRIT.
C'MON, I'LL TAKE YOU TO HIM.
THAT'S *EXACTLY* WHAT I WANT RIGHT NOW!!
?!
WHAT'S THIS...?
AREN'T YOU CURIOUS?
PSHHH—T
WE WERE NEVER ALLOWED IN HERE AS KIDS.
KTUNK..!!

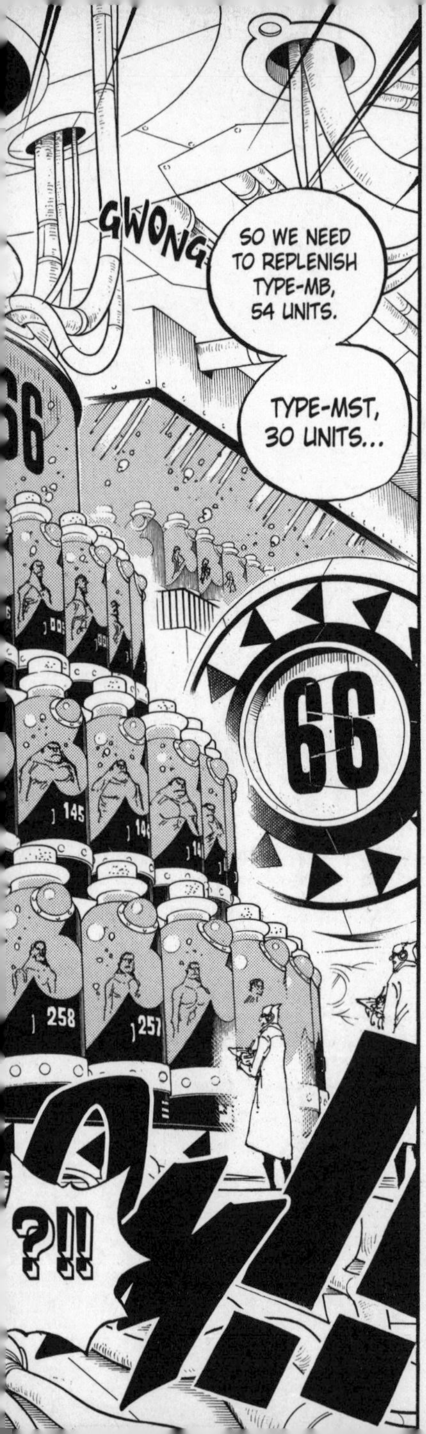
GWONG
SO WE NEED TO REPLENISH TYPE-MB, 54 UNITS.
TYPE-MST, 30 UNITS...
?!!

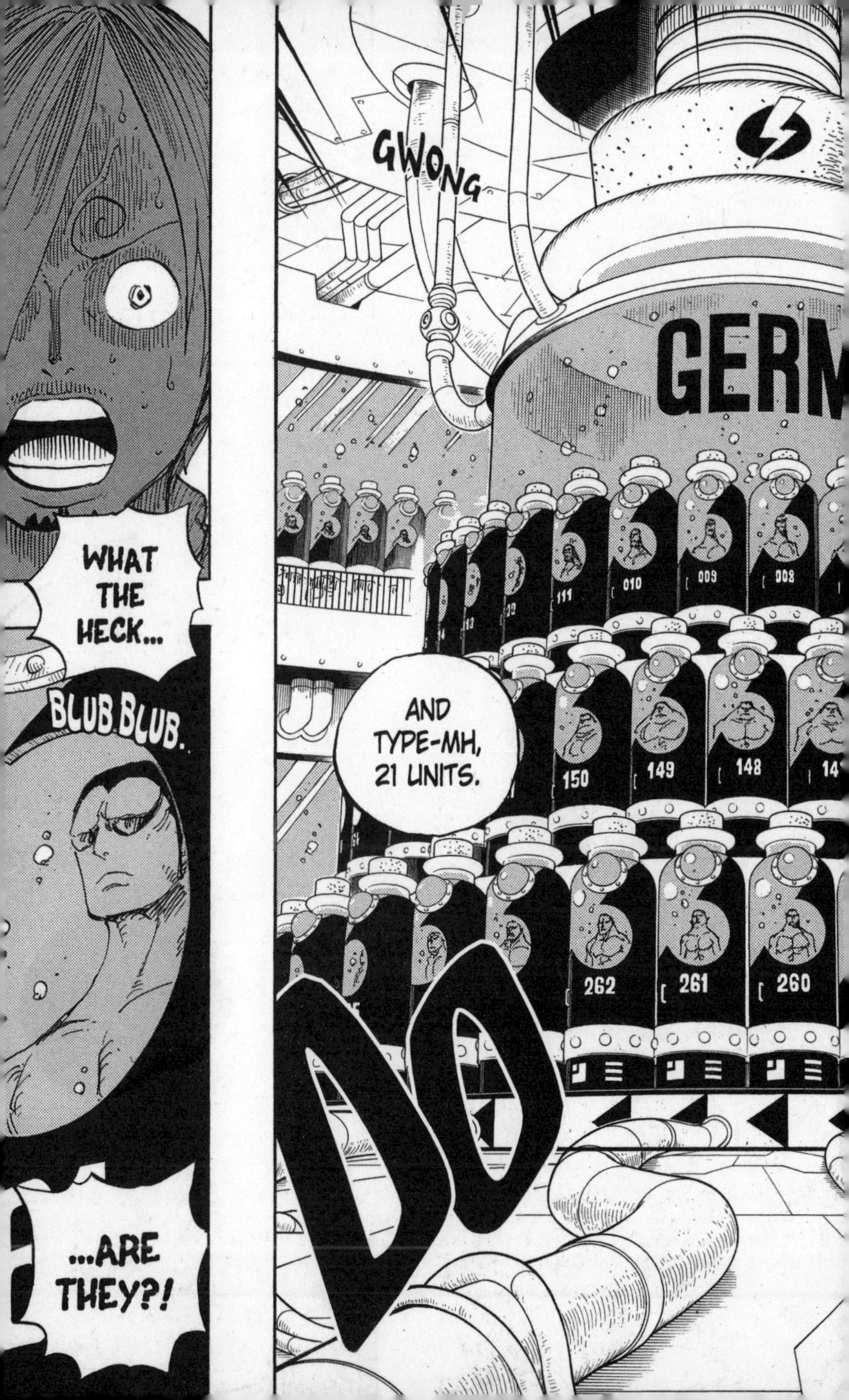
GWONG
GERM
AND TYPE-MH, 21 UNITS.
DO
WHAT THE HECK...
BLUB BLUB.
...ARE THEY?!

SBS Question Corner

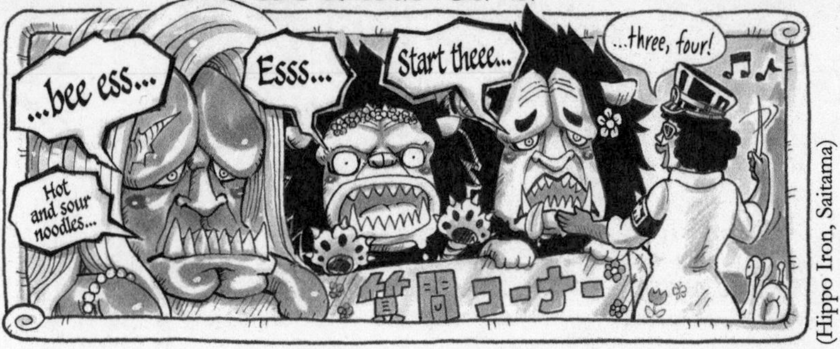
...three, four!
Start theee...
Esss...
...bee ess...
Hot and sour noodles...
質問コーナー

(Hippo Iron, Saitama)

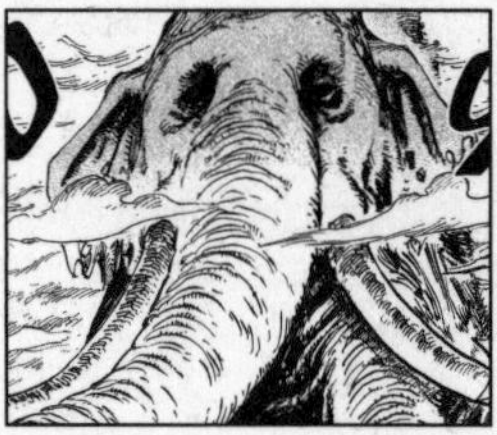

Q: One day, I heard a voice. "Give me the order!!" It was the voice of Zunesha. So I asked, "What order?" And Zunesha said, "Order me…to start the SBS!!!"
So…start the SBS!!!

--Middle-Aged Man Who Wants to Eat the Clear-Clear Fruit

A: Aaaah!! It's Zunesha!! Zunesha is starting the SBS!! Run away!! Aaah...eeek...

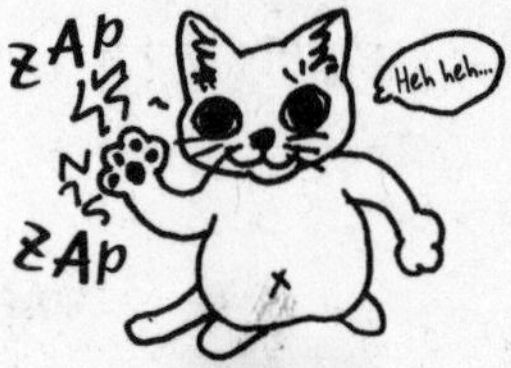
ZAP
Heh heh...
ZAP

Q: When I try to pet my cat during the dry season, I get a little electric prickle. Could my cat be a mink?

--Year of the China Rabbit Y

A: That is absolutely a mink. Watch out--it might be waiting for the dawn of the world, or hiding a ninja.

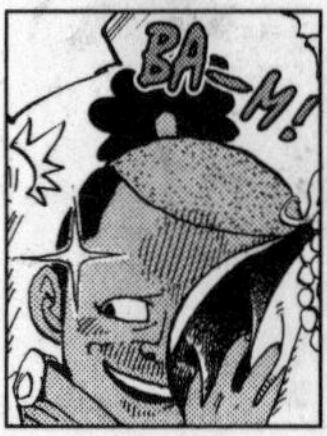
BA-M!

Q: I want to be Momonosuke!!

--Captain Nobuo

A: I understand. Let me be clear: "On the inside, every man was once Momonosuke." And your heart will be Momonosuke for eternity!! I'm not there yet, but I hope to be Momonosuke when I am an old geezer!!

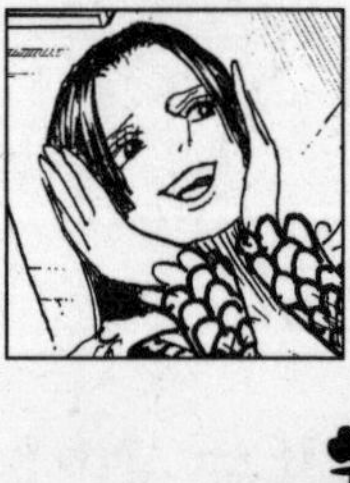

Q: Does Hancock's cooking taste good?

--Eryngii

A: It used to be bad, but she's gotten much better at cooking meat over the last two years. It looks good, but only Luffy's eaten it, so who really knows.

Chapter 840:
THE IRON MASK

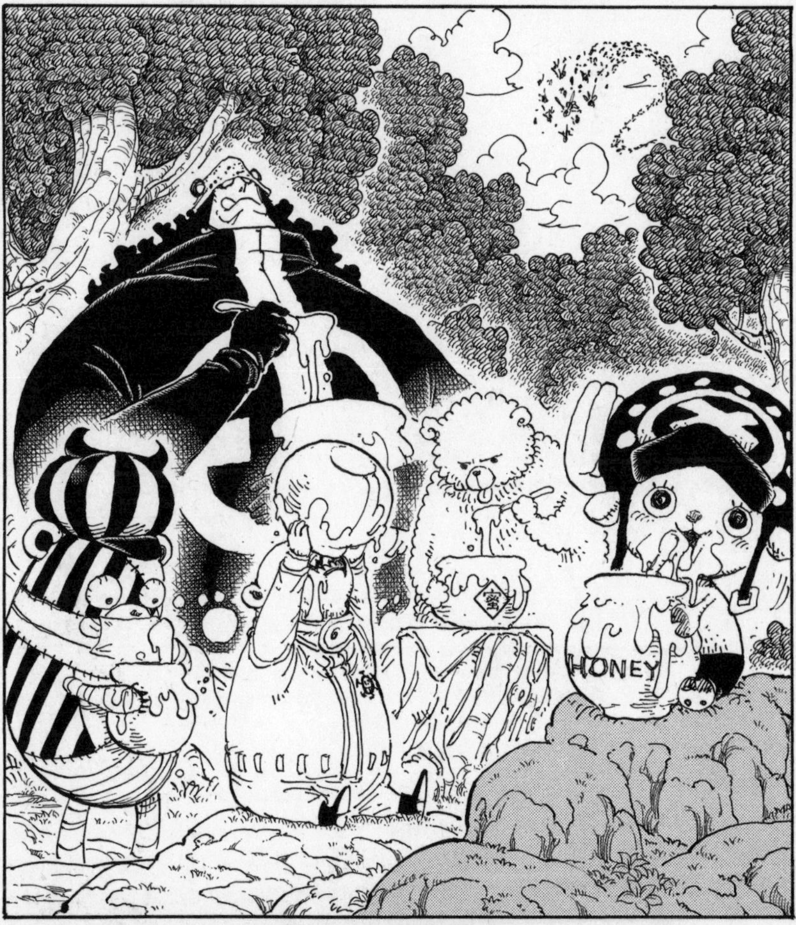
HONEY

REQUEST: "CHOPPER, BEPO, KUMACY, HIKING BEAR AND BARTHOLOMEW KUMA EATING HONEY LIKE POOH BEAR" BY HONEYLICKER FROM IBARAKI

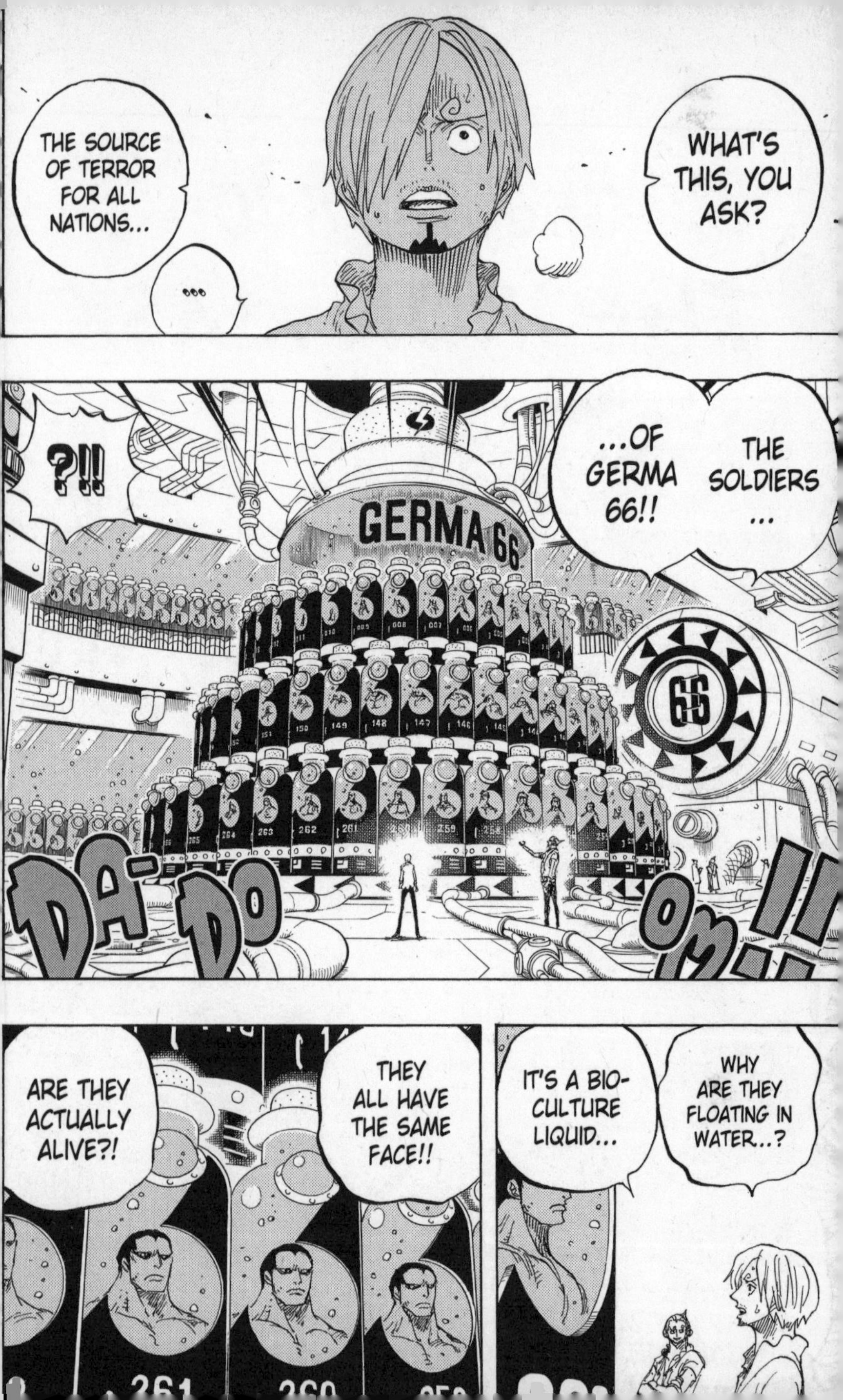
WHAT'S THIS, YOU ASK?
THE SOURCE OF TERROR FOR ALL NATIONS...
...
THE SOLDIERS ...
...OF GERMA 66!!
?!!
GERMA 66
DA-DOOM!!
WHY ARE THEY FLOATING IN WATER...?
IT'S A BIO-CULTURE LIQUID...
THEY ALL HAVE THE SAME FACE!!
ARE THEY ACTUALLY ALIVE?!

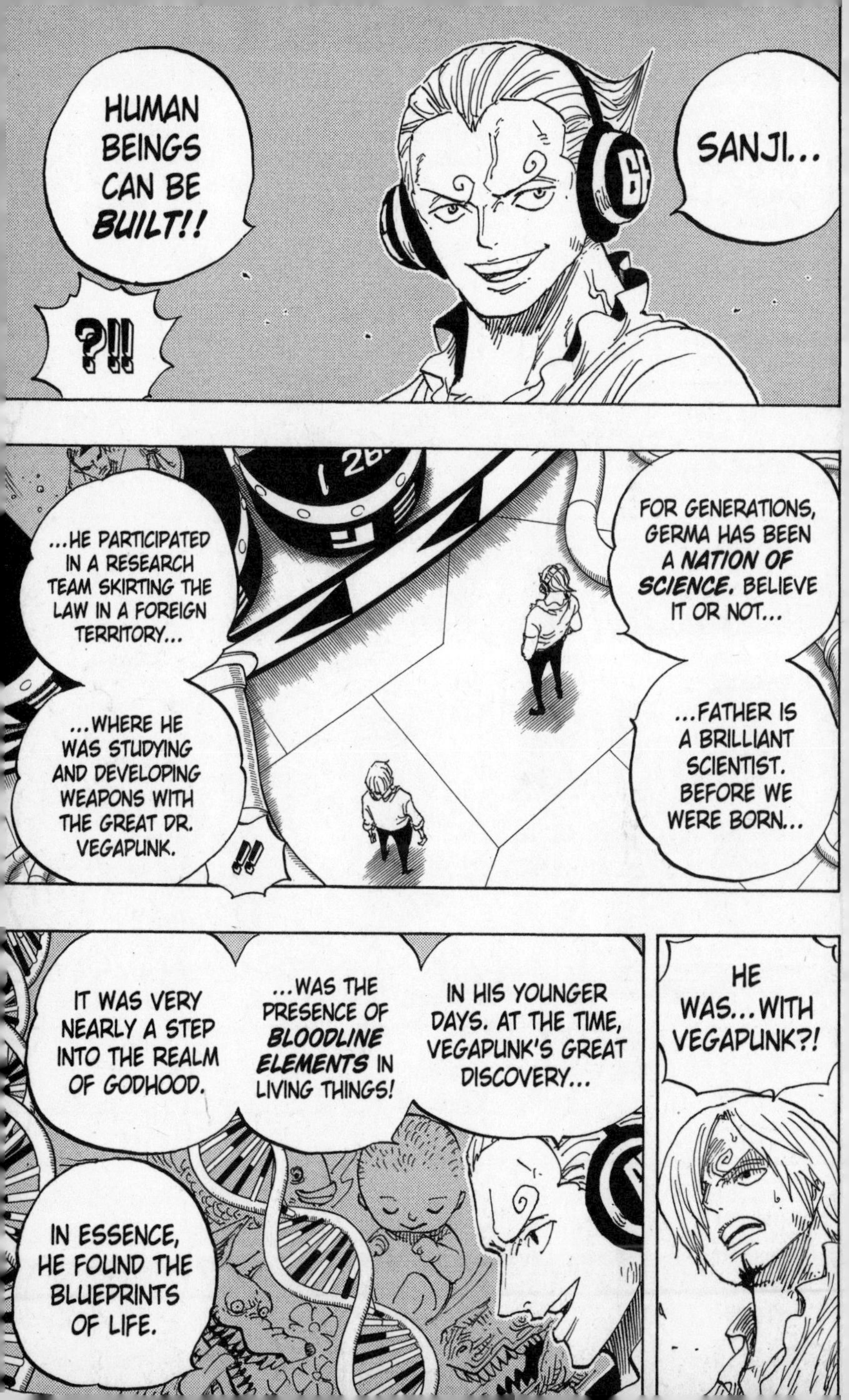
SANJI...
HUMAN BEINGS CAN BE BUILT!!
?!!
FOR GENERATIONS, GERMA HAS BEEN A NATION OF SCIENCE. BELIEVE IT OR NOT...
...FATHER IS A BRILLIANT SCIENTIST. BEFORE WE WERE BORN...
...HE PARTICIPATED IN A RESEARCH TEAM SKIRTING THE LAW IN A FOREIGN TERRITORY...
...WHERE HE WAS STUDYING AND DEVELOPING WEAPONS WITH THE GREAT DR. VEGAPUNK.
!!
HE WAS...WITH VEGAPUNK?!
IN HIS YOUNGER DAYS. AT THE TIME, VEGAPUNK'S GREAT DISCOVERY...
...WAS THE PRESENCE OF BLOODLINE ELEMENTS IN LIVING THINGS!
IT WAS VERY NEARLY A STEP INTO THE REALM OF GODHOOD.
IN ESSENCE, HE FOUND THE BLUEPRINTS OF LIFE.

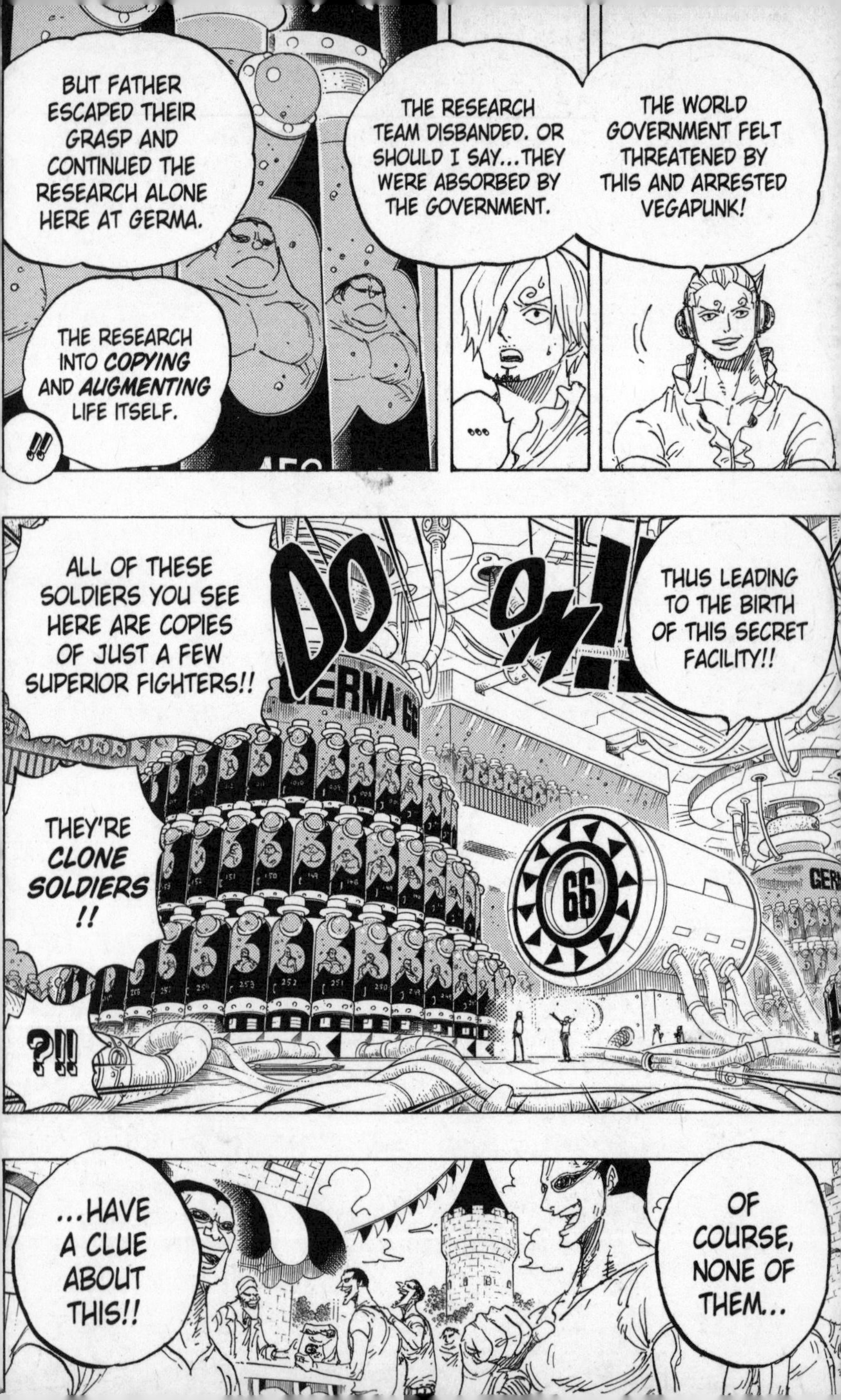
THE WORLD GOVERNMENT FELT THREATENED BY THIS AND ARRESTED VEGAPUNK!
THE RESEARCH TEAM DISBANDED. OR SHOULD I SAY...THEY WERE ABSORBED BY THE GOVERNMENT.
...
BUT FATHER ESCAPED THEIR GRASP AND CONTINUED THE RESEARCH ALONE HERE AT GERMA.
THE RESEARCH INTO *COPYING* AND *AUGMENTING* LIFE ITSELF.
!!
THUS LEADING TO THE BIRTH OF THIS SECRET FACILITY!!
DOOM!
ALL OF THESE SOLDIERS YOU SEE HERE ARE COPIES OF JUST A FEW SUPERIOR FIGHTERS!!
THEY'RE *CLONE SOLDIERS* !!
66
?!!
OF COURSE, NONE OF THEM...
...HAVE A CLUE ABOUT THIS!!

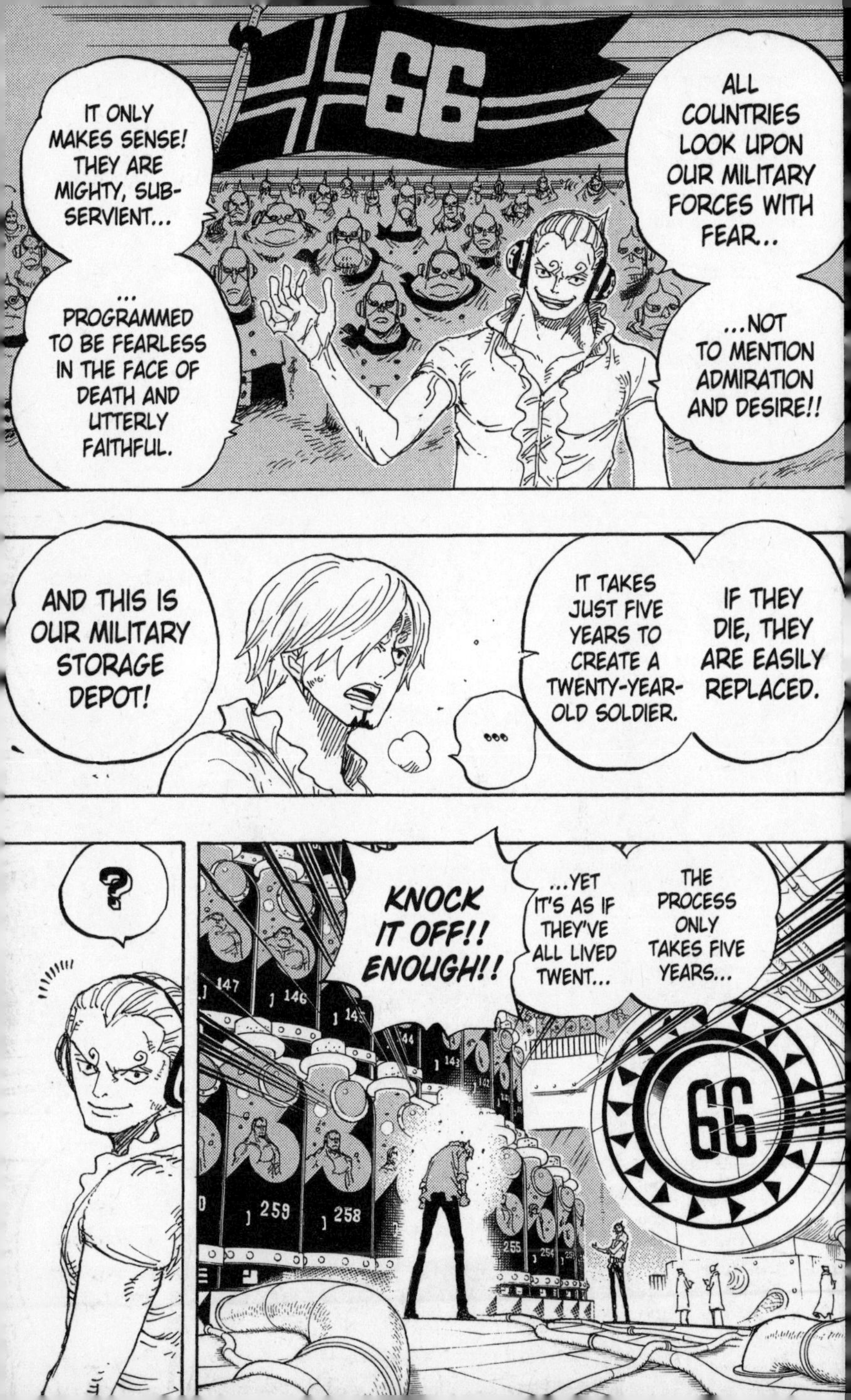
66
ALL COUNTRIES LOOK UPON OUR MILITARY FORCES WITH FEAR...
...NOT TO MENTION ADMIRATION AND DESIRE!!
IT ONLY MAKES SENSE! THEY ARE MIGHTY, SUB-SERVIENT...
... PROGRAMMED TO BE FEARLESS IN THE FACE OF DEATH AND UTTERLY FAITHFUL.
IF THEY DIE, THEY ARE EASILY REPLACED.
IT TAKES JUST FIVE YEARS TO CREATE A TWENTY-YEAR-OLD SOLDIER.
...
AND THIS IS OUR MILITARY STORAGE DEPOT!
THE PROCESS ONLY TAKES FIVE YEARS...
...YET IT'S AS IF THEY'VE ALL LIVED TWENT...
KNOCK IT OFF!! ENOUGH!!
147
146
259
258
255
66
?

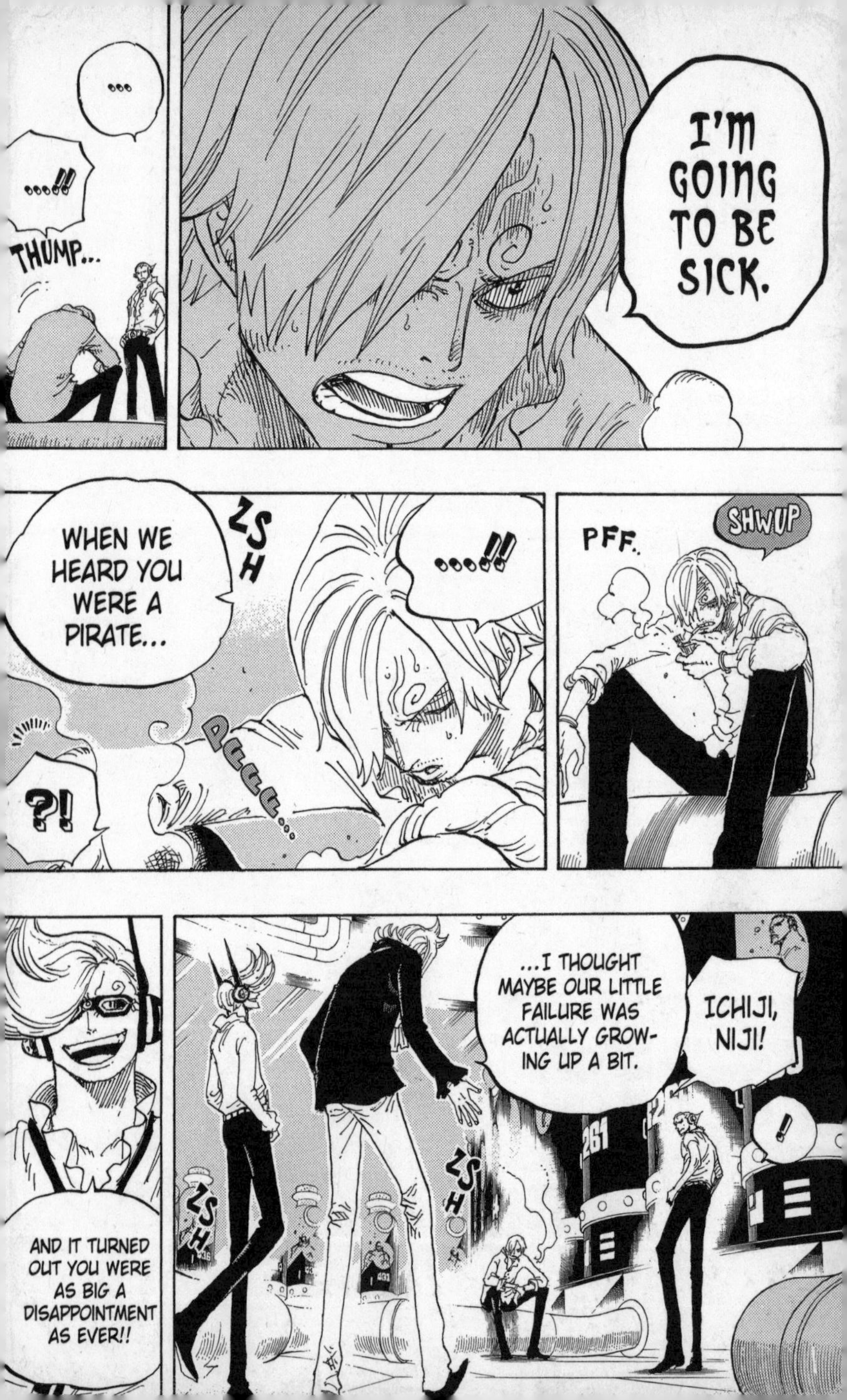
I'M GOING TO BE SICK.
...
...!!
THUMP...
SHWUP
PFF..
...!!
ZSH
WHEN WE HEARD YOU WERE A PIRATE...
DEEEE...
?!
ICHIJI, NIJI!
...I THOUGHT MAYBE OUR LITTLE FAILURE WAS ACTUALLY GROWING UP A BIT.
!
ZSH
ZSH
AND IT TURNED OUT YOU WERE AS BIG A DISAPPOINTMENT AS EVER!!

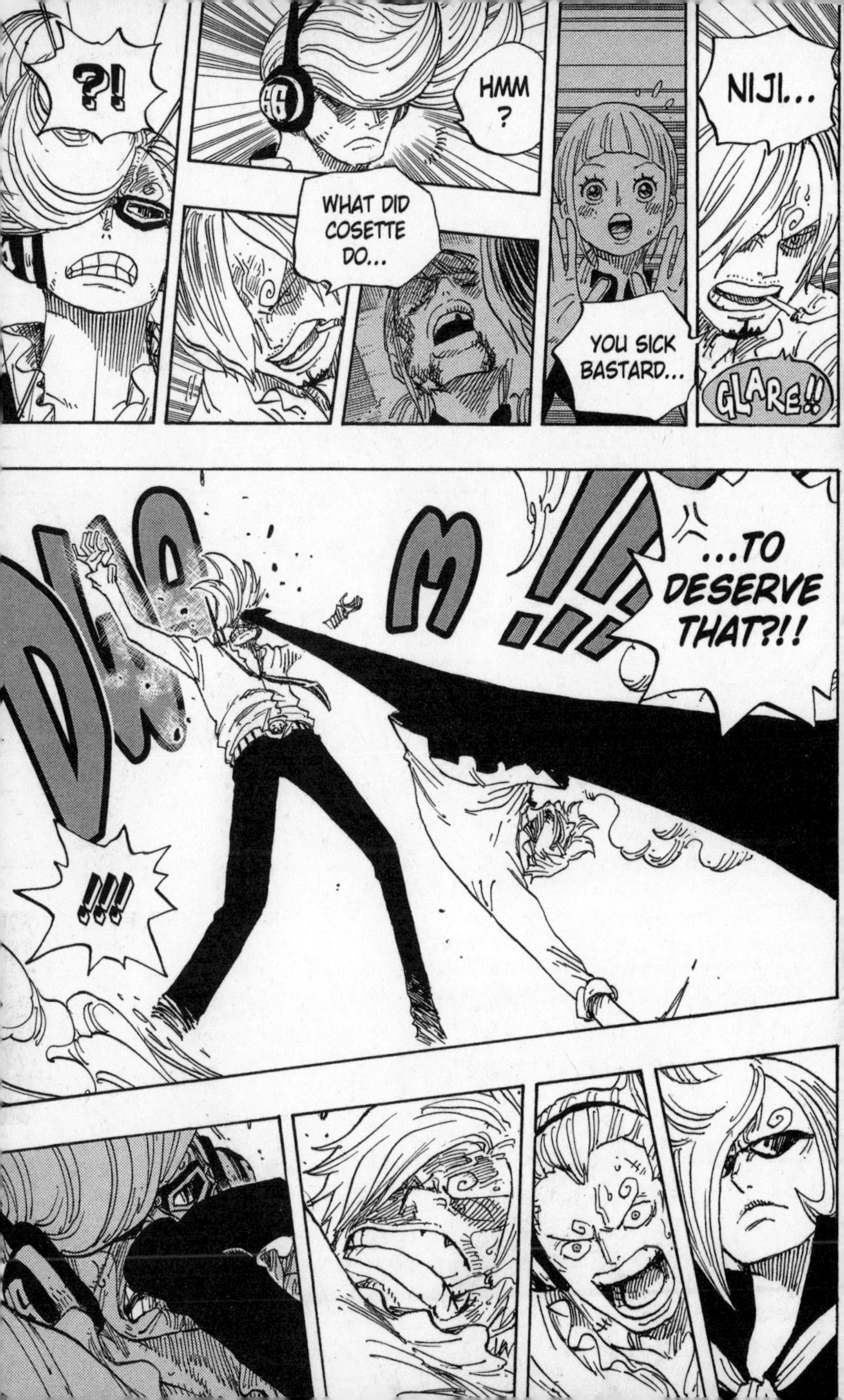
NIJI...
GLARE!!
YOU SICK BASTARD...
HMM ?
WHAT DID COSETTE DO...
?!
...TO DESERVE THAT?!!
DWOM!!
!!!

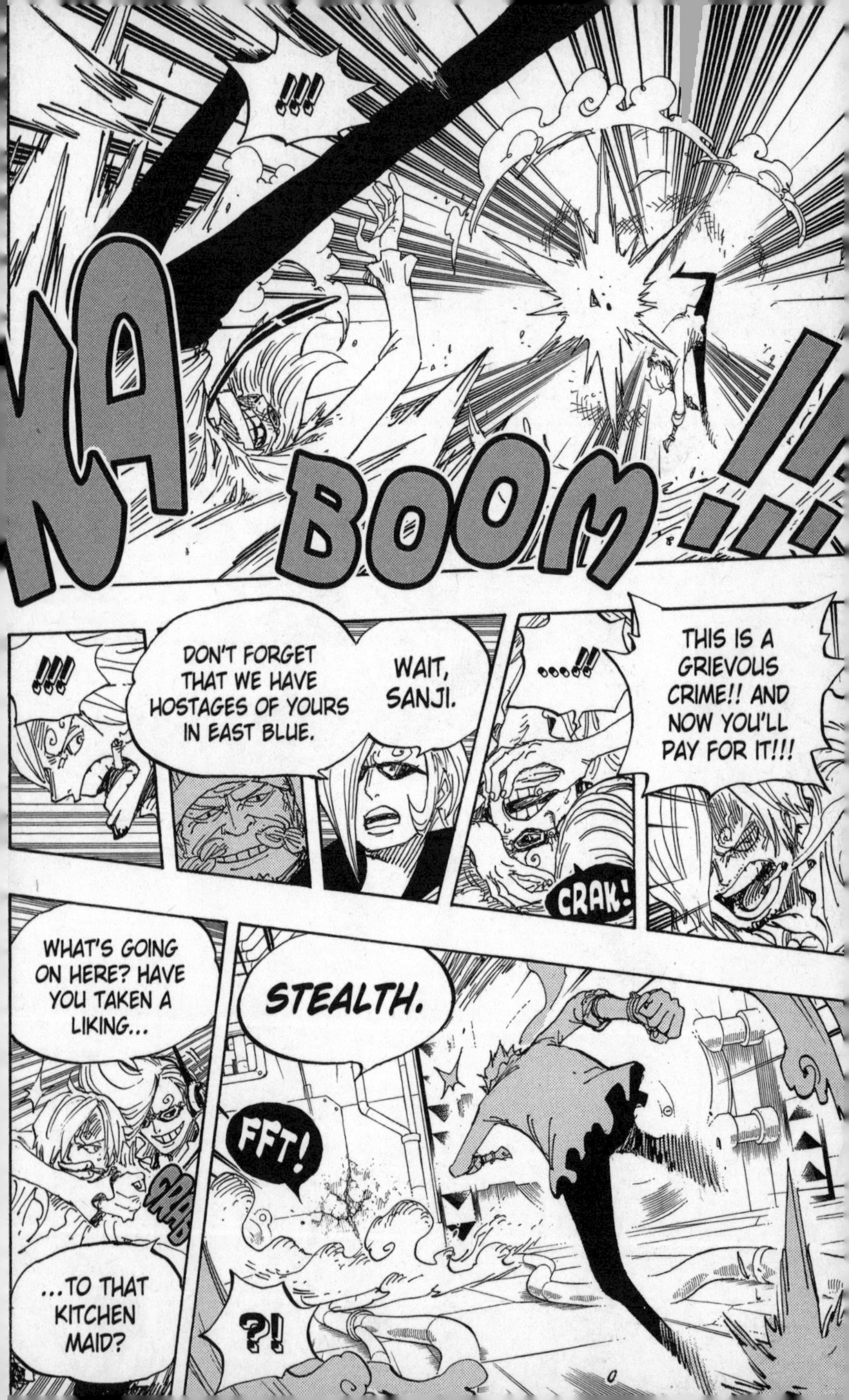
!!!
KA BOOM...!!!
THIS IS A GRIEVOUS CRIME!! AND NOW YOU'LL PAY FOR IT!!!
....!!
CRAK!
WAIT, SANJI.
DON'T FORGET THAT WE HAVE HOSTAGES OF YOURS IN EAST BLUE.
!!!
STEALTH.
FFT!
?!
WHAT'S GOING ON HERE? HAVE YOU TAKEN A LIKING...
GRAB
...TO THAT KITCHEN MAID?

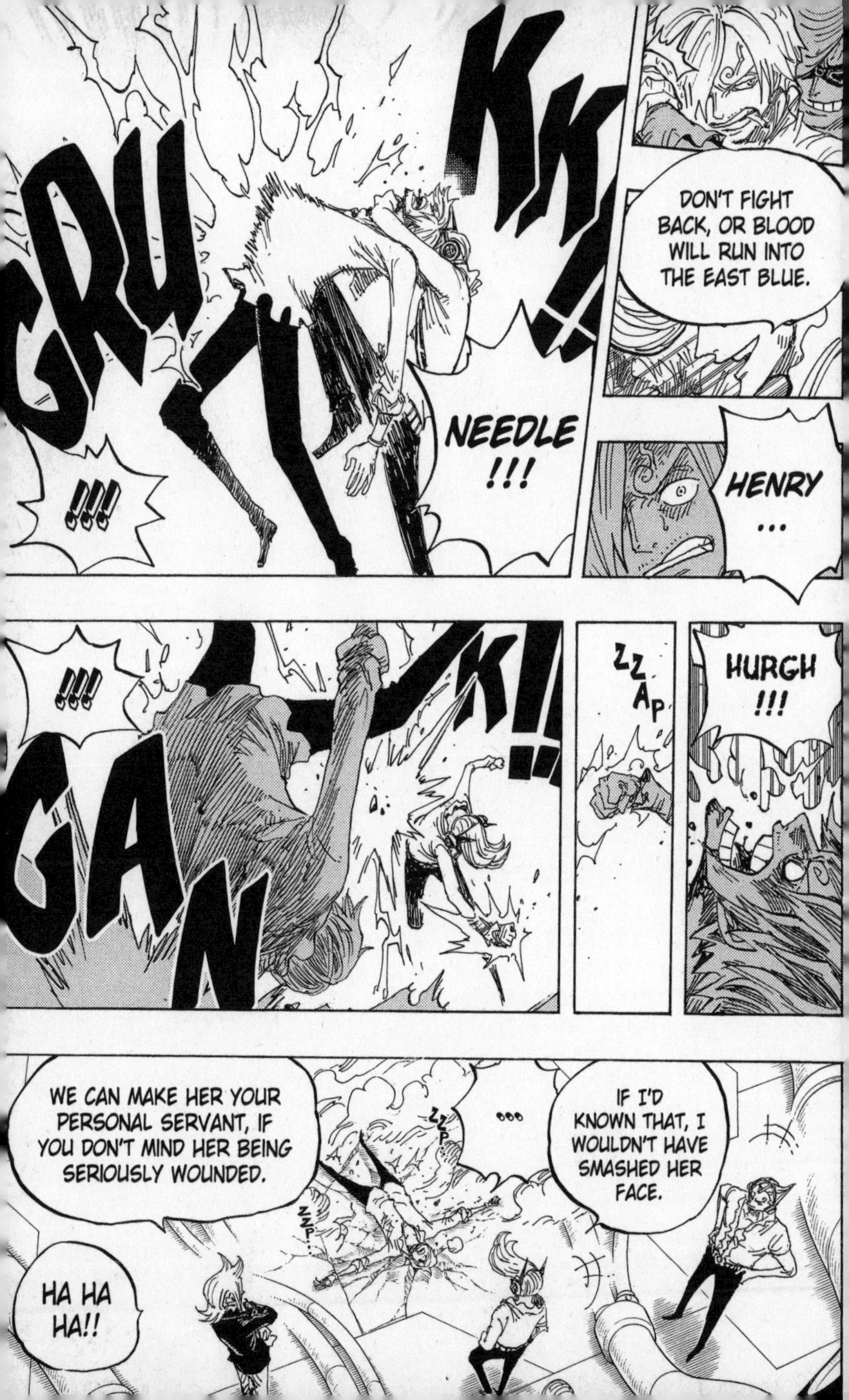
DON'T FIGHT BACK, OR BLOOD WILL RUN INTO THE EAST BLUE.
HENRY ...
KK
GRU
NEEDLE !!!
!!!
HURGH !!!
ZZAP
K!!
!!!
GAN
IF I'D KNOWN THAT, I WOULDN'T HAVE SMASHED HER FACE.
...
ZZP
WE CAN MAKE HER YOUR PERSONAL SERVANT, IF YOU DON'T MIND HER BEING SERIOUSLY WOUNDED.
ZZP...
HA HA HA!!

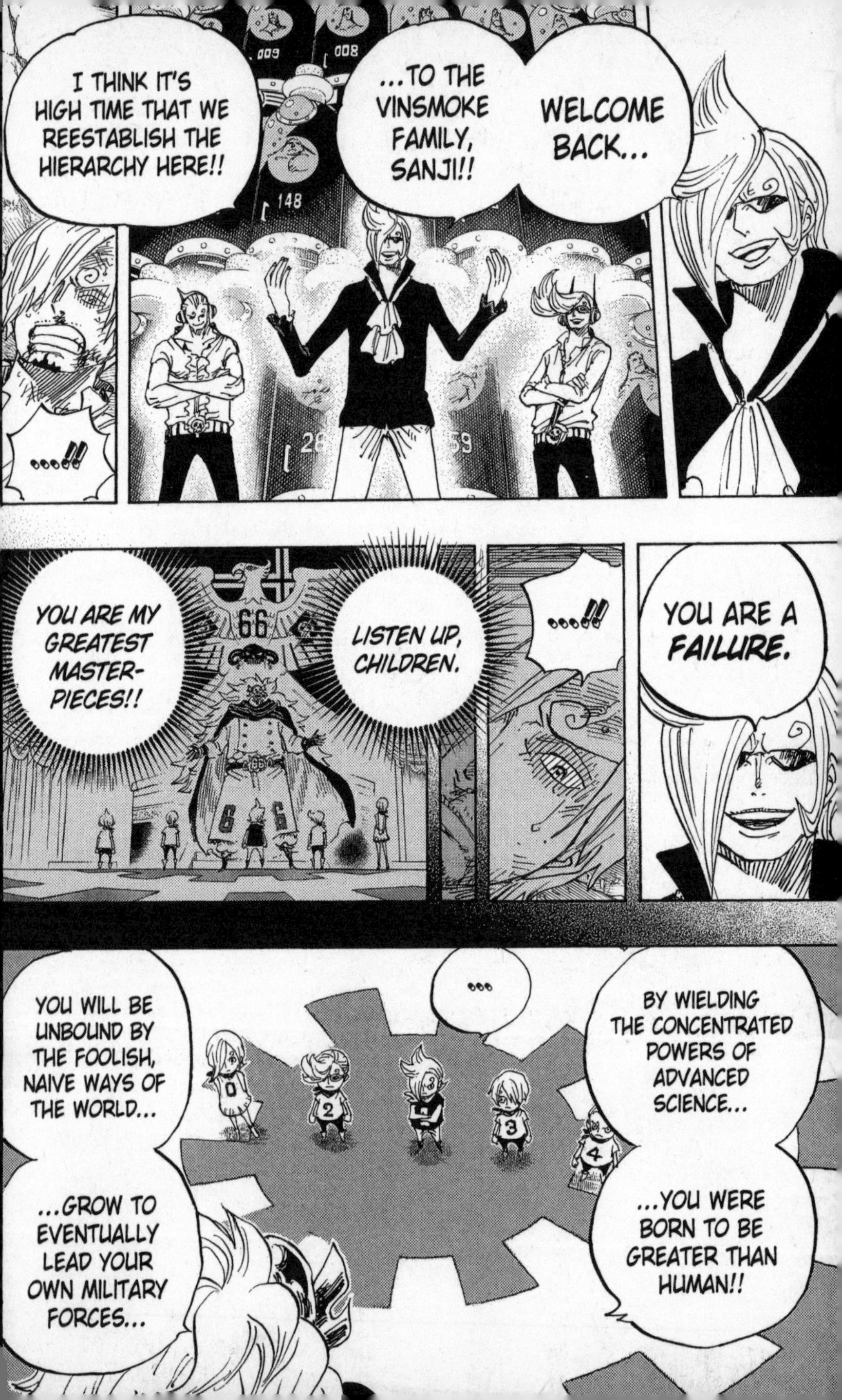
WELCOME BACK...
...TO THE VINSMOKE FAMILY, SANJI!!
I THINK IT'S HIGH TIME THAT WE REESTABLISH THE HIERARCHY HERE!!
....!!
YOU ARE A *FAILURE.*
....!!
LISTEN UP, CHILDREN.
YOU ARE MY GREATEST MASTER-PIECES!!
...
BY WIELDING THE CONCENTRATED POWERS OF ADVANCED SCIENCE...
...YOU WERE BORN TO BE GREATER THAN HUMAN!!
YOU WILL BE UNBOUND BY THE FOOLISH, NAIVE WAYS OF THE WORLD...
...GROW TO EVENTUALLY LEAD YOUR OWN MILITARY FORCES...

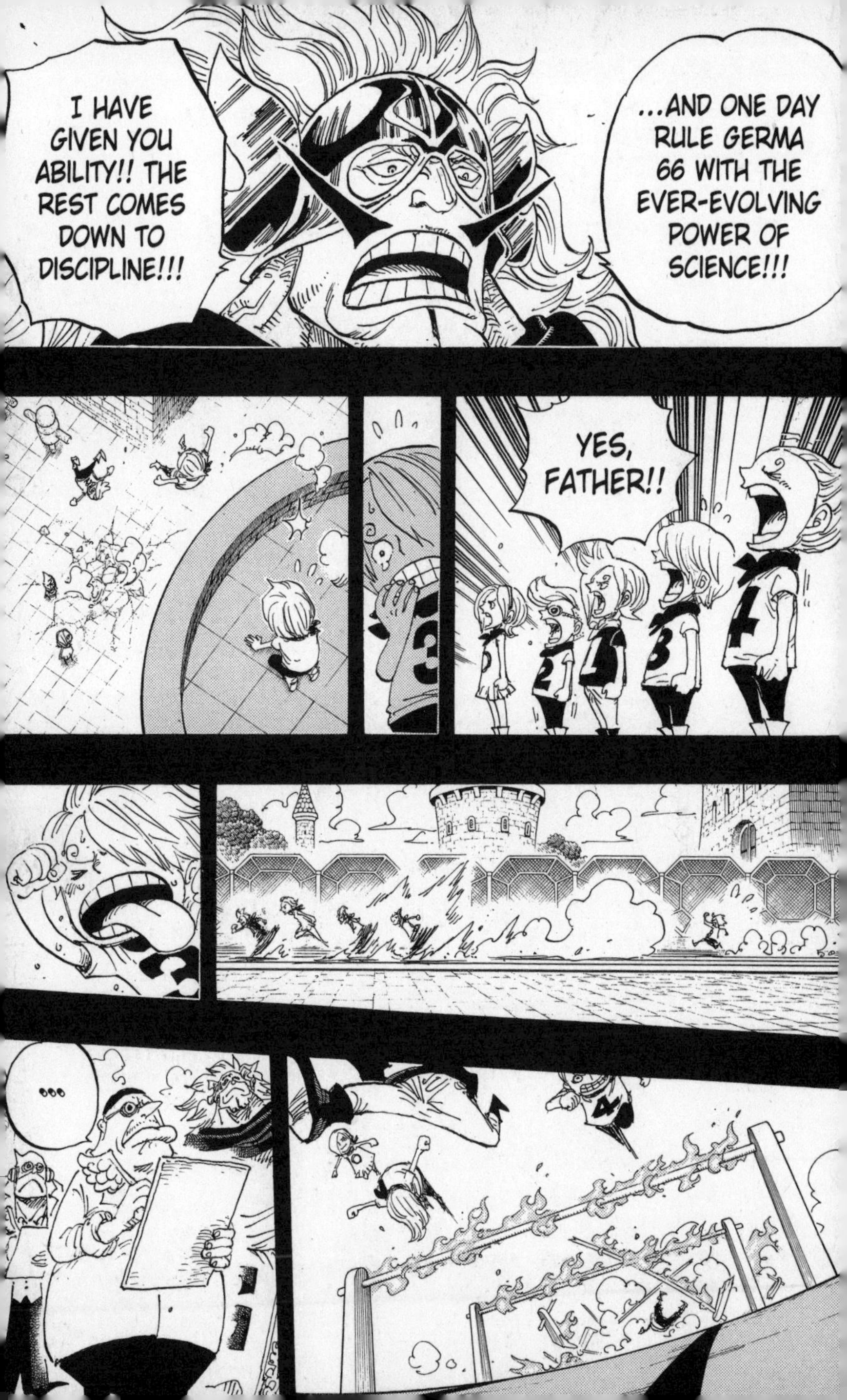
I HAVE GIVEN YOU ABILITY!! THE REST COMES DOWN TO DISCIPLINE!!!
...AND ONE DAY RULE GERMA 66 WITH THE EVER-EVOLVING POWER OF SCIENCE!!!
YES, FATHER!!
...

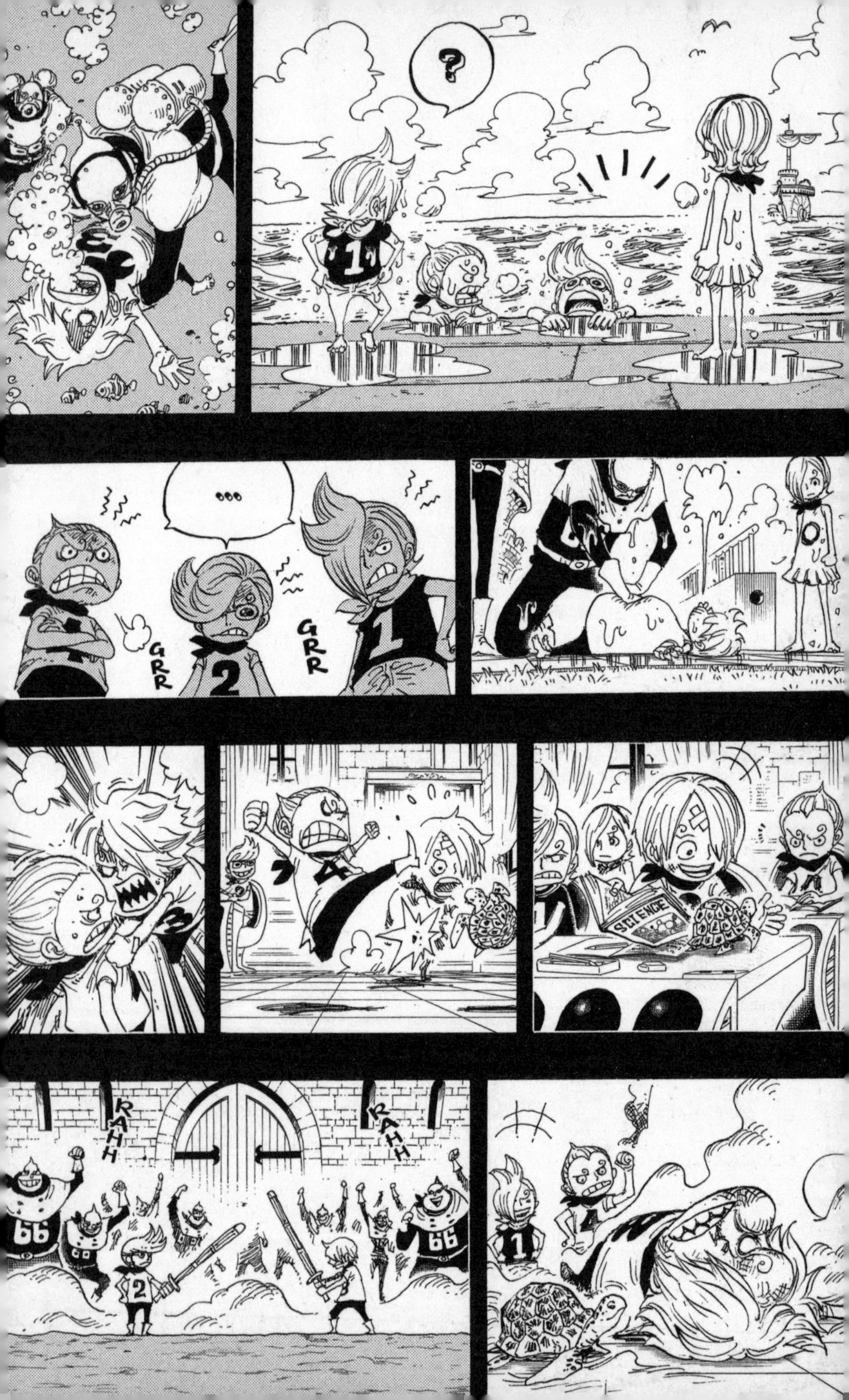
?
GRR
...
GRR
SCIENCE
RAHH
RAHH

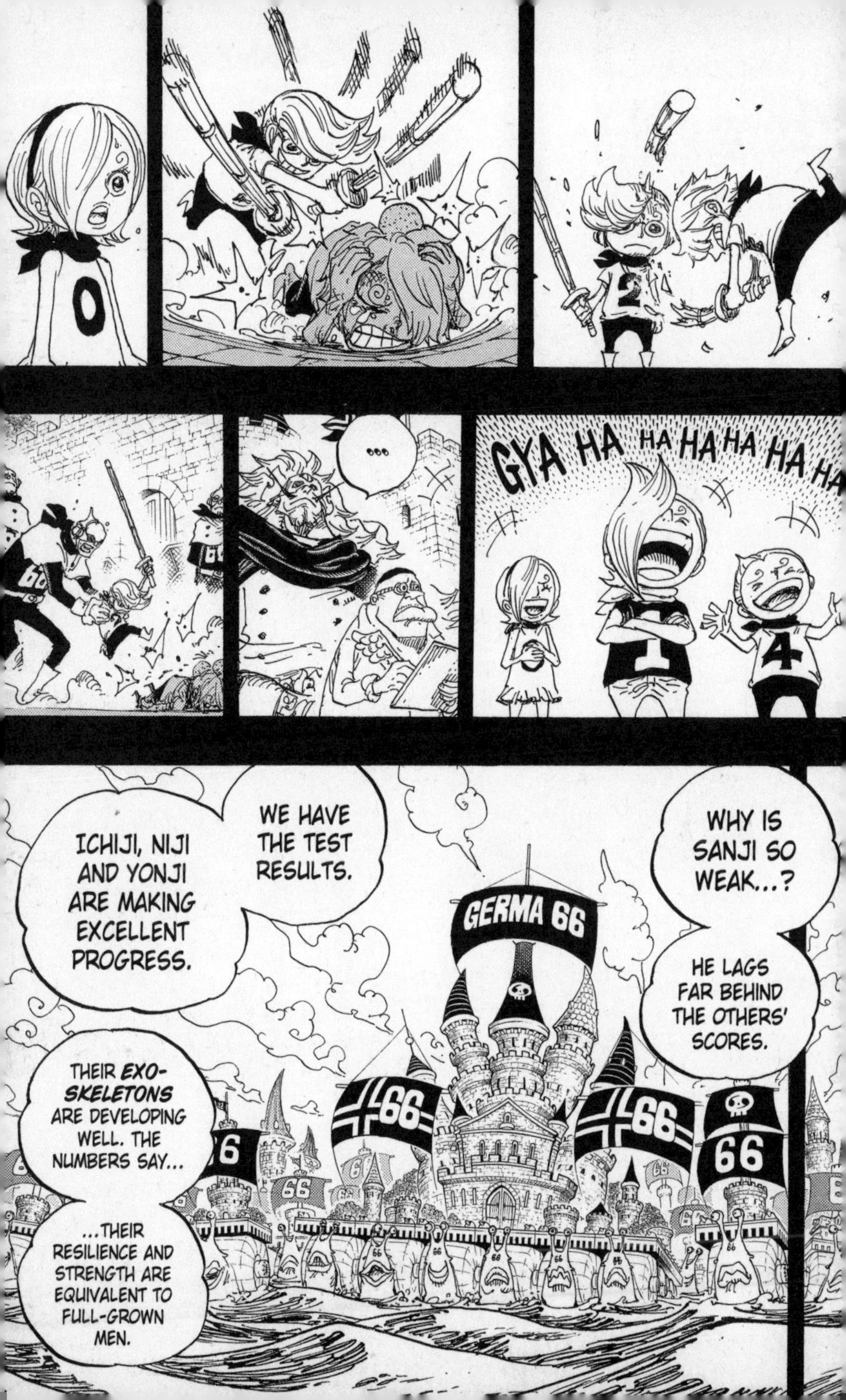
GYA HA HA HA HA HA HA
...
GERMA 66
WHY IS SANJI SO WEAK...?
HE LAGS FAR BEHIND THE OTHERS' SCORES.
WE HAVE THE TEST RESULTS.
ICHIJI, NIJI AND YONJI ARE MAKING EXCELLENT PROGRESS.
THEIR *EXO-SKELETONS* ARE DEVELOPING WELL. THE NUMBERS SAY...
...THEIR RESILIENCE AND STRENGTH ARE EQUIVALENT TO FULL-GROWN MEN.

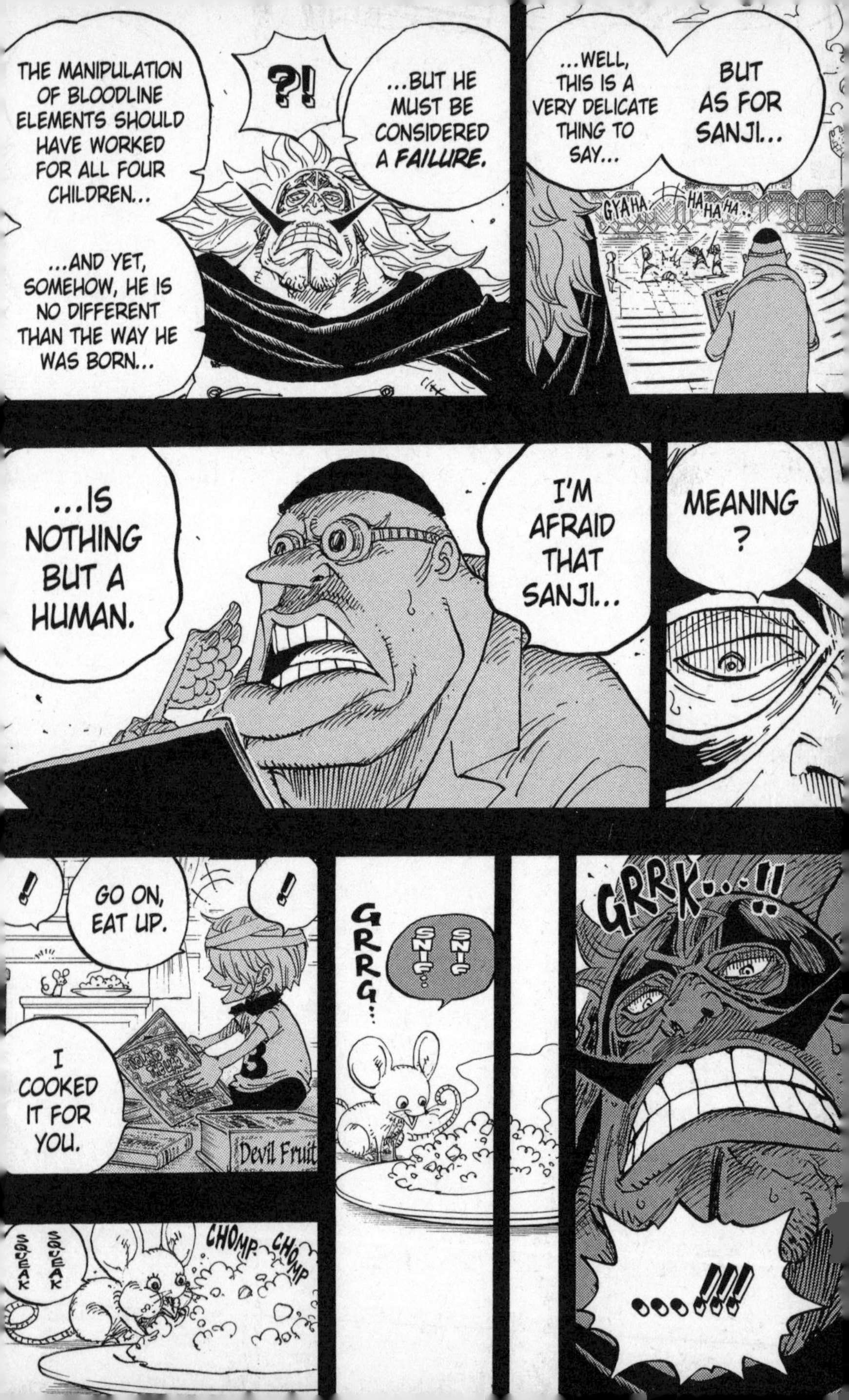
BUT AS FOR SANJI...
...WELL, THIS IS A VERY DELICATE THING TO SAY...
GYAHA HAHAHAHA...
...BUT HE MUST BE CONSIDERED A FAILURE.
?!
THE MANIPULATION OF BLOODLINE ELEMENTS SHOULD HAVE WORKED FOR ALL FOUR CHILDREN...
...AND YET, SOMEHOW, HE IS NO DIFFERENT THAN THE WAY HE WAS BORN...
MEANING?
I'M AFRAID THAT SANJI...
...IS NOTHING BUT A HUMAN.
GRRK...!!
...!!!
SNIF SNIF
GRRG...
!
GO ON, EAT UP.
!
I COOKED IT FOR YOU.
Devil Fruit
CHOMP CHOMP
SQUEAK SQUEAK

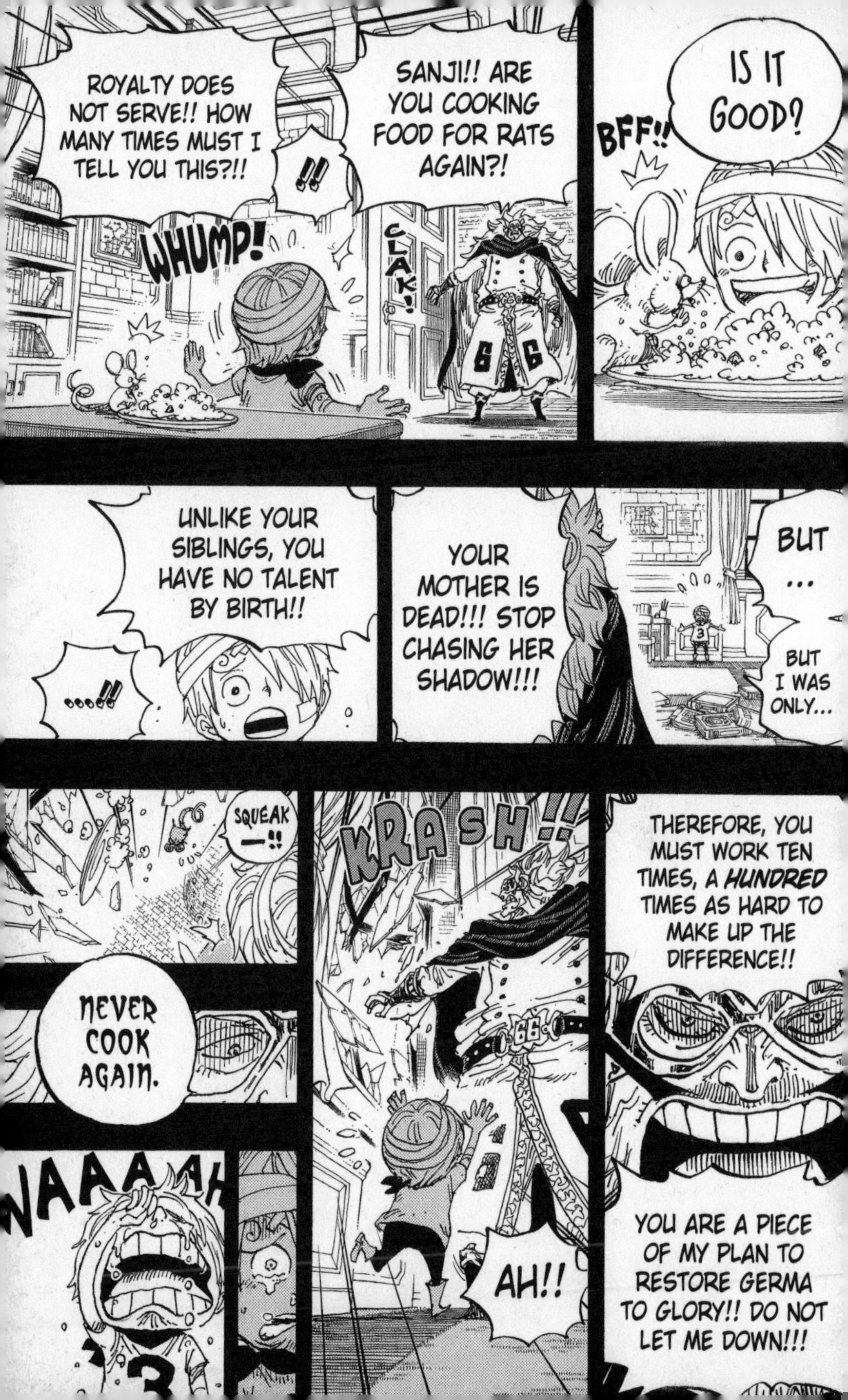
IS IT GOOD?
BFF!!
SANJI!! ARE YOU COOKING FOOD FOR RATS AGAIN?!
CLAK!
!!
ROYALTY DOES NOT SERVE!! HOW MANY TIMES MUST I TELL YOU THIS?!!
WHUMP!
BUT ...
BUT I WAS ONLY...
YOUR MOTHER IS DEAD!!! STOP CHASING HER SHADOW!!!
UNLIKE YOUR SIBLINGS, YOU HAVE NO TALENT BY BIRTH!!
....!!
THEREFORE, YOU MUST WORK TEN TIMES, A *HUNDRED* TIMES AS HARD TO MAKE UP THE DIFFERENCE!!
YOU ARE A PIECE OF MY PLAN TO RESTORE GERMA TO GLORY!! DO NOT LET ME DOWN!!!
KRASH!!
AH!!
SQUEAK—!!
NEVER COOK AGAIN.
WAAAAH

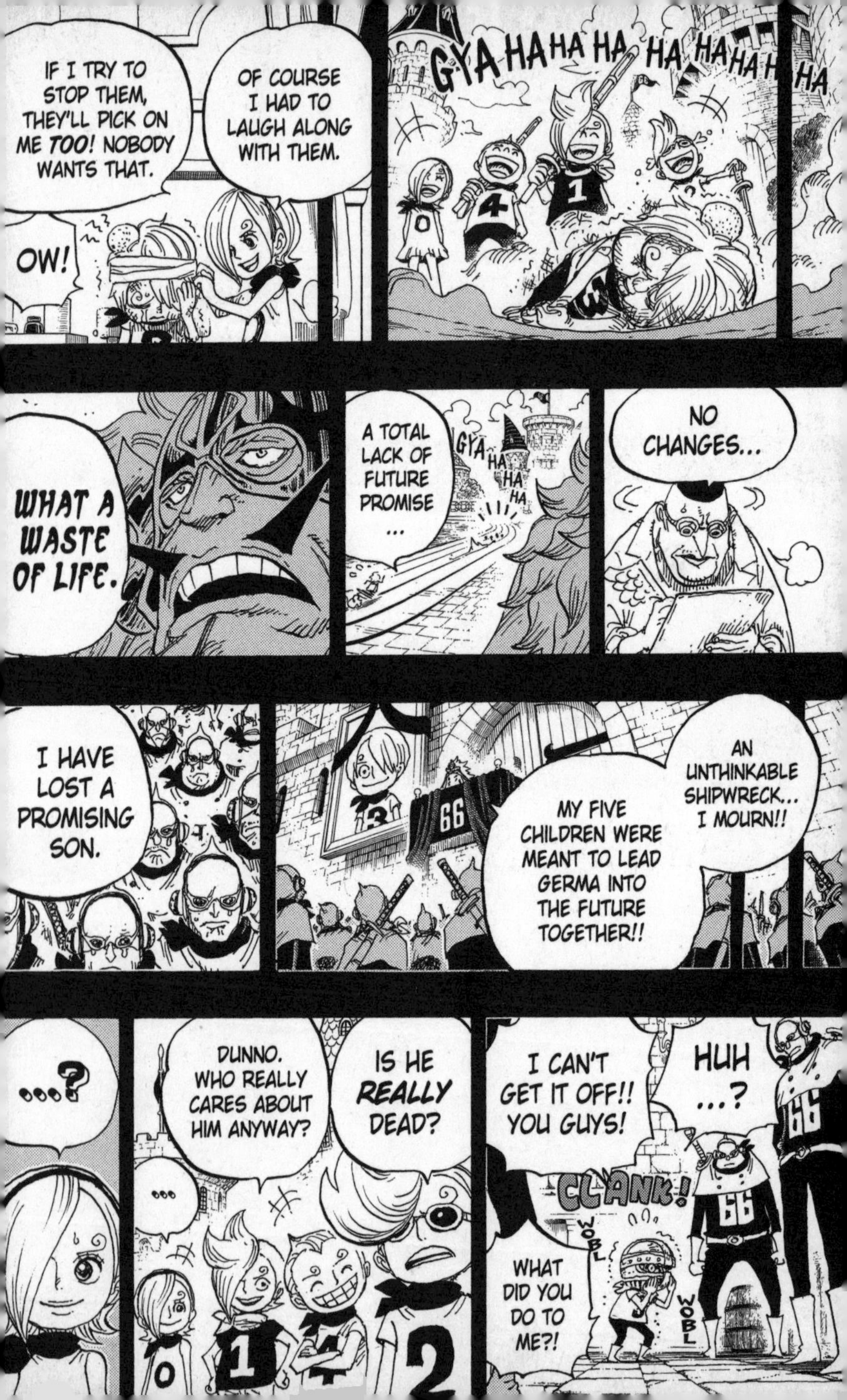
GYAHAHAHAHA HA HAHAHAHAHA
OF COURSE I HAD TO LAUGH ALONG WITH THEM.
IF I TRY TO STOP THEM, THEY'LL PICK ON ME *TOO*! NOBODY WANTS THAT.
OW!
NO CHANGES...
A TOTAL LACK OF FUTURE PROMISE ...
GYAHAHAHA
WHAT A WASTE OF LIFE.
AN UNTHINKABLE SHIPWRECK... I MOURN!!
MY FIVE CHILDREN WERE MEANT TO LEAD GERMA INTO THE FUTURE TOGETHER!!
I HAVE LOST A PROMISING SON.
HUH ...?
I CAN'T GET IT OFF!! YOU GUYS!
CLANK!
WOBL
WHAT DID YOU DO TO ME?!
WOBL
IS HE *REALLY* DEAD?
DUNNO. WHO REALLY CARES ABOUT HIM ANYWAY?
...
...?

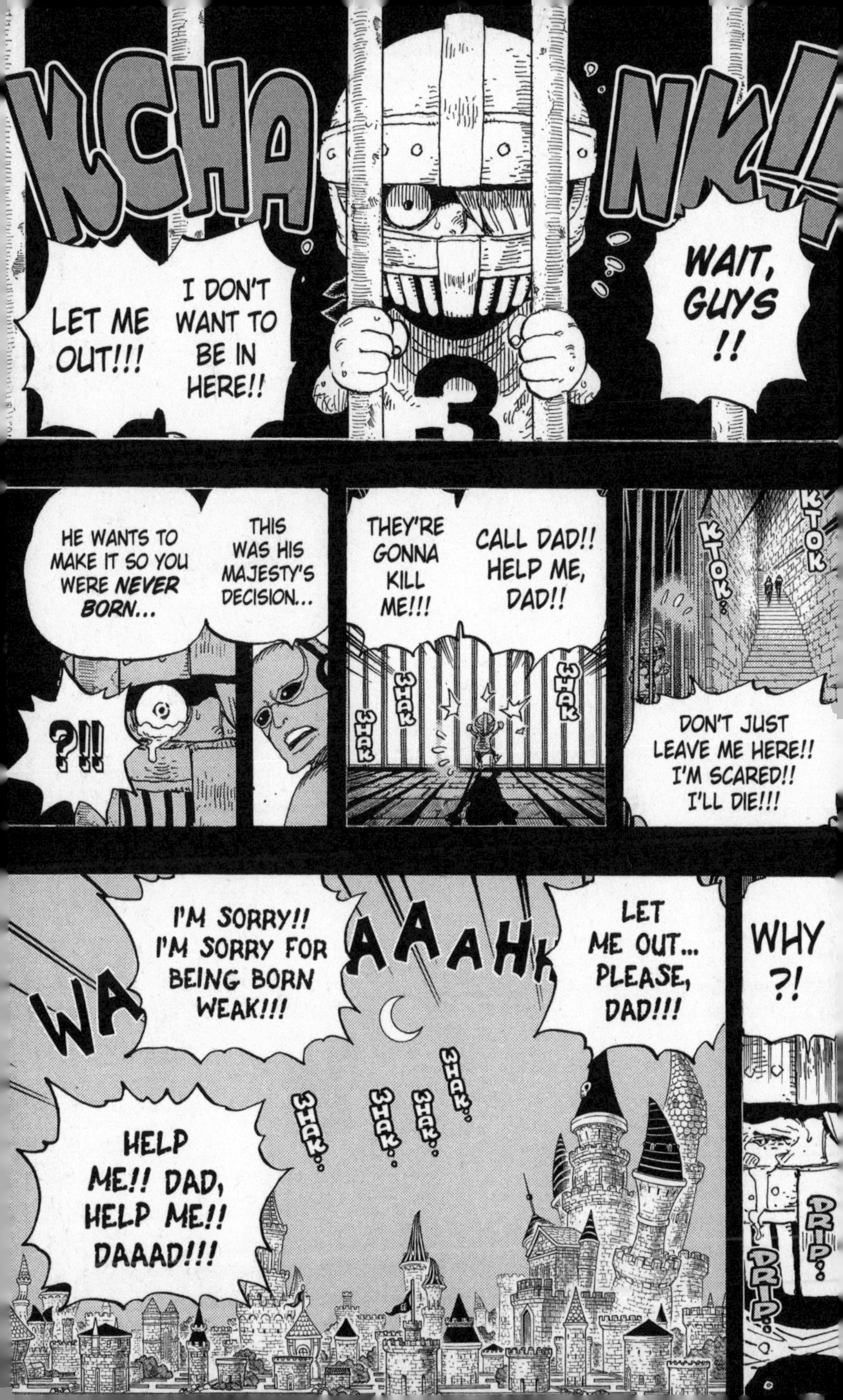
KCHANK!!
WAIT, GUYS!!
I DON'T WANT TO BE IN HERE!!
LET ME OUT!!!
KTOK
KTOK
DON'T JUST LEAVE ME HERE!! I'M SCARED!! I'LL DIE!!!
CALL DAD!! HELP ME, DAD!!
THEY'RE GONNA KILL ME!!!
WHAK
WHAK
WHAK
THIS WAS HIS MAJESTY'S DECISION...
HE WANTS TO MAKE IT SO YOU WERE *NEVER BORN*...
?!!
WHY ?!
DRIP
DRIP
LET ME OUT... PLEASE, DAD!!!
WAAAAHK
I'M SORRY!! I'M SORRY FOR BEING BORN WEAK!!!
WHAK
WHAK
WHAK
WHAK
HELP ME!! DAD, HELP ME!! DAAAD!!!

SBS Question Corner

エス ビー エス
SBS
質問コーナー

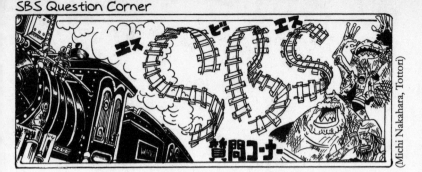

(Michi Nakahara, Tottori)

Q: In what order did Bepo, Penguin and Shachi join the Heart Pirates?

--Amefurashi

A: It's a long answer, but so many people asked that I decided to run through it here. You've read the backstory of Law in volumes 76 and 77. After the incident 13 years ago, Law wandered into the next town over on Swallow Island, crying his eyes out.

Law
Shachi
Penguin
Bepo

- Shachi and Penguin were snotty little kids growing up on Swallow Island in the North Blue.
- Fourteen years ago, Bepo left Zou in search of his older brother, got on a ship to the North Blue, and wound up on Swallow Island a year later.

PAT..!
NOW ANY NOISE THAT YOU CREATE WILL BE SILENCED!
SLIP AWAY WHEN YOU CAN, AND WE'LL MEET UP AT THE NEXT TOWN.

- On the edge of the town, Law spotted two young ruffians picking on a polar bear. When they turned on him next, he ended up beating them and saving the polar bear.
  Ultimately, all three of them wound up respecting and following him.
- Law, age 13 (now 26)
  Penguin, age 15 (now 28)
  Shachi, age 14 (now 27)
  Bepo, age 9 (now 22)

- Bepo studied seafaring and navigation in the hopes of returning to Zou. Eventually, the four of them founded the Heart Pirates together. So the answer to your question is "at the same time"! You won't see this in the manga!

Chapter 841:

TO THE EAST BLUE

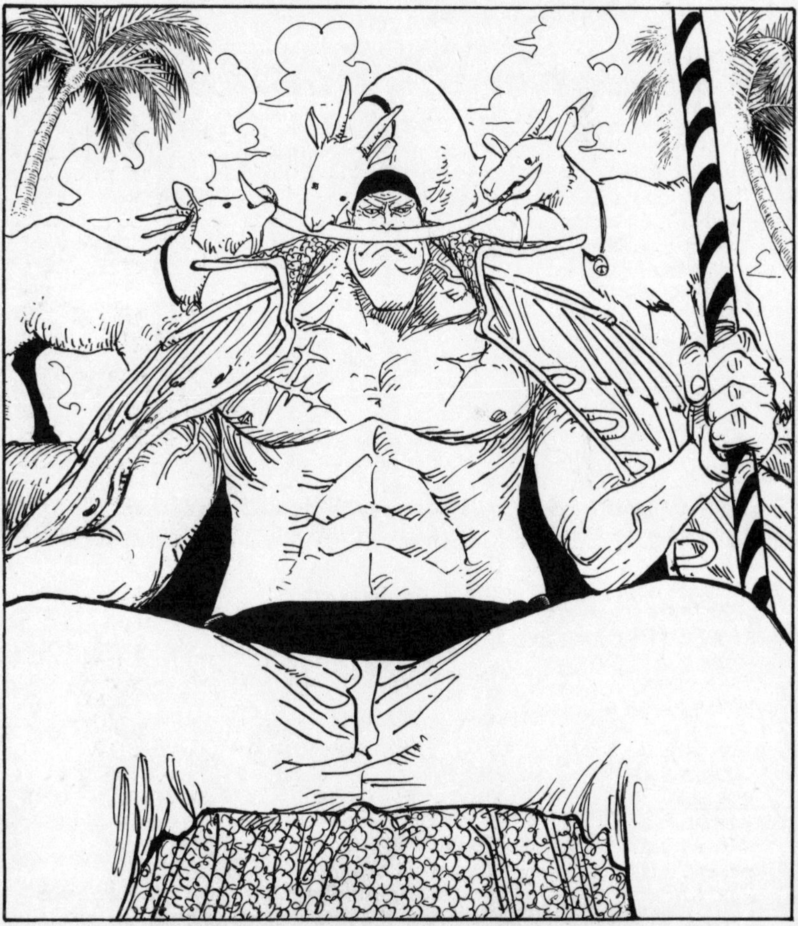

REQUEST: "GOATS CHOWING DOWN ON WHITEBEARD'S 'STACHE" BY WHITE GOAT ATE THE LETTER FROM OKAYAMA

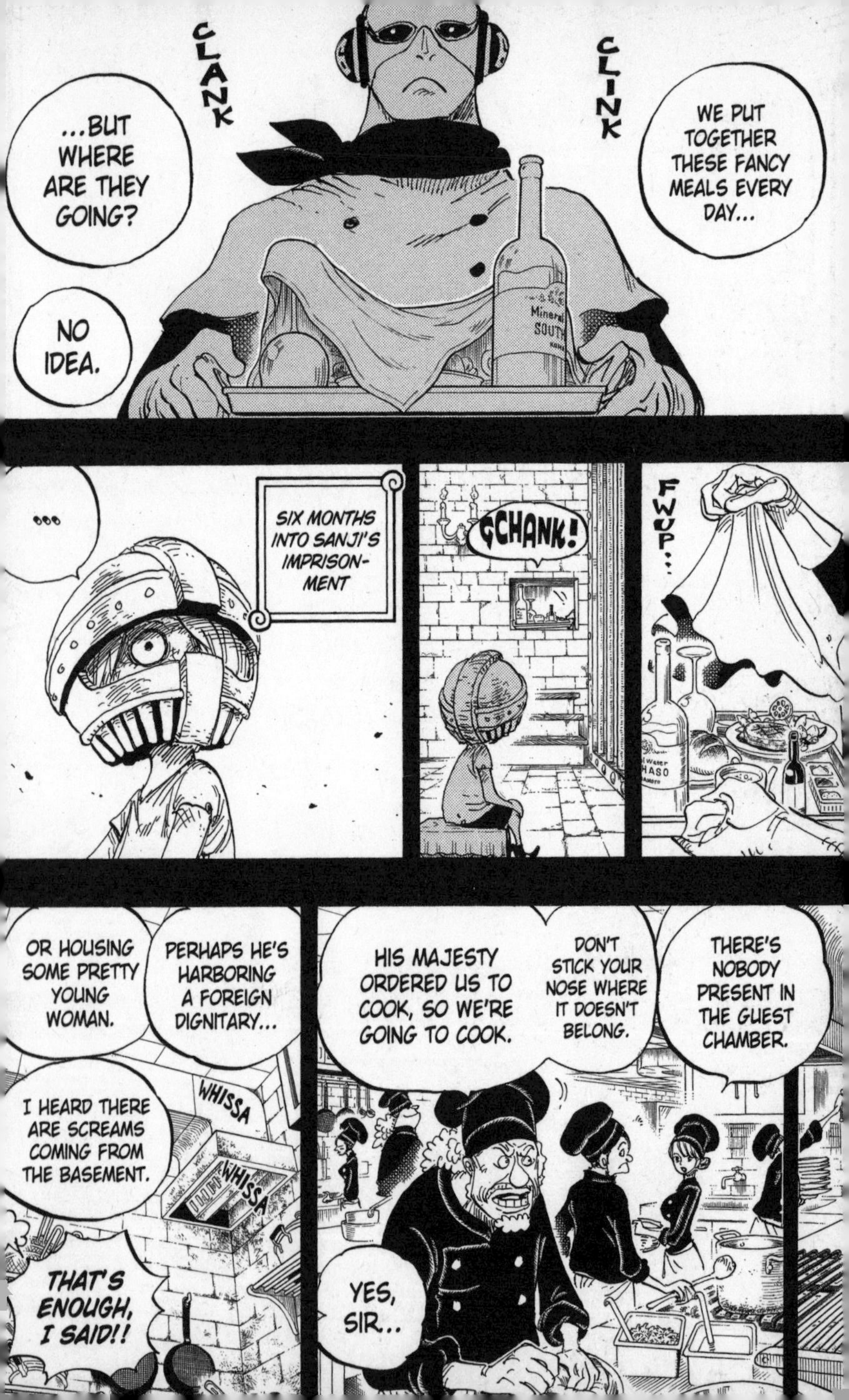

WE PUT TOGETHER THESE FANCY MEALS EVERY DAY...
CLINK
CLANK
...BUT WHERE ARE THEY GOING?
NO IDEA.
FWUP..
CHANK!
SIX MONTHS INTO SANJI'S IMPRISONMENT
...
THERE'S NOBODY PRESENT IN THE GUEST CHAMBER.
DON'T STICK YOUR NOSE WHERE IT DOESN'T BELONG.
HIS MAJESTY ORDERED US TO COOK, SO WE'RE GOING TO COOK.
YES, SIR...
PERHAPS HE'S HARBORING A FOREIGN DIGNITARY...
OR HOUSING SOME PRETTY YOUNG WOMAN.
WHISSA
I HEARD THERE ARE SCREAMS COMING FROM THE BASEMENT.
WHISSA
THAT'S ENOUGH, I SAID!!

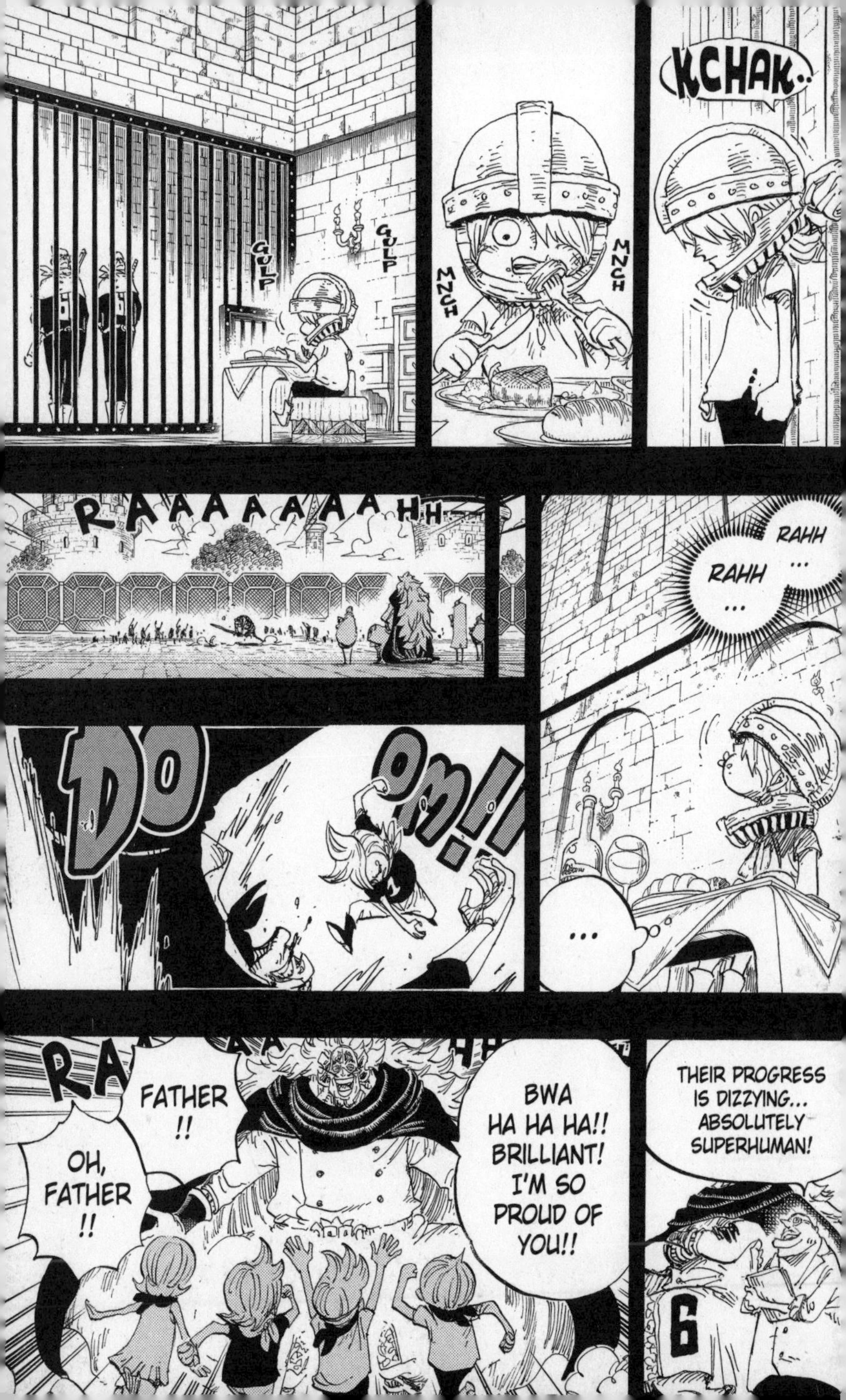
KCHAK..
MNCH
MNCH
GULP
GULP
RAHH ...
RAHH ...
...
RAAAAAAAAHH
DOOM!!
THEIR PROGRESS IS DIZZYING... ABSOLUTELY SUPERHUMAN!
BWA HA HA HA!! BRILLIANT! I'M SO PROUD OF YOU!!
FATHER !!
OH, FATHER !!

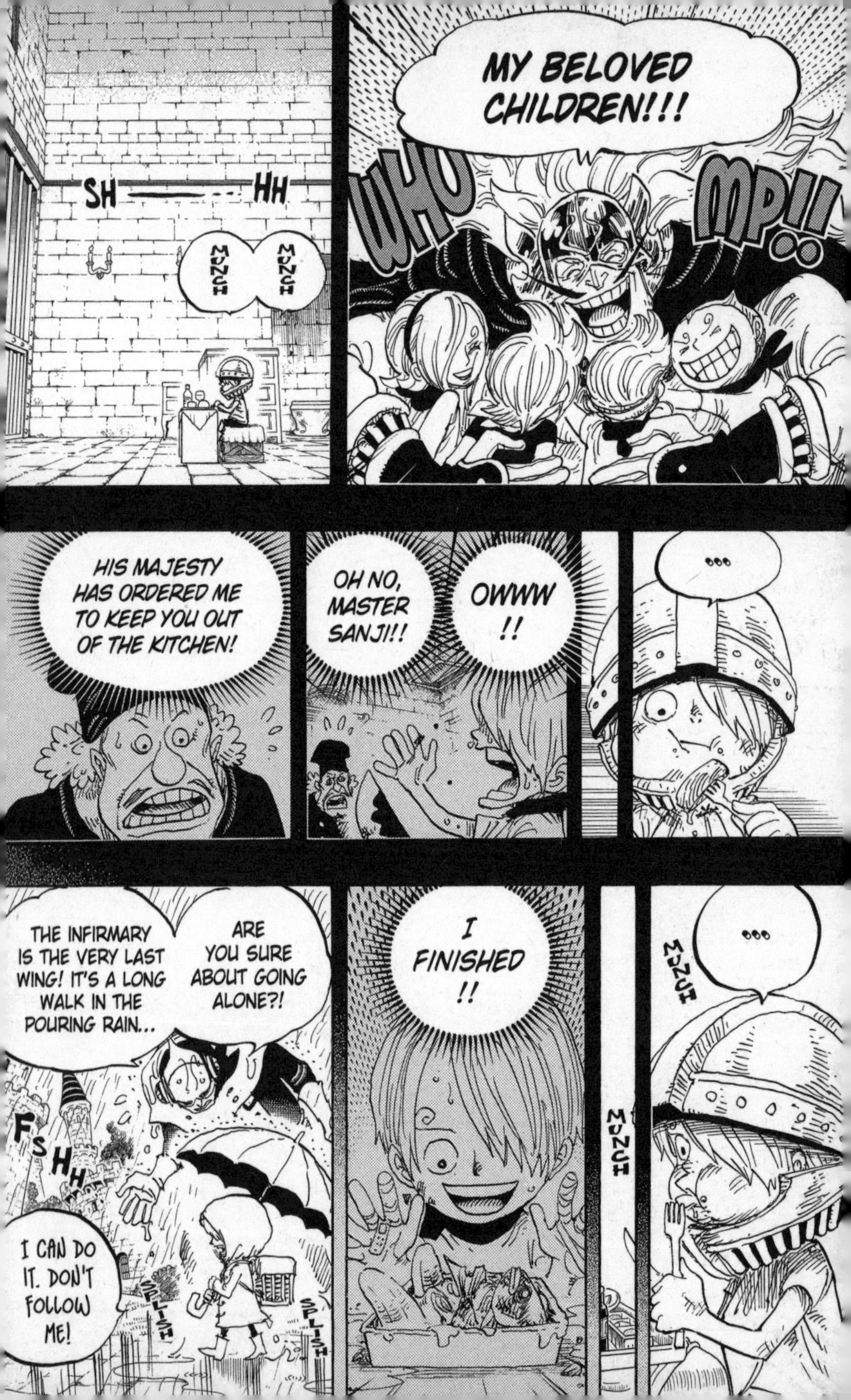
MY BELOVED CHILDREN!!!
WHUMP!!
SH—HH
MUNCH
MUNCH
...
OWWW!!
OH NO, MASTER SANJI!!
HIS MAJESTY HAS ORDERED ME TO KEEP YOU OUT OF THE KITCHEN!
...
MUNCH
MUNCH
I FINISHED!!
ARE YOU SURE ABOUT GOING ALONE?!
THE INFIRMARY IS THE VERY LAST WING! IT'S A LONG WALK IN THE POURING RAIN...
FSHHH
I CAN DO IT. DON'T FOLLOW ME!
SPLISH
SPLISH

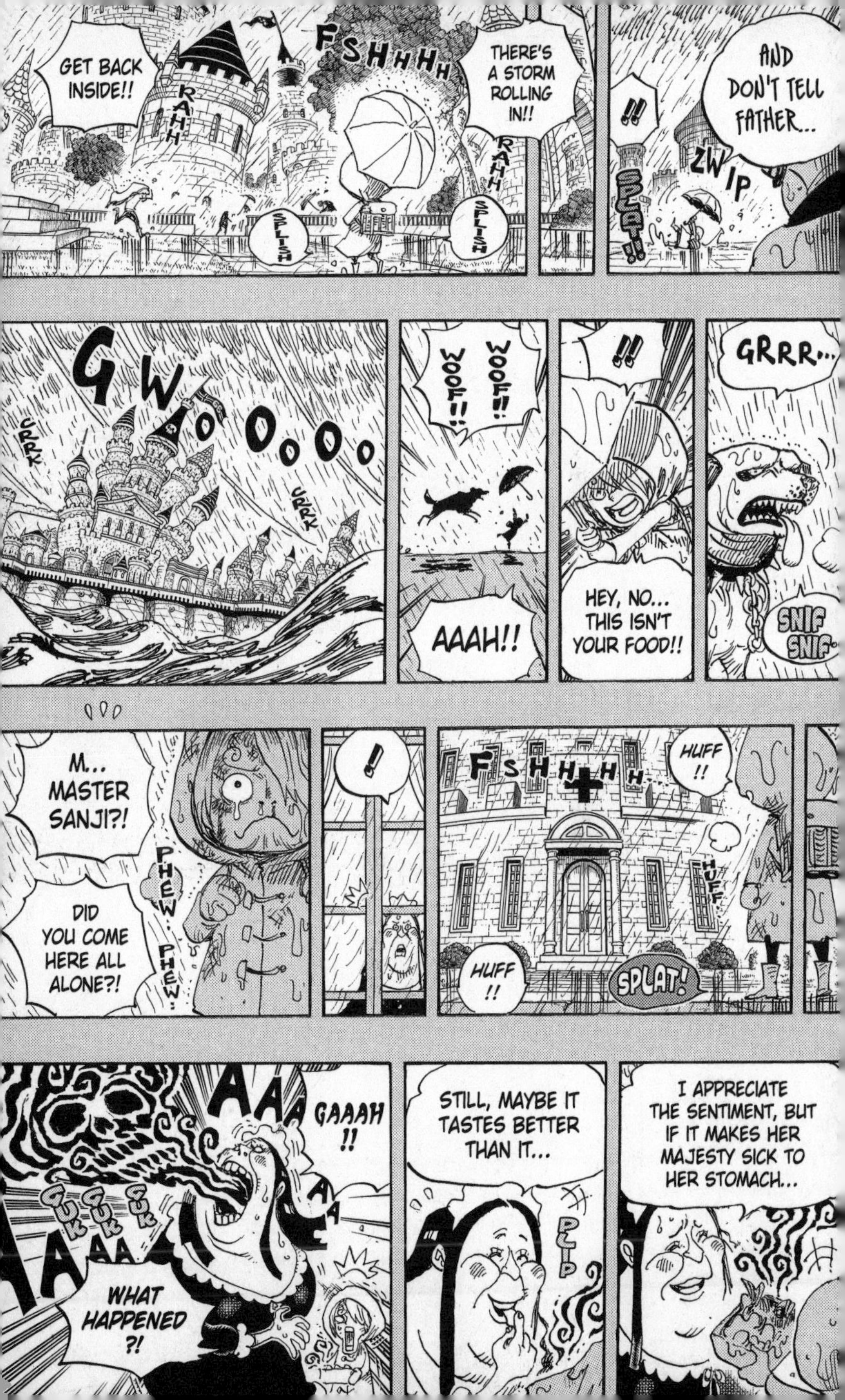
AND DON'T TELL FATHER...
!!
ZWIP
SPLAT!!
THERE'S A STORM ROLLING IN!!
FSHHHHH
GET BACK INSIDE!!
RAHH
RAHH
SPLISH
SPLISH
GRRR...
SNIF SNIF
!!
HEY, NO... THIS ISN'T YOUR FOOD!!
WOOF!! WOOF!!
AAAH!!
GWOOOOO
CRRK
CRRK
HUFF !!
FSHHHHH
HUFF...
HUFF !!
SPLAT!
!
M... MASTER SANJI?!
PHEW... PHEW...
DID YOU COME HERE ALL ALONE?!
I APPRECIATE THE SENTIMENT, BUT IF IT MAKES HER MAJESTY SICK TO HER STOMACH...
STILL, MAYBE IT TASTES BETTER THAN IT...
PLIP
GAAAH!!
AAAA
GUK GUK GUK
WHAT HAPPENED?!

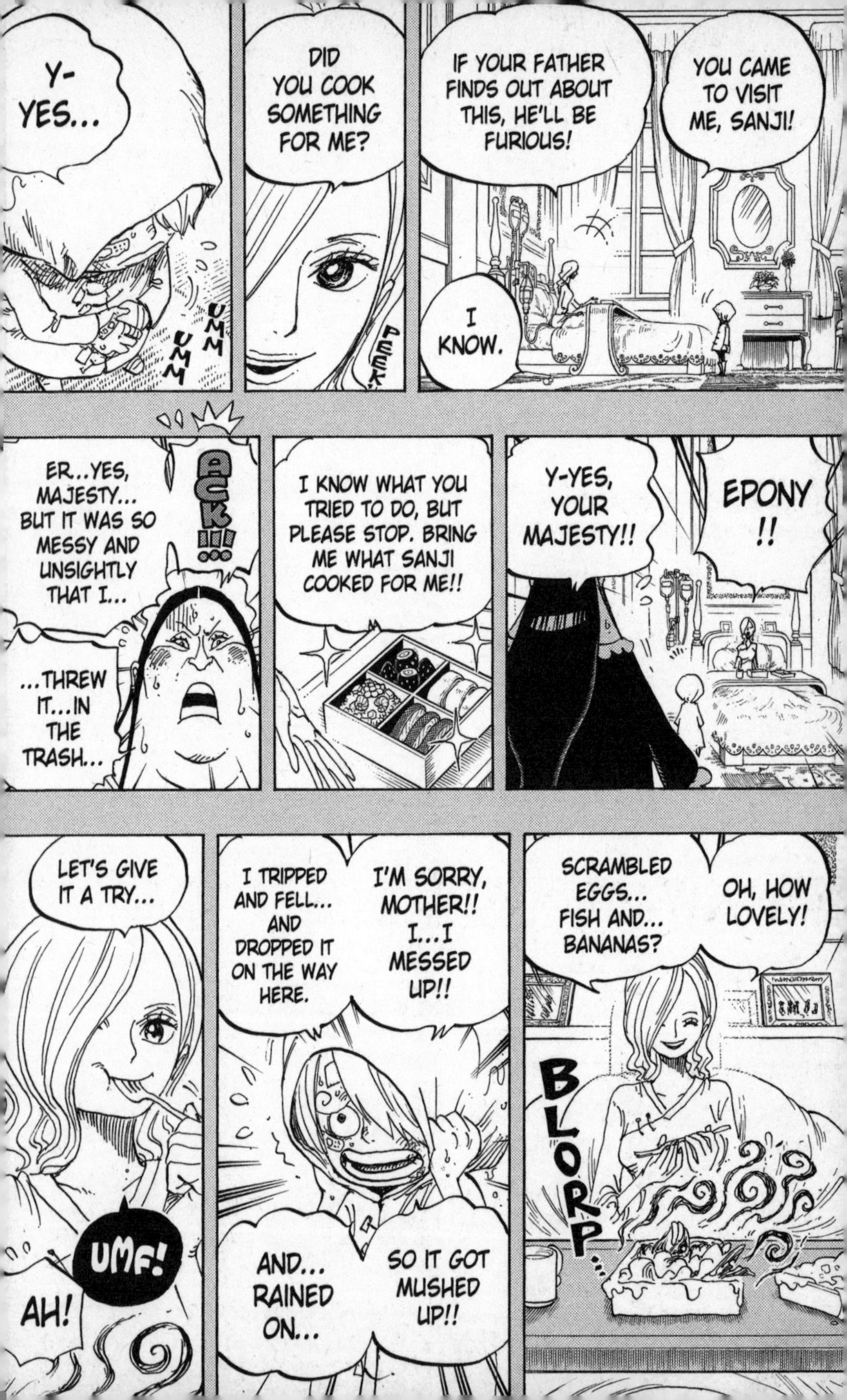
YOU CAME TO VISIT ME, SANJI!
IF YOUR FATHER FINDS OUT ABOUT THIS, HE'LL BE FURIOUS!
I KNOW.
DID YOU COOK SOMETHING FOR ME?
PEEK
Y- YES...
UMM
UMM
EPONY !!
Y-YES, YOUR MAJESTY!!
I KNOW WHAT YOU TRIED TO DO, BUT PLEASE STOP. BRING ME WHAT SANJI COOKED FOR ME!!
ACK!!!
ER...YES, MAJESTY... BUT IT WAS SO MESSY AND UNSIGHTLY THAT I...
...THREW IT...IN THE TRASH...
OH, HOW LOVELY!
SCRAMBLED EGGS... FISH AND... BANANAS?
BLORP...
I'M SORRY, MOTHER!! I...I MESSED UP!!
I TRIPPED AND FELL... AND DROPPED IT ON THE WAY HERE.
SO IT GOT MUSHED UP!!
AND... RAINED ON...
LET'S GIVE IT A TRY...
UMF!
AH!

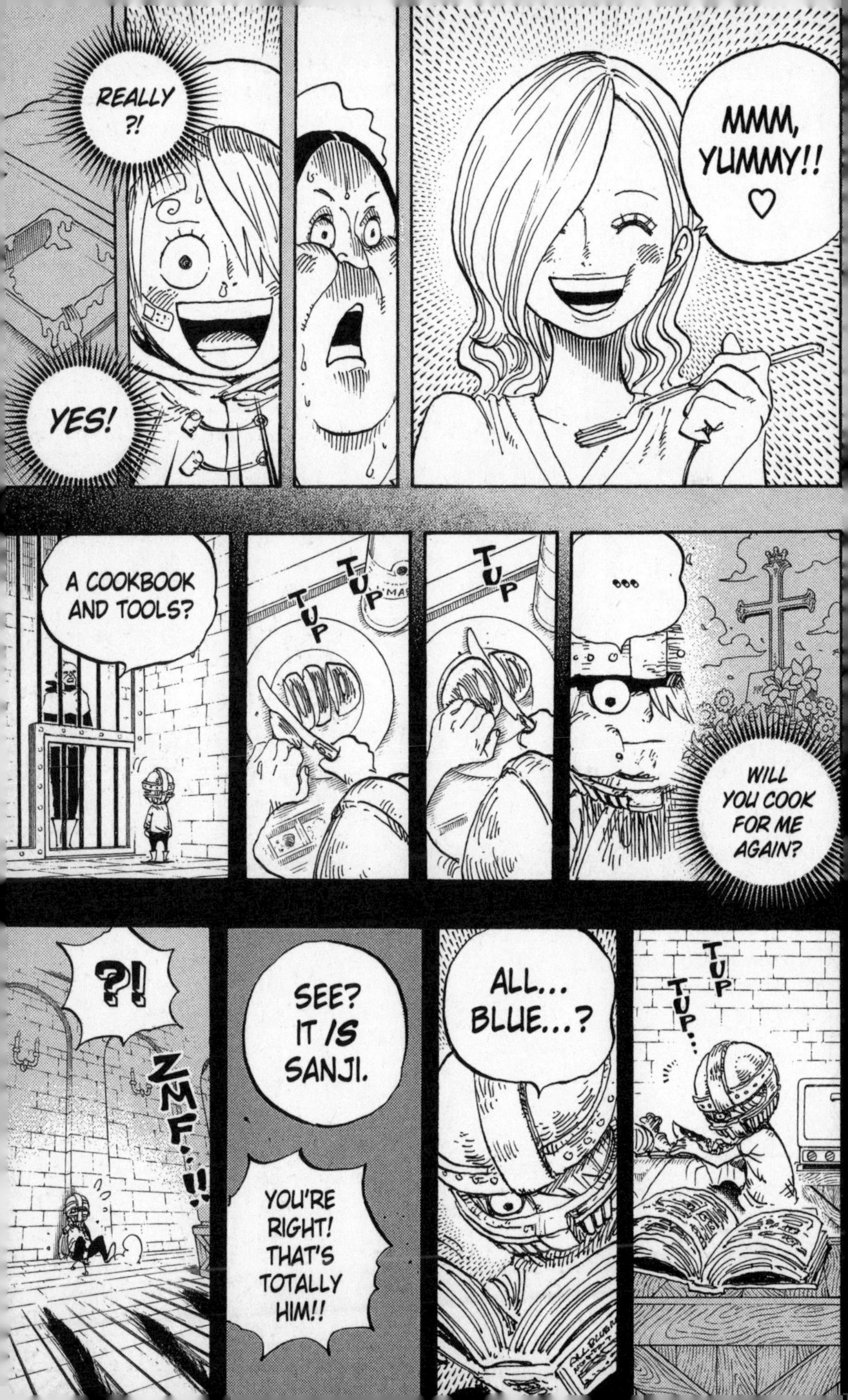
MMM, YUMMY!! ♡
REALLY ?!
YES!
...
WILL YOU COOK FOR ME AGAIN?
TUP
TUP TUP
A COOKBOOK AND TOOLS?
TUP TUP...
ALL... BLUE...?
SEE? IT *IS* SANJI.
YOU'RE RIGHT! THAT'S TOTALLY HIM!!
?!
ZMF...!!

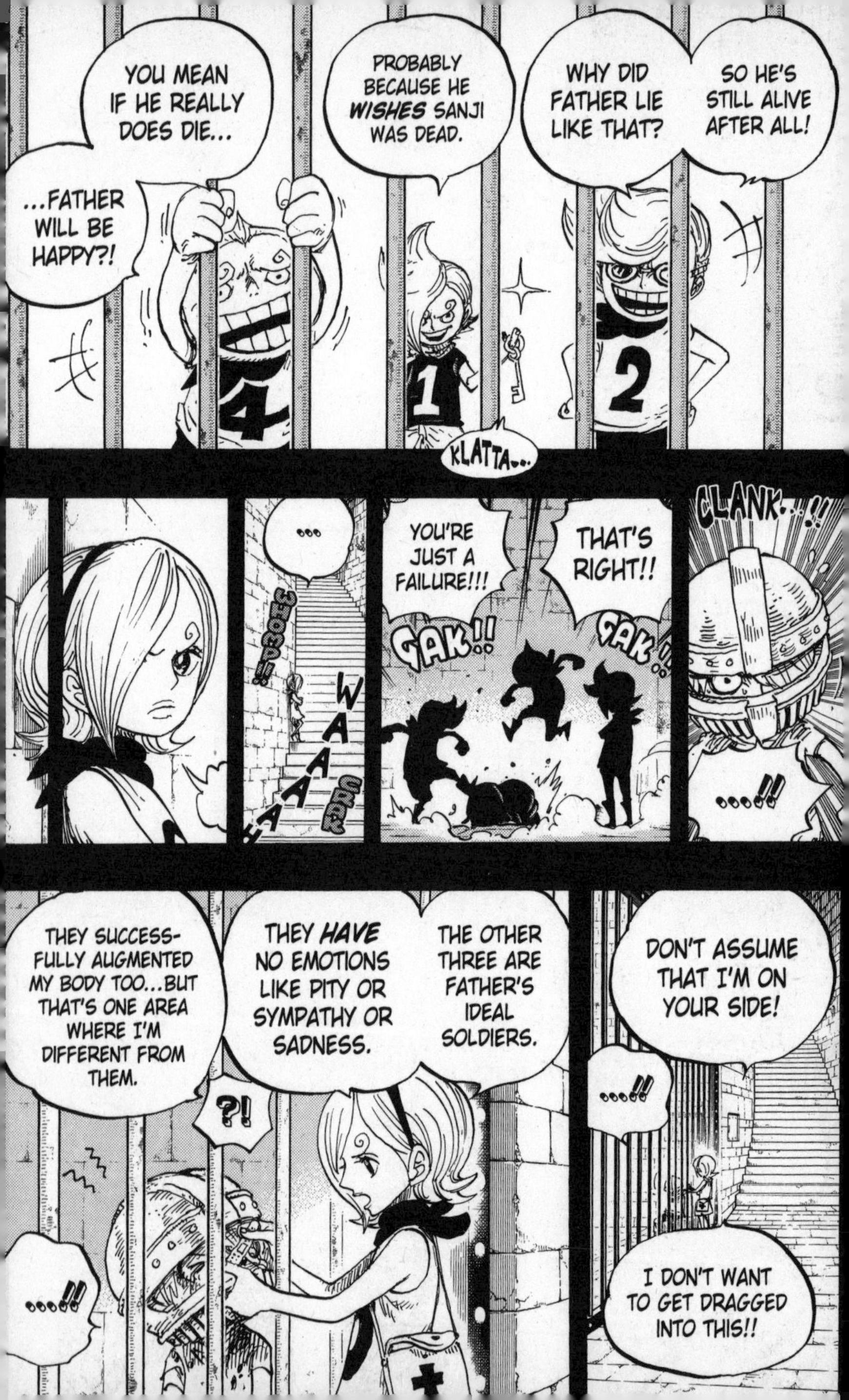
SO HE'S STILL ALIVE AFTER ALL!
WHY DID FATHER LIE LIKE THAT?
PROBABLY BECAUSE HE *WISHES* SANJI WAS DEAD.
YOU MEAN IF HE REALLY DOES DIE...
...FATHER WILL BE HAPPY?!
KLATTA...
CLANK...!!
...!!
THAT'S RIGHT!!
YOU'RE JUST A FAILURE!!!
GAK!!
GAK!!
...
WHOMP!!
WAAAAAH
GRR
DON'T ASSUME THAT I'M ON YOUR SIDE!
...!!
I DON'T WANT TO GET DRAGGED INTO THIS!!
THE OTHER THREE ARE FATHER'S IDEAL SOLDIERS.
THEY *HAVE* NO EMOTIONS LIKE PITY OR SYMPATHY OR SADNESS.
THEY SUCCESSFULLY AUGMENTED MY BODY TOO...BUT THAT'S ONE AREA WHERE I'M DIFFERENT FROM THEM.
?!
...!!

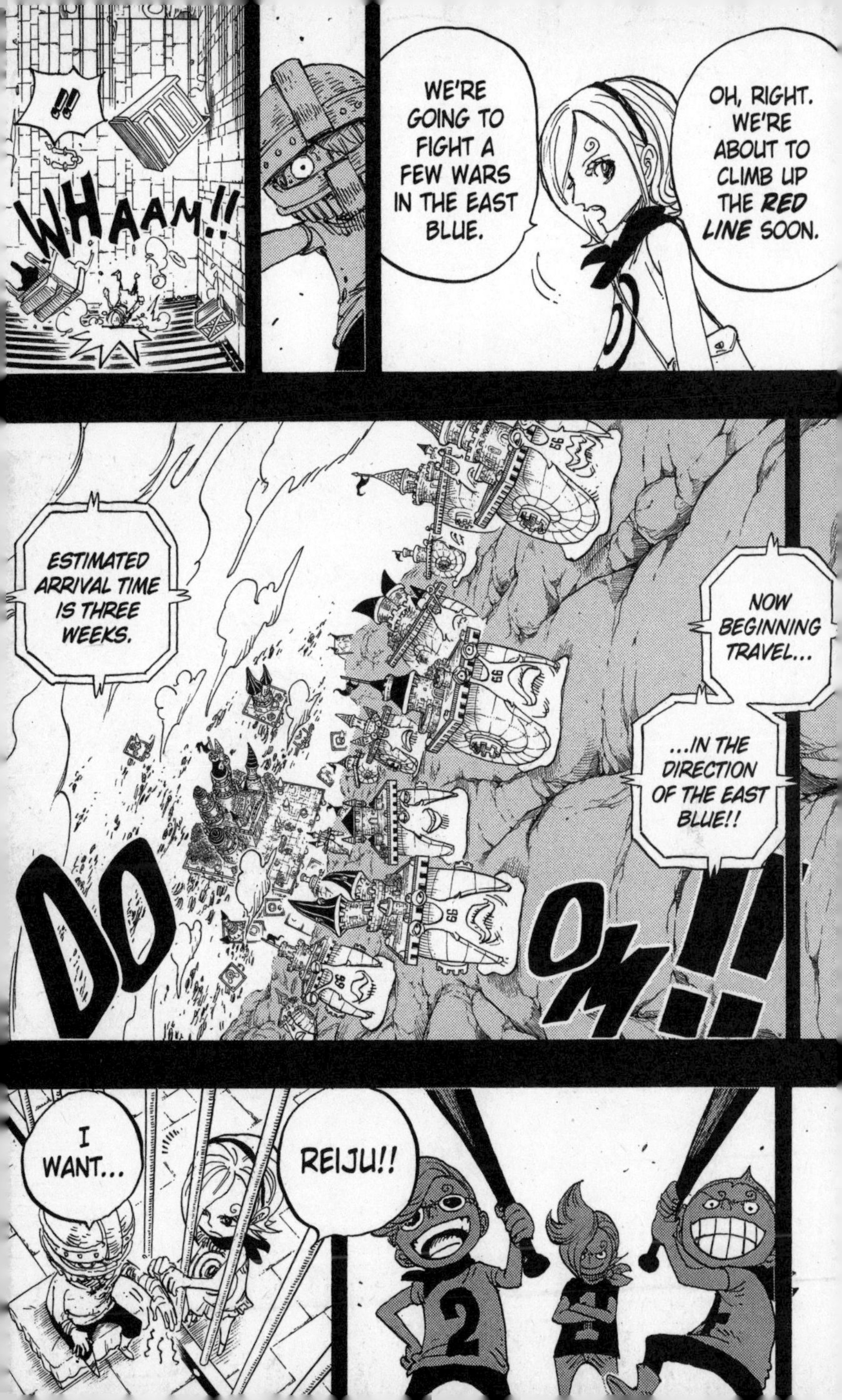

OH, RIGHT. WE'RE ABOUT TO CLIMB UP THE RED LINE SOON.
WE'RE GOING TO FIGHT A FEW WARS IN THE EAST BLUE.
!!
WHAAM!!
NOW BEGINNING TRAVEL...
...IN THE DIRECTION OF THE EAST BLUE!!
ESTIMATED ARRIVAL TIME IS THREE WEEKS.
DOOM!!
REIJU!!
I WANT...

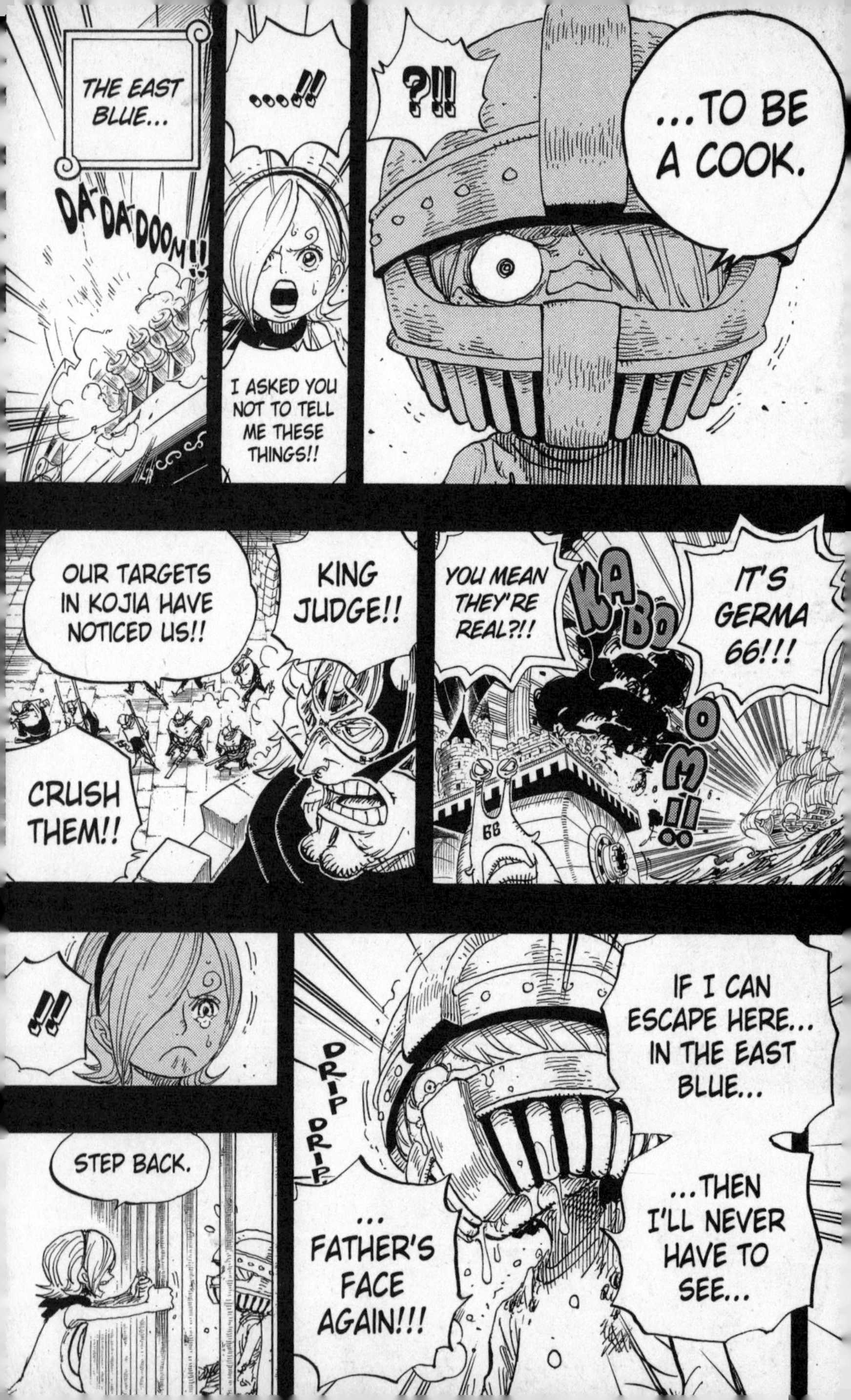
?!!
...TO BE A COOK.
....!!
I ASKED YOU NOT TO TELL ME THESE THINGS!!
THE EAST BLUE...
DA-DA-DOOM!!
IT'S GERMA 66!!!
KABOOM!!
YOU MEAN THEY'RE REAL?!!
KING JUDGE!!
OUR TARGETS IN KOJIA HAVE NOTICED US!!
CRUSH THEM!!
IF I CAN ESCAPE HERE... IN THE EAST BLUE...
...THEN I'LL NEVER HAVE TO SEE...
DRIP DRIP
...FATHER'S FACE AGAIN!!!
!!
STEP BACK.

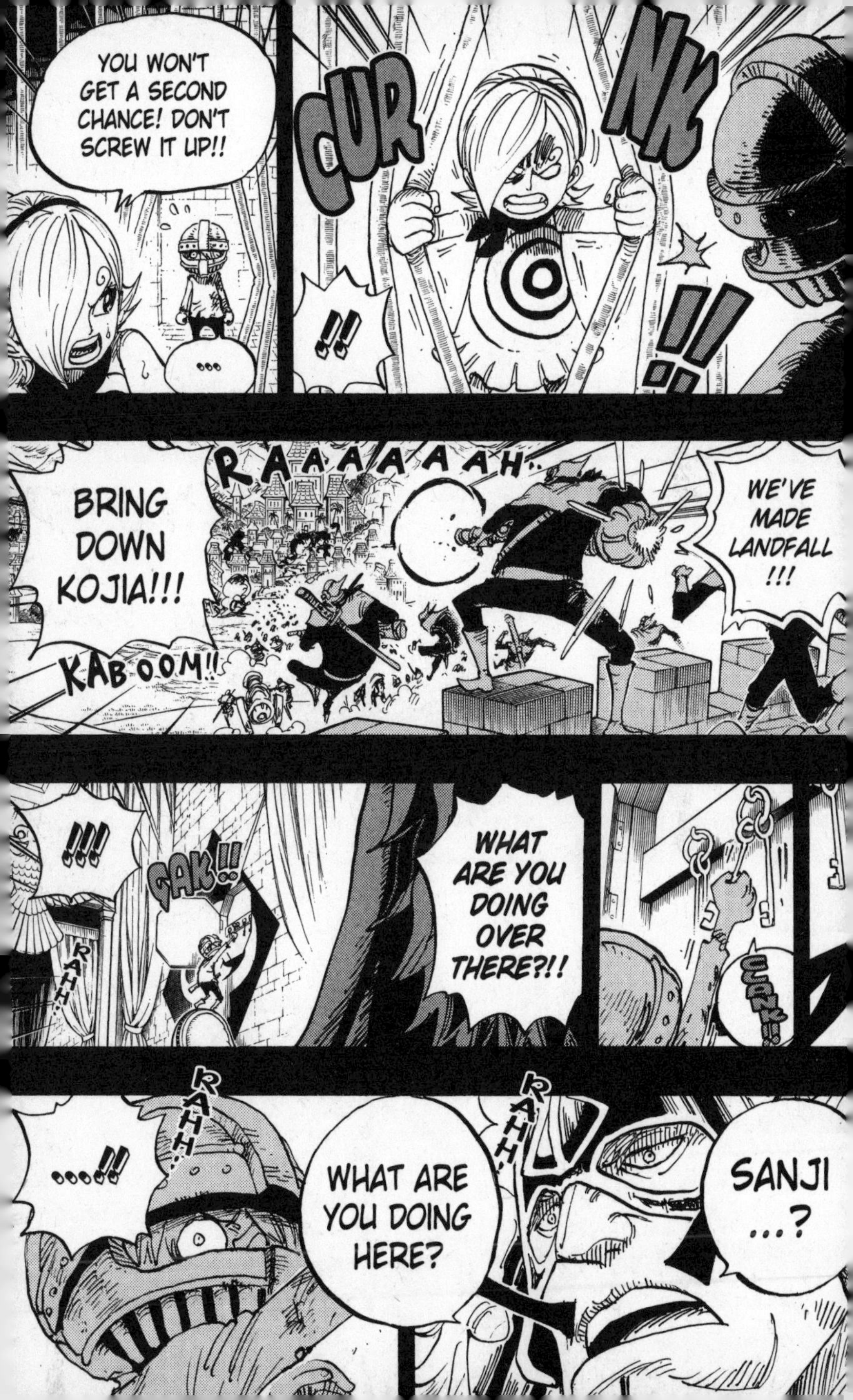

CURNK
!!
!!
YOU WON'T GET A SECOND CHANCE! DON'T SCREW IT UP!!
...
WE'VE MADE LANDFALL!!!
RAAAAAAAH..
BRING DOWN KOJIA!!!
KABOOM!!
CLANK!!
WHAT ARE YOU DOING OVER THERE?!!
GAK!!
!!!
RAHH...
SANJI ...?
RAHH...
WHAT ARE YOU DOING HERE?
RAHH...
...!!

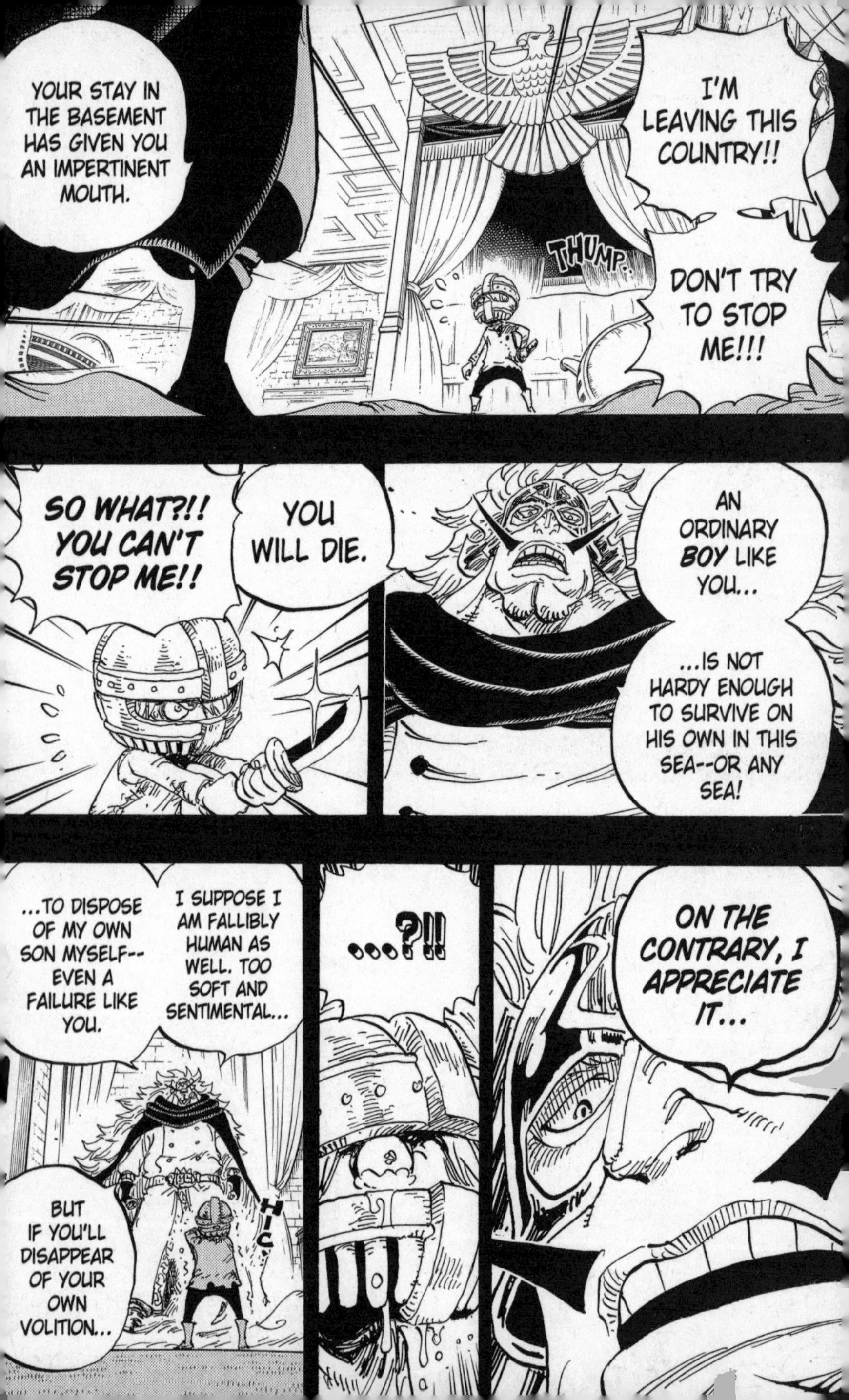

I'M LEAVING THIS COUNTRY!!
DON'T TRY TO STOP ME!!!
THUMP
YOUR STAY IN THE BASEMENT HAS GIVEN YOU AN IMPERTINENT MOUTH.
AN ORDINARY *BOY* LIKE YOU...
...IS NOT HARDY ENOUGH TO SURVIVE ON HIS OWN IN THIS SEA--OR ANY SEA!
YOU WILL DIE.
SO WHAT?!! YOU CAN'T STOP ME!!
ON THE CONTRARY, I APPRECIATE IT...
...?!!
I SUPPOSE I AM FALLIBLY HUMAN AS WELL. TOO SOFT AND SENTIMENTAL...
...TO DISPOSE OF MY OWN SON MYSELF--EVEN A FAILURE LIKE YOU.
BUT IF YOU'LL DISAPPEAR OF YOUR OWN VOLITION...
HIC

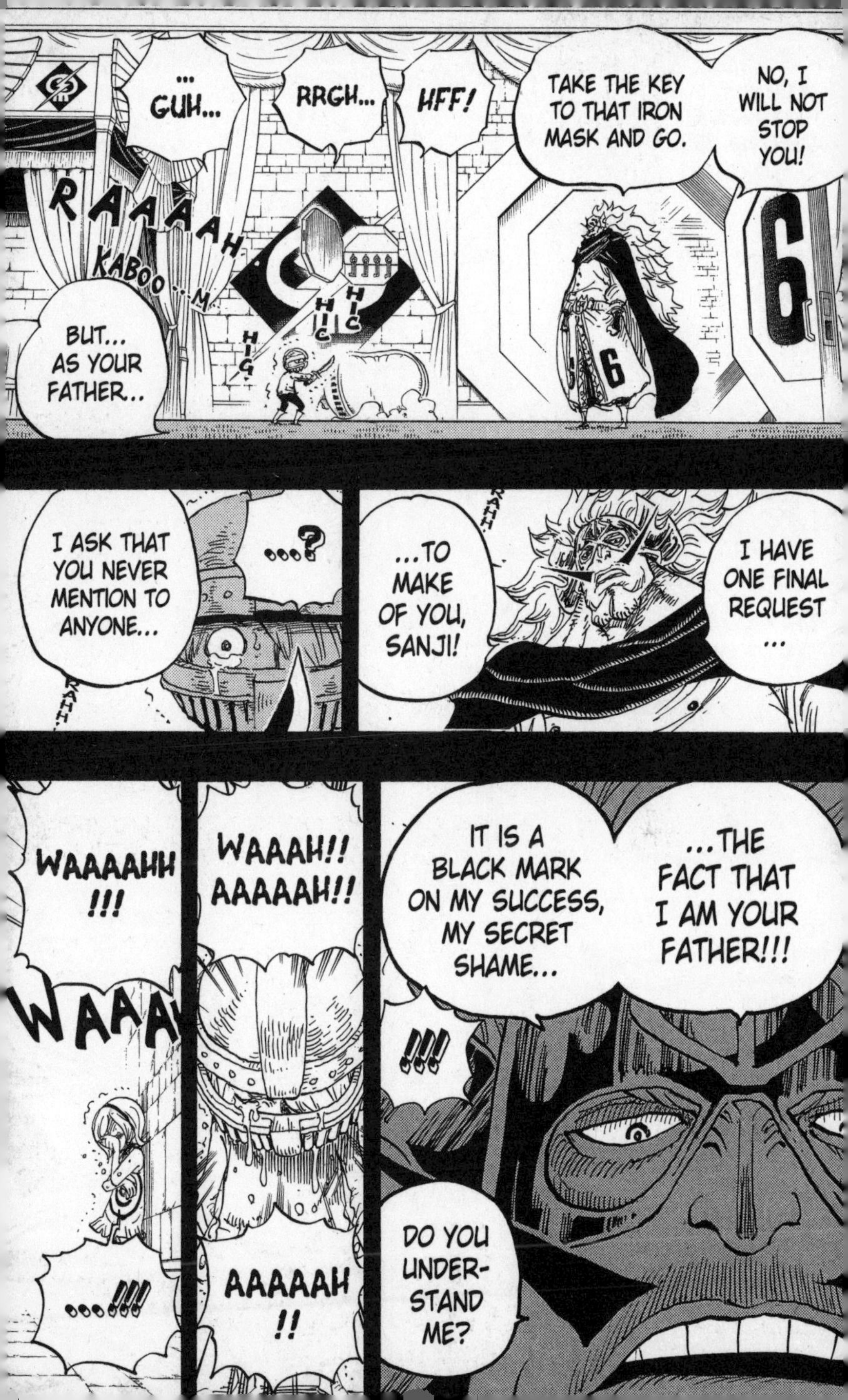
NO, I WILL NOT STOP YOU!
TAKE THE KEY TO THAT IRON MASK AND GO.
HFF!
RRGH...
... GUH...
RAAAAAH
KABOO...M
HIC
HIC
HIG
BUT... AS YOUR FATHER...
I HAVE ONE FINAL REQUEST ...
...TO MAKE OF YOU, SANJI!
RAHH
...?
I ASK THAT YOU NEVER MENTION TO ANYONE...
RAHH
...THE FACT THAT I AM YOUR FATHER!!!
IT IS A BLACK MARK ON MY SUCCESS, MY SECRET SHAME...
!!!
DO YOU UNDER-STAND ME?
WAAAH!! AAAAAH!!
AAAAAH !!
WAAAAHH !!!
WAAA
....!!!

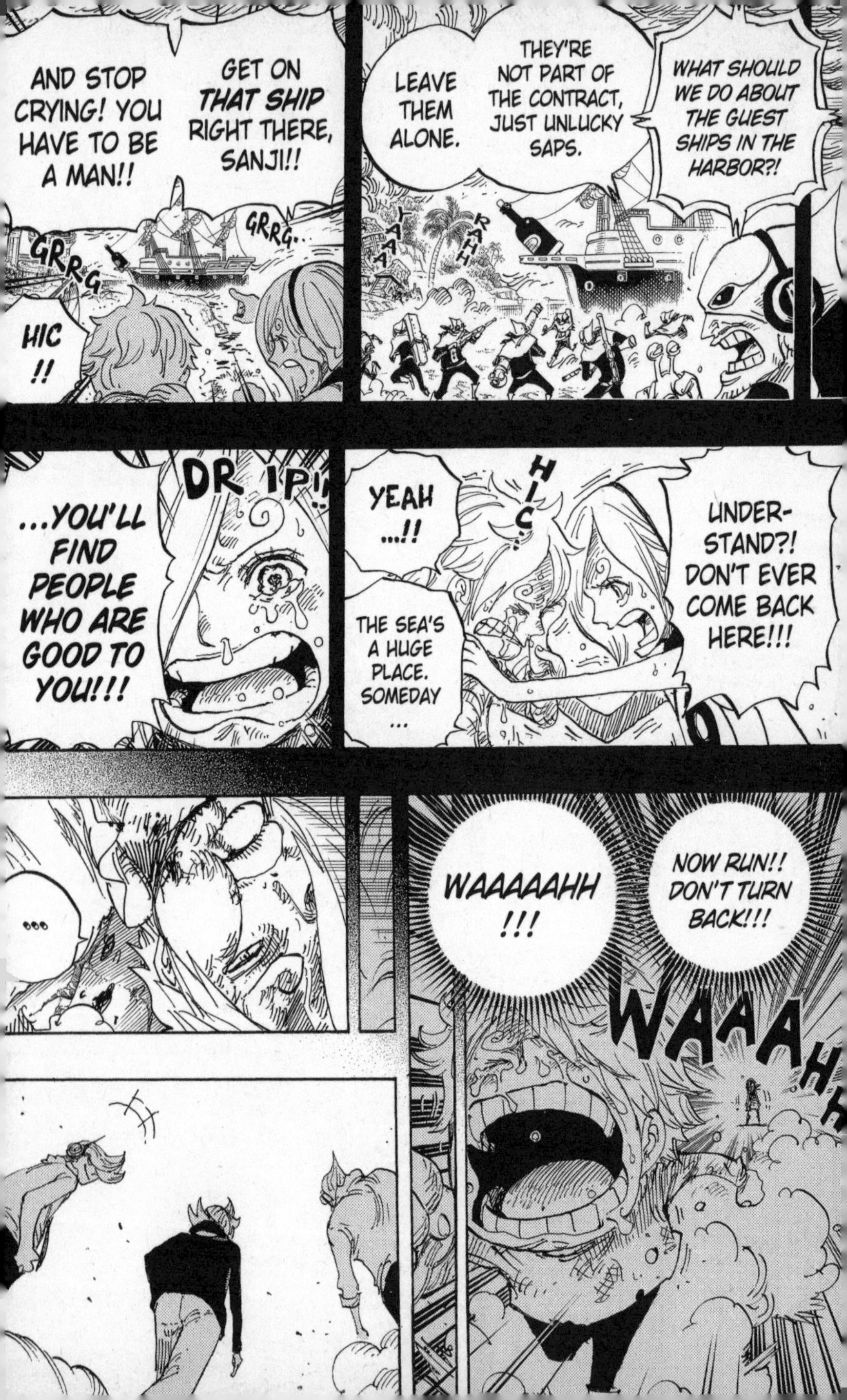
WHAT SHOULD WE DO ABOUT THE GUEST SHIPS IN THE HARBOR?!
THEY'RE NOT PART OF THE CONTRACT, JUST UNLUCKY SAPS.
LEAVE THEM ALONE.
RAHH
YAAA
GET ON THAT SHIP RIGHT THERE, SANJI!!
AND STOP CRYING! YOU HAVE TO BE A MAN!!
GRRG...
GRRG
HIC !!
UNDER-STAND?! DON'T EVER COME BACK HERE!!!
HIC
YEAH ...!!
THE SEA'S A HUGE PLACE. SOMEDAY ...
DRIP!!
...YOU'LL FIND PEOPLE WHO ARE GOOD TO YOU!!!
NOW RUN!! DON'T TURN BACK!!!
WAAAAAHH !!!
WAAAHH
...

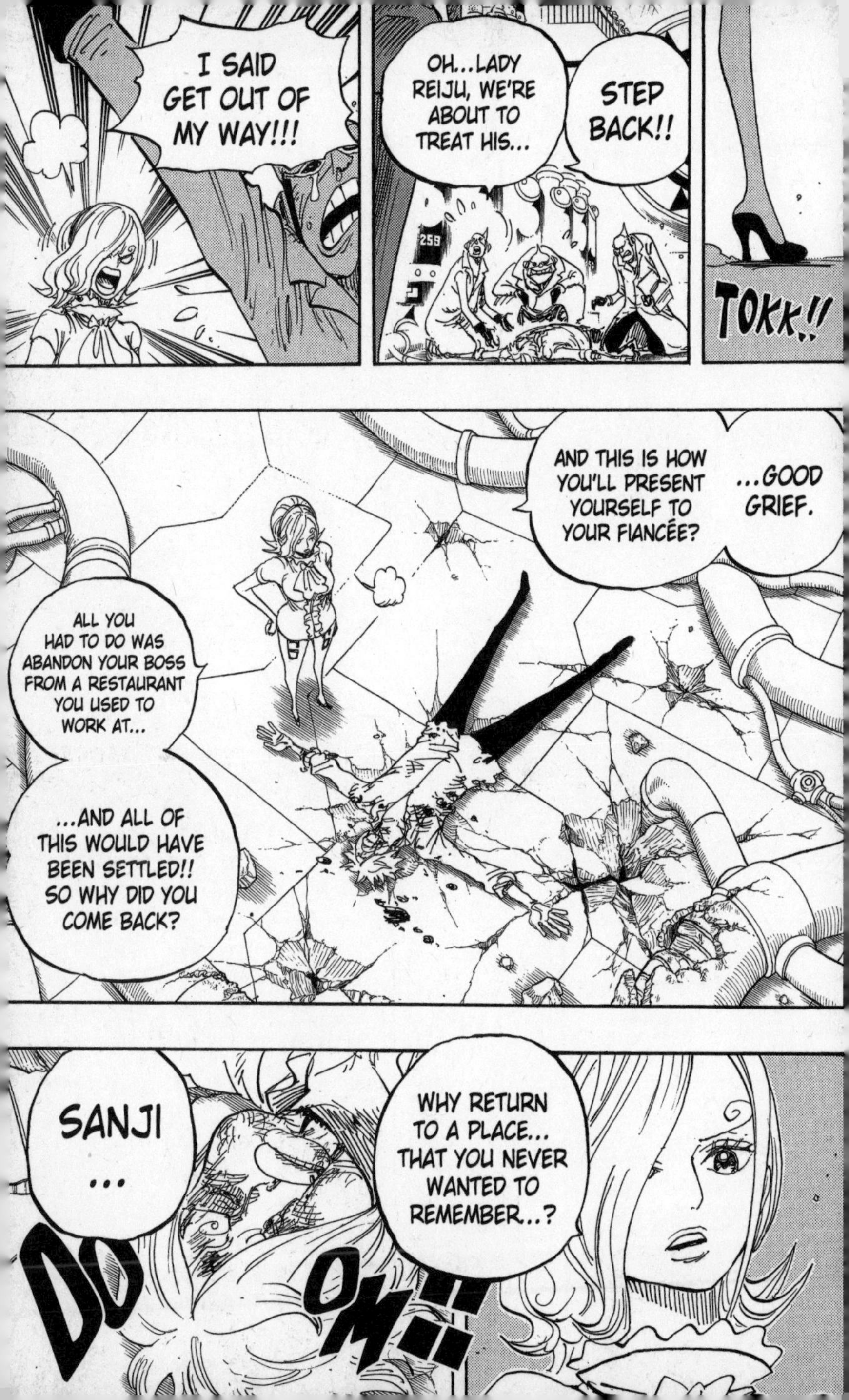
TOKK!!
OH...LADY REIJU, WE'RE ABOUT TO TREAT HIS...
STEP BACK!!
I SAID GET OUT OF MY WAY!!!
...GOOD GRIEF.
AND THIS IS HOW YOU'LL PRESENT YOURSELF TO YOUR FIANCÉE?
ALL YOU HAD TO DO WAS ABANDON YOUR BOSS FROM A RESTAURANT YOU USED TO WORK AT...
...AND ALL OF THIS WOULD HAVE BEEN SETTLED!! SO WHY DID YOU COME BACK?
WHY RETURN TO A PLACE... THAT YOU NEVER WANTED TO REMEMBER...?
SANJI ...
DOOM!!

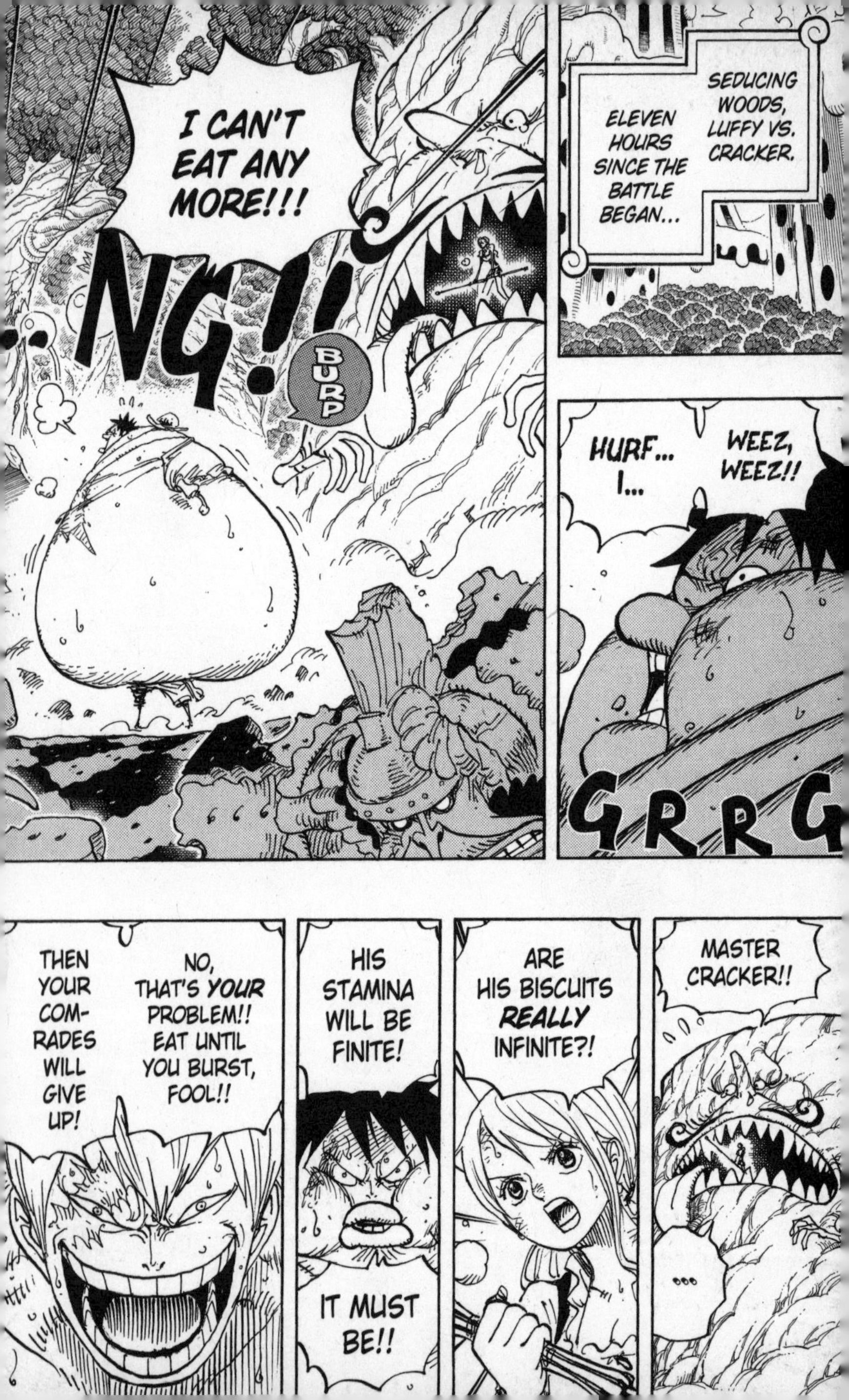

SEDUCING WOODS, LUFFY VS. CRACKER.
ELEVEN HOURS SINCE THE BATTLE BEGAN...
WEEZ, WEEZ!!
HURF... I...
GRRG
I CAN'T EAT ANY MORE!!!
NG!!
BURP
MASTER CRACKER!!
...
ARE HIS BISCUITS REALLY INFINITE?!
HIS STAMINA WILL BE FINITE!
IT MUST BE!!
NO, THAT'S YOUR PROBLEM!! EAT UNTIL YOU BURST, FOOL!!
THEN YOUR COM-RADES WILL GIVE UP!

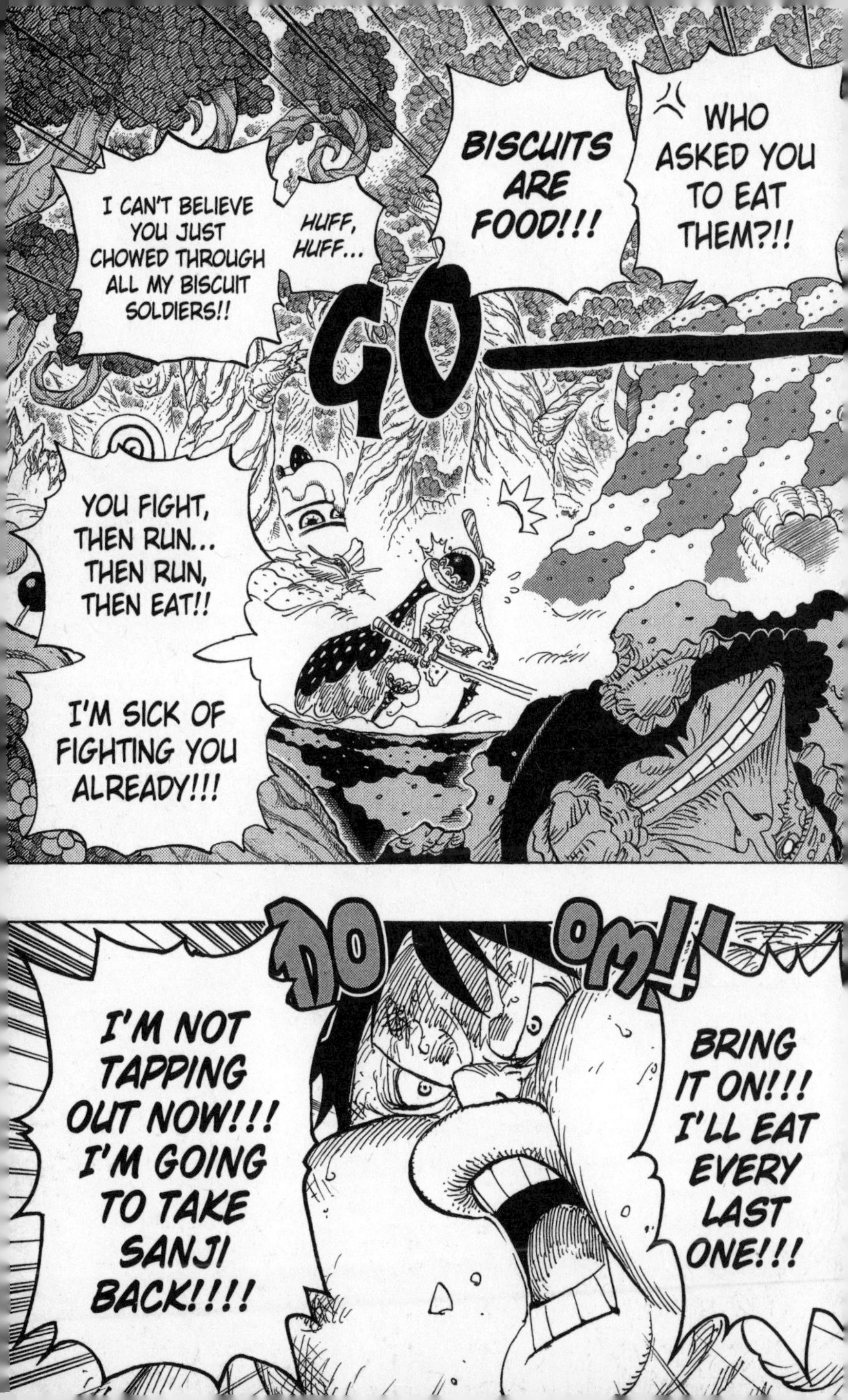

WHO ASKED YOU TO EAT THEM?!!
BISCUITS ARE FOOD!!!
HUFF, HUFF...
I CAN'T BELIEVE YOU JUST CHOWED THROUGH ALL MY BISCUIT SOLDIERS!!
GO
YOU FIGHT, THEN RUN... THEN RUN, THEN EAT!!
I'M SICK OF FIGHTING YOU ALREADY!!!
BRING IT ON!!! I'LL EAT EVERY LAST ONE!!!
DOOM!!
I'M NOT TAPPING OUT NOW!!! I'M GOING TO TAKE SANJI BACK!!!!

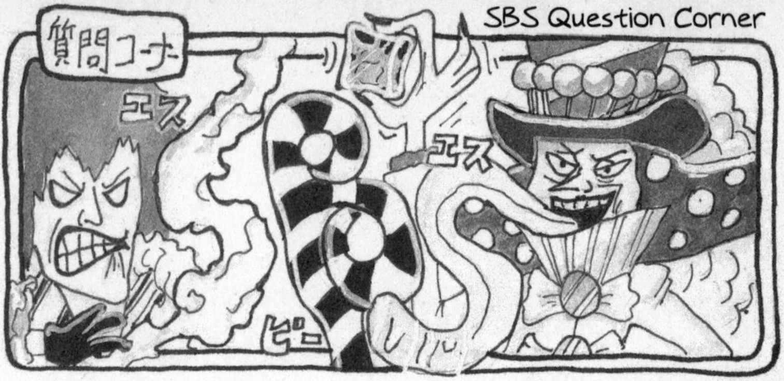
質問コーナー
エス
エス

(HayatoAsami, Kanagawa)

Q: I was born on June 13, but I don't share a birthday with any character. I was trying to think of one so I didn't feel so lonely, and then I realized that 6 can stand for *mugiwara* ("straw hat") and 13 can be read *ichimi* ("gang")! So how about if June 13 is "Straw Hat Crew Day"?! It's a party!!!

--cherry

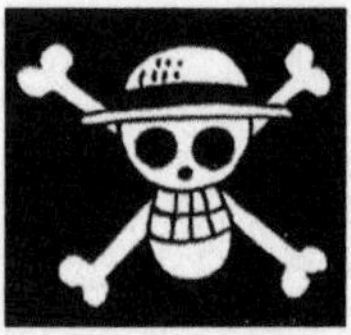

A: What?! If you think you can get away with that... you're right! I also got some suggestions for the Don Quixote Family members from Andy and Mary's Lamb...but I won't just take them without a fight! Here are the birthdays and the phrases the numbers stand for in Japanese...

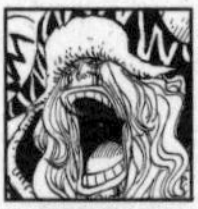

Diamante
May 29
("Coliseum Flag")

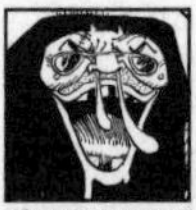

Trebol
March 18
("Chief of Staff's Boogers")

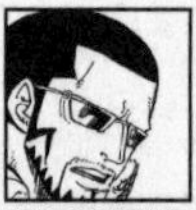

Vergo
July 5
(G-5, G is the 7th letter)

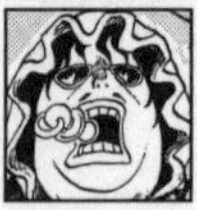

Señor Pink
June 12
(Lover's Day)

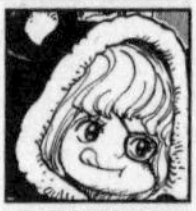

Sugar
October 22
(Looks 10, Actually 22)

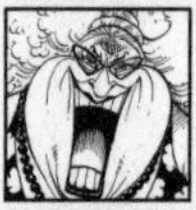

Giolla
January 25
(National Beauty Day)

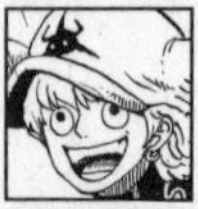

Dellinger
August 11
("High-heels")

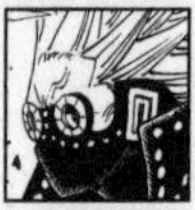

Gladius
August 6
("Pop-Pop Fruit")

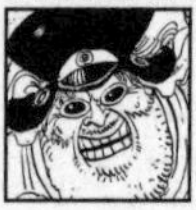

Machvise
August 13
("Vise")

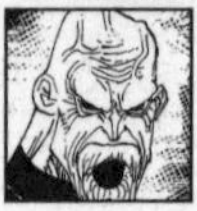

Lao G
October 7
("Old Geezer")

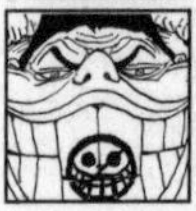

Buffalo
April 8
(National Tire Day)

Q: Is this all right?

Q: What do you think?

A: Hey, you!! I'm sorry to say that I've taken a hard look at these, and...they pass!!

Q: Hello, Oda Sensei. Please tell me the ages of Buggy, Kuro, Krieg, Wapol, and Foxy.

--Mr. Mugiwara

A: Them?!! Why?! Why would you want to know?! I mean, okay, but...!

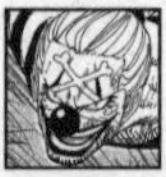

39 (same as Shanks)

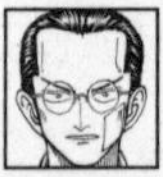

35

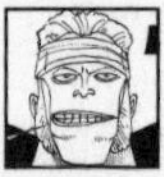

44

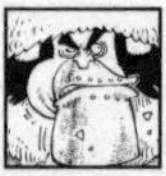

29

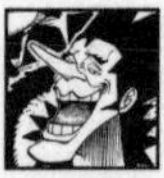

38

Chapter 842:
THE POWER OF A FULL STOMACH

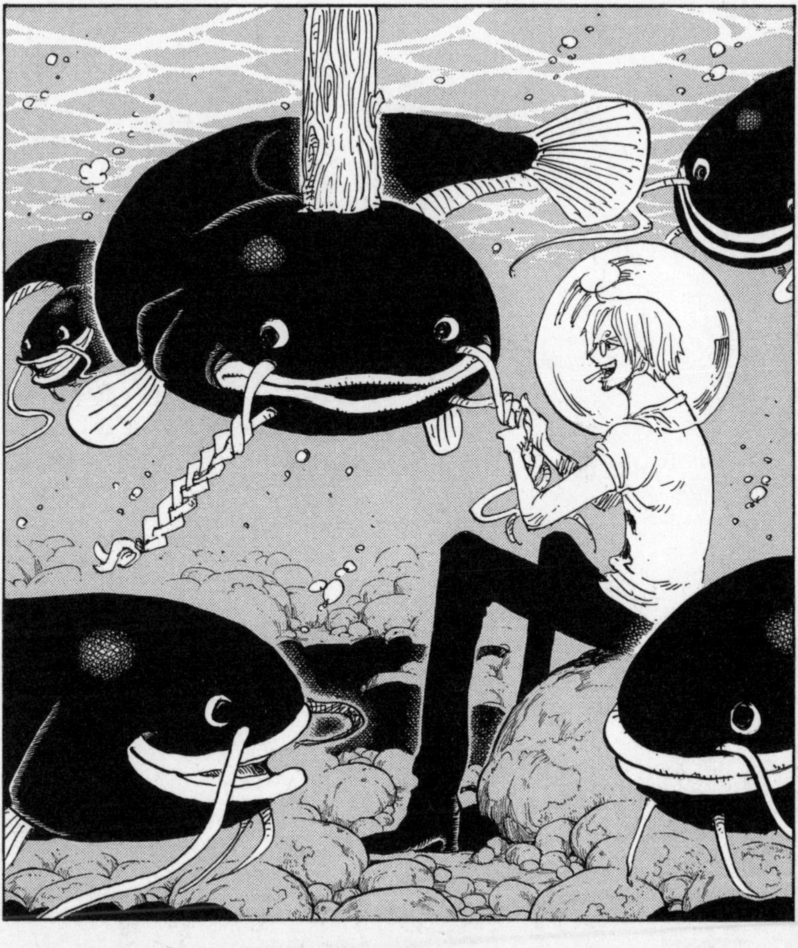

REQUEST: "SANJI HAPPILY TYING CATFISH WHISKERS TO LOOK LIKE LIKE ZEFF'S" BY NODA SKYWALKER FROM OSAKA

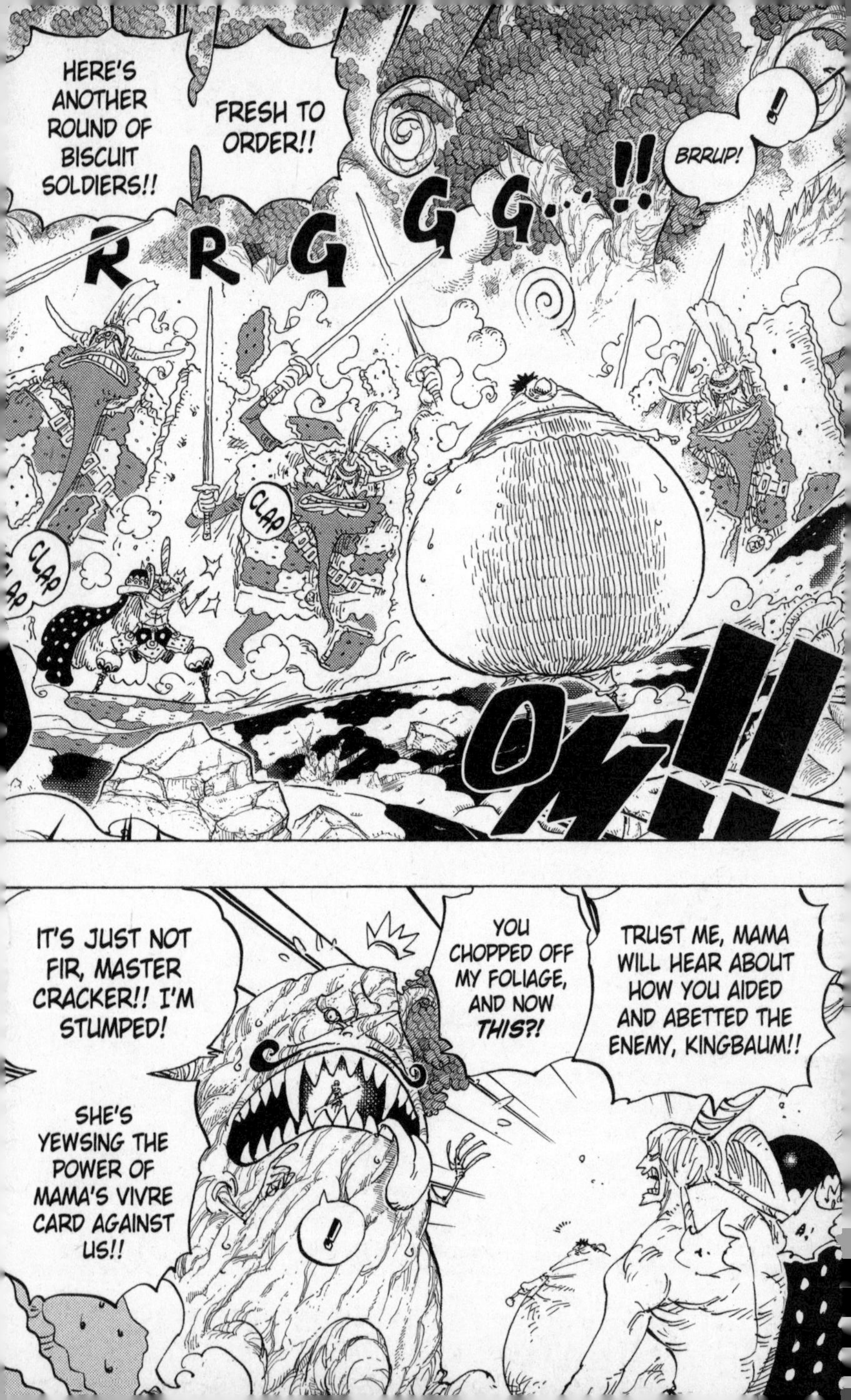
!
BRRUP!
RRGGGG...!!
FRESH TO ORDER!!
HERE'S ANOTHER ROUND OF BISCUIT SOLDIERS!!
CLAP
CLAP
ON!!
TRUST ME, MAMA WILL HEAR ABOUT HOW YOU AIDED AND ABETTED THE ENEMY, KINGBAUM!!
YOU CHOPPED OFF MY FOLIAGE, AND NOW *THIS?!*
IT'S JUST NOT FIR, MASTER CRACKER!! I'M STUMPED!
SHE'S YEWSING THE POWER OF MAMA'S VIVRE CARD AGAINST US!!
!

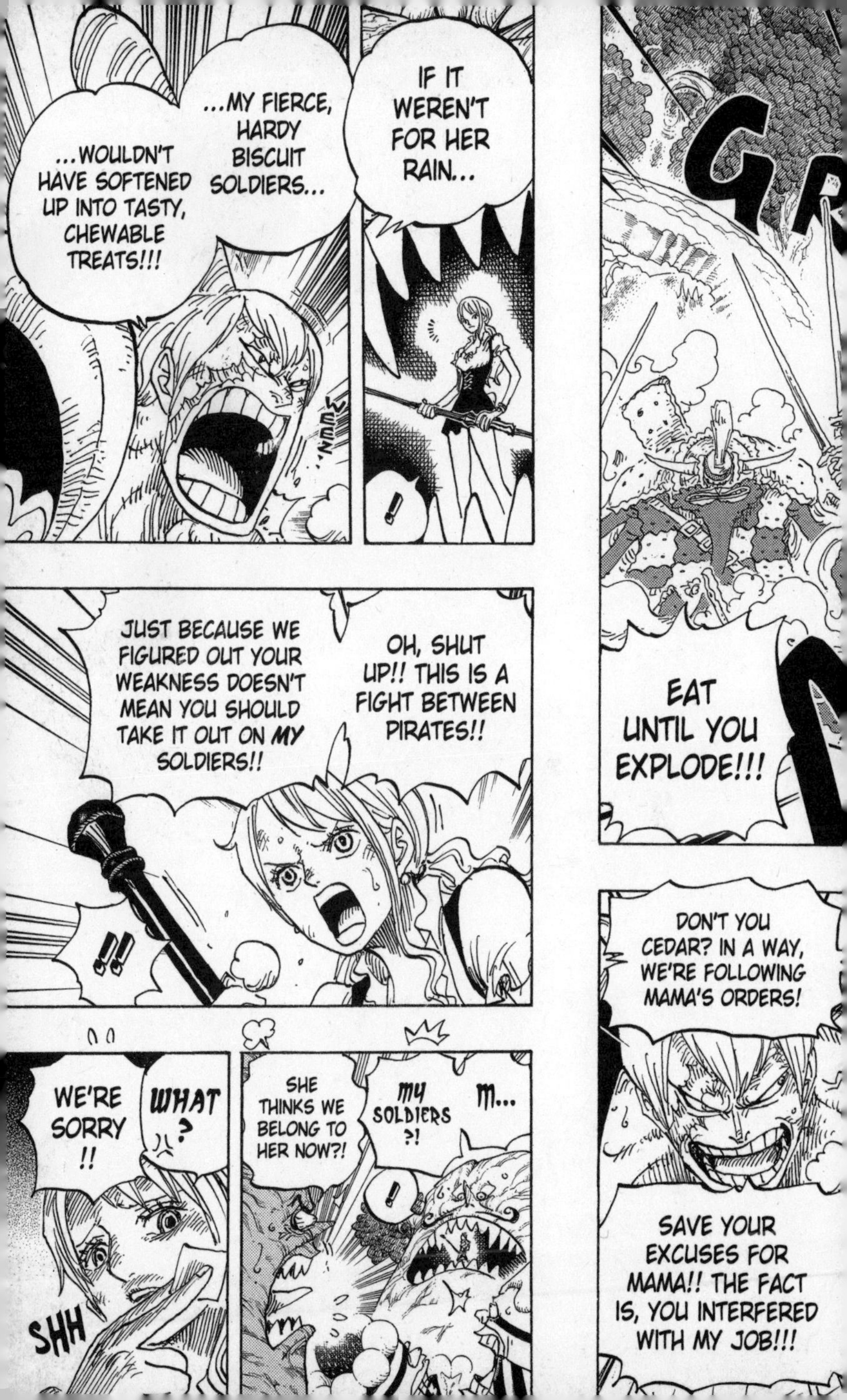
GR
EAT UNTIL YOU EXPLODE!!!
DON'T YOU CEDAR? IN A WAY, WE'RE FOLLOWING MAMA'S ORDERS!
SAVE YOUR EXCUSES FOR MAMA!! THE FACT IS, YOU INTERFERED WITH MY JOB!!!
IF IT WEREN'T FOR HER RAIN...
...MY FIERCE, HARDY BISCUIT SOLDIERS...
...WOULDN'T HAVE SOFTENED UP INTO TASTY, CHEWABLE TREATS!!!
WEEN
OH, SHUT UP!! THIS IS A FIGHT BETWEEN PIRATES!!
JUST BECAUSE WE FIGURED OUT YOUR WEAKNESS DOESN'T MEAN YOU SHOULD TAKE IT OUT ON MY SOLDIERS!!
M...
MY SOLDIERS?!
SHE THINKS WE BELONG TO HER NOW?!
WHAT?
WE'RE SORRY!!
SHH

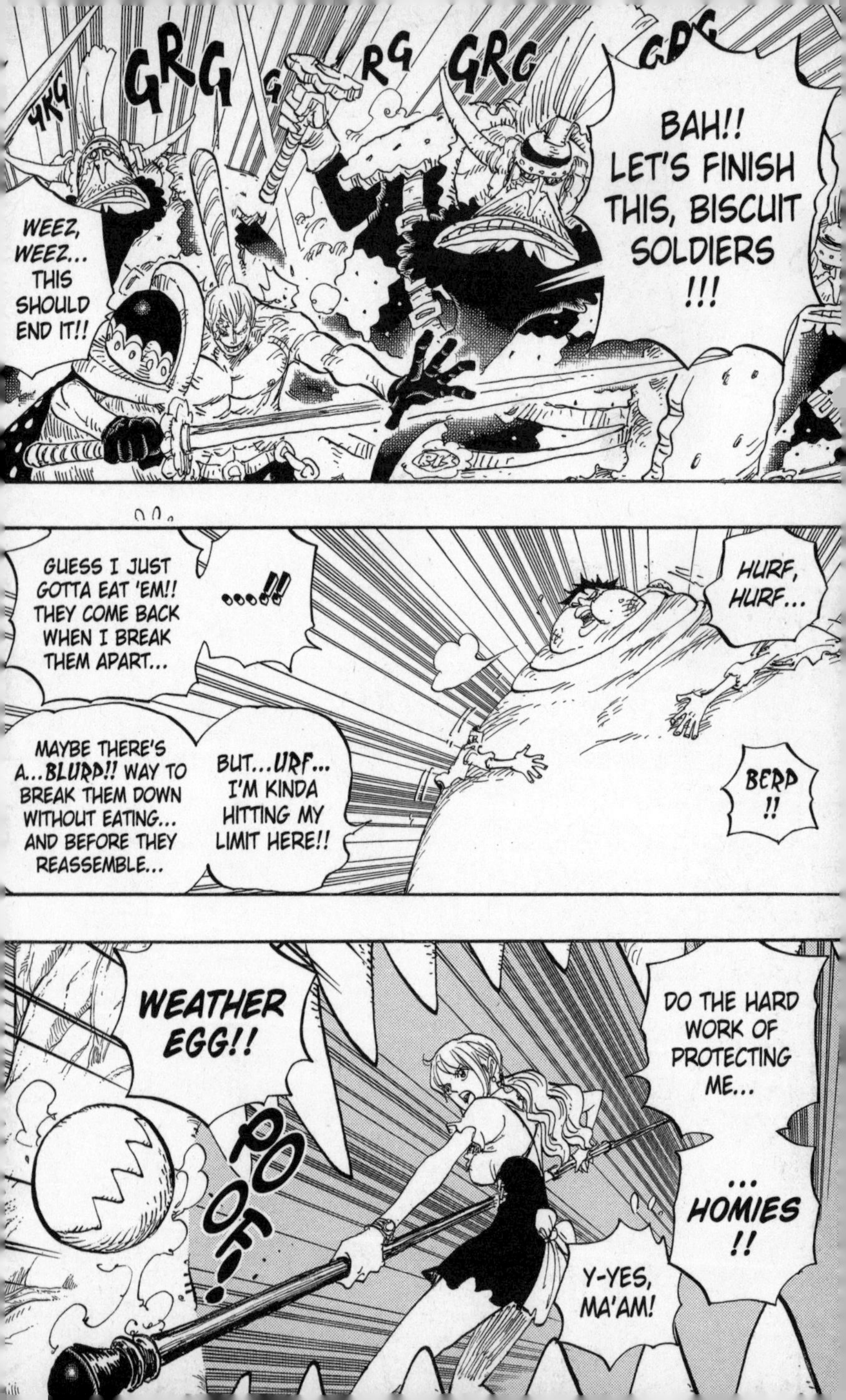

GDG
BAH!! LET'S FINISH THIS, BISCUIT SOLDIERS!!!
GRG
RG
G
GRG
YKG
WEEZ, WEEZ... THIS SHOULD END IT!!
HURF, HURF...
BERP!!
...!!
GUESS I JUST GOTTA EAT 'EM!! THEY COME BACK WHEN I BREAK THEM APART...
BUT...URF... I'M KINDA HITTING MY LIMIT HERE!!
MAYBE THERE'S A...BLURP!! WAY TO BREAK THEM DOWN WITHOUT EATING... AND BEFORE THEY REASSEMBLE...
DO THE HARD WORK OF PROTECTING ME...
...HOMIES!!
Y-YES, MA'AM!
WEATHER EGG!!
POOF!!

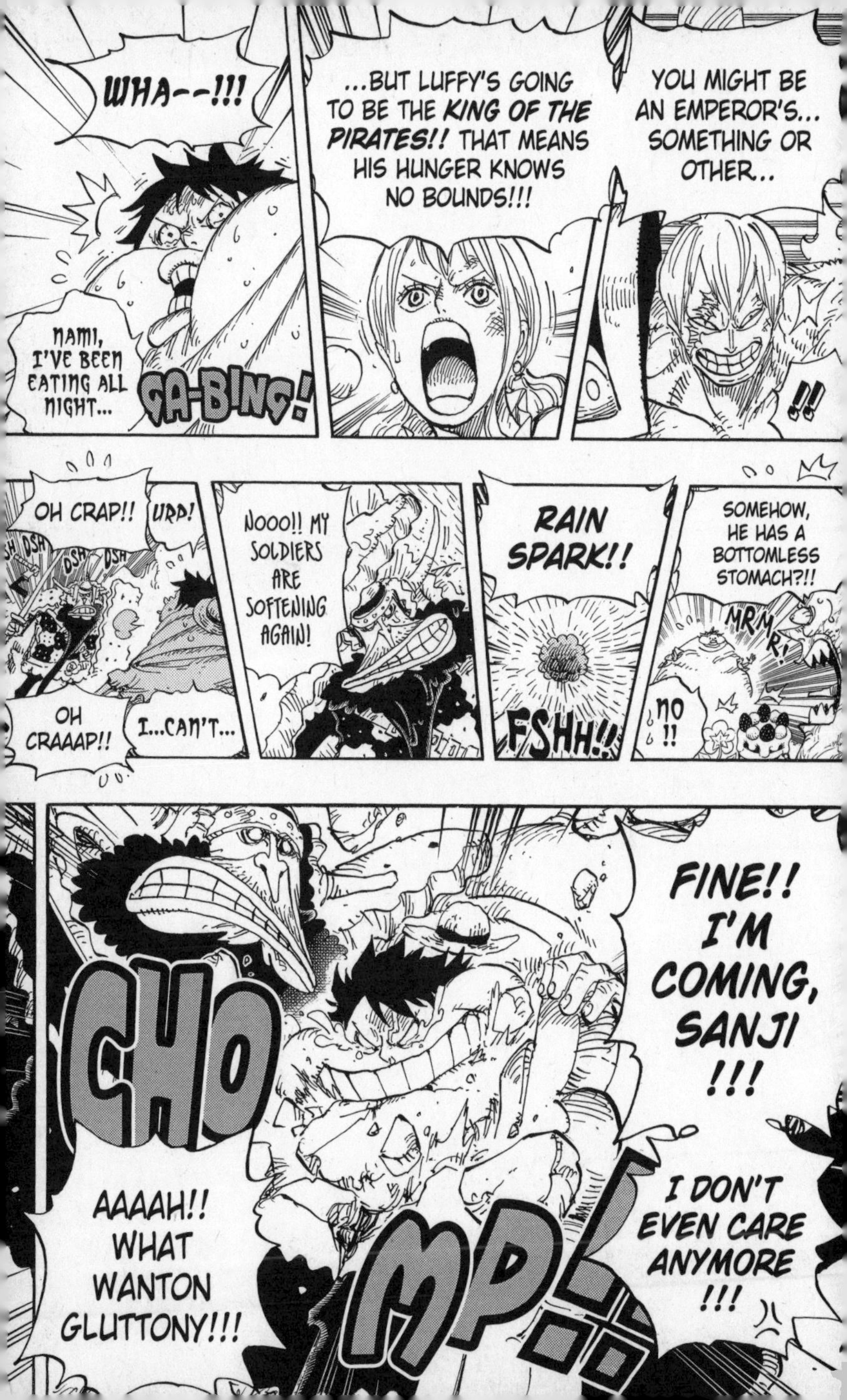
YOU MIGHT BE AN EMPEROR'S... SOMETHING OR OTHER..
!!
...BUT LUFFY'S GOING TO BE THE ***KING OF THE PIRATES!!*** THAT MEANS HIS HUNGER KNOWS NO BOUNDS!!!
WHA--!!!
NAMI, I'VE BEEN EATING ALL NIGHT...
GA-BING!
SOMEHOW, HE HAS A BOTTOMLESS STOMACH?!!
MRMR!
NO !!
RAIN SPARK!!
FSHH!!
NOOO!! MY SOLDIERS ARE SOFTENING AGAIN!
URP!
OH CRAP!!
DSH DSH DSH
I...CAN'T...
OH CRAAAP!!
FINE!! I'M COMING, SANJI!!!
CHO
I DON'T EVEN CARE ANYMORE!!!
MP!!
AAAAH!! WHAT WANTON GLUTTONY!!!

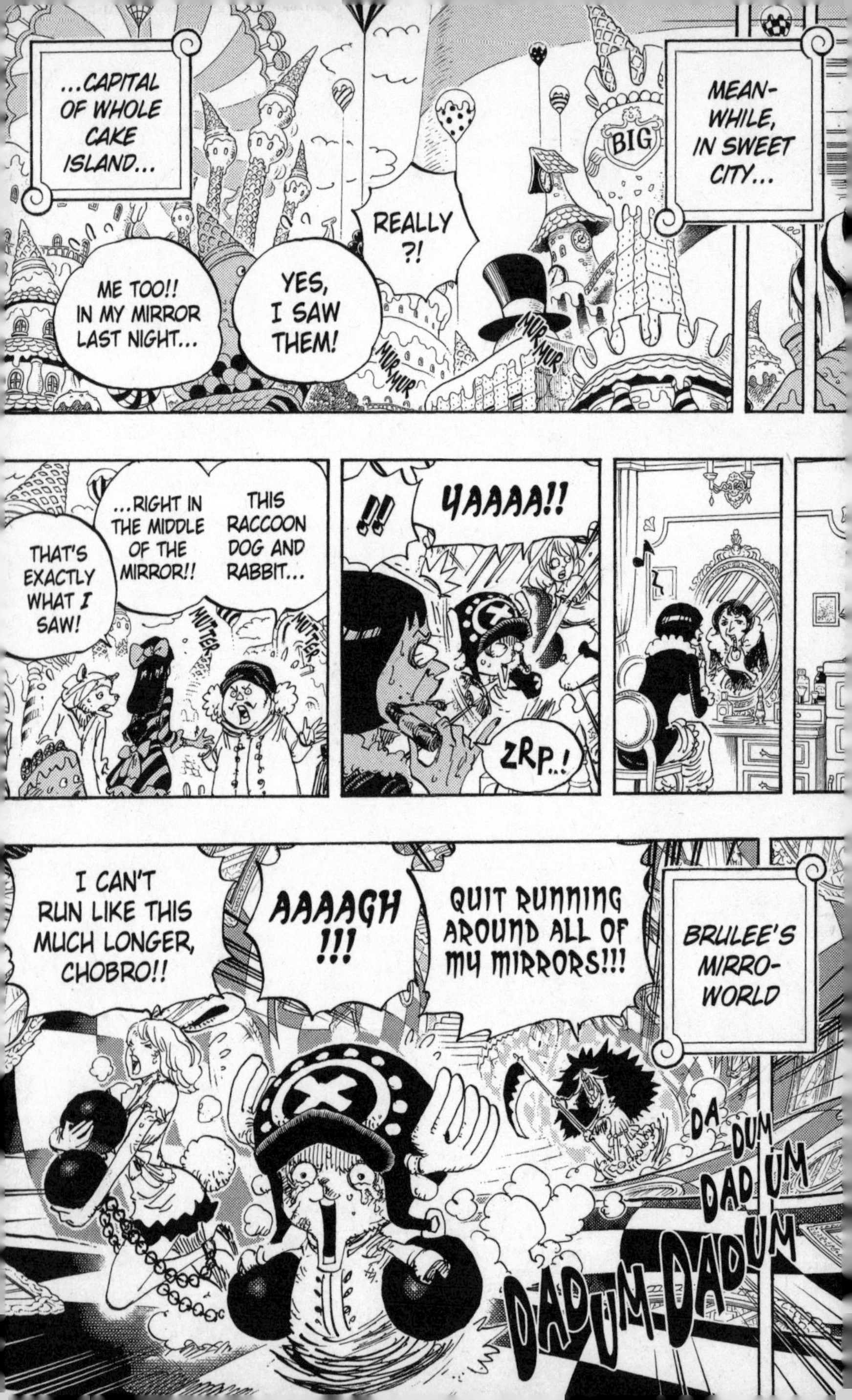
MEAN-WHILE, IN SWEET CITY...
...CAPITAL OF WHOLE CAKE ISLAND...
REALLY?!
MUR MUR
YES, I SAW THEM!
MUR MUR
ME TOO!! IN MY MIRROR LAST NIGHT...
YAAAA!!
!!
ZRP..!
THIS RACCOON DOG AND RABBIT...
...RIGHT IN THE MIDDLE OF THE MIRROR!!
MUTTER
MUTTER
THAT'S EXACTLY WHAT I SAW!
BRULEE'S MIRRO-WORLD
QUIT RUNNING AROUND ALL OF MY MIRRORS!!!
AAAAGH!!!
I CAN'T RUN LIKE THIS MUCH LONGER, CHOBRO!!
DA DUM DADUM
DADUM DADUM

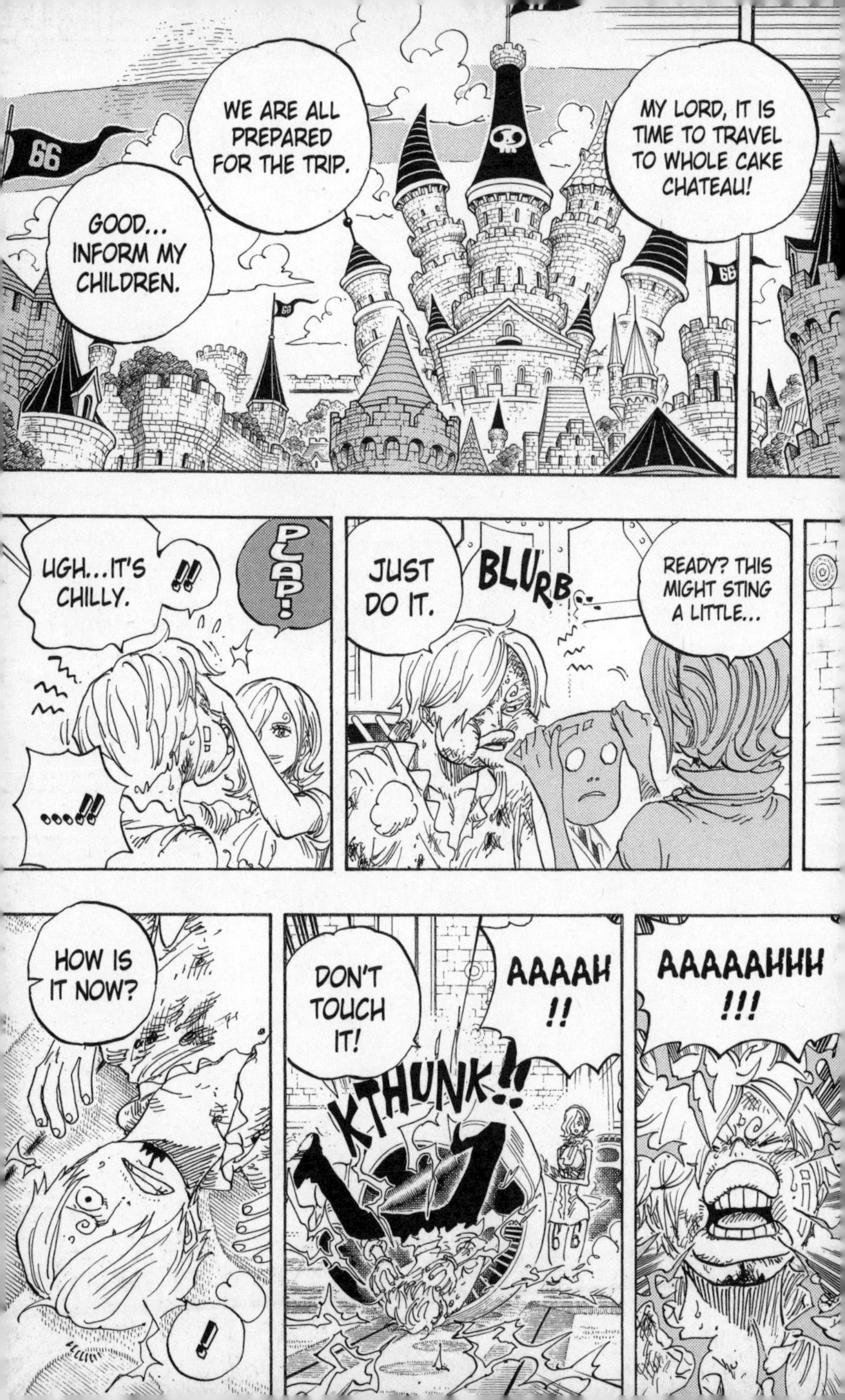
MY LORD, IT IS TIME TO TRAVEL TO WHOLE CAKE CHATEAU!
WE ARE ALL PREPARED FOR THE TRIP.
GOOD... INFORM MY CHILDREN.
READY? THIS MIGHT STING A LITTLE...
BLURB
JUST DO IT.
PLAP!
!!
UGH...IT'S CHILLY.
....!!
AAAAAHHH !!!
AAAAH !!
DON'T TOUCH IT!
KTHUNK!!
HOW IS IT NOW?
!

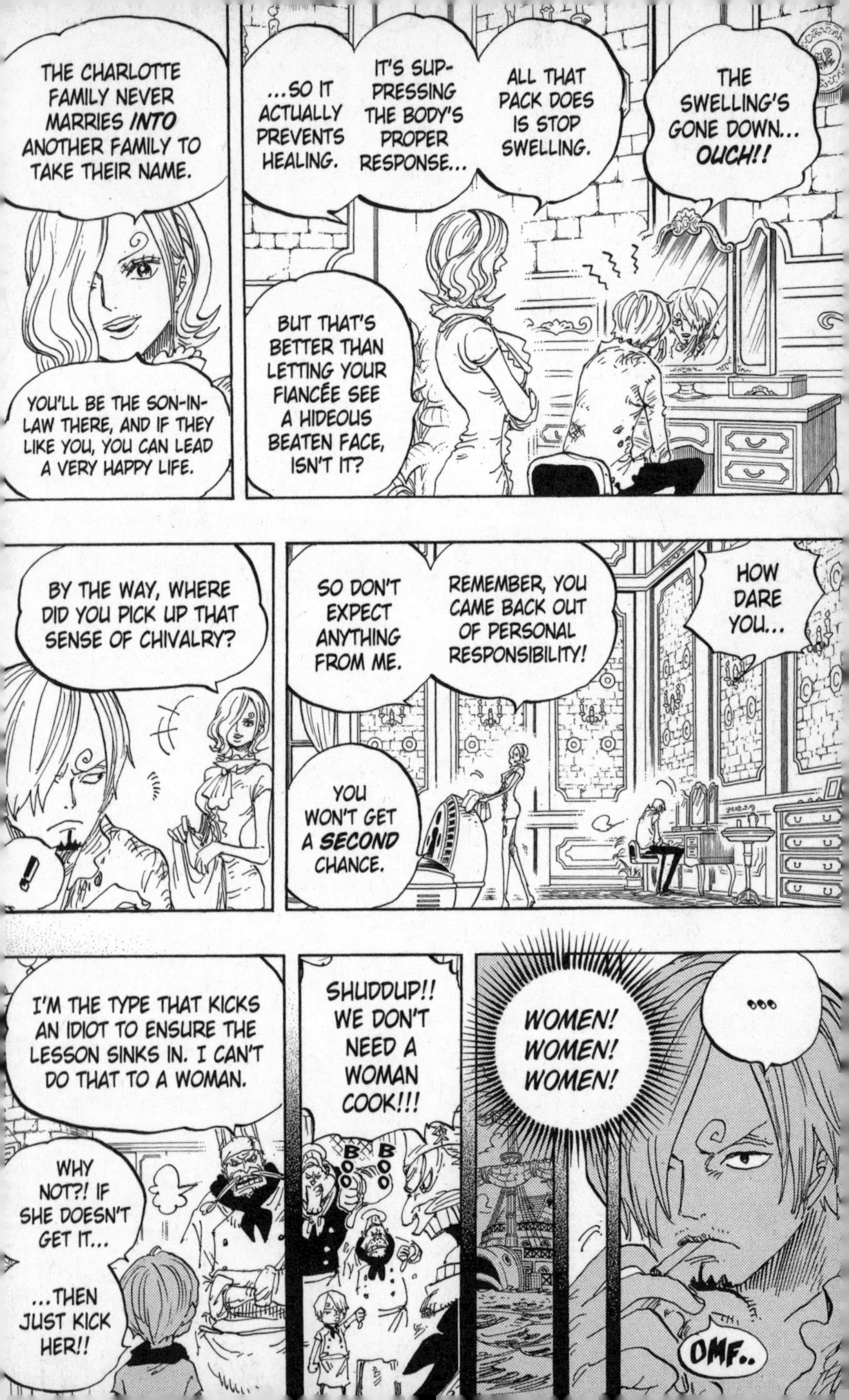
THE SWELLING'S GONE DOWN... *OUCH!!*
ALL THAT PACK DOES IS STOP SWELLING.
IT'S SUPPRESSING THE BODY'S PROPER RESPONSE...
...SO IT ACTUALLY PREVENTS HEALING.
BUT THAT'S BETTER THAN LETTING YOUR FIANCÉE SEE A HIDEOUS BEATEN FACE, ISN'T IT?
THE CHARLOTTE FAMILY NEVER MARRIES *INTO* ANOTHER FAMILY TO TAKE THEIR NAME.
YOU'LL BE THE SON-IN-LAW THERE, AND IF THEY LIKE YOU, YOU CAN LEAD A VERY HAPPY LIFE.
HOW DARE YOU...
REMEMBER, YOU CAME BACK OUT OF PERSONAL RESPONSIBILITY!
SO DON'T EXPECT ANYTHING FROM ME.
YOU WON'T GET A *SECOND* CHANCE.
BY THE WAY, WHERE DID YOU PICK UP THAT SENSE OF CHIVALRY?
!
...
OMF..
WOMEN! WOMEN! WOMEN!
SHUDDUP!! WE DON'T NEED A WOMAN COOK!!!
BOO
BOO
I'M THE TYPE THAT KICKS AN IDIOT TO ENSURE THE LESSON SINKS IN. I CAN'T DO THAT TO A WOMAN.
WHY NOT?! IF SHE DOESN'T GET IT...
...THEN JUST KICK HER!!

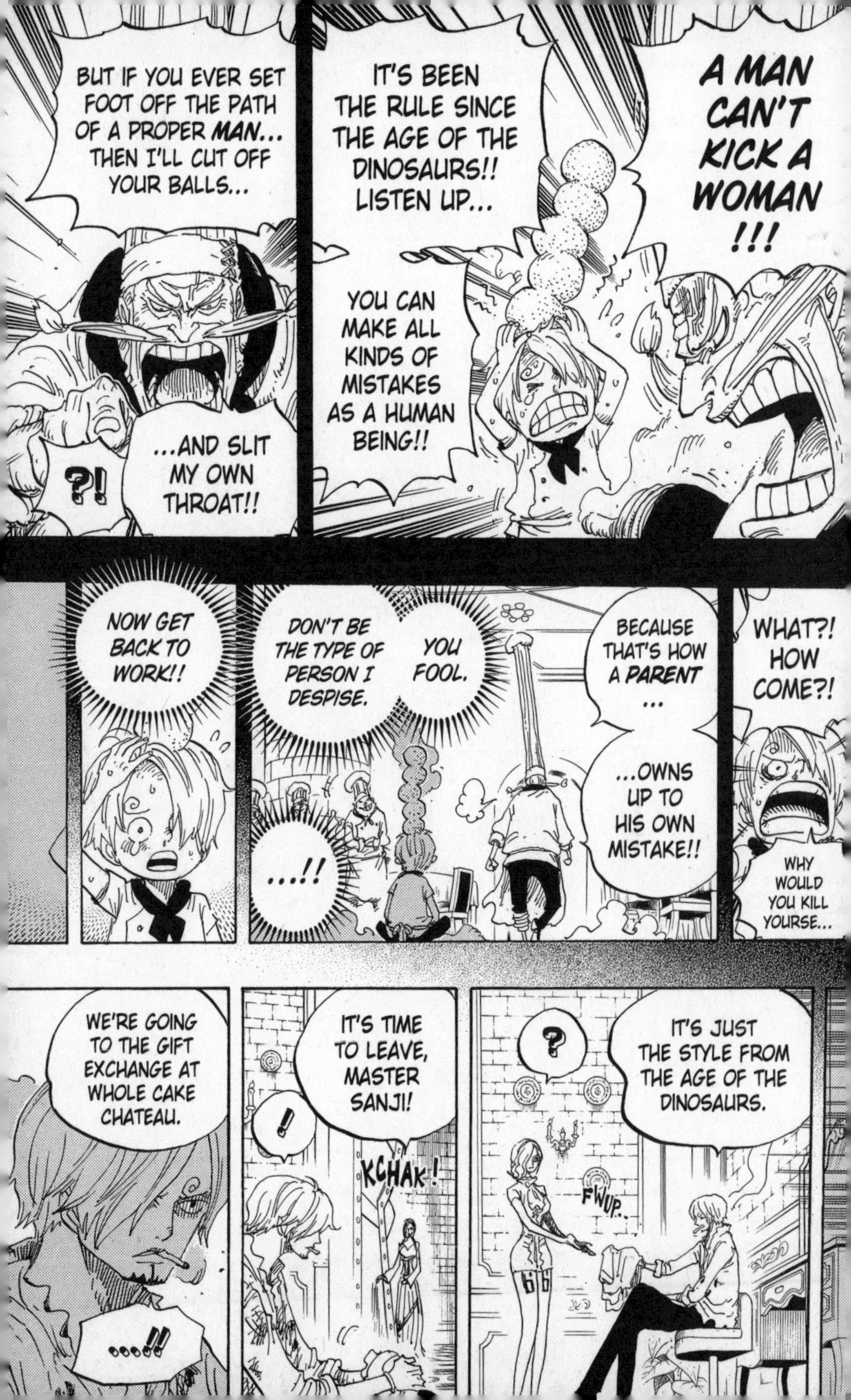
A MAN CAN'T KICK A WOMAN!!!
IT'S BEEN THE RULE SINCE THE AGE OF THE DINOSAURS!! LISTEN UP...
YOU CAN MAKE ALL KINDS OF MISTAKES AS A HUMAN BEING!!
BUT IF YOU EVER SET FOOT OFF THE PATH OF A PROPER MAN... THEN I'LL CUT OFF YOUR BALLS...
...AND SLIT MY OWN THROAT!!
?!
WHAT?! HOW COME?!
WHY WOULD YOU KILL YOURSE...
BECAUSE THAT'S HOW A PARENT...
...OWNS UP TO HIS OWN MISTAKE!!
YOU FOOL.
DON'T BE THE TYPE OF PERSON I DESPISE.
...!!
NOW GET BACK TO WORK!!
?
IT'S JUST THE STYLE FROM THE AGE OF THE DINOSAURS.
FWUP...
IT'S TIME TO LEAVE, MASTER SANJI!
KCHAK!
!
WE'RE GOING TO THE GIFT EXCHANGE AT WHOLE CAKE CHATEAU.
....!!

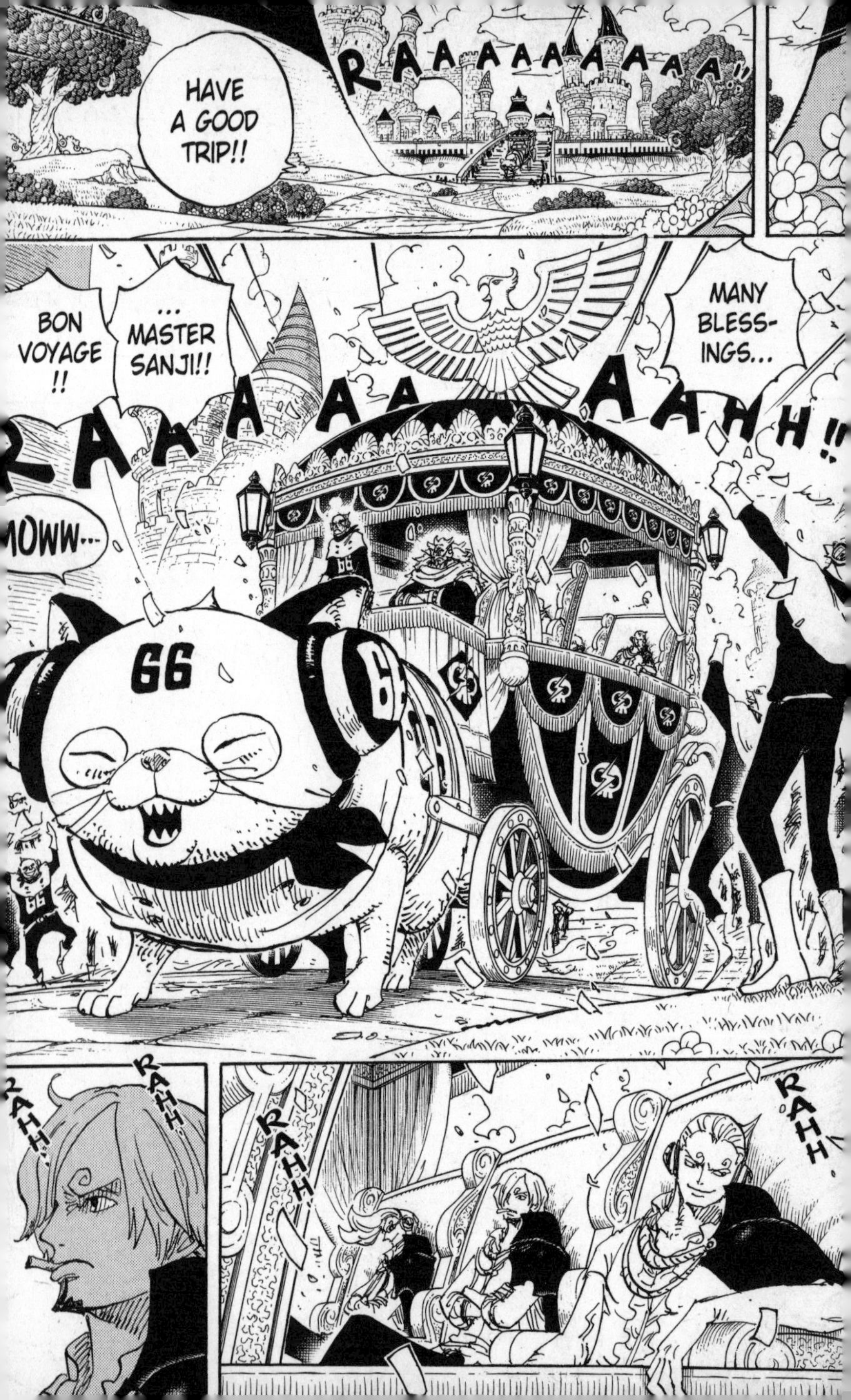

RAAAAAAAAA!!
HAVE A GOOD TRIP!!
MANY BLESS-INGS...
RAAAAAAAAAHH!!
... MASTER SANJI!!
BON VOYAGE!!
MOWW...
RAHH
RAHH
RAHH
RAHH

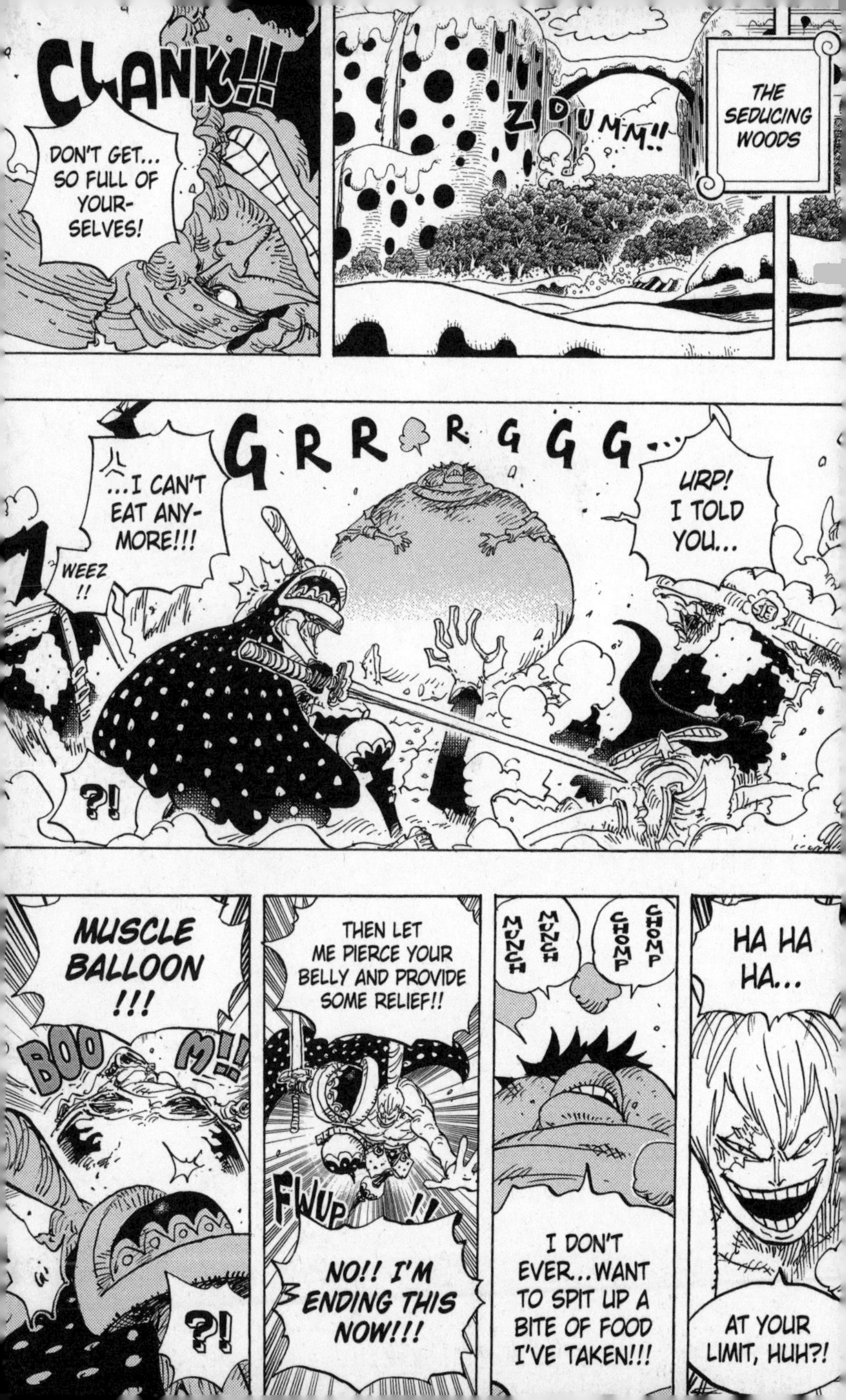
THE SEDUCING WOODS
ZDUMM!!
CLANK!!
DON'T GET... SO FULL OF YOUR-SELVES!
URP! I TOLD YOU...
GRRRRGGG...
...I CAN'T EAT ANY-MORE!!!
WEEZ!!
?!
HA HA HA...
AT YOUR LIMIT, HUH?!
CHOMP CHOMP
MUNCH MUNCH
I DON'T EVER...WANT TO SPIT UP A BITE OF FOOD I'VE TAKEN!!!
THEN LET ME PIERCE YOUR BELLY AND PROVIDE SOME RELIEF!!
FWUP!!
NO!! I'M ENDING THIS NOW!!!
MUSCLE BALLOON!!!
BOOM!!
?!

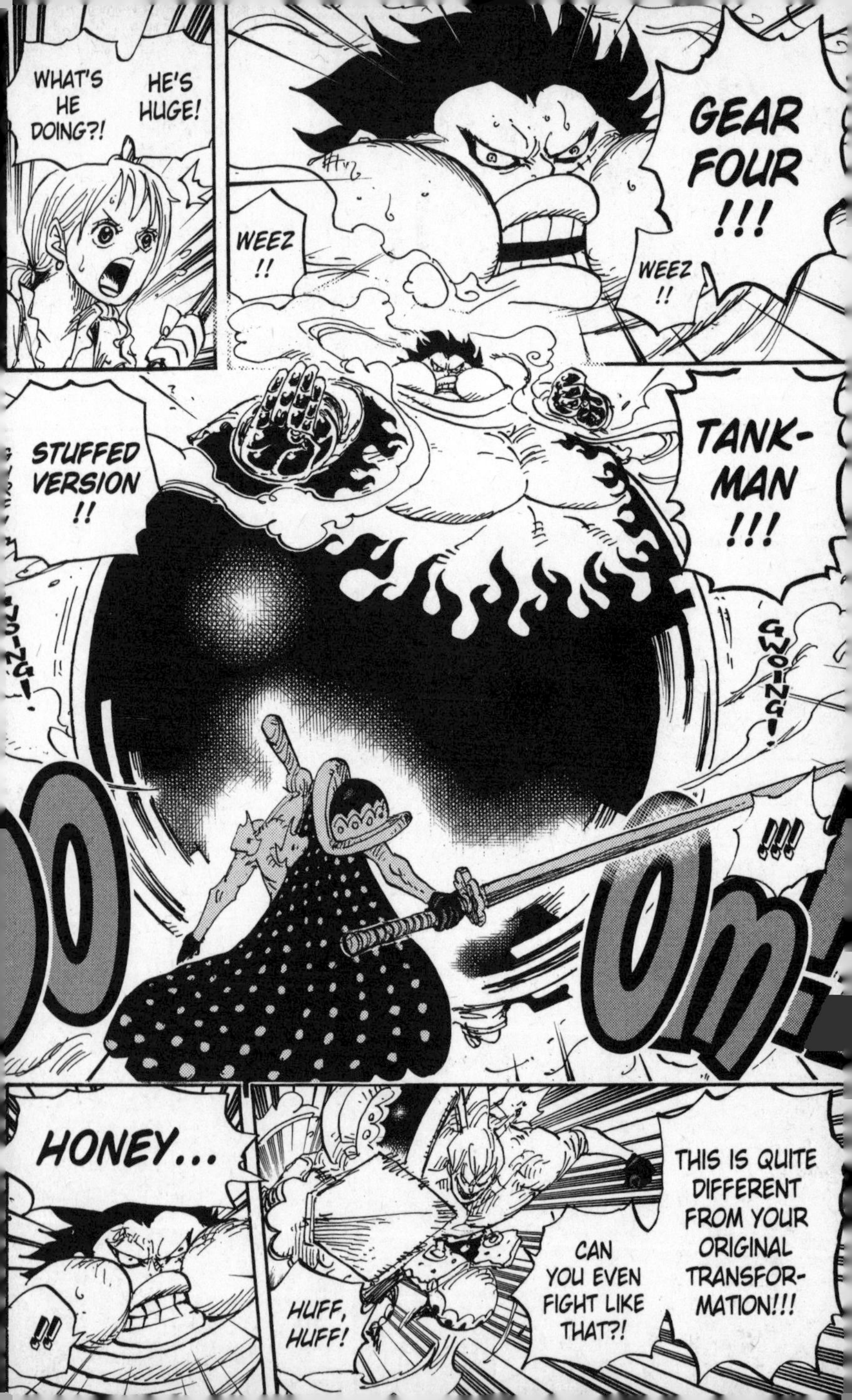
GEAR FOUR!!!
WEEZ!!
WEEZ!!
HE'S HUGE!
WHAT'S HE DOING?!
TANK-MAN!!!
STUFFED VERSION!!
GWOING!
!!!
THIS IS QUITE DIFFERENT FROM YOUR ORIGINAL TRANSFORMATION!!!
CAN YOU EVEN FIGHT LIKE THAT?!
HUFF, HUFF!
HONEY...
!!

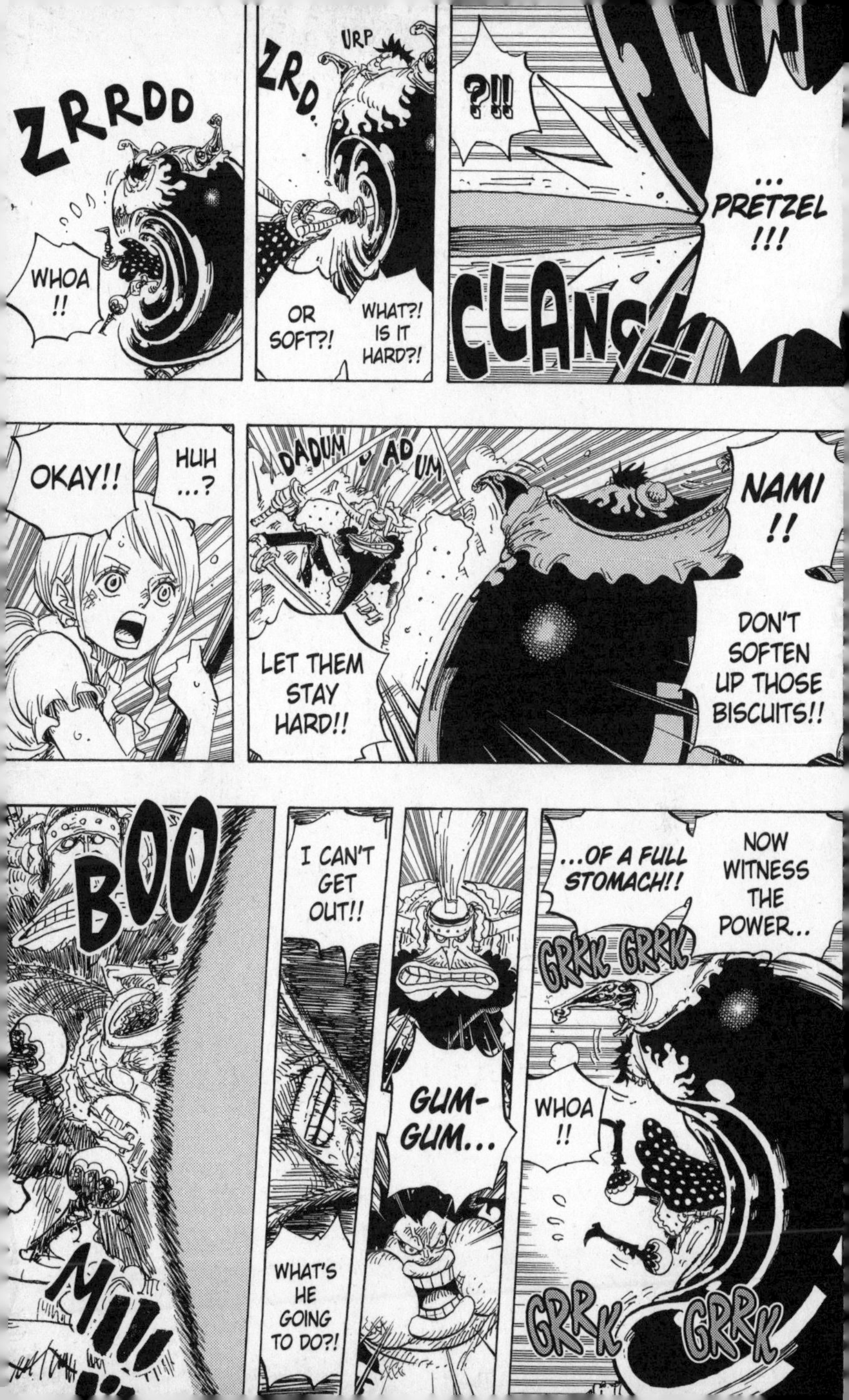
... PRETZEL!!!
?!!
CLANG!!
URP
ZRRD.
WHAT?! IS IT HARD?!
OR SOFT?!
ZRRDD
WHOA!!
NAMI!!
DON'T SOFTEN UP THOSE BISCUITS!!
DADUM DADUM
LET THEM STAY HARD!!
HUH...?
OKAY!!
NOW WITNESS THE POWER...
...OF A FULL STOMACH!!
GRRK GRRK
WHOA!!
GRRK GRRK
GUM-GUM...
I CAN'T GET OUT!!
WHAT'S HE GOING TO DO?!
BOOM!!!

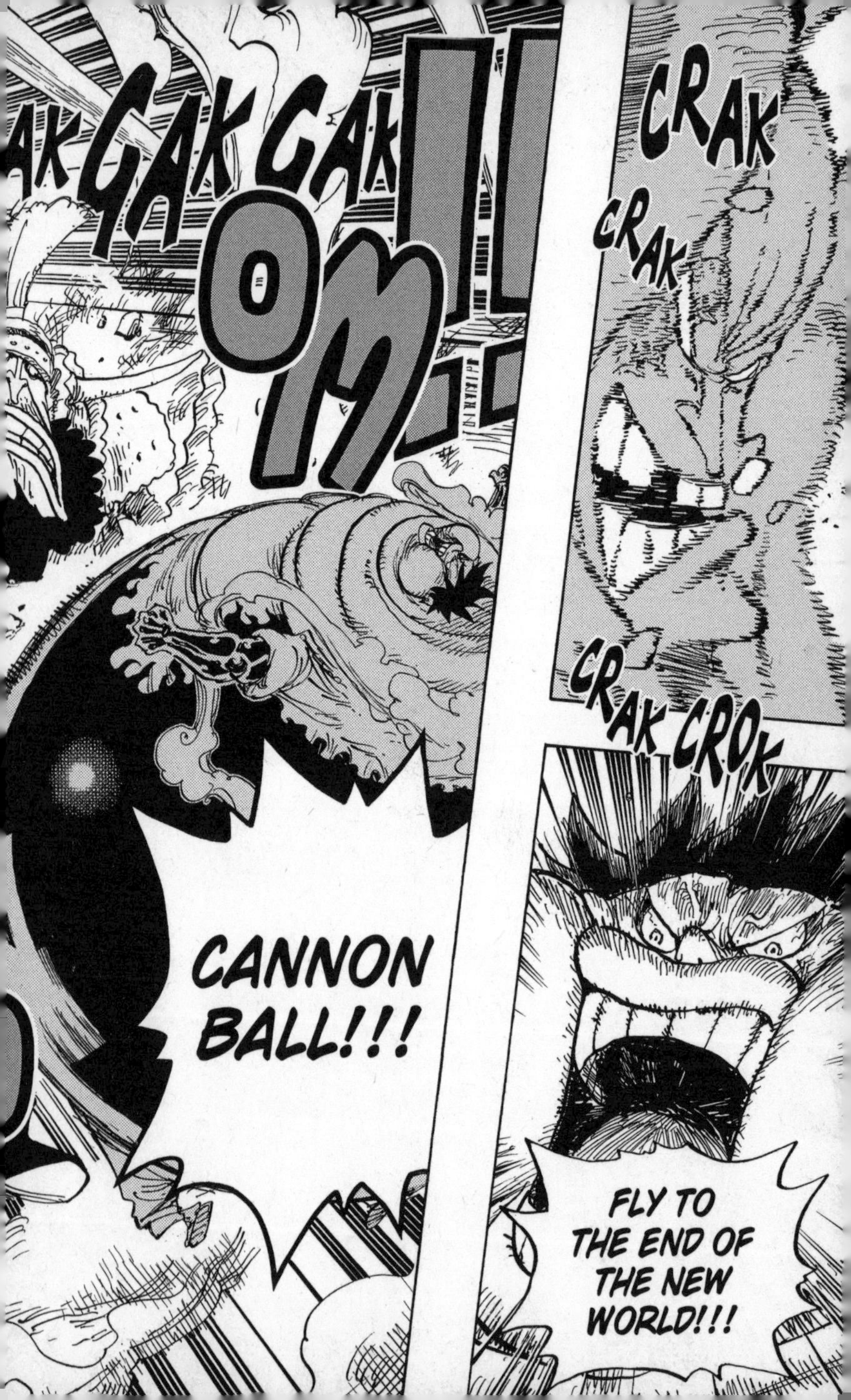
CRAK
CRAK
CRAK
CRAK CROK
FLY TO THE END OF THE NEW WORLD!!!
AK GAK GAK
OM!!
CANNON BALL!!!

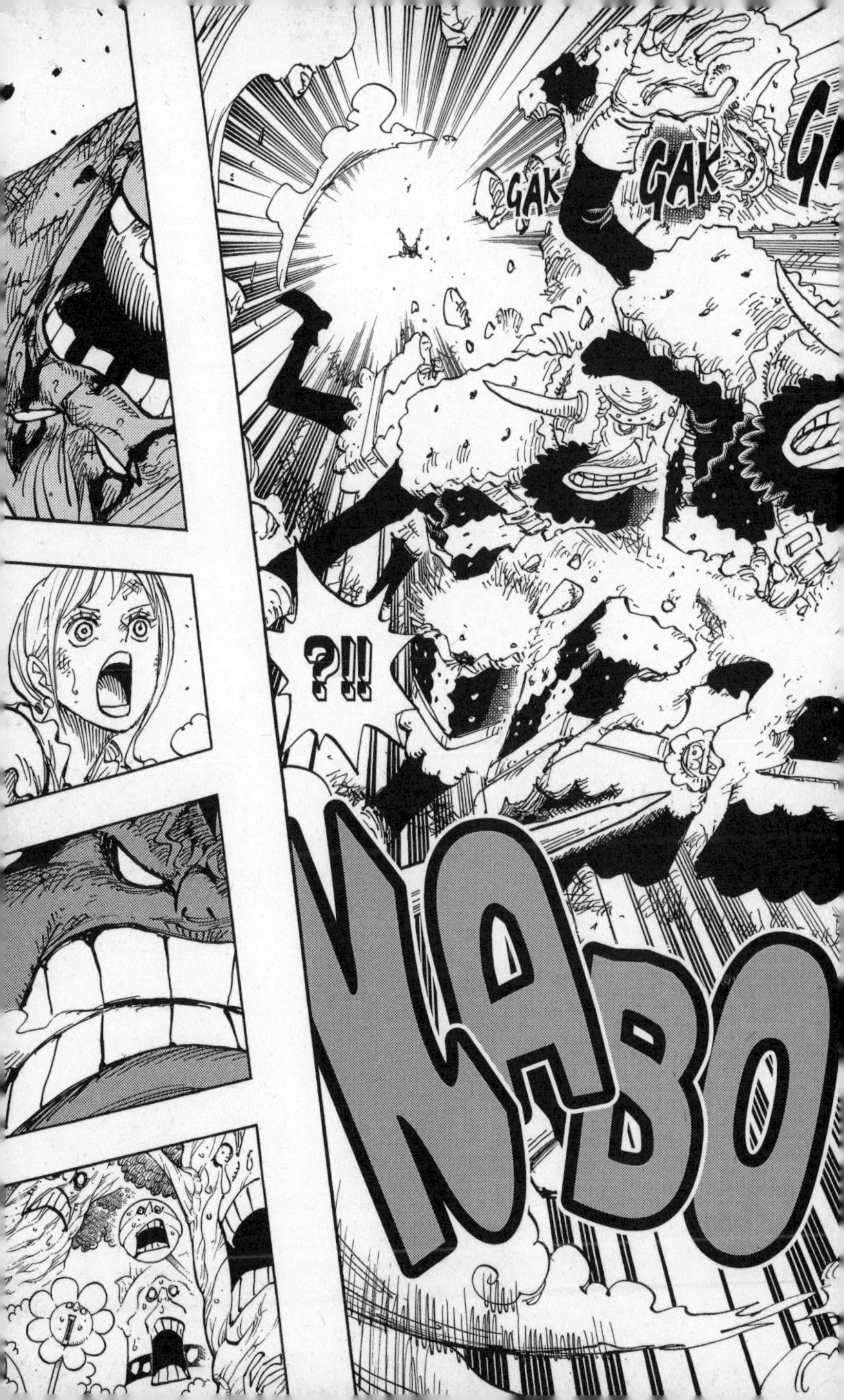

GAK
GAK
?!!
KABO

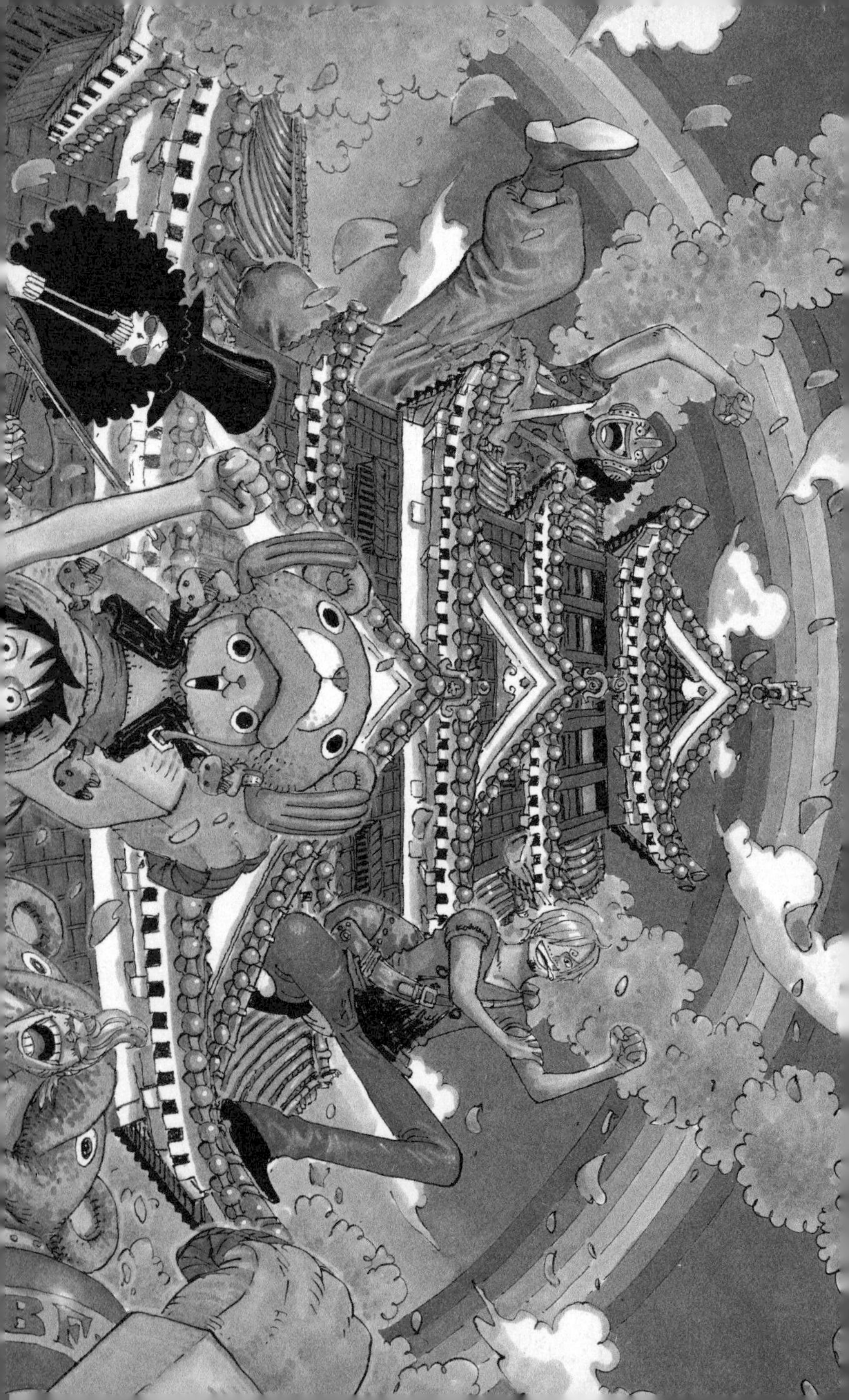

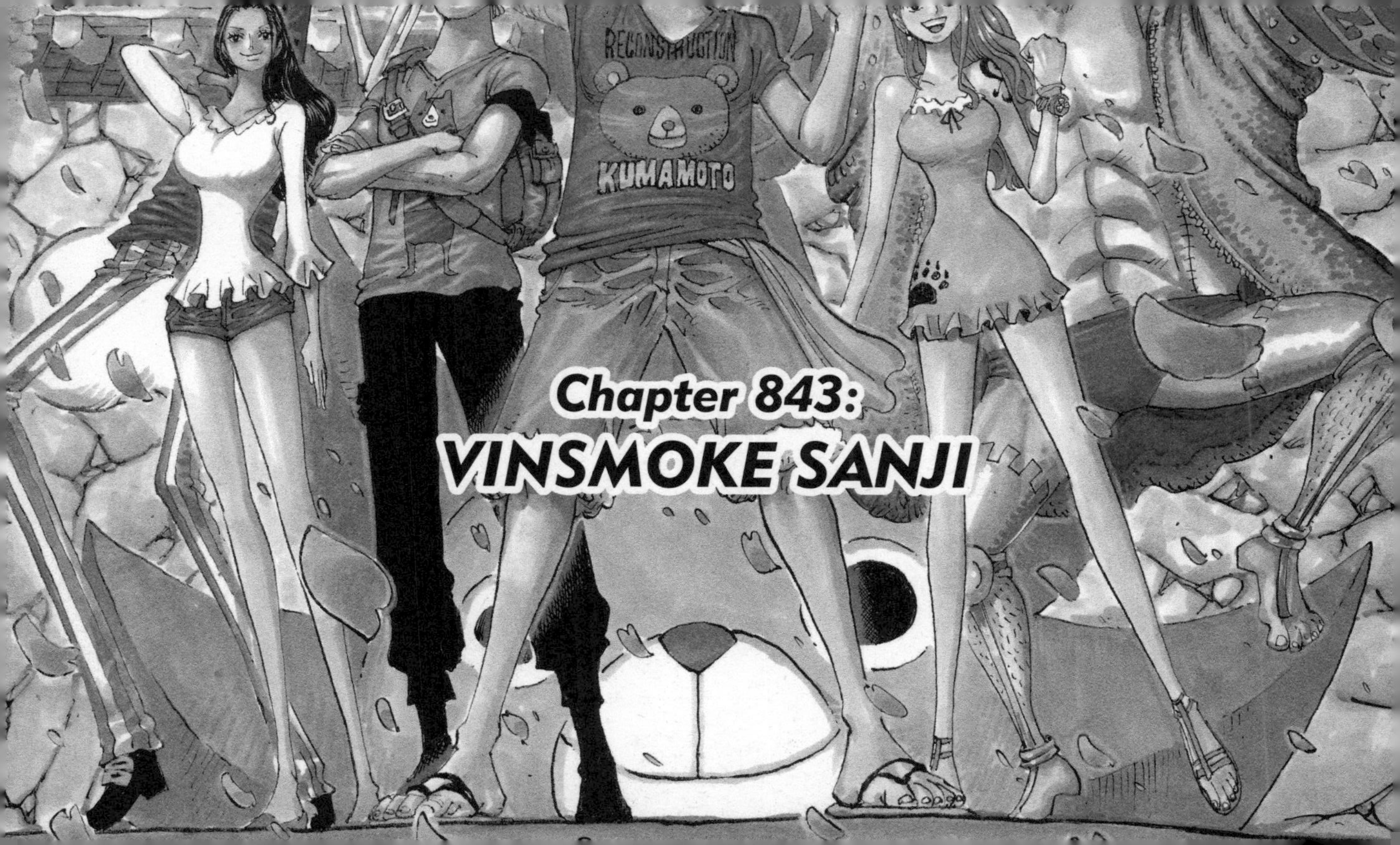
RECONSTRUCTION
KUMAMOTO

Chapter 843: VINSMOKE SANJI

vol.84
ONE PIECE

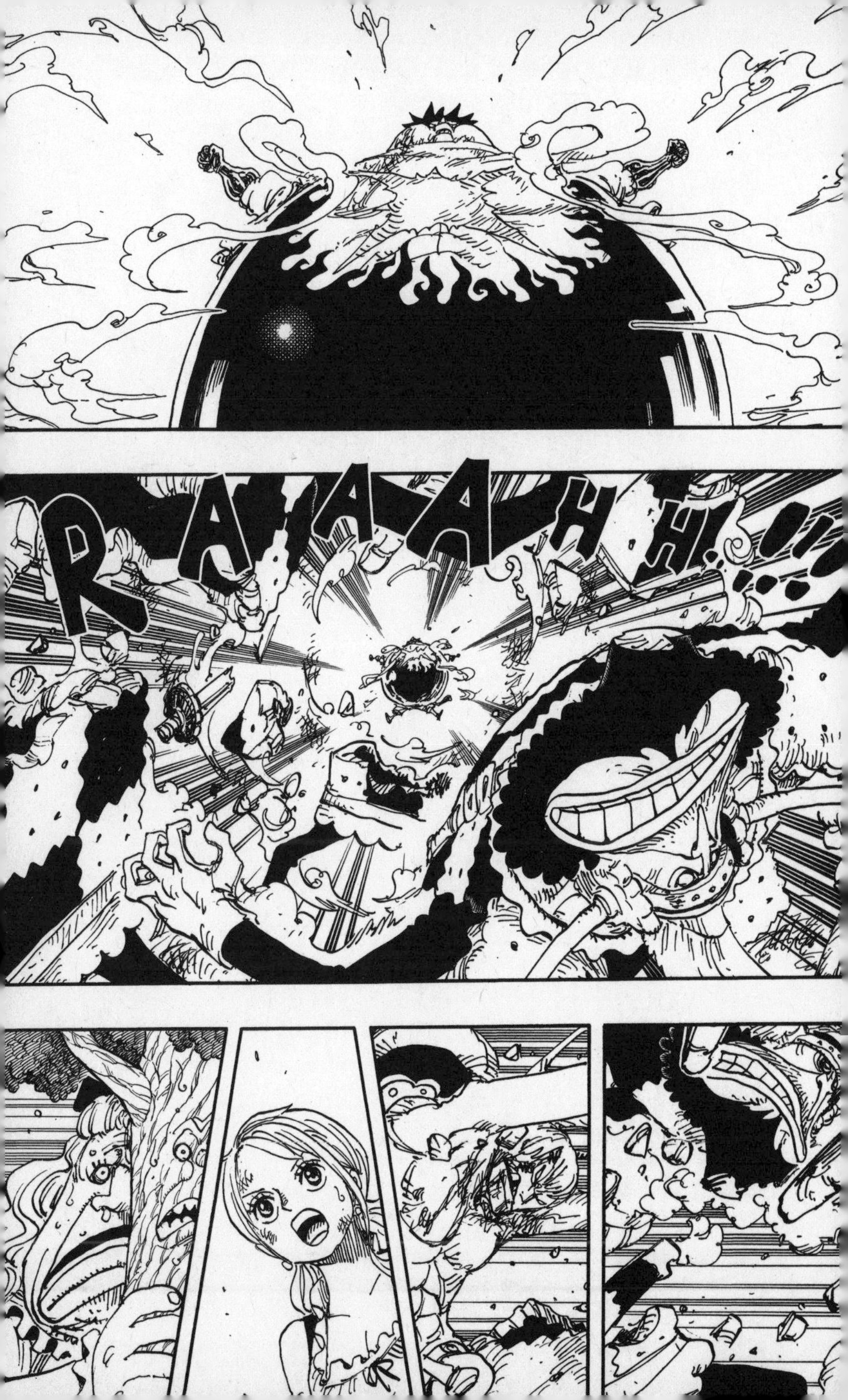
RAAAHHH!!!

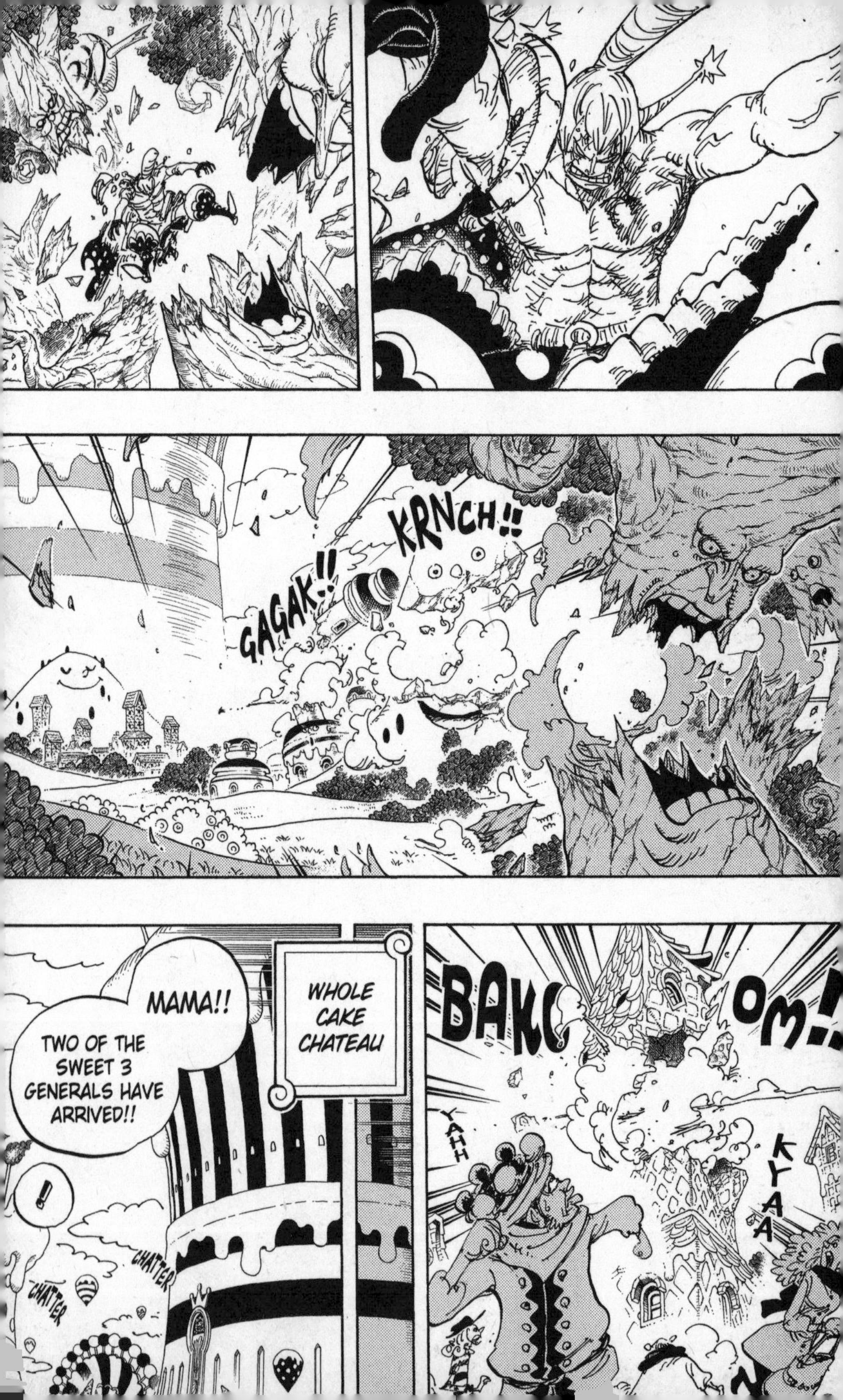
KRNCH!!
GAGAK!!
BAKOOM!!
YAHH
KYAA
WHOLE CAKE CHATEAU
MAMA!! TWO OF THE SWEET 3 GENERALS HAVE ARRIVED!!
!
CHATTER
CHATTER

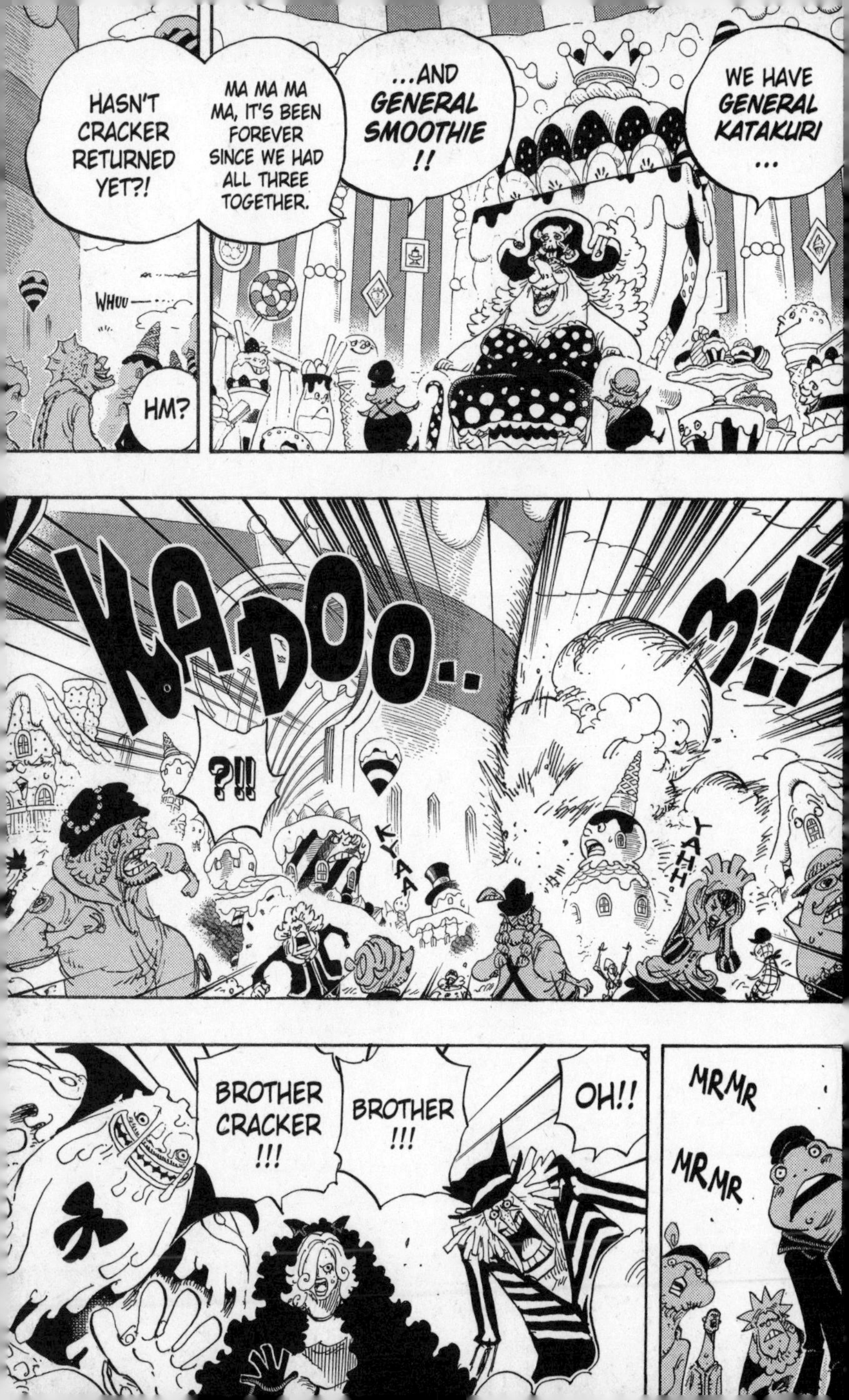

WE HAVE GENERAL KATAKURI...
...AND GENERAL SMOOTHIE!!
MA MA MA MA, IT'S BEEN FOREVER SINCE WE HAD ALL THREE TOGETHER.
HASN'T CRACKER RETURNED YET?!
WHUU——
HM?
KADOOM!!
YAHH
KYAA
?!!
MRMR
MRMR
OH!!
BROTHER!!!
BROTHER CRACKER!!!

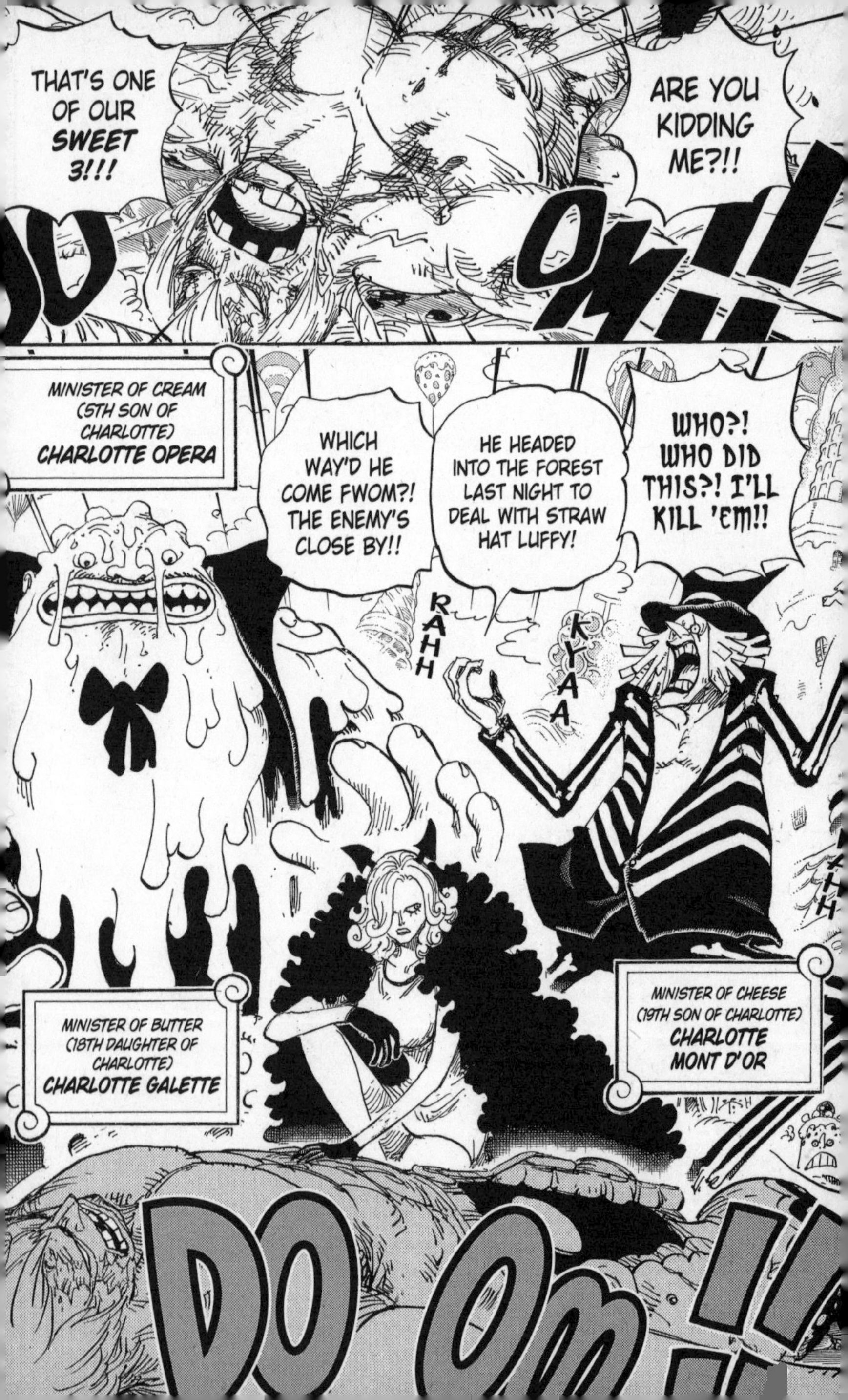
ARE YOU KIDDING ME?!!
THAT'S ONE OF OUR SWEET 3!!!
WHO?! WHO DID THIS?! I'LL KILL 'EM!!
HE HEADED INTO THE FOREST LAST NIGHT TO DEAL WITH STRAW HAT LUFFY!
WHICH WAY'D HE COME FWOM?! THE ENEMY'S CLOSE BY!!
MINISTER OF CREAM (5TH SON OF CHARLOTTE) CHARLOTTE OPERA
KYAA
RAHH
MINISTER OF CHEESE (19TH SON OF CHARLOTTE) CHARLOTTE MONT D'OR
MINISTER OF BUTTER (18TH DAUGHTER OF CHARLOTTE) CHARLOTTE GALETTE
DOOM!!

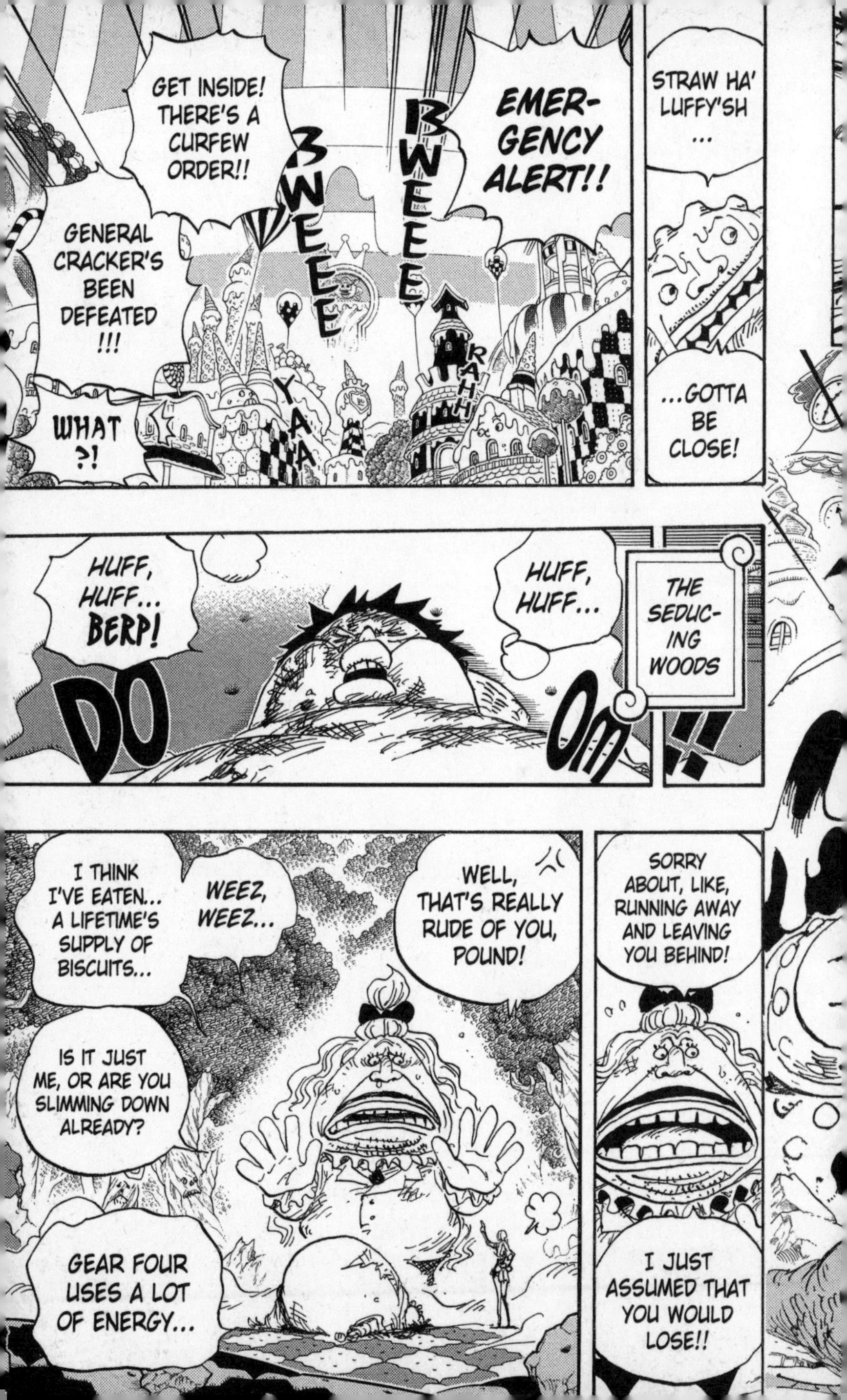
STRAW HA' LUFFY'SH ...
...GOTTA BE CLOSE!
EMERGENCY ALERT!!
BWEEEE
BWEEEE
GET INSIDE! THERE'S A CURFEW ORDER!!
RAHH
YAA
GENERAL CRACKER'S BEEN DEFEATED!!!
WHAT ?!
THE SEDUCING WOODS
HUFF, HUFF...
DOOM!!
HUFF, HUFF... BERP!
SORRY ABOUT, LIKE, RUNNING AWAY AND LEAVING YOU BEHIND!
I JUST ASSUMED THAT YOU WOULD LOSE!!
WELL, THAT'S REALLY RUDE OF YOU, POUND!
WEEZ, WEEZ...
I THINK I'VE EATEN... A LIFETIME'S SUPPLY OF BISCUITS...
IS IT JUST ME, OR ARE YOU SLIMMING DOWN ALREADY?
GEAR FOUR USES A LOT OF ENERGY...

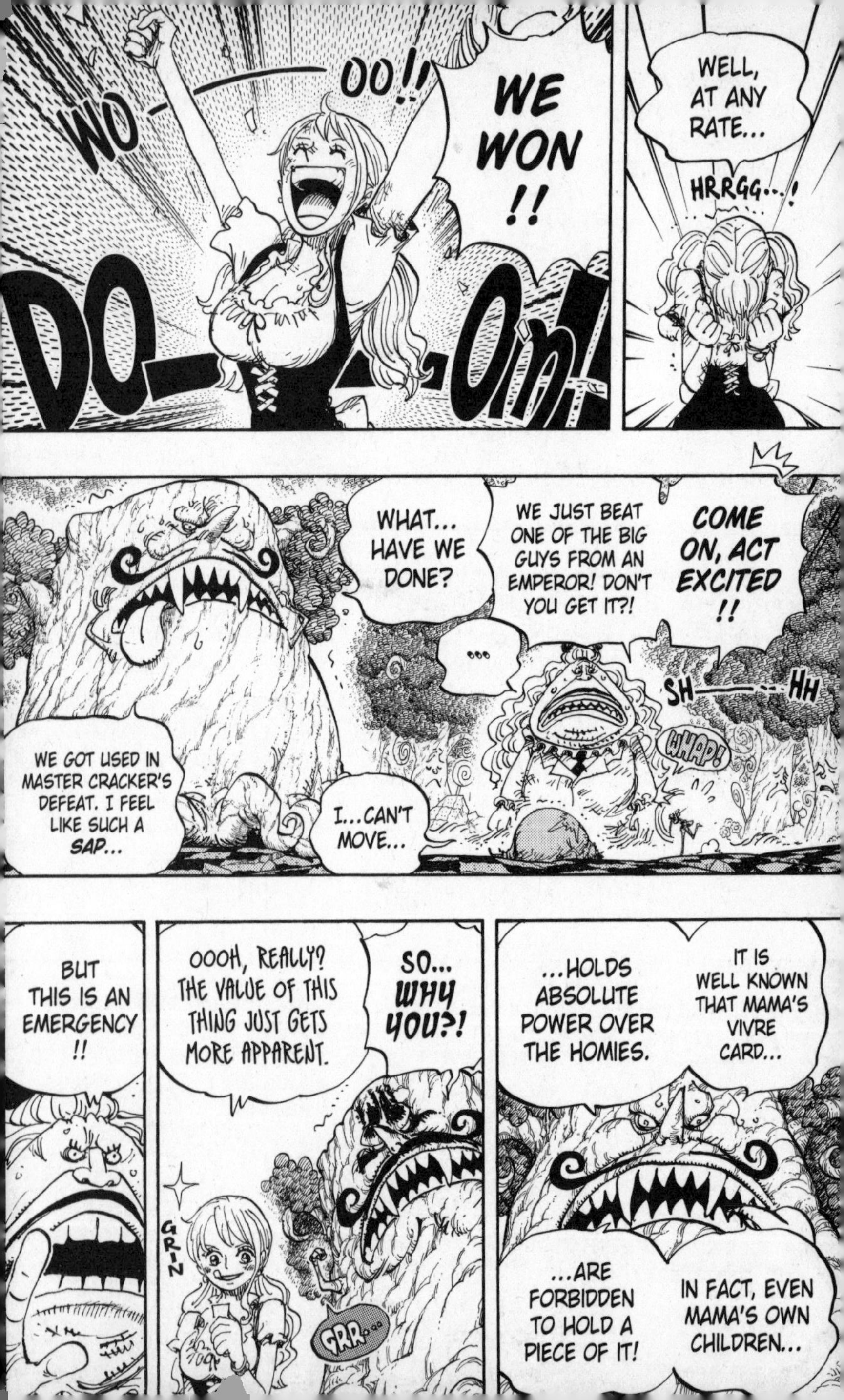
WELL, AT ANY RATE...
HRRGG...!
WO—OO!!
WE WON!!
DO—OM!
COME ON, ACT EXCITED!!
SH—HH
WE JUST BEAT ONE OF THE BIG GUYS FROM AN EMPEROR! DON'T YOU GET IT?!
WHAT... HAVE WE DONE?
WHAP!
...
I...CAN'T MOVE...
WE GOT USED IN MASTER CRACKER'S DEFEAT. I FEEL LIKE SUCH A SAP...
IT IS WELL KNOWN THAT MAMA'S VIVRE CARD...
...HOLDS ABSOLUTE POWER OVER THE HOMIES.
IN FACT, EVEN MAMA'S OWN CHILDREN...
...ARE FORBIDDEN TO HOLD A PIECE OF IT!
SO... WHY YOU?!
OOOH, REALLY? THE VALUE OF THIS THING JUST GETS MORE APPARENT.
GRIN
GRR...
BUT THIS IS AN EMERGENCY!!

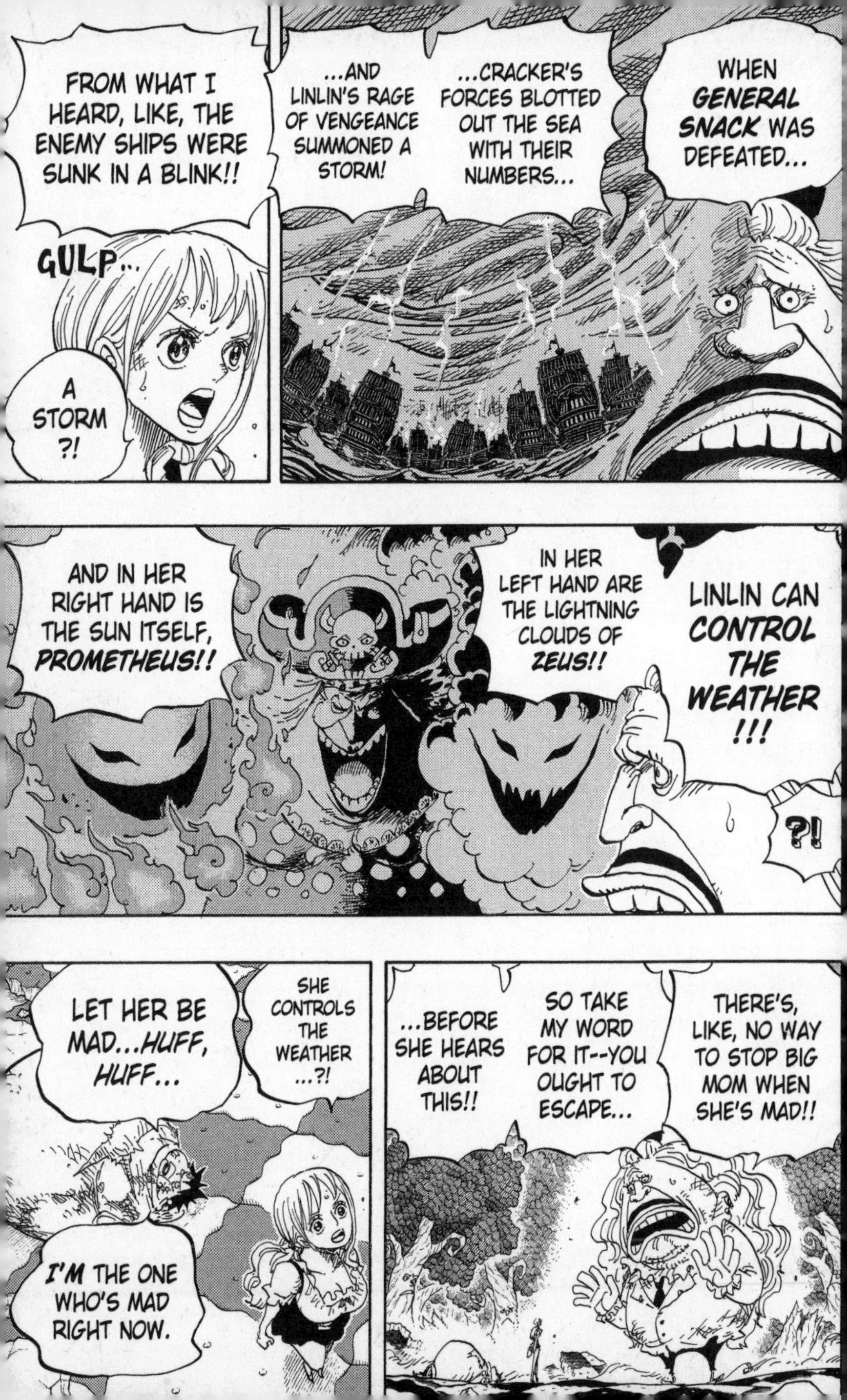
WHEN GENERAL SNACK WAS DEFEATED...
...CRACKER'S FORCES BLOTTED OUT THE SEA WITH THEIR NUMBERS...
...AND LINLIN'S RAGE OF VENGEANCE SUMMONED A STORM!
FROM WHAT I HEARD, LIKE, THE ENEMY SHIPS WERE SUNK IN A BLINK!!
GULP...
A STORM ?!
LINLIN CAN CONTROL THE WEATHER !!!
?!
IN HER LEFT HAND ARE THE LIGHTNING CLOUDS OF ZEUS!!
AND IN HER RIGHT HAND IS THE SUN ITSELF, PROMETHEUS!!
THERE'S, LIKE, NO WAY TO STOP BIG MOM WHEN SHE'S MAD!!
SO TAKE MY WORD FOR IT--YOU OUGHT TO ESCAPE...
...BEFORE SHE HEARS ABOUT THIS!!
SHE CONTROLS THE WEATHER ...?!
LET HER BE MAD...HUFF, HUFF...
I'M THE ONE WHO'S MAD RIGHT NOW.

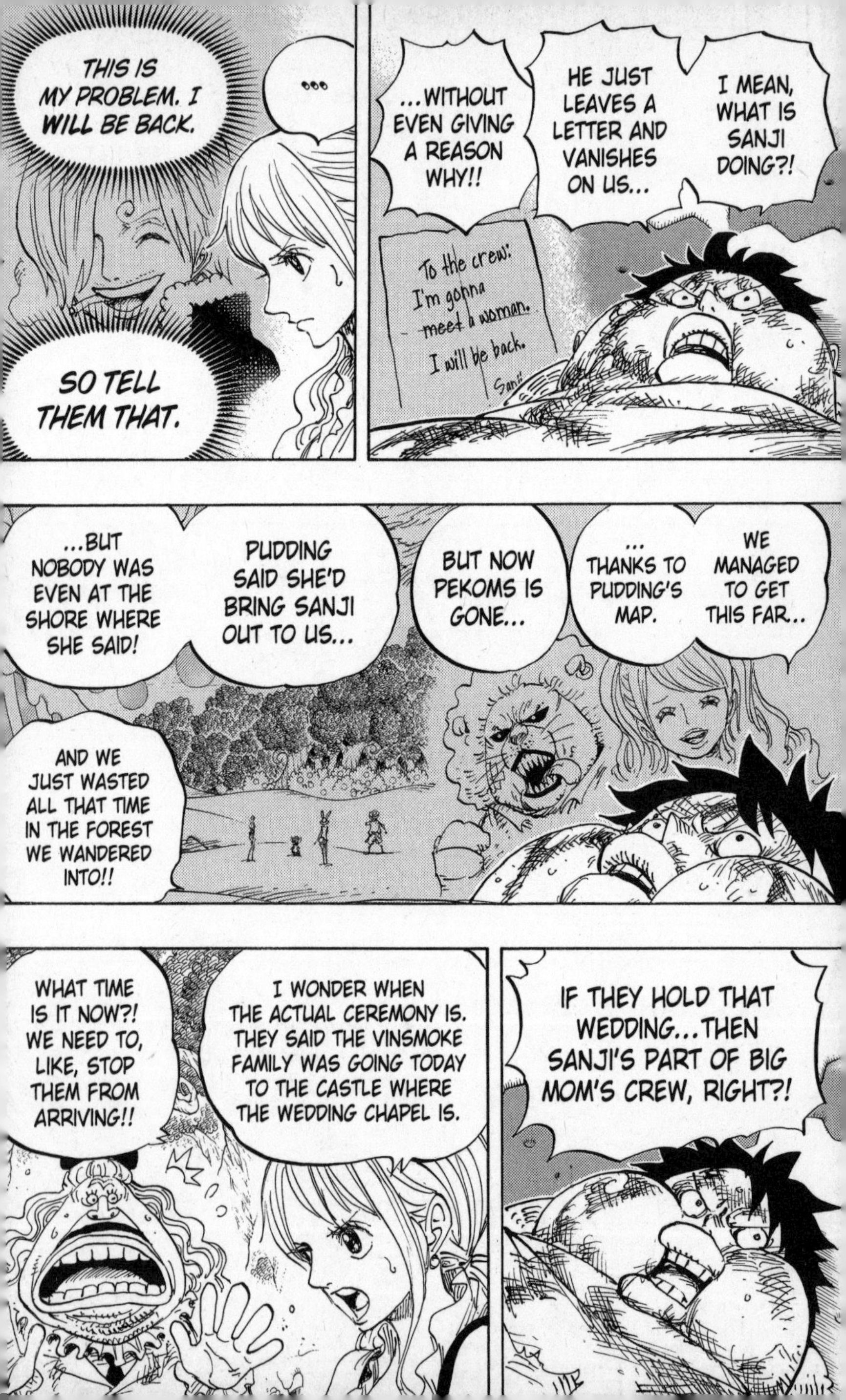
I MEAN, WHAT IS SANJI DOING?!
HE JUST LEAVES A LETTER AND VANISHES ON US...
...WITHOUT EVEN GIVING A REASON WHY!!
To the crew: I'm gonna meet a woman. I will be back.
Sanji
...
THIS IS MY PROBLEM. I WILL BE BACK.
SO TELL THEM THAT.
WE MANAGED TO GET THIS FAR...
... THANKS TO PUDDING'S MAP.
BUT NOW PEKOMS IS GONE...
PUDDING SAID SHE'D BRING SANJI OUT TO US...
...BUT NOBODY WAS EVEN AT THE SHORE WHERE SHE SAID!
AND WE JUST WASTED ALL THAT TIME IN THE FOREST WE WANDERED INTO!!
IF THEY HOLD THAT WEDDING...THEN SANJI'S PART OF BIG MOM'S CREW, RIGHT?!
I WONDER WHEN THE ACTUAL CEREMONY IS. THEY SAID THE VINSMOKE FAMILY WAS GOING TODAY TO THE CASTLE WHERE THE WEDDING CHAPEL IS.
WHAT TIME IS IT NOW?! WE NEED TO, LIKE, STOP THEM FROM ARRIVING!!

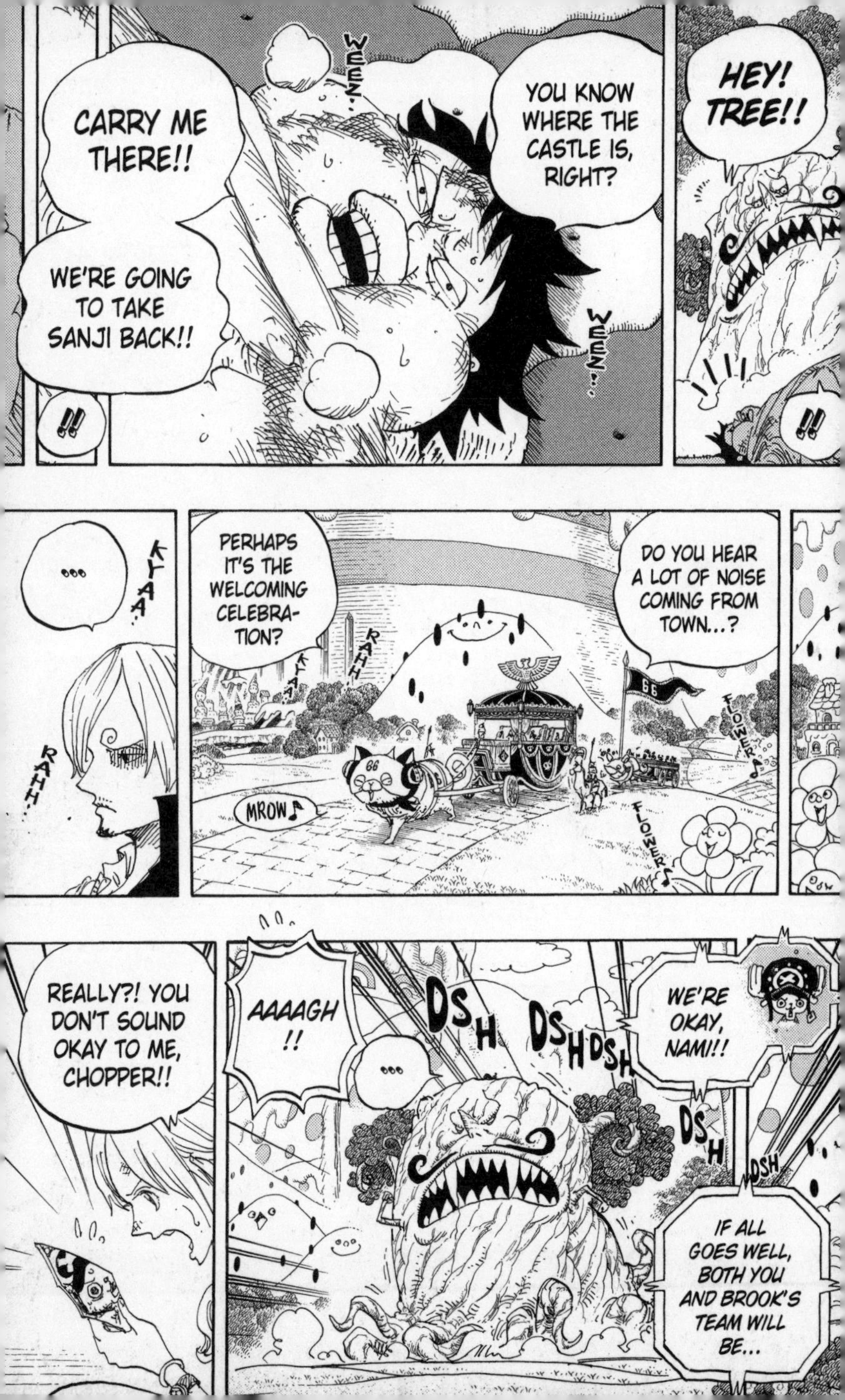
HEY! TREE!!
!!
YOU KNOW WHERE THE CASTLE IS, RIGHT?
WEEZ...
WEEZ...
CARRY ME THERE!!
WE'RE GOING TO TAKE SANJI BACK!!
!!
DO YOU HEAR A LOT OF NOISE COMING FROM TOWN...?
PERHAPS IT'S THE WELCOMING CELEBRATION?
RAHH
KYAA
FLOWER♪
FLOWER♪
MROW♪
...
KYAA...
RAHH...
WE'RE OKAY, NAMI!!
DSH DSH DSH DSH
DSH
DSH
AAAAGH!!
...
IF ALL GOES WELL, BOTH YOU AND BROOK'S TEAM WILL BE...
REALLY?! YOU DON'T SOUND OKAY TO ME, CHOPPER!!

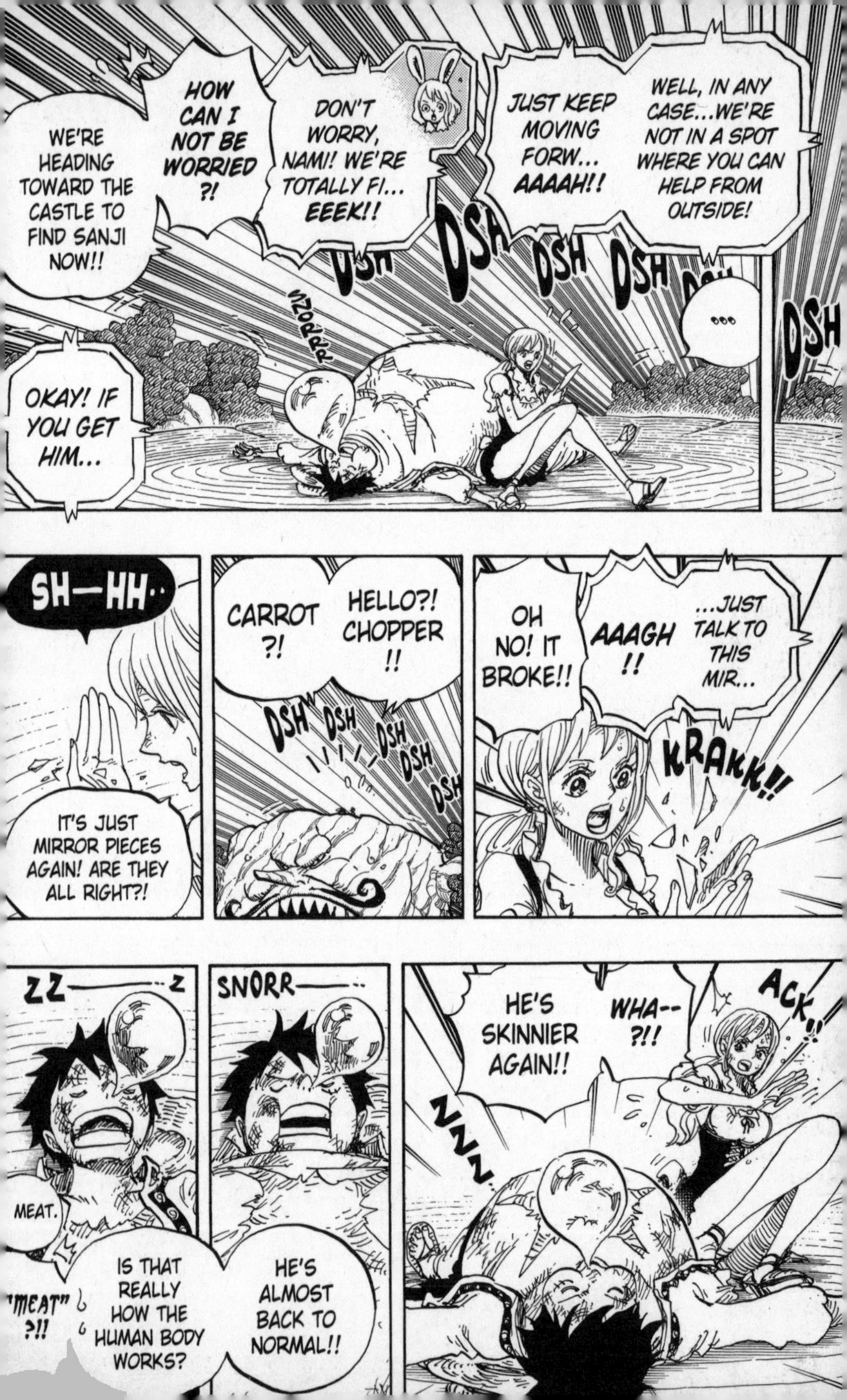
WELL, IN ANY CASE...WE'RE NOT IN A SPOT WHERE YOU CAN HELP FROM OUTSIDE!
JUST KEEP MOVING FORW... AAAAH!!
DON'T WORRY, NAMI! WE'RE TOTALLY FI... EEEK!!
HOW CAN I NOT BE WORRIED?!
WE'RE HEADING TOWARD THE CASTLE TO FIND SANJI NOW!!
DSH
DSH
DSH
DSH
DSH
...
SNORRR
OKAY! IF YOU GET HIM...
...JUST TALK TO THIS MIR...
AAAGH!!
OH NO! IT BROKE!!
KRAKK!!
HELLO?! CHOPPER!!
CARROT?!
DSH DSH DSH DSH DSH
SH—HH..
IT'S JUST MIRROR PIECES AGAIN! ARE THEY ALL RIGHT?!
ACK!!
WHA-- ?!!
HE'S SKINNIER AGAIN!!
ZZZ...
SNORR——
HE'S ALMOST BACK TO NORMAL!!
ZZ——Z
MEAT.
IS THAT REALLY HOW THE HUMAN BODY WORKS?
"MEAT" ?!!

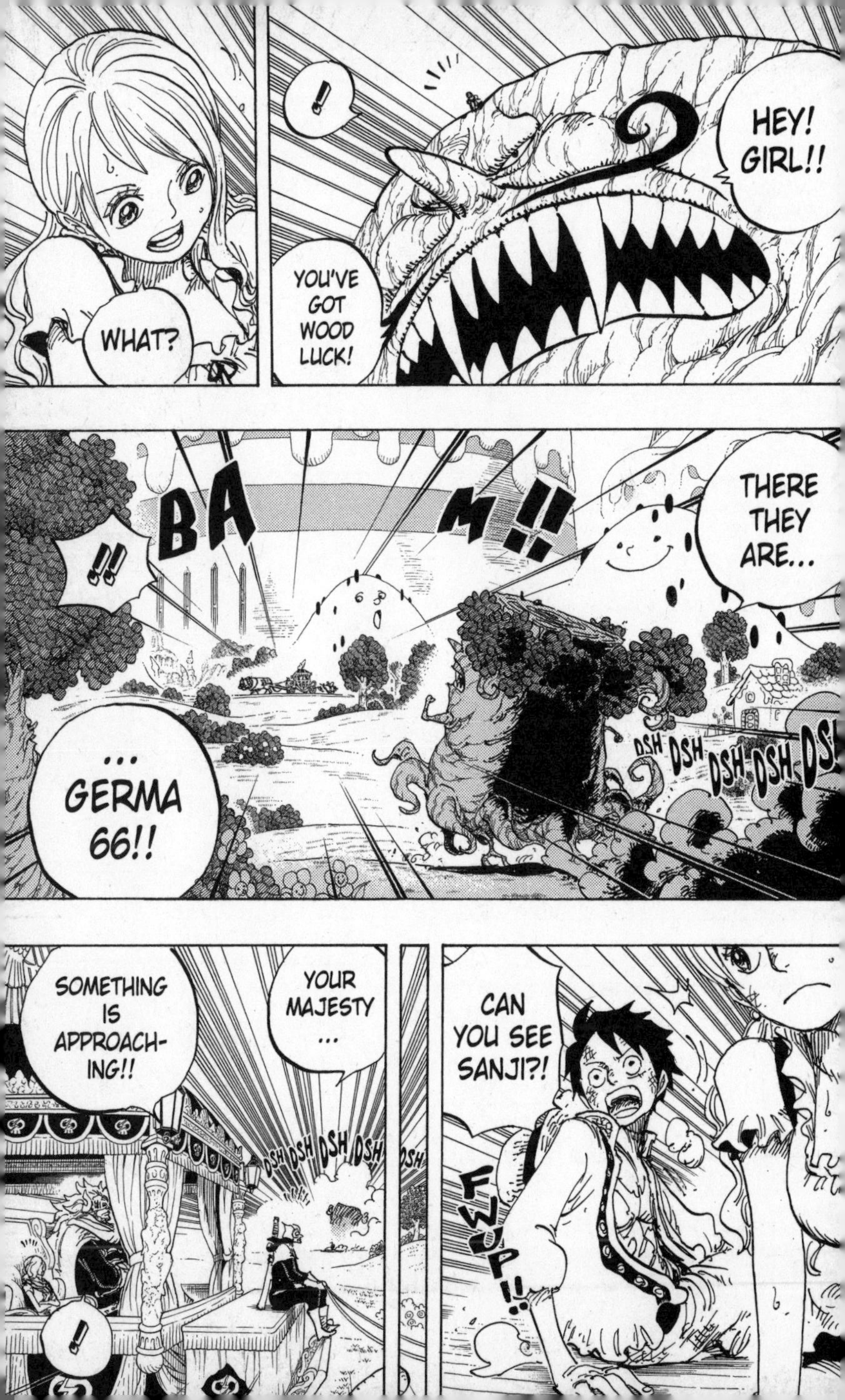
HEY! GIRL!!
!
YOU'VE GOT WOOD LUCK!
WHAT?
THERE THEY ARE...
BAM!!
!!
DSH DSH DSH DSH DSH
... GERMA 66!!
CAN YOU SEE SANJI?!
FWUP!!
YOUR MAJESTY ...
SOMETHING IS APPROACH-ING!!
DSH DSH DSH DSH DSH
!

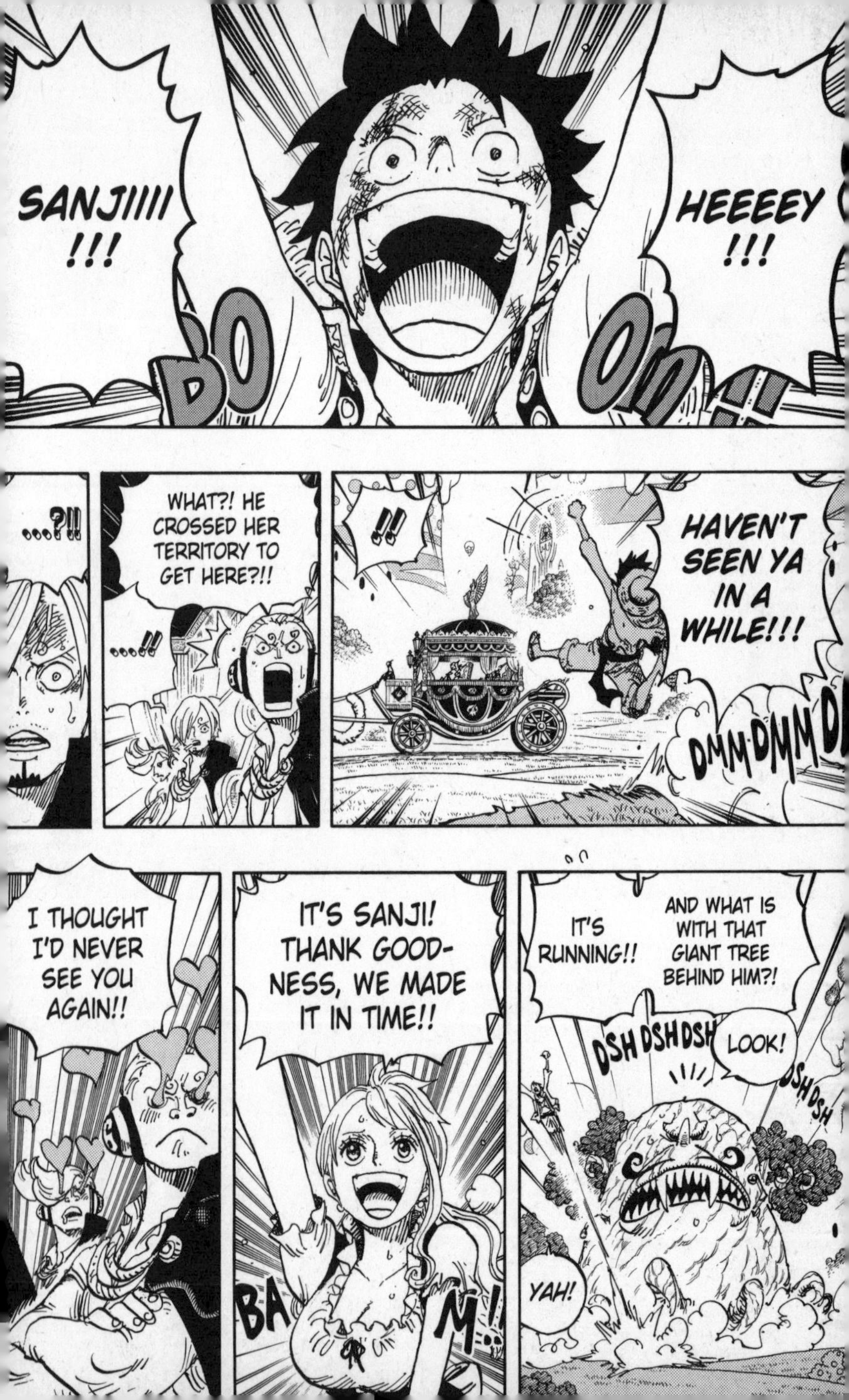
HEEEEY !!!
SANJIIII !!!
BOOM!!
!!
HAVEN'T SEEN YA IN A WHILE!!!
DMM DMM D
WHAT?! HE CROSSED HER TERRITORY TO GET HERE?!!
...!!
...?!!
AND WHAT IS WITH THAT GIANT TREE BEHIND HIM?!
IT'S RUNNING!!
DSH DSH DSH
LOOK!
DSH DSH
YAH!
IT'S SANJI! THANK GOOD-NESS, WE MADE IT IN TIME!!
BAM!!
I THOUGHT I'D NEVER SEE YOU AGAIN!!

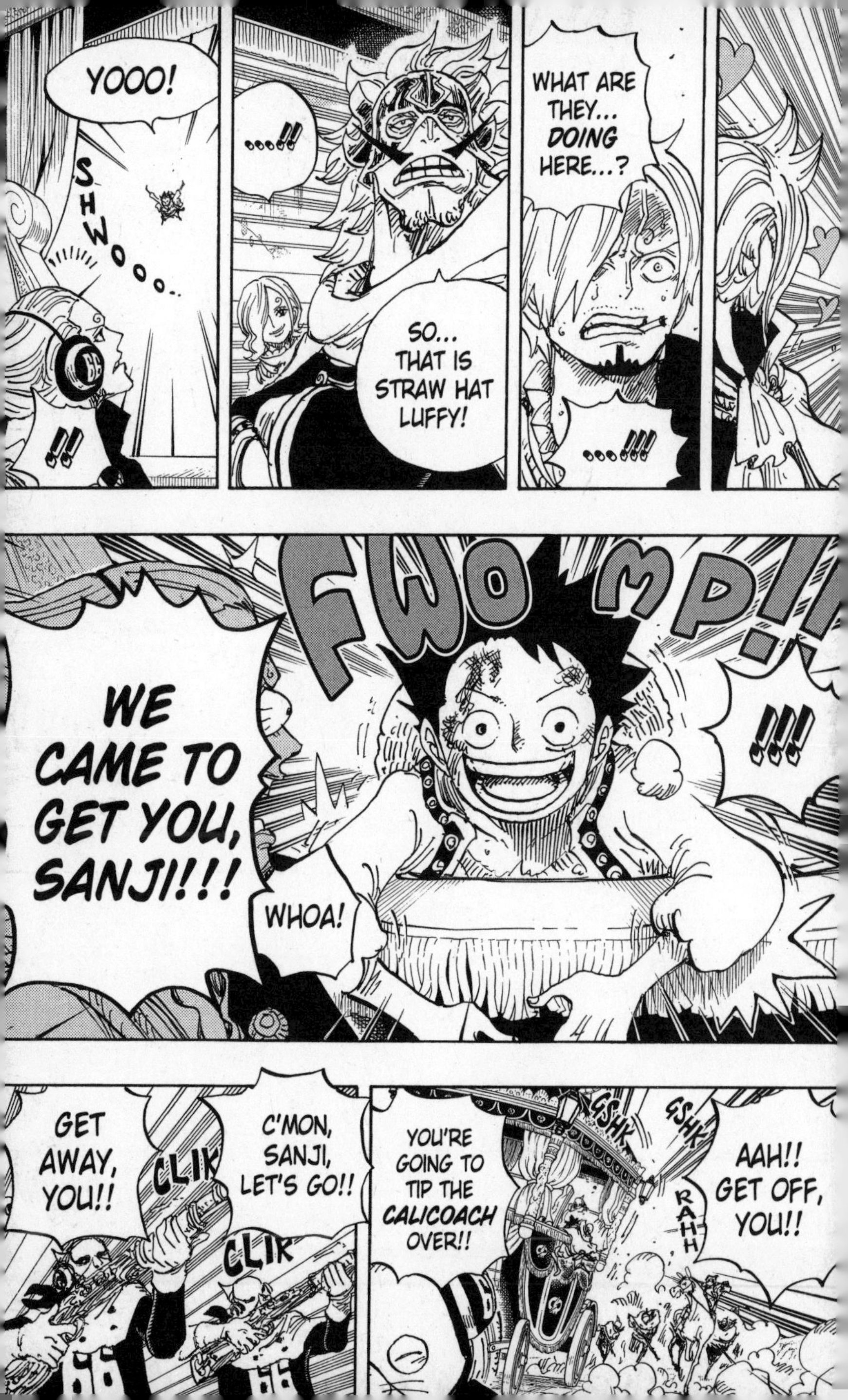
WHAT ARE THEY... DOING HERE...?
...!!!
....!!
SO... THAT IS STRAW HAT LUFFY!
YOOO!
SHWOOOO...
!!
FWOMP!!!
!!!
WE CAME TO GET YOU, SANJI!!!
WHOA!
AAH!! GET OFF, YOU!!
GSHK
GSHK
RAHH
YOU'RE GOING TO TIP THE CALICOACH OVER!!
C'MON, SANJI, LET'S GO!!
CLIK
GET AWAY, YOU!!
CLIK

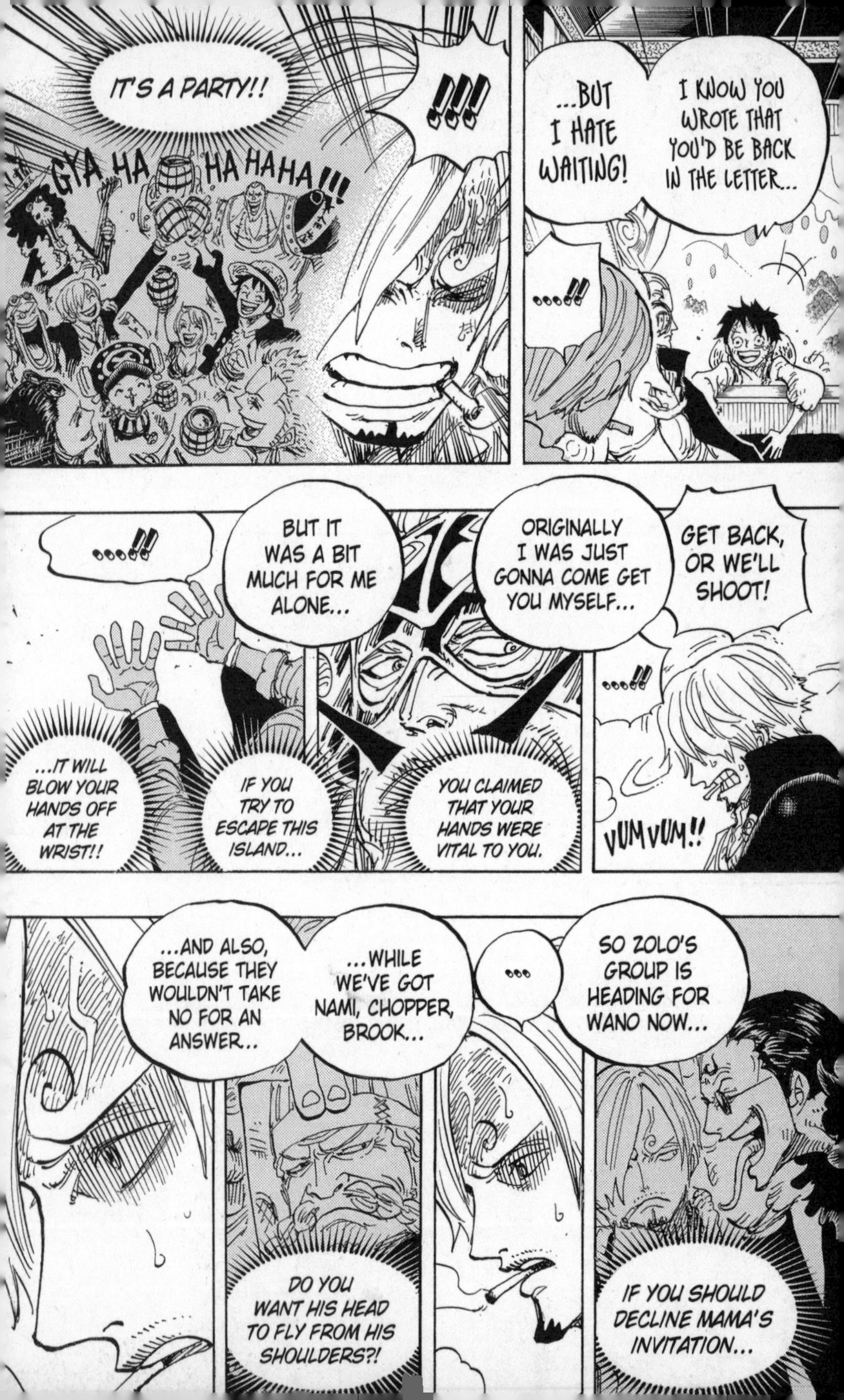
I KNOW YOU WROTE THAT YOU'D BE BACK IN THE LETTER...
...BUT I HATE WAITING!
...!!
!!!
IT'S A PARTY!!
GYA HA HA HAHA!!!
GET BACK, OR WE'LL SHOOT!
...!!
VUM VUM!!
ORIGINALLY I WAS JUST GONNA COME GET YOU MYSELF...
BUT IT WAS A BIT MUCH FOR ME ALONE...
YOU CLAIMED THAT YOUR HANDS WERE VITAL TO YOU.
IF YOU TRY TO ESCAPE THIS ISLAND...
...!!
...IT WILL BLOW YOUR HANDS OFF AT THE WRIST!!
SO ZOLO'S GROUP IS HEADING FOR WANO NOW...
IF YOU SHOULD DECLINE MAMA'S INVITATION...
...
...WHILE WE'VE GOT NAMI, CHOPPER, BROOK...
DO YOU WANT HIS HEAD TO FLY FROM HIS SHOULDERS?!
...AND ALSO, BECAUSE THEY WOULDN'T TAKE NO FOR AN ANSWER...

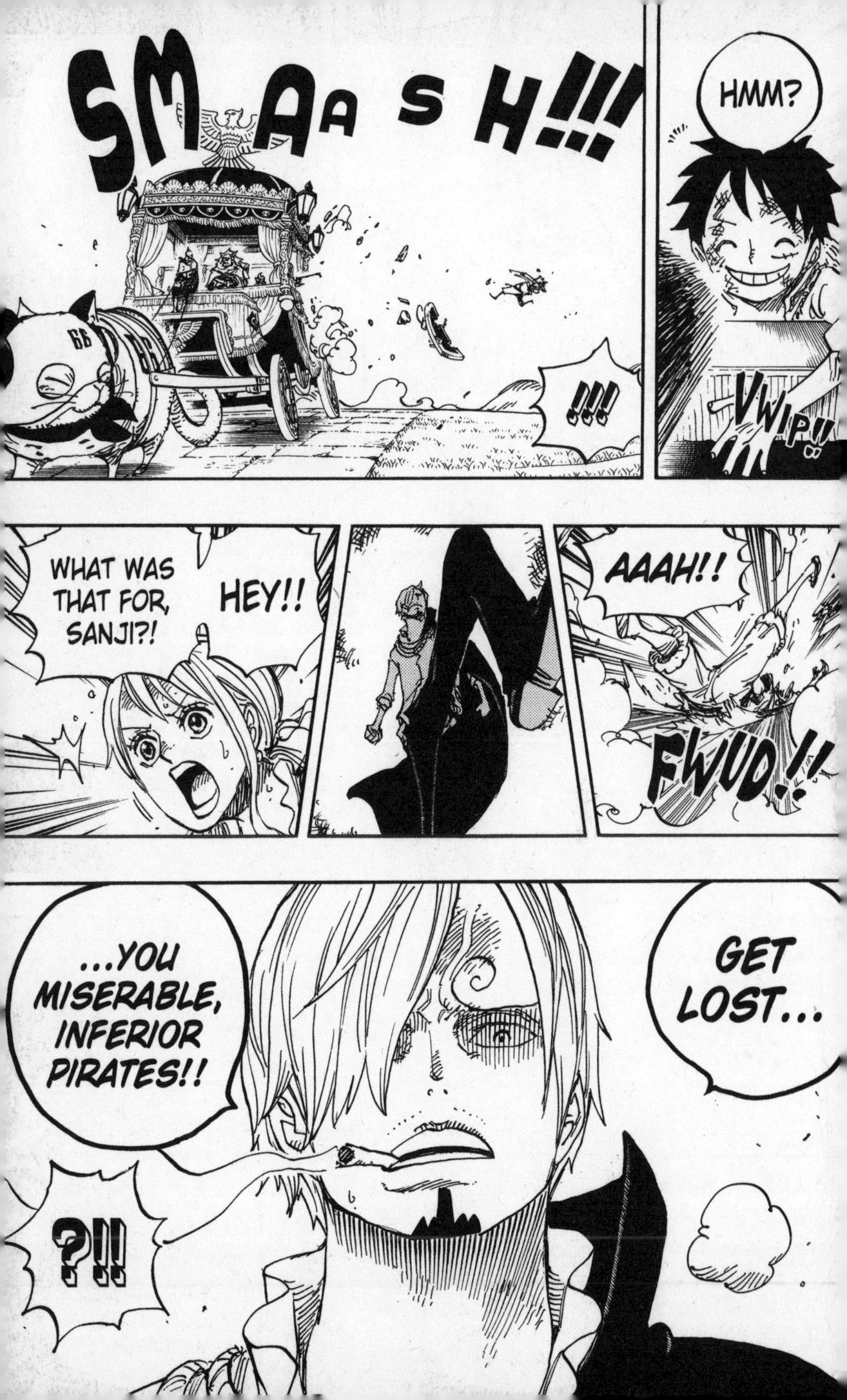
HMM?
VWIP!!
SMAASH!!!
!!!
AAAH!!
FWUD!!
HEY!!
WHAT WAS THAT FOR, SANJI?!
GET LOST...
...YOU MISERABLE, INFERIOR PIRATES!!
?!!

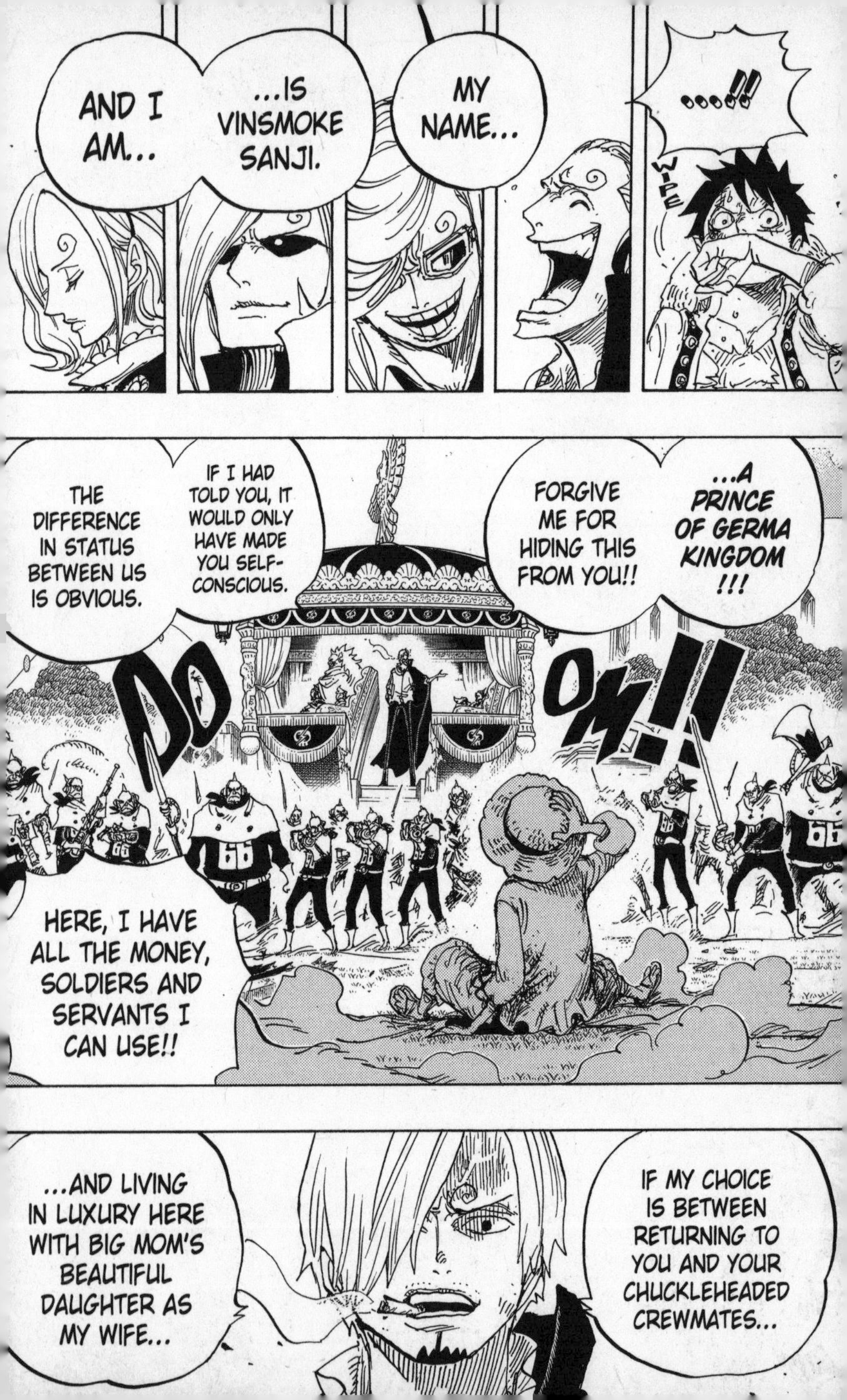
....!!
WIPE
MY NAME...
...IS VINSMOKE SANJI.
AND I AM...
...A PRINCE OF GERMA KINGDOM!!!
FORGIVE ME FOR HIDING THIS FROM YOU!!
IF I HAD TOLD YOU, IT WOULD ONLY HAVE MADE YOU SELF-CONSCIOUS.
THE DIFFERENCE IN STATUS BETWEEN US IS OBVIOUS.
DOOM!!
HERE, I HAVE ALL THE MONEY, SOLDIERS AND SERVANTS I CAN USE!!
IF MY CHOICE IS BETWEEN RETURNING TO YOU AND YOUR CHUCKLEHEADED CREWMATES...
...AND LIVING IN LUXURY HERE WITH BIG MOM'S BEAUTIFUL DAUGHTER AS MY WIFE...

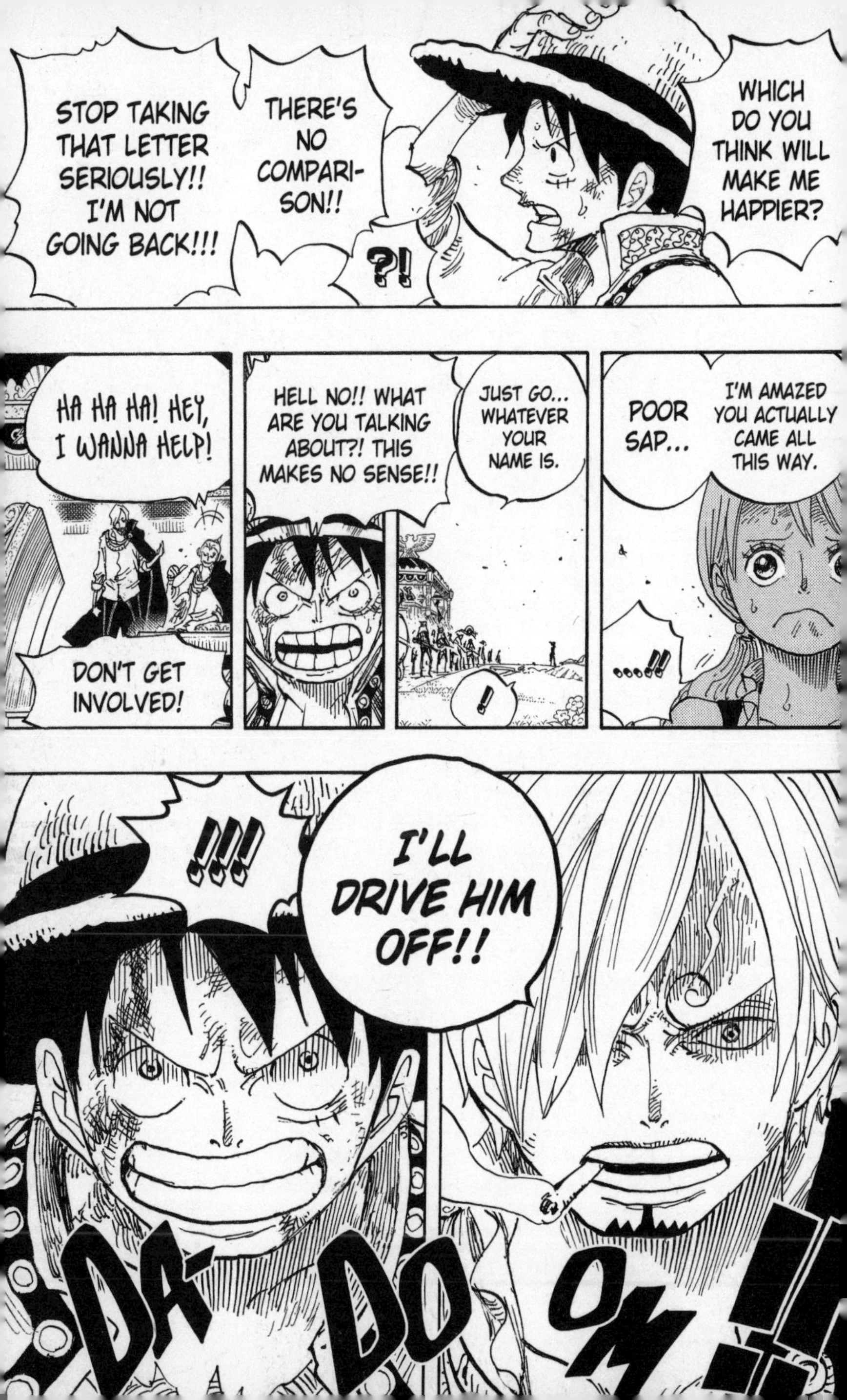
WHICH DO YOU THINK WILL MAKE ME HAPPIER?
THERE'S NO COMPARI-SON!!
STOP TAKING THAT LETTER SERIOUSLY!! I'M NOT GOING BACK!!!
?!
I'M AMAZED YOU ACTUALLY CAME ALL THIS WAY.
POOR SAP...
...!!
JUST GO... WHATEVER YOUR NAME IS.
HELL NO!! WHAT ARE YOU TALKING ABOUT?! THIS MAKES NO SENSE!!
!
HA HA HA! HEY, I WANNA HELP!
DON'T GET INVOLVED!
I'LL DRIVE HIM OFF!!
!!!
DA-DO-OM!!

SBS Question Corner

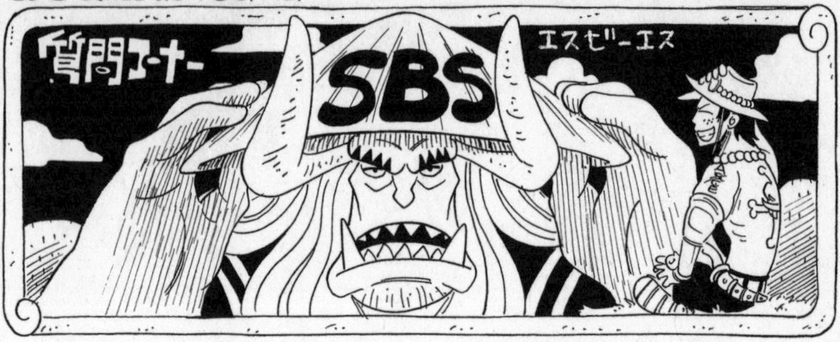

質問コーナー
SBS
エスビーエス

(BiagioPanzani, Italy)

Q: The Germa castle is kinda *werrrp*. Does that mean the people inside live their lives kind of *werpy?*

--Luck

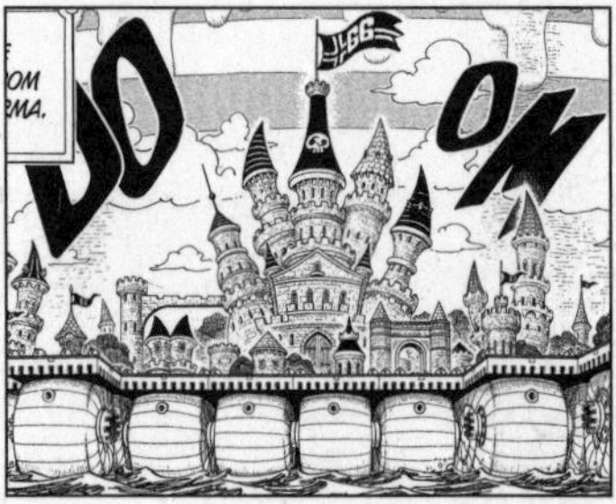

DOON

A: Actually, it's not that they built a castle that turned all *werrrp*, it's that they built it to exact specifications to achieve that level of *werrrp*. If anything, the people who live there are extremely exacting and uptight!!

Q: Hello, Oda Sensei! Basil Hawkins takes his horoscopes and fortunes seriously when he acts. If his lucky item for the day was a miniskirt, would he wear it?

--Moss Mink

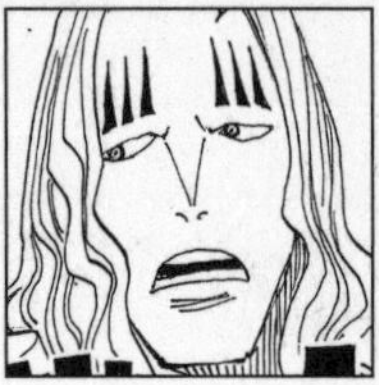

A: Well, he's very confident in his fortune-telling, so I daresay he would wear it. His leg hair is quite thick.

Q: In chapter 823, you introduced Sally Isntoinette, queen of Goa. Is she based on Marie Antoinette? I'm so jealous of Stelly--he's ugly and horrible, yet he snagged a beautiful wife. I'm ugly and not rich, but I snagged **my** angry wife with my heart!!

--Chores Are Easy

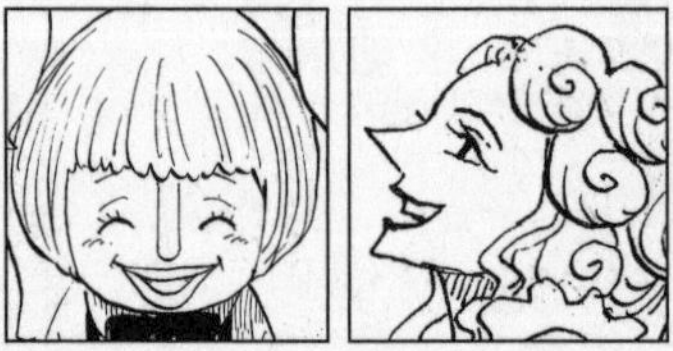

A: Does everyone remember Stelly? He was Sabo's foster brother in Luffy's flashback from Volume 60. Somehow, in the present day, he's worked himself into the royal family and become king! What a punk! And I figured his queen was probably a horrible person too, so I gave her a lazy name! Isntoinette! What kind of name is that?! Don't worry! I'm sure your angry wife is way better than her!

Chapter 844:
LUFFY VS. SANJI

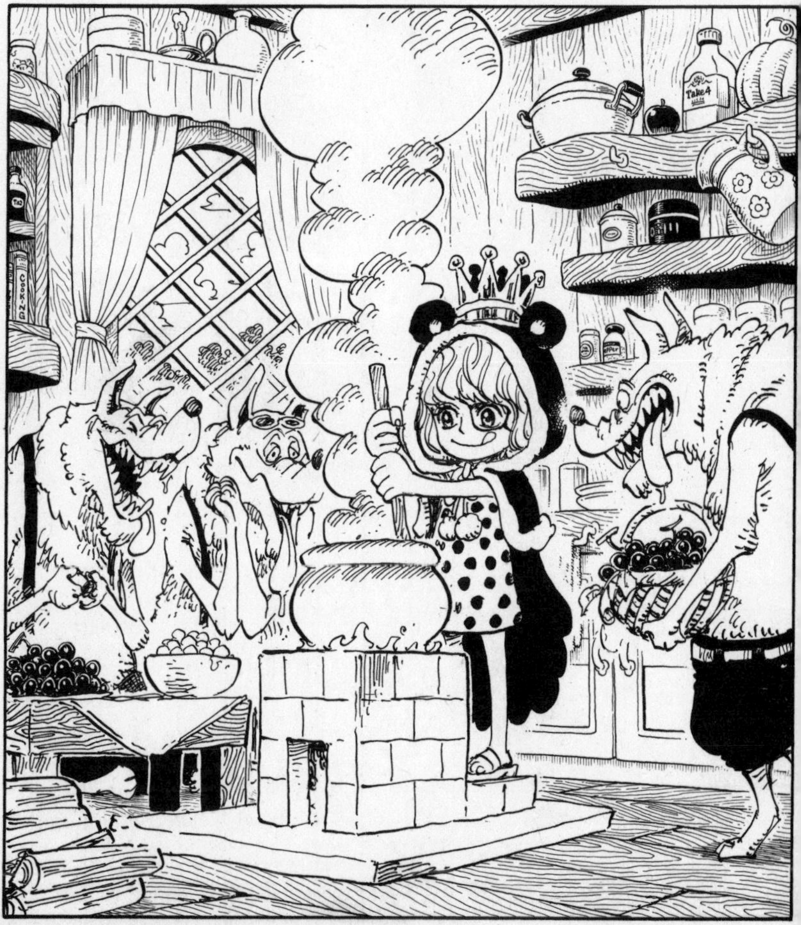

REQUEST: "SUGAR WHIPPING UP SOME GRAPE JAM WITH WOLVES" BY NODA SKYWALKER FROM OSAKA

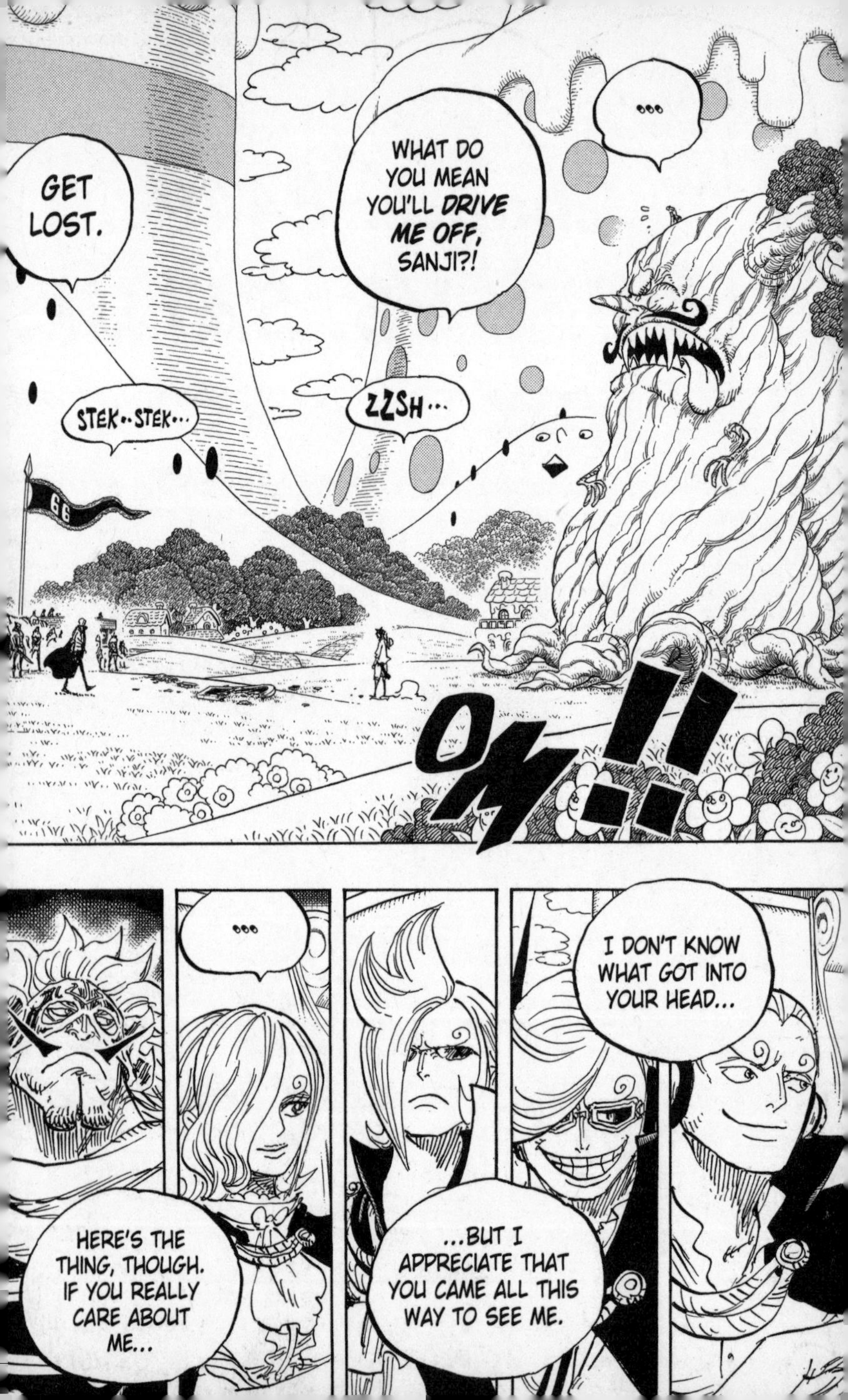
...
WHAT DO YOU MEAN YOU'LL DRIVE ME OFF, SANJI?!
GET LOST.
ZZSH...
STEK..STEK...
OH!!
I DON'T KNOW WHAT GOT INTO YOUR HEAD...
...BUT I APPRECIATE THAT YOU CAME ALL THIS WAY TO SEE ME.
...
HERE'S THE THING, THOUGH. IF YOU REALLY CARE ABOUT ME...

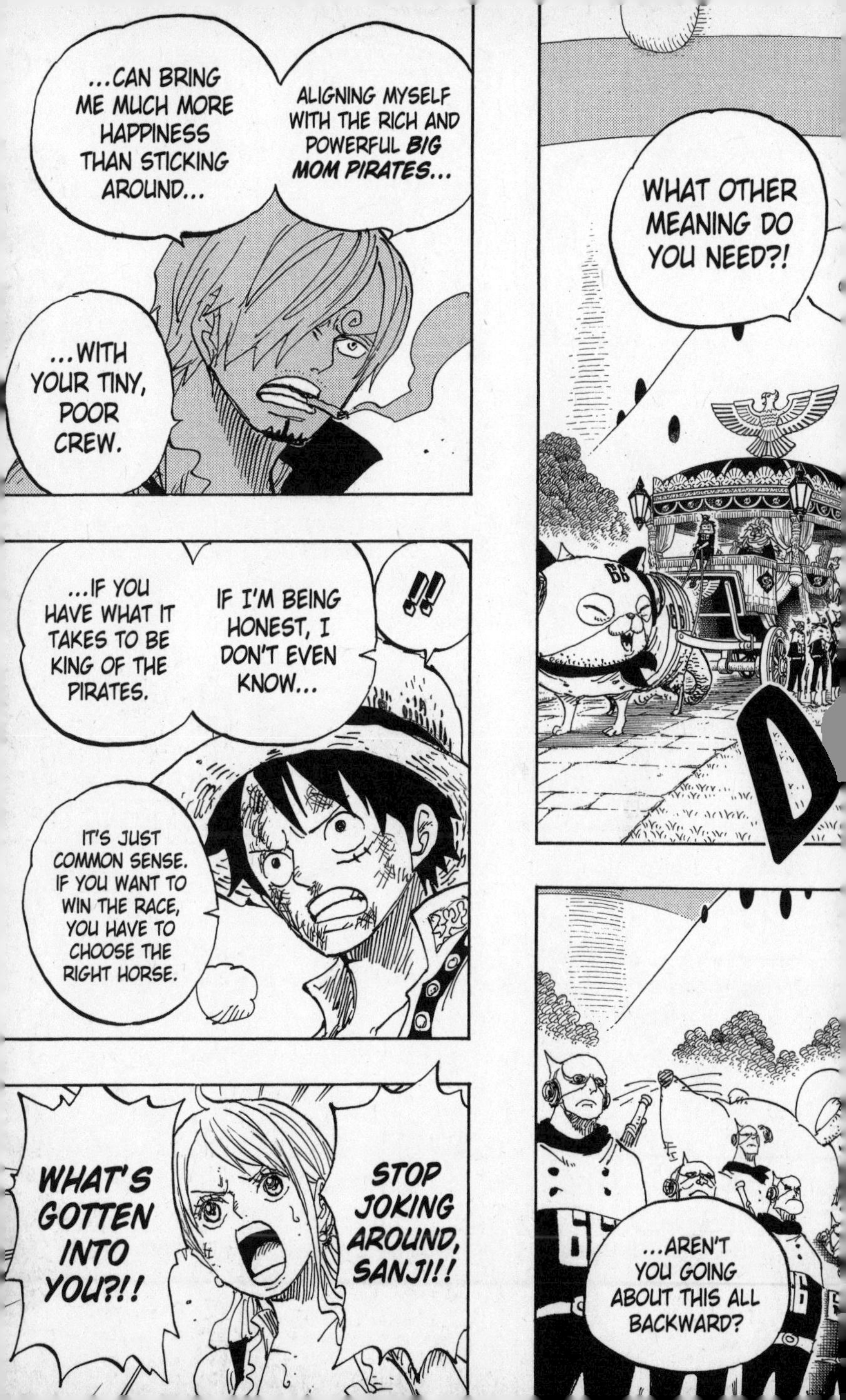
WHAT OTHER MEANING DO YOU NEED?!
...AREN'T YOU GOING ABOUT THIS ALL BACKWARD?
ALIGNING MYSELF WITH THE RICH AND POWERFUL BIG MOM PIRATES...
...CAN BRING ME MUCH MORE HAPPINESS THAN STICKING AROUND...
...WITH YOUR TINY, POOR CREW.
!!
IF I'M BEING HONEST, I DON'T EVEN KNOW...
...IF YOU HAVE WHAT IT TAKES TO BE KING OF THE PIRATES.
IT'S JUST COMMON SENSE. IF YOU WANT TO WIN THE RACE, YOU HAVE TO CHOOSE THE RIGHT HORSE.
STOP JOKING AROUND, SANJI!!
WHAT'S GOTTEN INTO YOU?!!

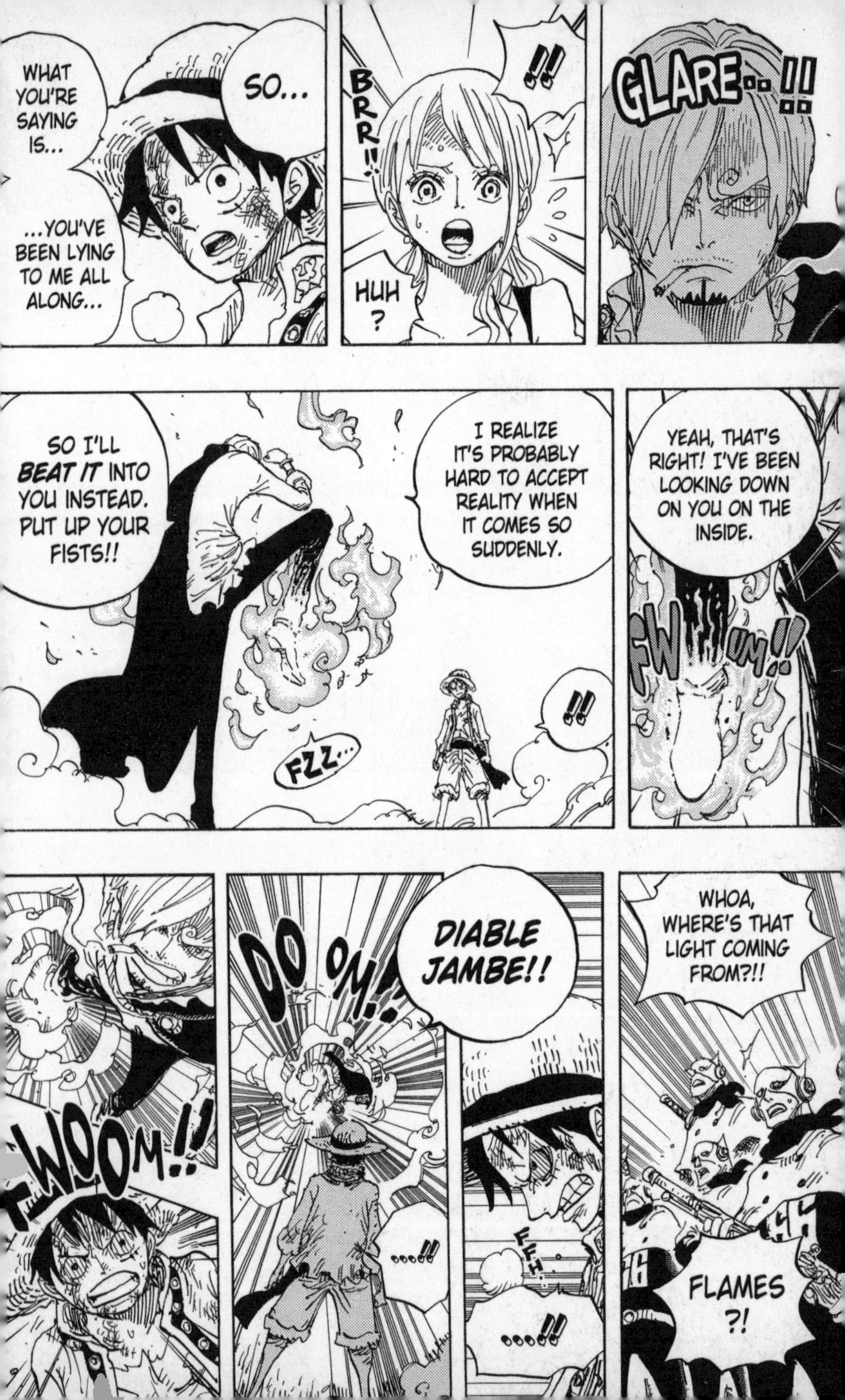
GLARE..!!
BRR!!
!!
HUH?
SO...
WHAT YOU'RE SAYING IS...
...YOU'VE BEEN LYING TO ME ALL ALONG...
YEAH, THAT'S RIGHT! I'VE BEEN LOOKING DOWN ON YOU ON THE INSIDE.
FWUM!!
I REALIZE IT'S PROBABLY HARD TO ACCEPT REALITY WHEN IT COMES SO SUDDENLY.
!!
SO I'LL *BEAT IT* INTO YOU INSTEAD. PUT UP YOUR FISTS!!
FZZ...
WHOA, WHERE'S THAT LIGHT COMING FROM?!!
FLAMES?!
DIABLE JAMBE!!
FFH...
.....!!
DOOM!!
....!!
FWOOM!!

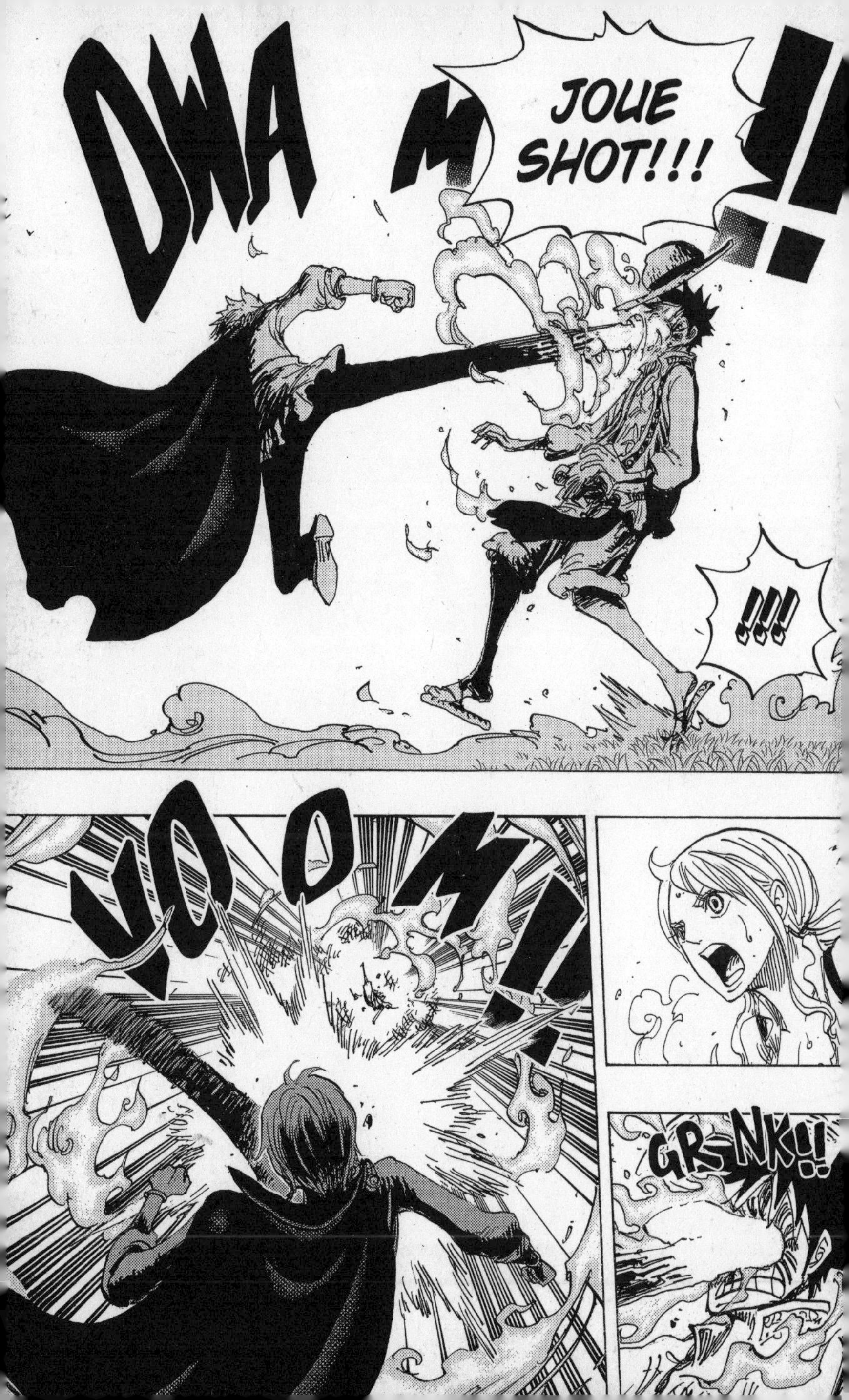
JOUE SHOT!!!
DWAM!!
!!!
GRNK!!
VOOM!!

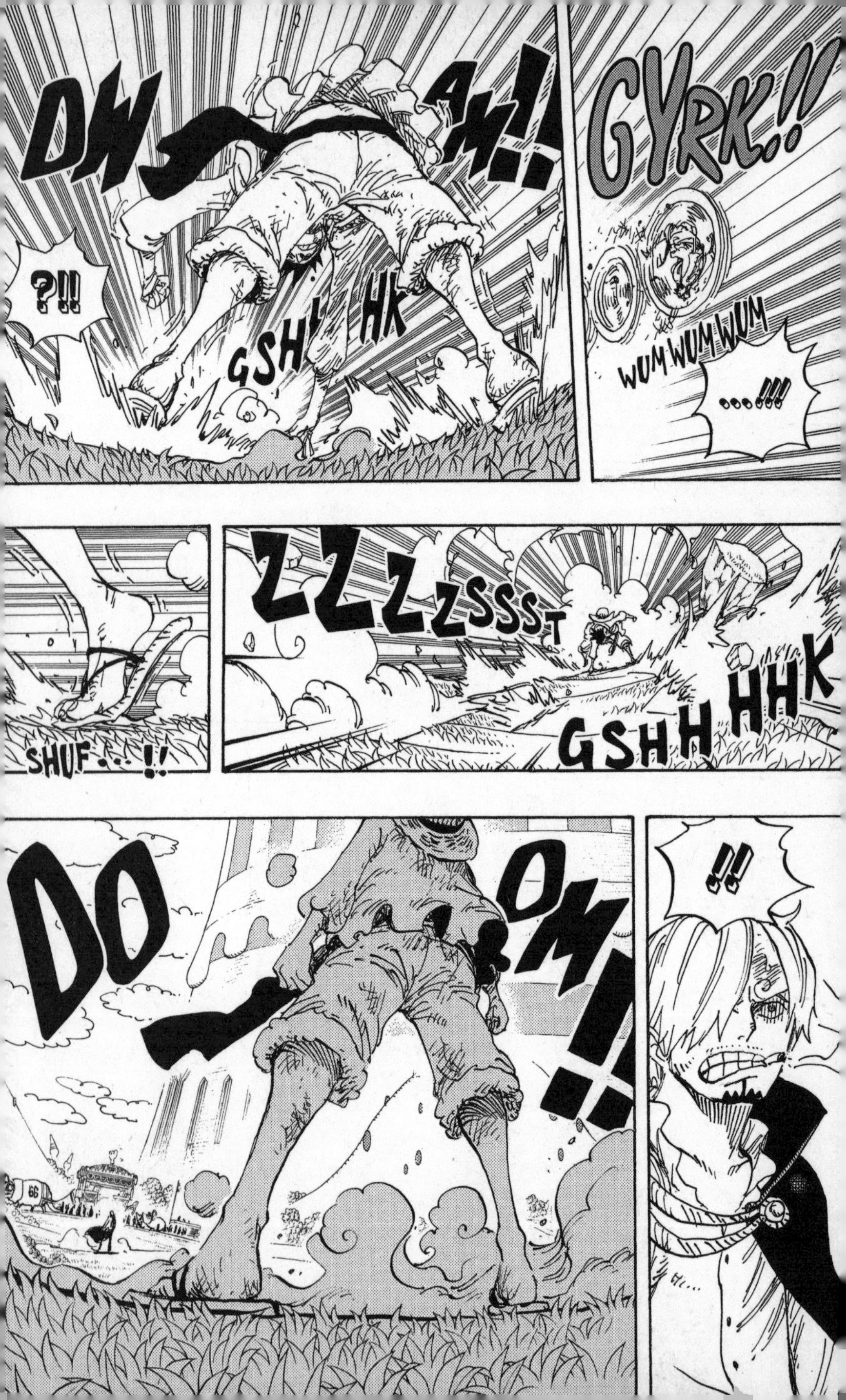
GYRK!!
WUM WUM WUM
...!!!
DW—AM!!
?!!
GSHHK
ZZZZSSST
GSHHHHK
SHUF...!!
!!
DO—OM!!

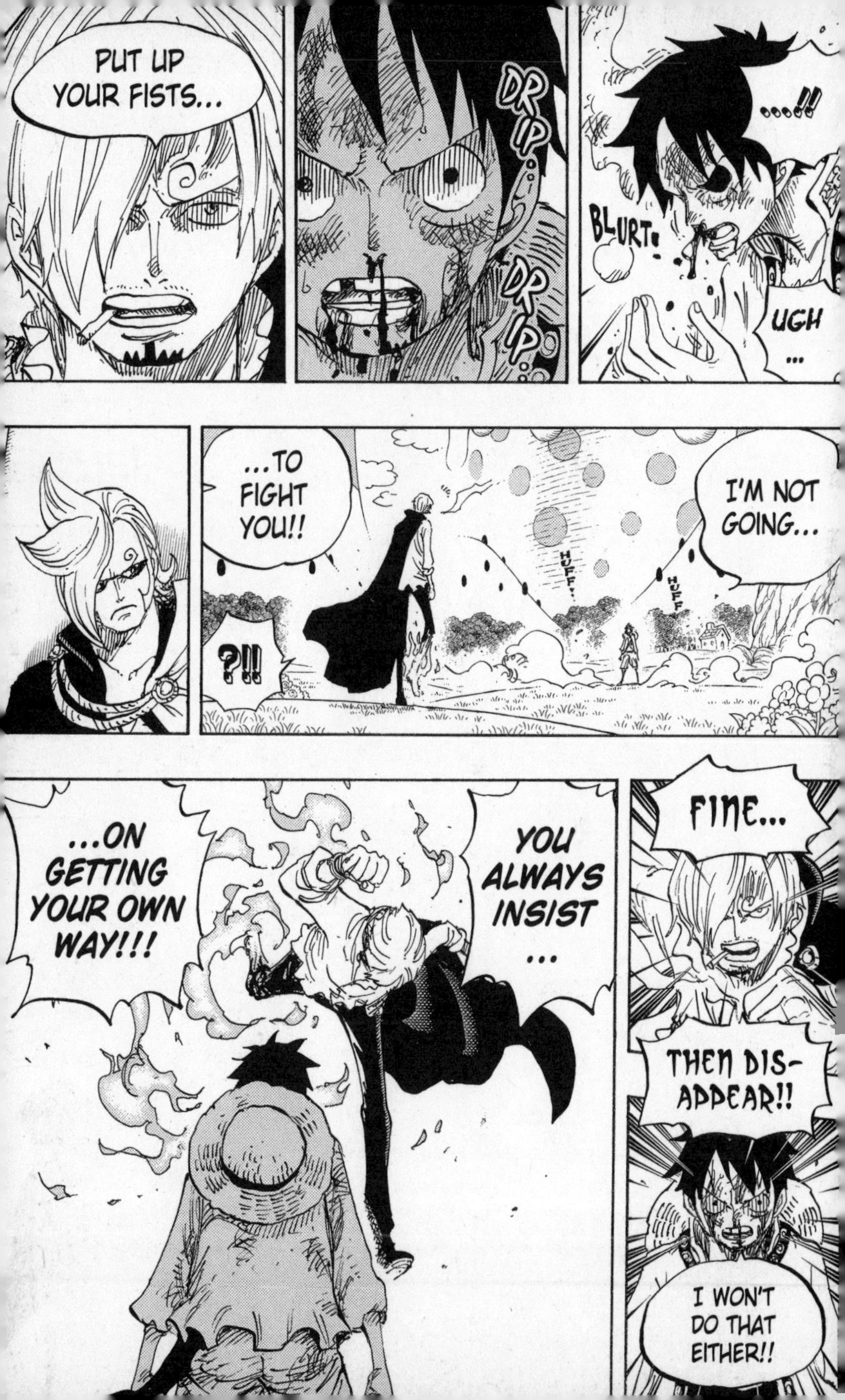
....!!
BLURT
UGH...
DRIP
DRIP
PUT UP YOUR FISTS...
I'M NOT GOING...
HUFF
HUFF
...TO FIGHT YOU!!
?!!
FINE...
THEN DIS-APPEAR!!
I WON'T DO THAT EITHER!!
YOU ALWAYS INSIST...
...ON GETTING YOUR OWN WAY!!!

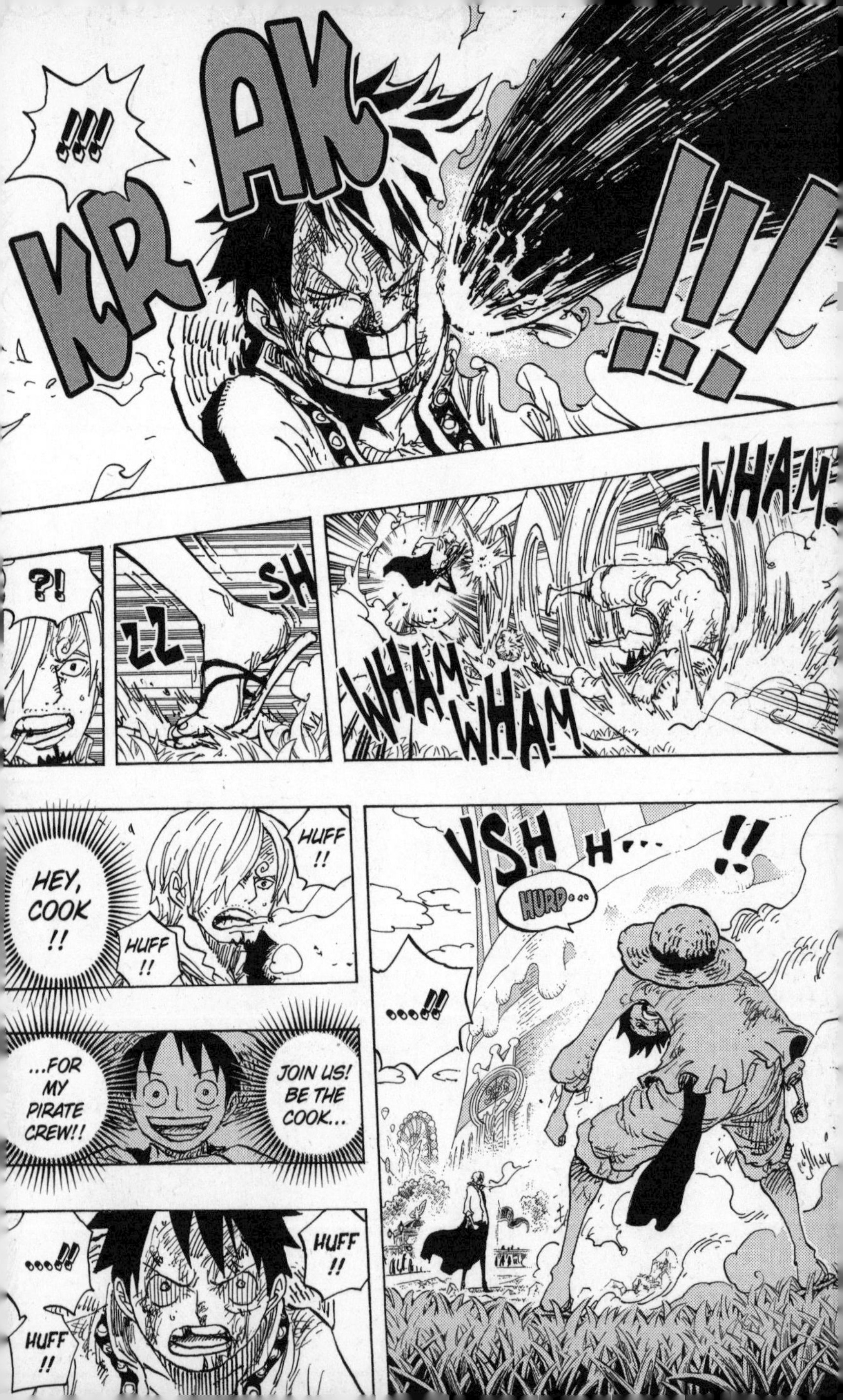
KRAK!!!
!!!
WHAM
WHAM
WHAM
SH
ZZ
?!
VSH H...
!!
HURP...
....!!
HUFF !!
HEY, COOK !!
HUFF !!
JOIN US! BE THE COOK...
...FOR MY PIRATE CREW!!
HUFF !!
....!!
HUFF !!

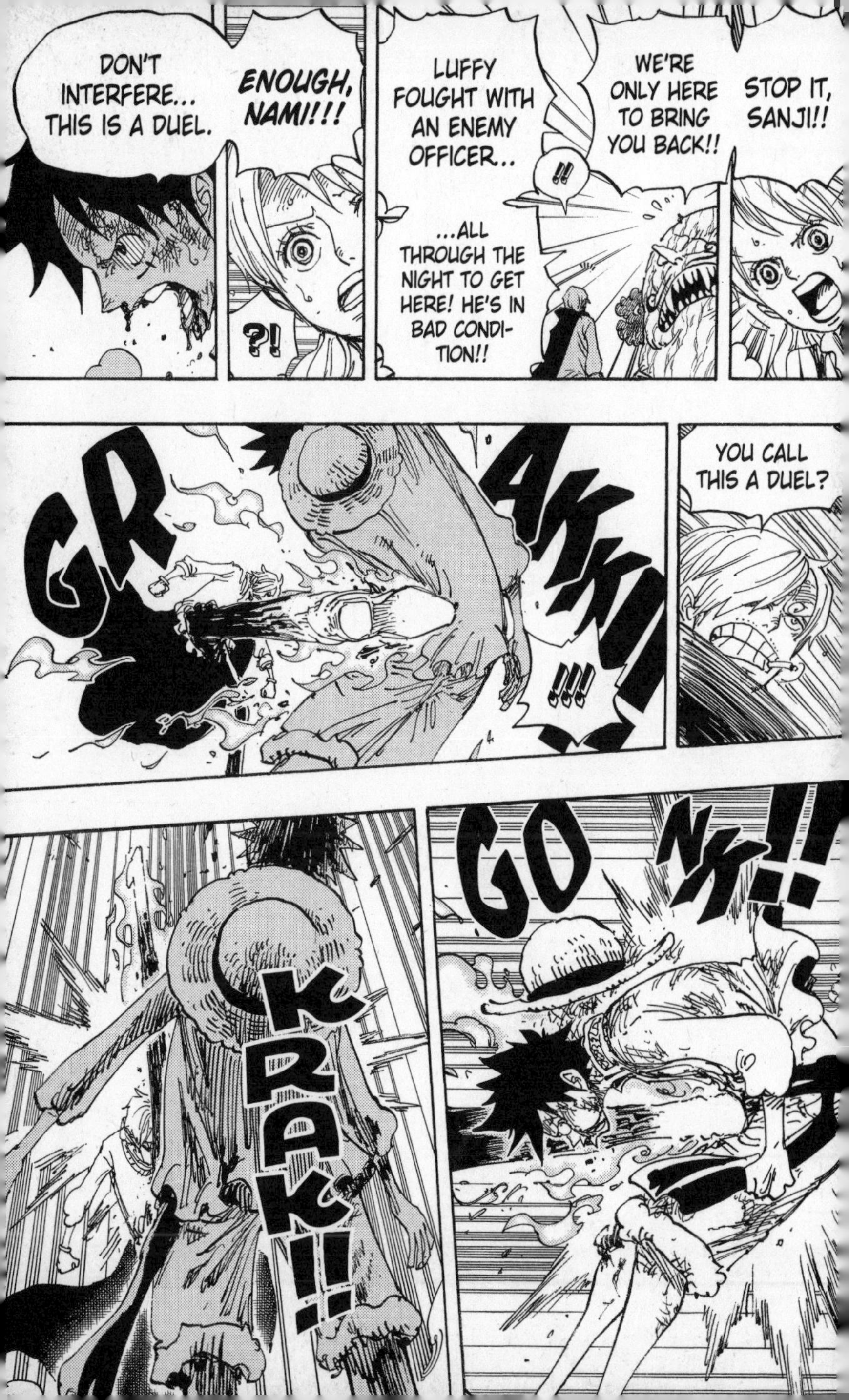
STOP IT, SANJI!!
WE'RE ONLY HERE TO BRING YOU BACK!!
!!
LUFFY FOUGHT WITH AN ENEMY OFFICER...
...ALL THROUGH THE NIGHT TO GET HERE! HE'S IN BAD CONDITION!!
ENOUGH, NAMI!!!
?!
DON'T INTERFERE... THIS IS A DUEL.
YOU CALL THIS A DUEL?
GRAKK!!!
GONK!!
KRAK!!

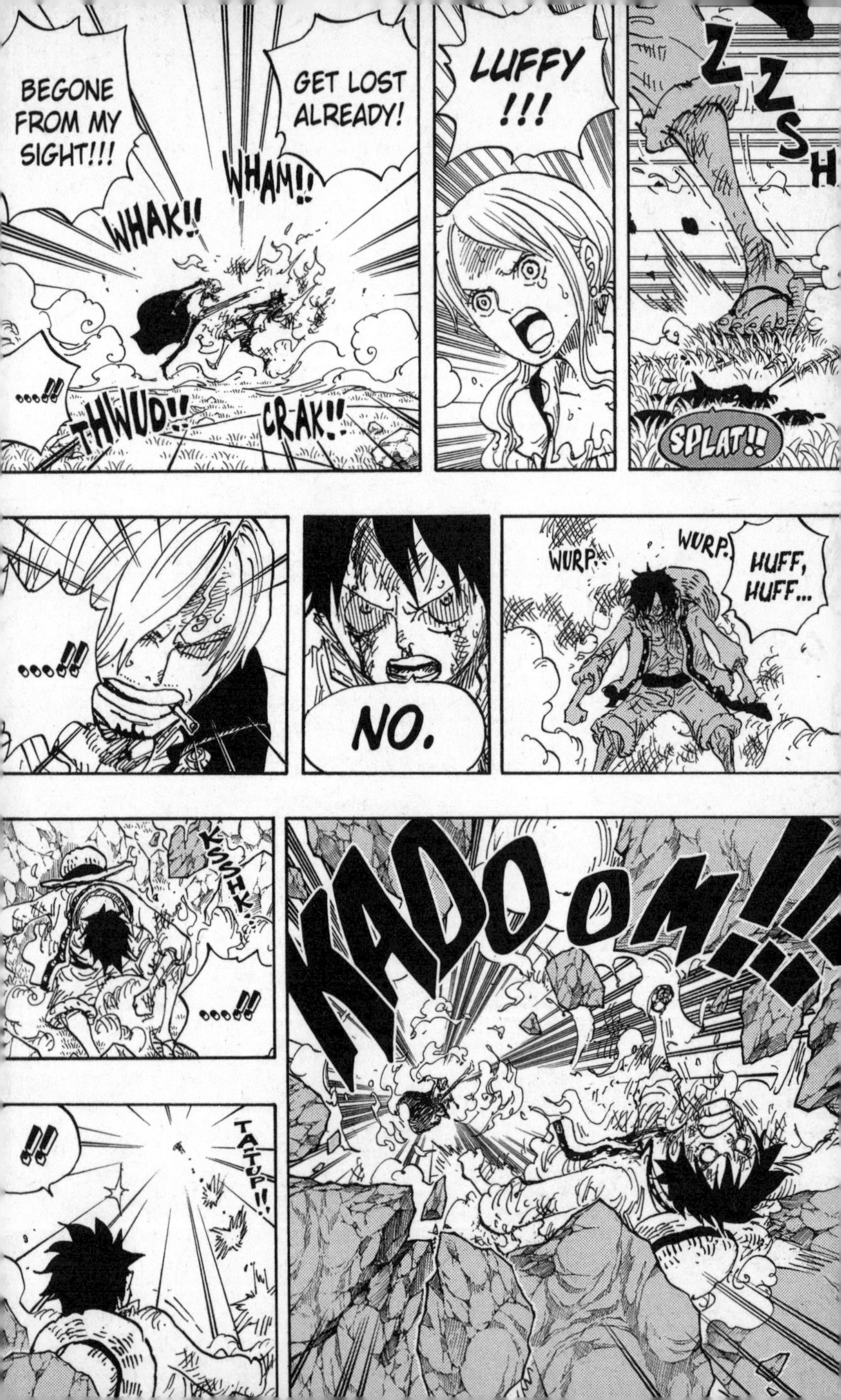
ZZSH
SPLAT!!
LUFFY!!!
GET LOST ALREADY!
BEGONE FROM MY SIGHT!!!
WHAM!!
WHAK!!
CRAK!!
...!!
THWUD!!
WURP.
HUFF, HUFF...
WURP.
NO.
...!!
KADOOM!!!
KSSHK...
...!!
!!
TATUP!!

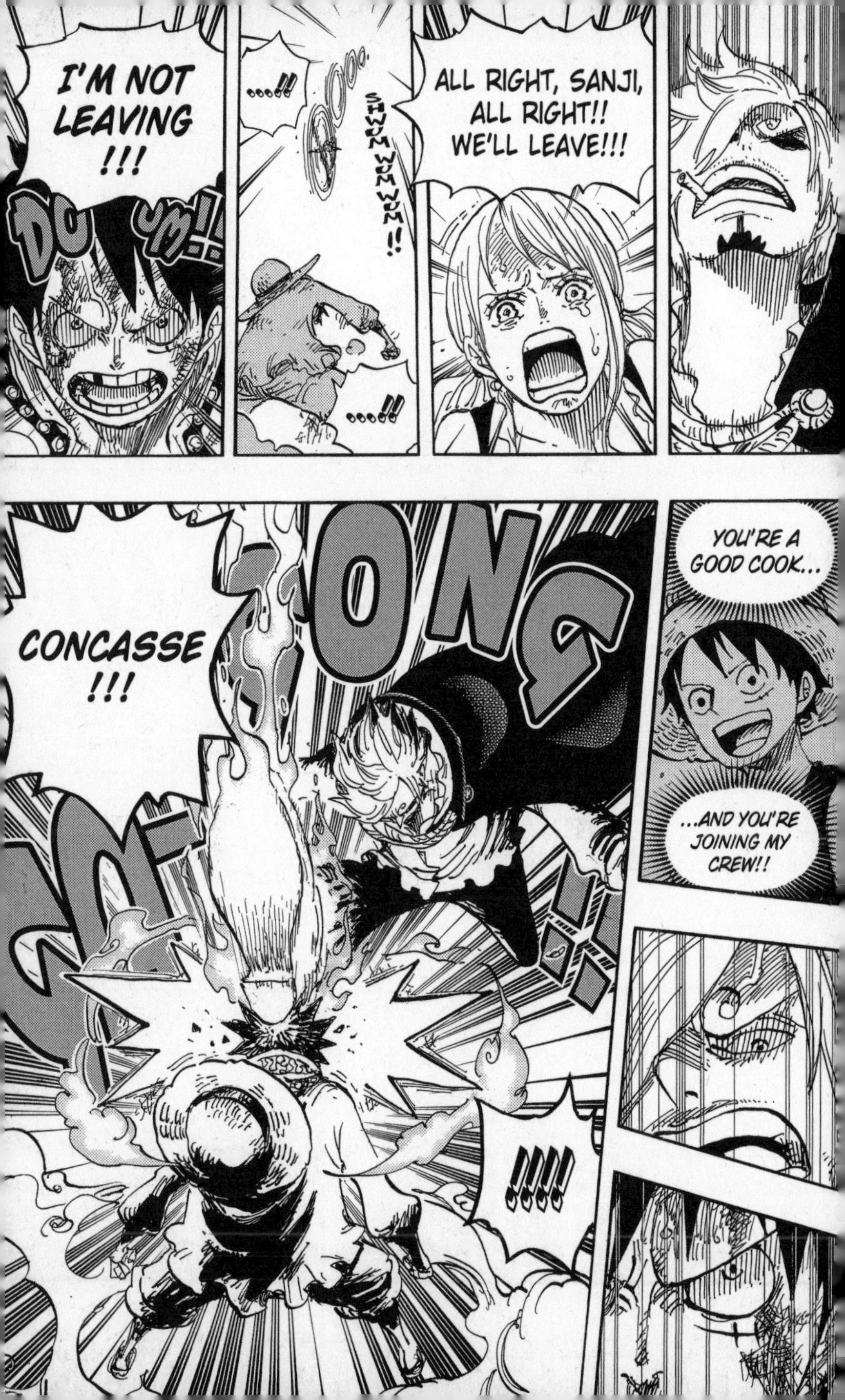
ALL RIGHT, SANJI, ALL RIGHT!! WE'LL LEAVE!!!
...!!
SHWUM WUM WUM!!
...!!
I'M NOT LEAVING !!!
DO UM!!
YOU'RE A GOOD COOK...
...AND YOU'RE JOINING MY CREW!!
CONCASSE !!!
ONG
!!!!

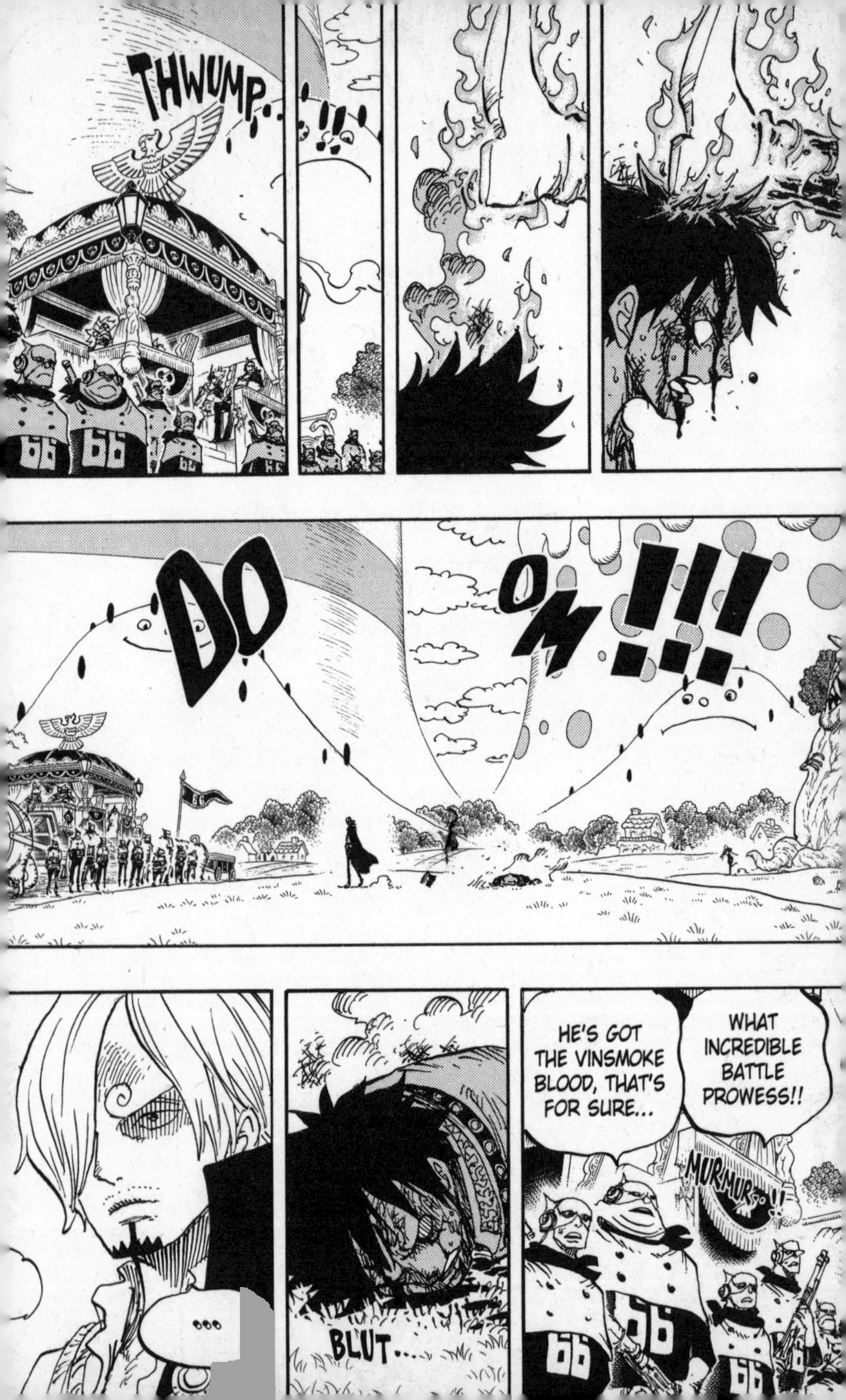
THWUMP...!!
DOOM!!!
WHAT INCREDIBLE BATTLE PROWESS!!
HE'S GOT THE VINSMOKE BLOOD, THAT'S FOR SURE...
MURMUR...!!
BLUT...
...

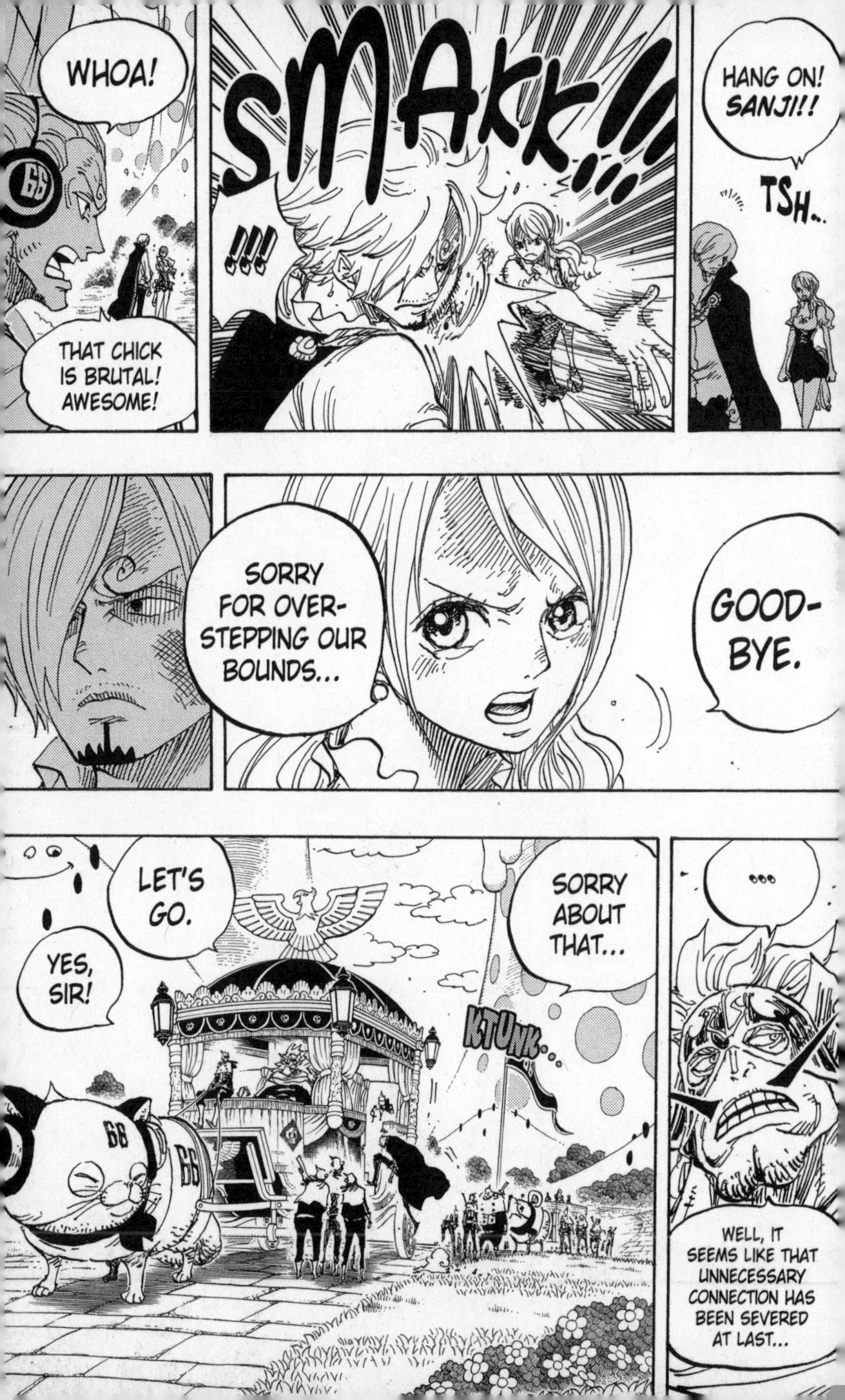
HANG ON! SANJI!!
TSH..
SMAKK!!!
!!!
WHOA!
THAT CHICK IS BRUTAL! AWESOME!
SORRY FOR OVER-STEPPING OUR BOUNDS...
GOOD-BYE.
...
WELL, IT SEEMS LIKE THAT UNNECESSARY CONNECTION HAS BEEN SEVERED AT LAST...
SORRY ABOUT THAT...
KTUNK...
LET'S GO.
YES, SIR!

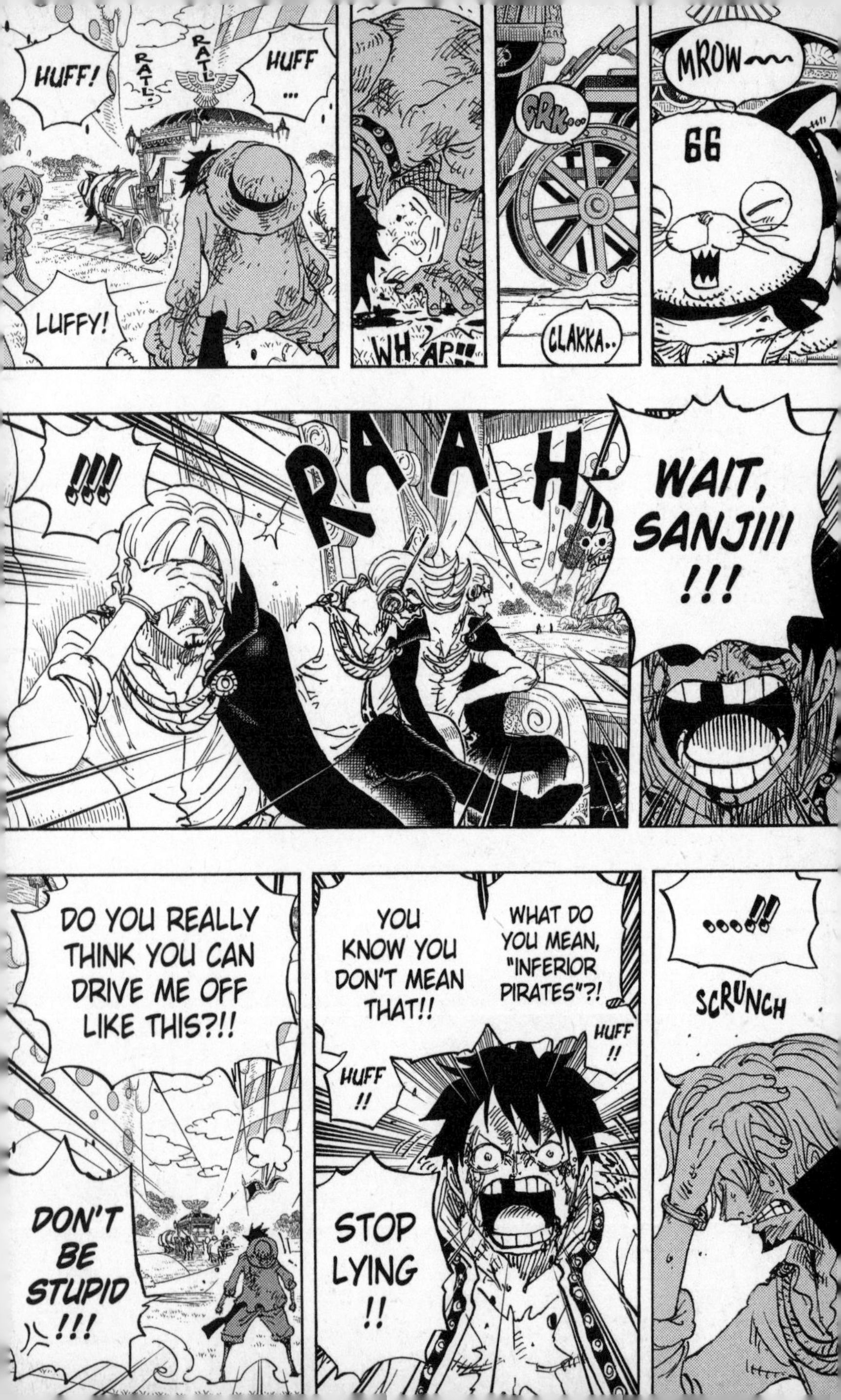
MROW~~
66
GRK...
CLAKKA..
WHAP!!
HUFF ...
RATL
RATL
HUFF!
LUFFY!
WAIT, SANJIII !!!
RAAH
!!!
...!!
SCRUNCH
WHAT DO YOU MEAN, "INFERIOR PIRATES"?!
YOU KNOW YOU DON'T MEAN THAT!!
HUFF !!
HUFF !!
STOP LYING !!
DO YOU REALLY THINK YOU CAN DRIVE ME OFF LIKE THIS?!!
DON'T BE STUPID !!!

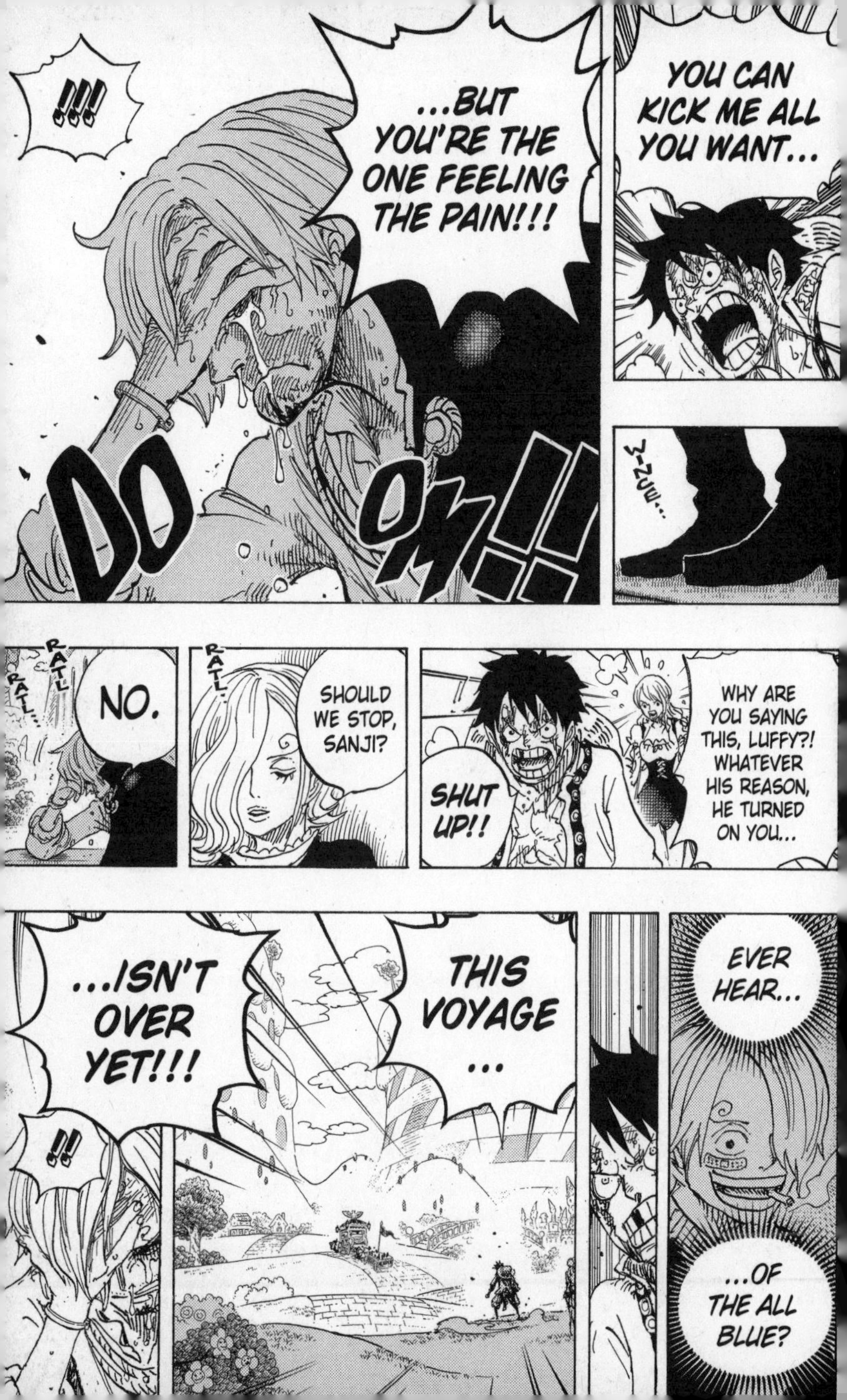
YOU CAN KICK ME ALL YOU WANT...
W-ZUU...
...BUT YOU'RE THE ONE FEELING THE PAIN!!!
!!!
DOOM!!
WHY ARE YOU SAYING THIS, LUFFY?! WHATEVER HIS REASON, HE TURNED ON YOU...
SHUT UP!!
RATL
SHOULD WE STOP, SANJI?
RATL
RATL...
NO.
EVER HEAR...
...OF THE ALL BLUE?
THIS VOYAGE ...
...ISN'T OVER YET!!!
!!

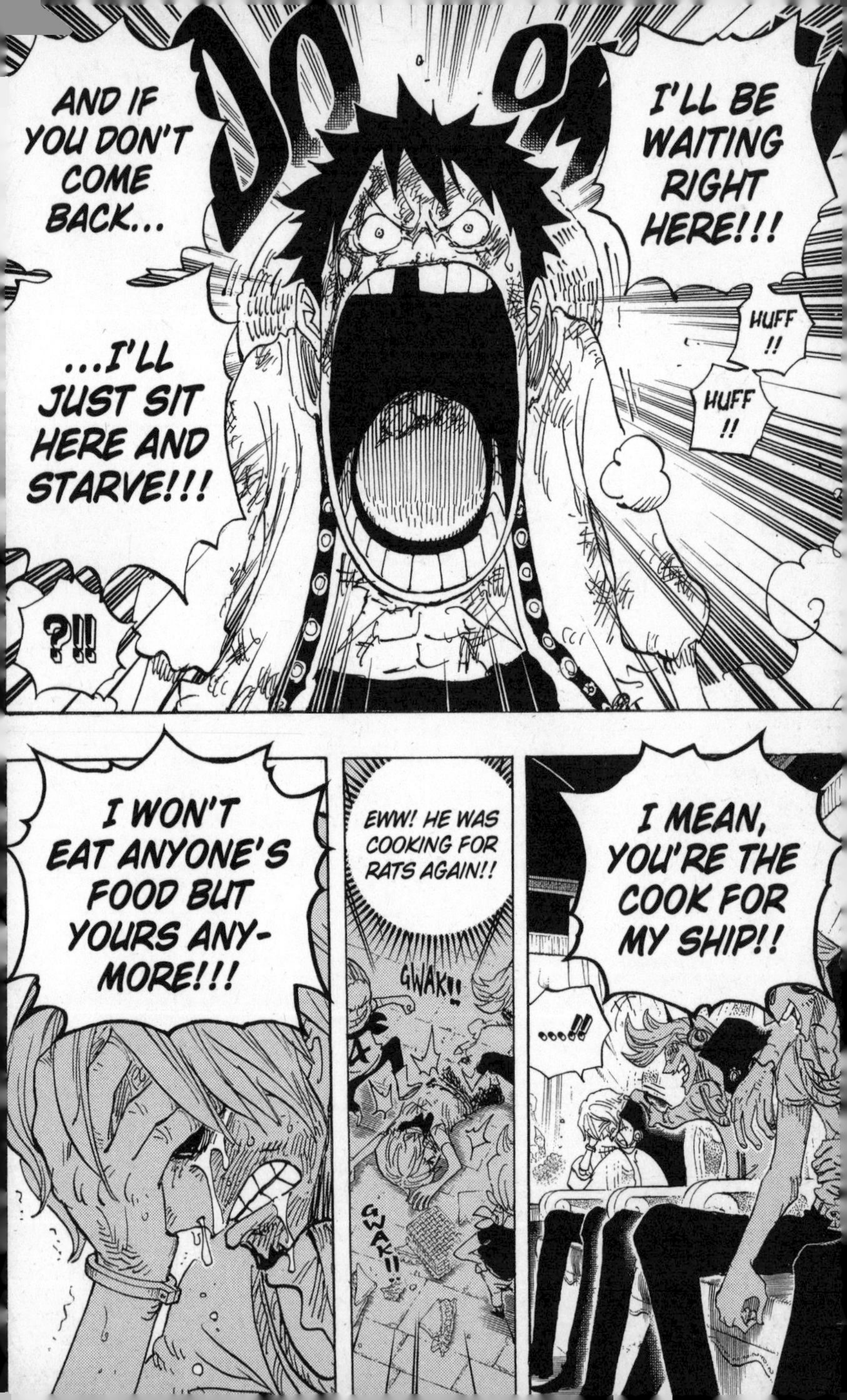
I'LL BE WAITING RIGHT HERE!!!
AND IF YOU DON'T COME BACK...
HUFF !!
HUFF !!
...I'LL JUST SIT HERE AND STARVE!!!
?!!
I MEAN, YOU'RE THE COOK FOR MY SHIP!!
...!!
EWW! HE WAS COOKING FOR RATS AGAIN!!
GWAK!!
GWAK!!
I WON'T EAT ANYONE'S FOOD BUT YOURS ANY-MORE!!!

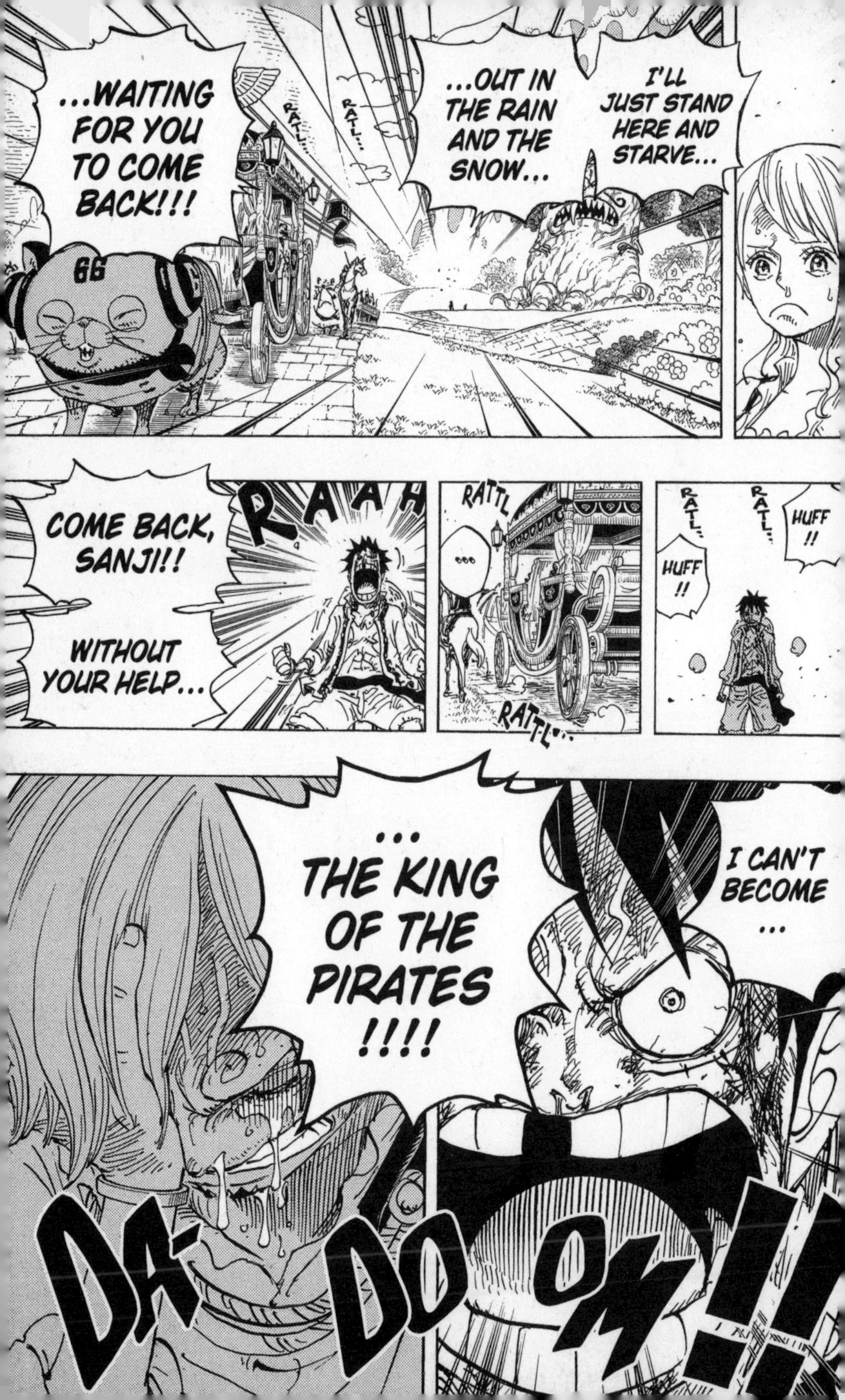
I'LL JUST STAND HERE AND STARVE...
...OUT IN THE RAIN AND THE SNOW...
RATL...
RATL...
...WAITING FOR YOU TO COME BACK!!!
RATL...
RATL...
HUFF !!
HUFF !!
RATTL
...
RATT-L...
RAAAH
COME BACK, SANJI!!
WITHOUT YOUR HELP...
I CAN'T BECOME ...
... THE KING OF THE PIRATES !!!!
DA-DOOM!!

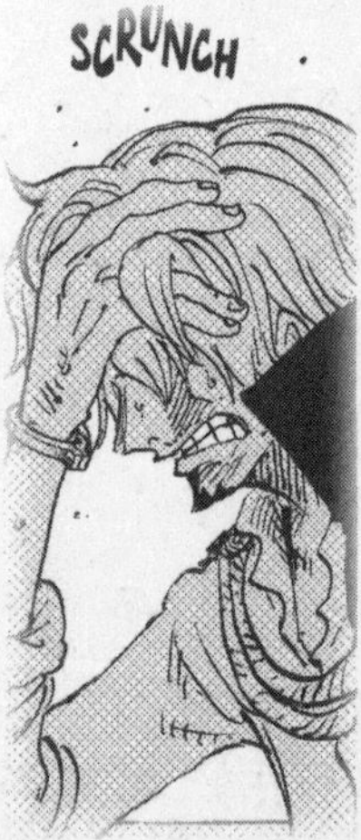
SCRUNCH

Chapter 845:
FORCES OF RAGE

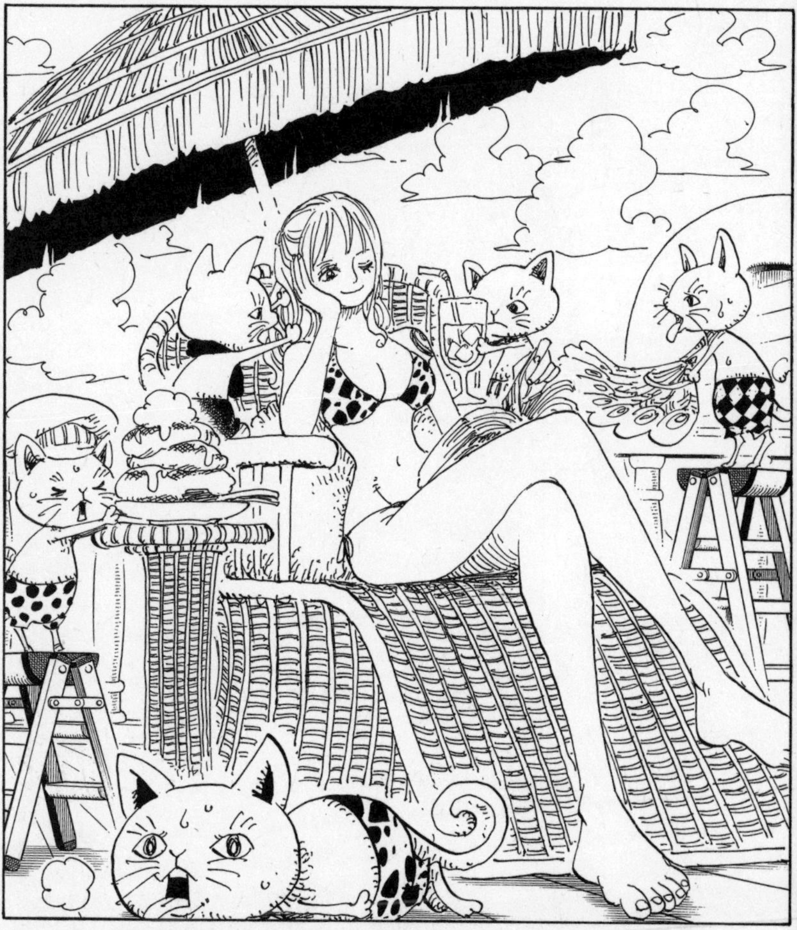

REQUEST(?): "NAMI BEING WAITED UPON BY QUINTUPLET KITTENS" BY AKUA NOICHIGO FROM OSAKA

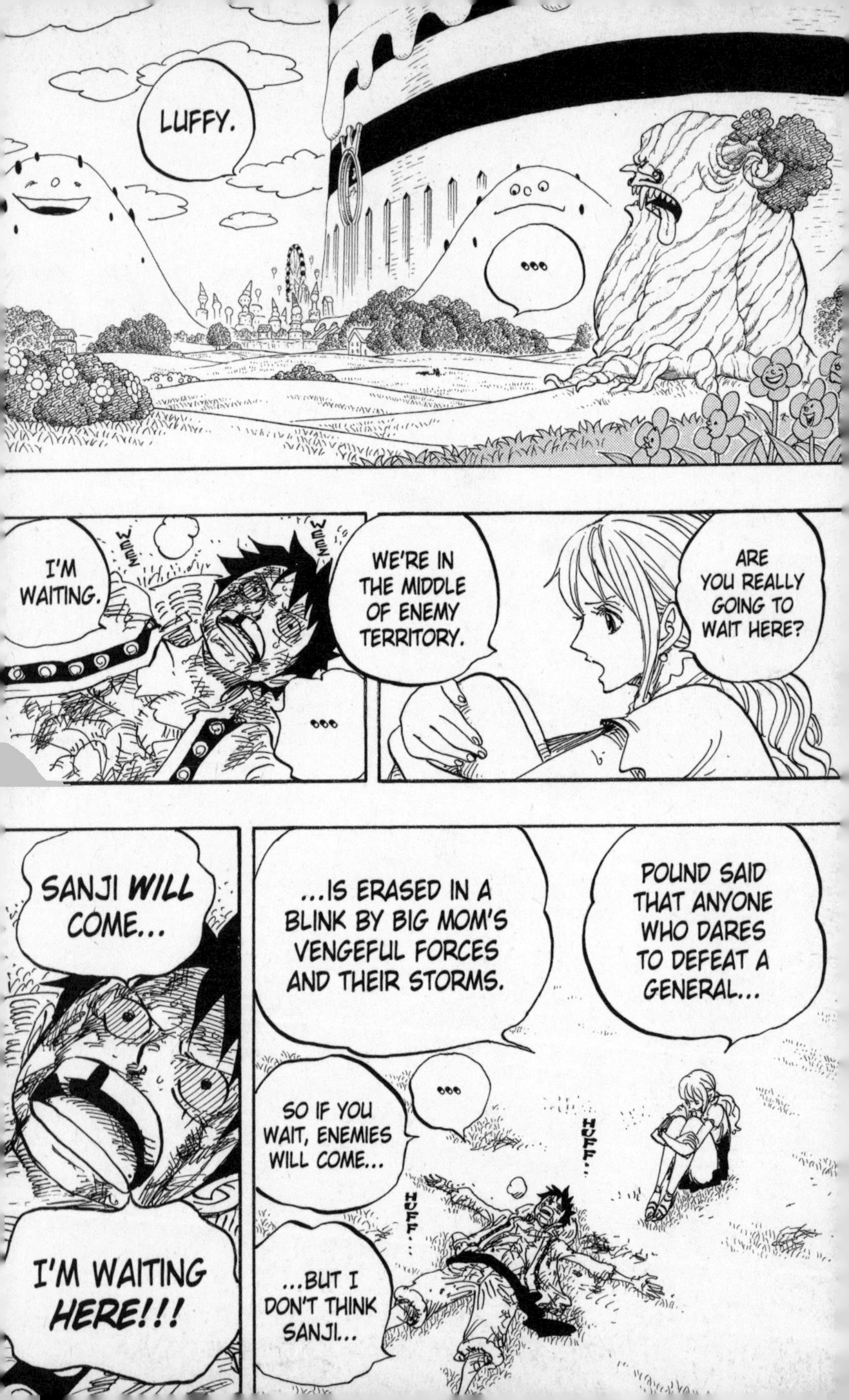
LUFFY.
...
ARE YOU REALLY GOING TO WAIT HERE?
WE'RE IN THE MIDDLE OF ENEMY TERRITORY.
WEEZ
WEEZ
I'M WAITING.
...
POUND SAID THAT ANYONE WHO DARES TO DEFEAT A GENERAL...
...IS ERASED IN A BLINK BY BIG MOM'S VENGEFUL FORCES AND THEIR STORMS.
...
SO IF YOU WAIT, ENEMIES WILL COME...
HUFF...
HUFF...
...BUT I DON'T THINK SANJI...
SANJI WILL COME...
I'M WAITING HERE!!!

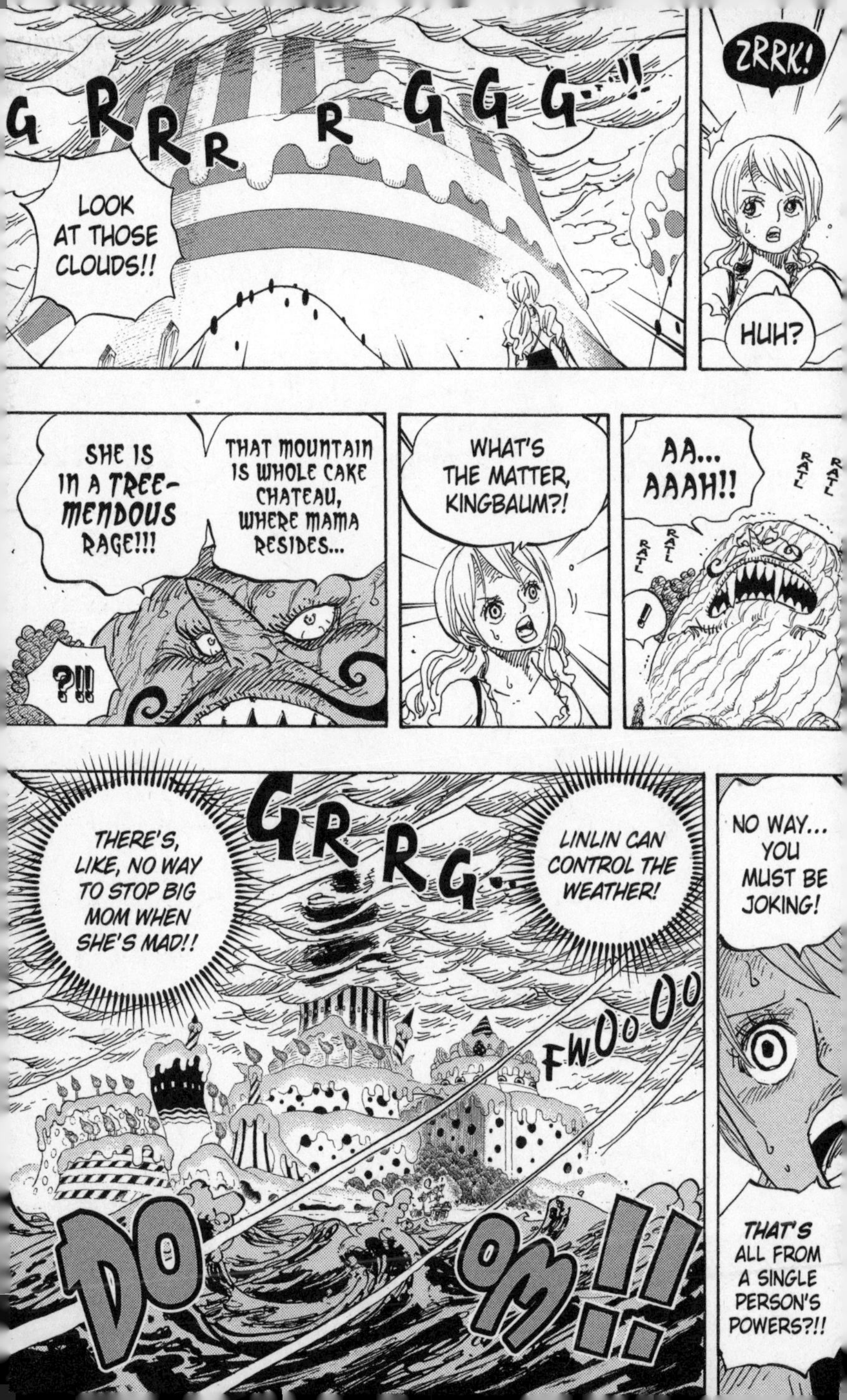
ZRRK!
HUH?
GRRRRGGG!!
LOOK AT THOSE CLOUDS!!
AA... AAAH!!
RATL RATL
RATL RATL
!
WHAT'S THE MATTER, KINGBAUM?!
THAT MOUNTAIN IS WHOLE CAKE CHATEAU, WHERE MAMA RESIDES...
SHE IS IN A *TREE-MENDOUS* RAGE!!!
?!!
NO WAY... YOU MUST BE JOKING!
THAT'S ALL FROM A SINGLE PERSON'S POWERS?!!
GRRRG...
LINLIN CAN CONTROL THE WEATHER!
THERE'S, LIKE, NO WAY TO STOP BIG MOM WHEN SHE'S MAD!!
FWOOOOO
DOOM!!

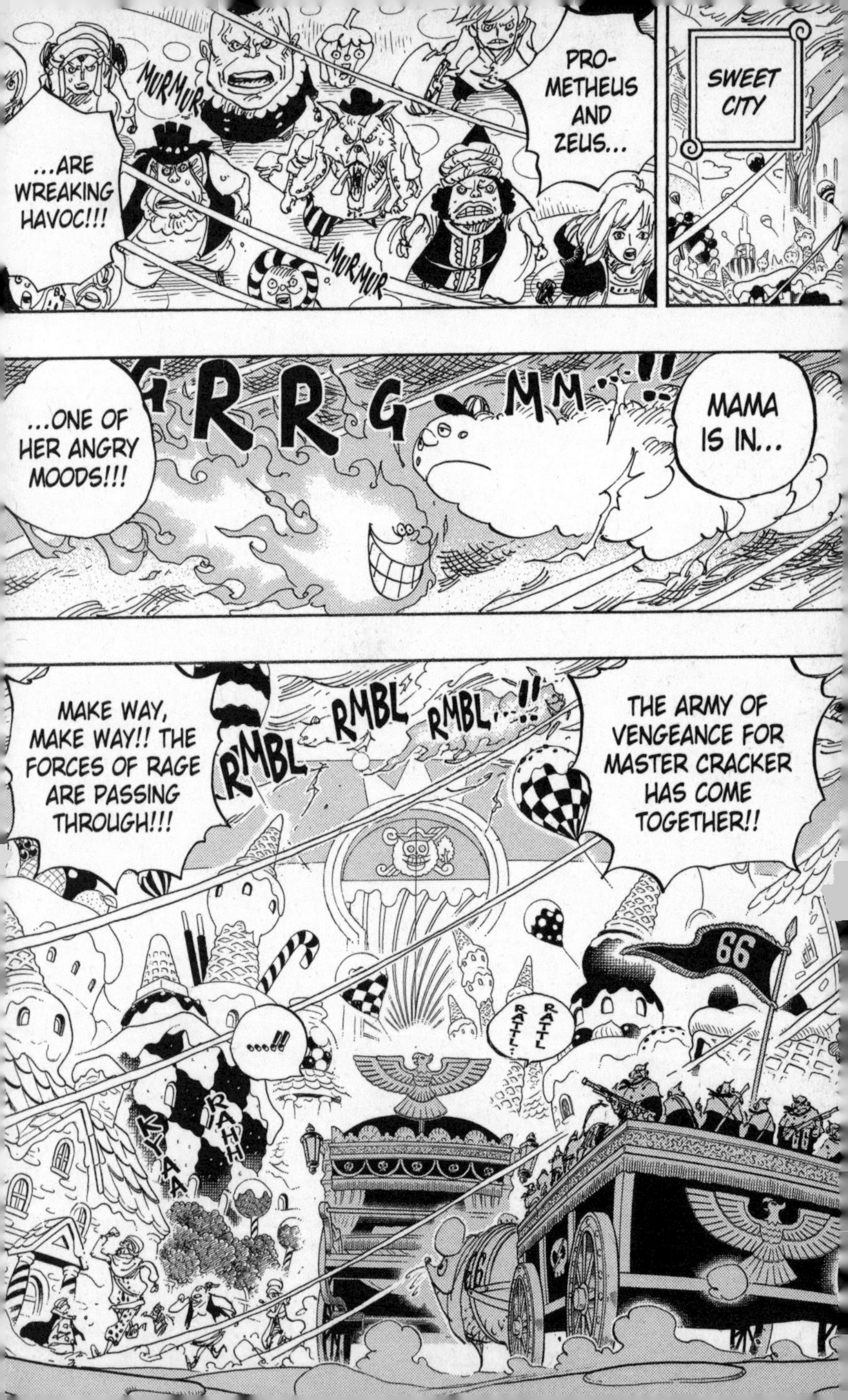
SWEET CITY
PRO-METHEUS AND ZEUS...
MURMUR
...ARE WREAKING HAVOC!!!
MURMUR
MAMA IS IN...
RRGMM...!!
...ONE OF HER ANGRY MOODS!!!
THE ARMY OF VENGEANCE FOR MASTER CRACKER HAS COME TOGETHER!!
RMBL RMBL RMBL...!!
MAKE WAY, MAKE WAY!! THE FORCES OF RAGE ARE PASSING THROUGH!!!
66
RATTL RATTL
....!!
RAHH
KYAA

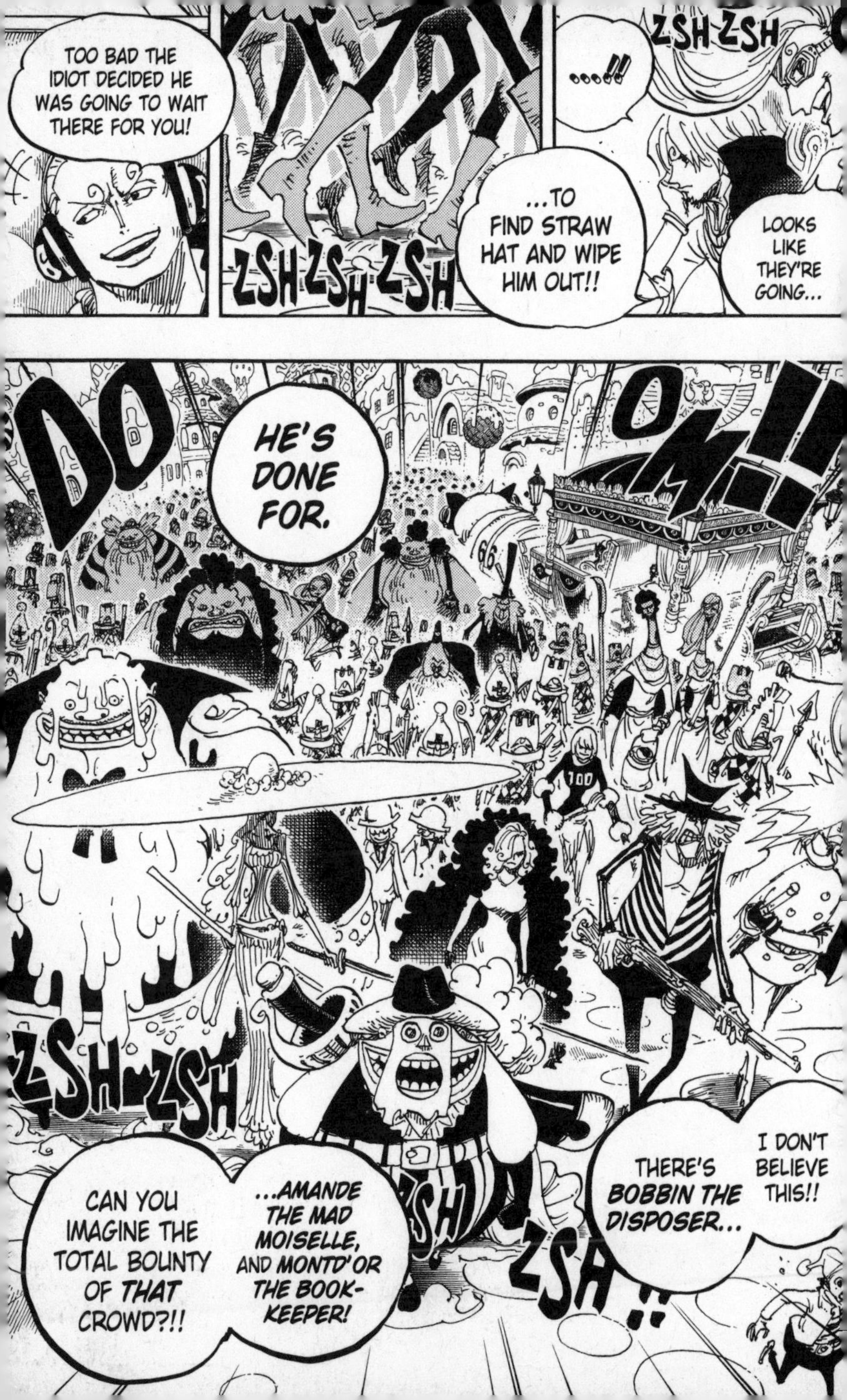
ZSH ZSH
...!!
LOOKS LIKE THEY'RE GOING...
...TO FIND STRAW HAT AND WIPE HIM OUT!!
ZSH ZSH ZSH
TOO BAD THE IDIOT DECIDED HE WAS GOING TO WAIT THERE FOR YOU!
OM!!
DO
HE'S DONE FOR.
I DON'T BELIEVE THIS!!
THERE'S BOBBIN THE DISPOSER...
...AMANDE THE MAD MOISELLE, AND MONTD'OR THE BOOK-KEEPER!
ZSH ZSH!!
CAN YOU IMAGINE THE TOTAL BOUNTY OF THAT CROWD?!!
ZSH ZSH

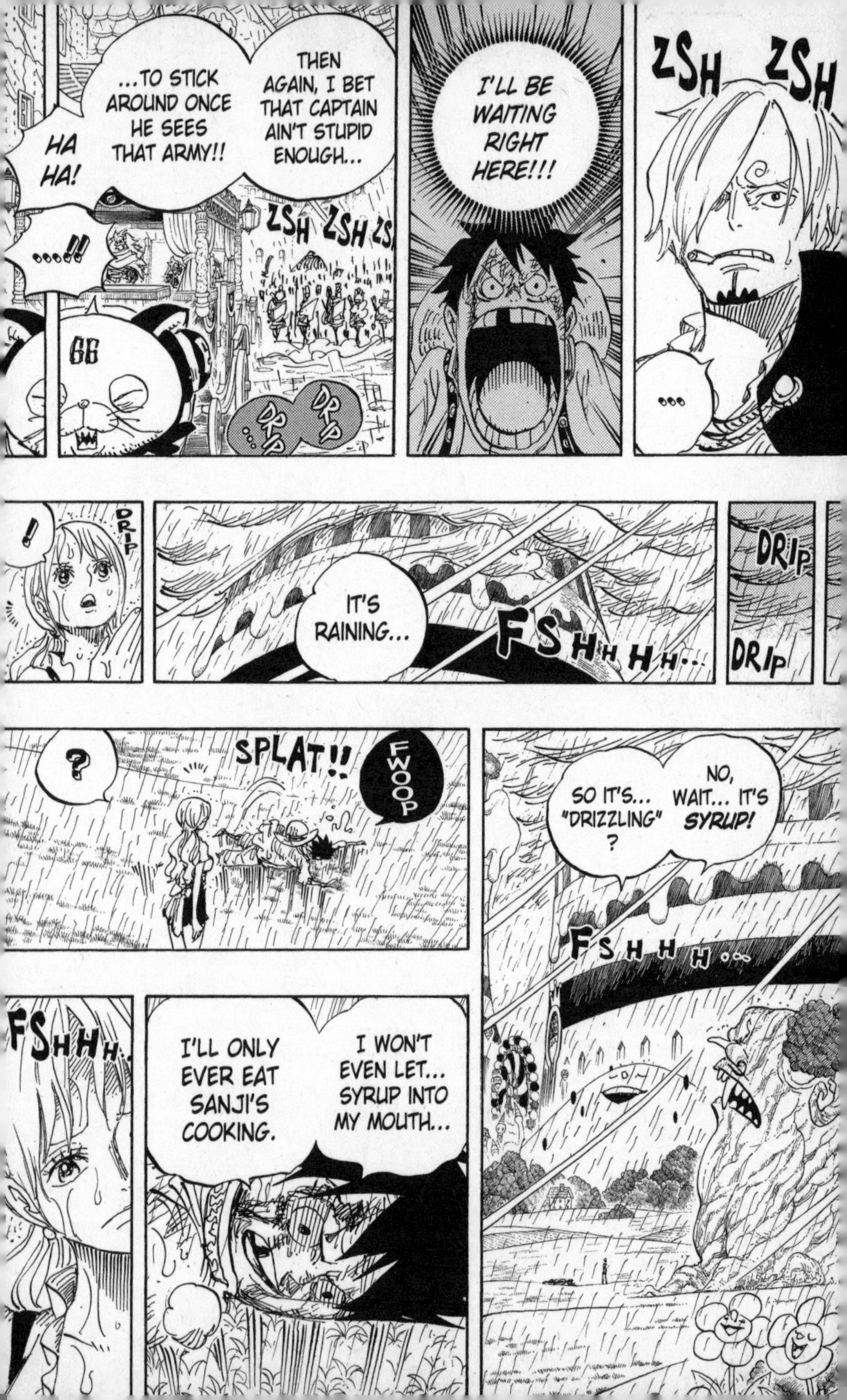
ZSH ZSH
...
I'LL BE WAITING RIGHT HERE!!!
THEN AGAIN, I BET THAT CAPTAIN AIN'T STUPID ENOUGH...
...TO STICK AROUND ONCE HE SEES THAT ARMY!!
HA HA!
ZSH ZSH ZSH
....!!
DRIP DRIP...
DRIP
DRIP
IT'S RAINING...
FSHHHH...
DRIP
!
NO, WAIT... IT'S SYRUP!
SO IT'S... "DRIZZLING" ?
FSHHHH...
FWOOP
SPLAT!!
?
I WON'T EVEN LET... SYRUP INTO MY MOUTH...
I'LL ONLY EVER EAT SANJI'S COOKING.
FSHHHH..

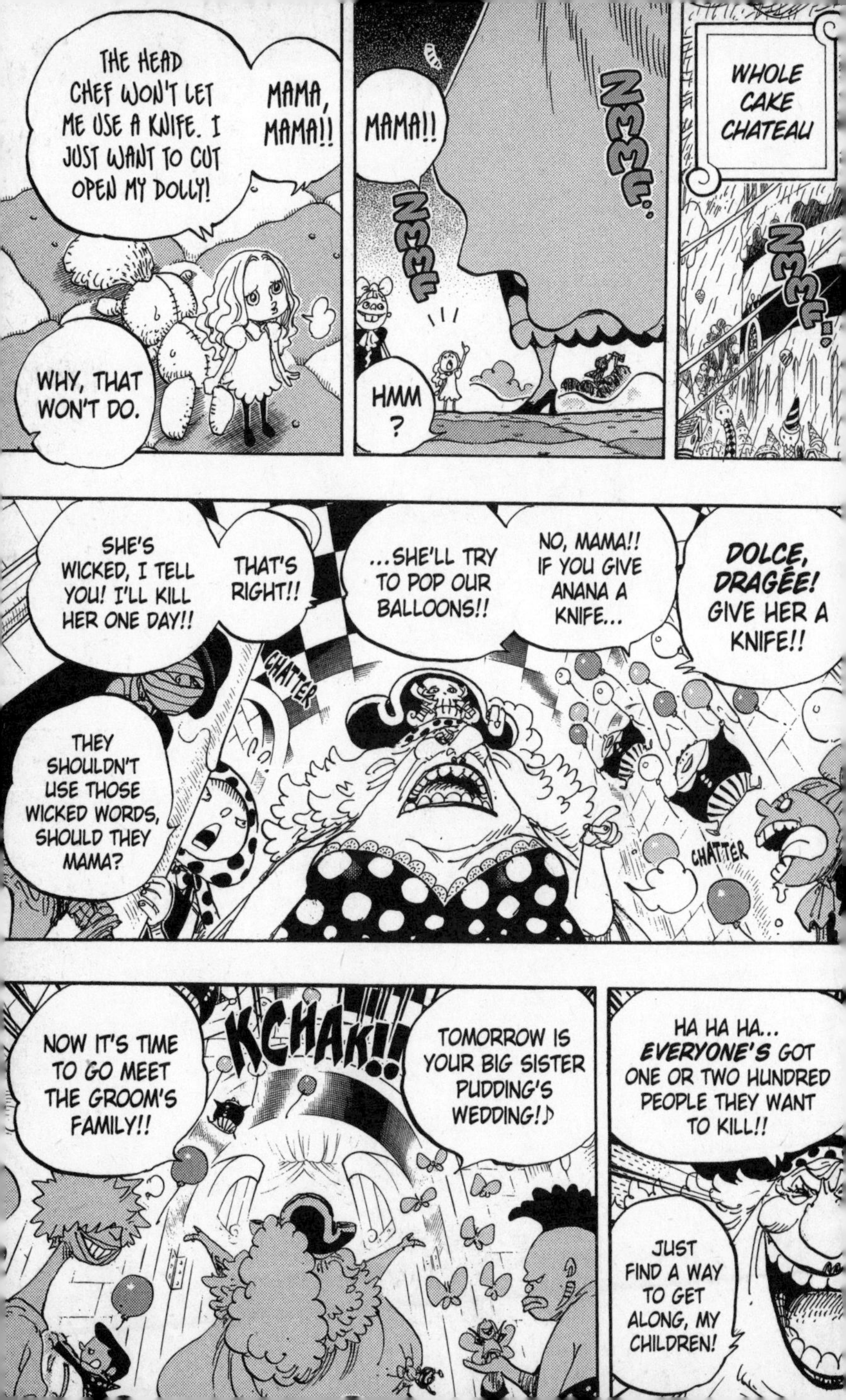
WHOLE CAKE CHATEAU
ZMMF!
ZMMF..
MAMA!!
ZMMF
HMM ?
MAMA, MAMA!!
THE HEAD CHEF WON'T LET ME USE A KNIFE. I JUST WANT TO CUT OPEN MY DOLLY!
WHY, THAT WON'T DO.
DOLCE, DRAGÉE! GIVE HER A KNIFE!!
NO, MAMA!! IF YOU GIVE ANANA A KNIFE...
...SHE'LL TRY TO POP OUR BALLOONS!!
THAT'S RIGHT!!
SHE'S WICKED, I TELL YOU! I'LL KILL HER ONE DAY!!
CHATTER
THEY SHOULDN'T USE THOSE WICKED WORDS, SHOULD THEY MAMA?
CHATTER
HA HA HA... EVERYONE'S GOT ONE OR TWO HUNDRED PEOPLE THEY WANT TO KILL!!
JUST FIND A WAY TO GET ALONG, MY CHILDREN!
TOMORROW IS YOUR BIG SISTER PUDDING'S WEDDING!♪
KCHAK!!
NOW IT'S TIME TO GO MEET THE GROOM'S FAMILY!!

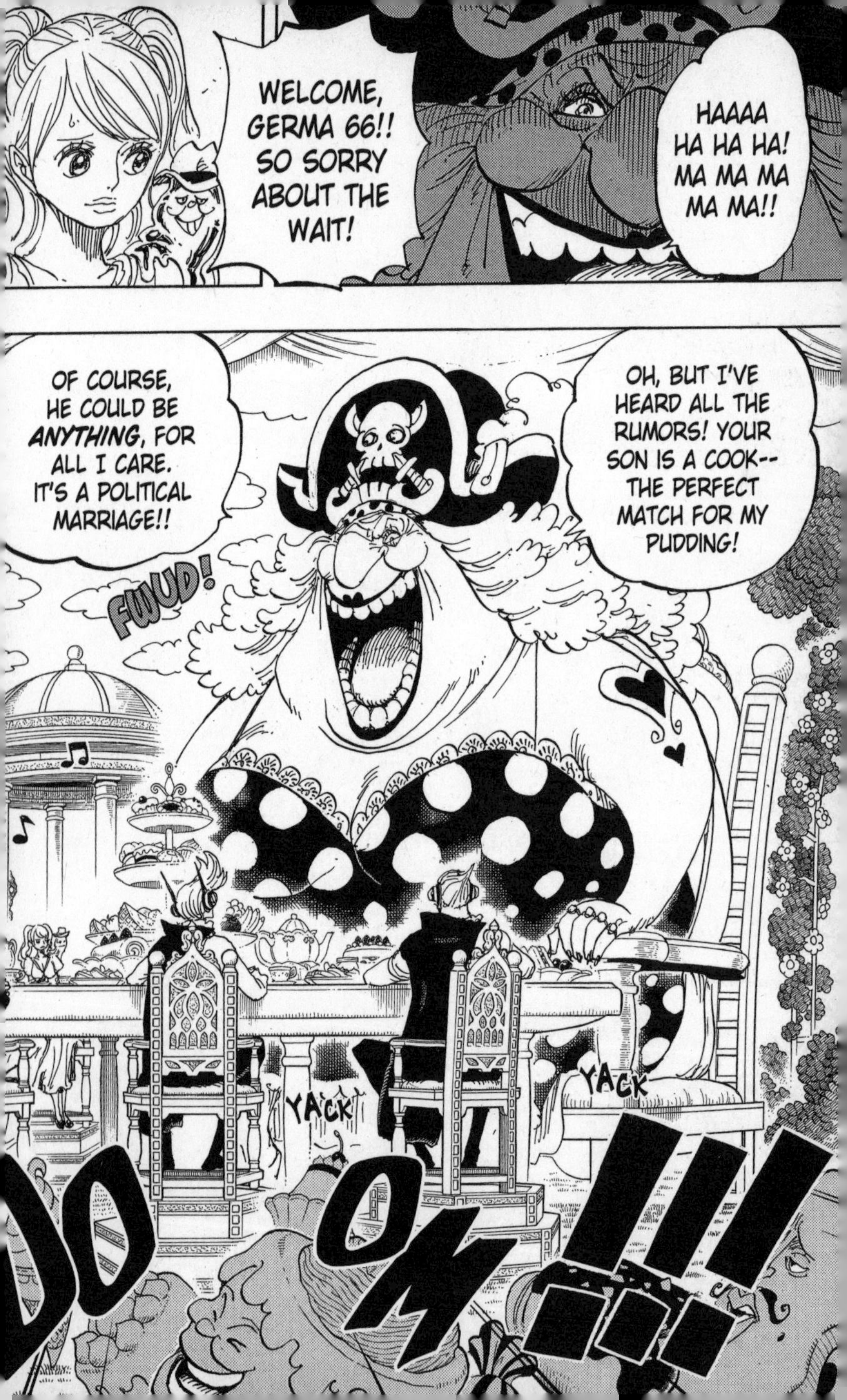
HAAAA HA HA HA! MA MA MA MA MA!!
WELCOME, GERMA 66!! SO SORRY ABOUT THE WAIT!
OH, BUT I'VE HEARD ALL THE RUMORS! YOUR SON IS A COOK-- THE PERFECT MATCH FOR MY PUDDING!
OF COURSE, HE COULD BE ANYTHING, FOR ALL I CARE. IT'S A POLITICAL MARRIAGE!!
FWUD!
YACK
YACK
DOOM!!!

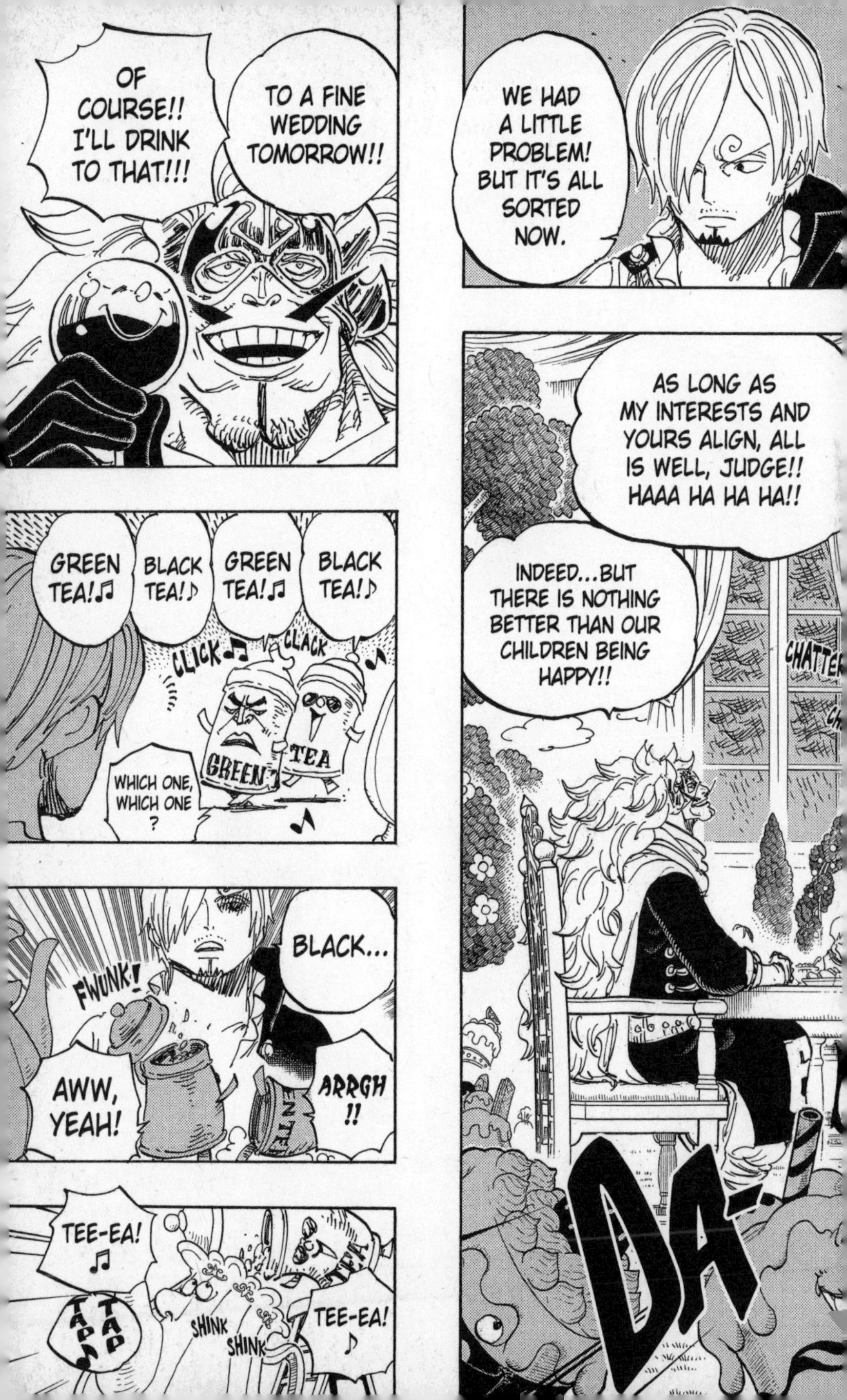
WE HAD A LITTLE PROBLEM! BUT IT'S ALL SORTED NOW.
TO A FINE WEDDING TOMORROW!!
OF COURSE!! I'LL DRINK TO THAT!!!
AS LONG AS MY INTERESTS AND YOURS ALIGN, ALL IS WELL, JUDGE!! HAAA HA HA HA!!
INDEED...BUT THERE IS NOTHING BETTER THAN OUR CHILDREN BEING HAPPY!!
CHATTER
DA-
BLACK TEA!♪
GREEN TEA!♫
BLACK TEA!♪
GREEN TEA!♫
CLACK
CLICK
TEA
GREEN
WHICH ONE, WHICH ONE ?
BLACK...
FWUNK!
ARRGH !!
AWW, YEAH!
TEE-EA! ♪
SHINK
SHINK
TEE-EA! ♫
TAP TAP

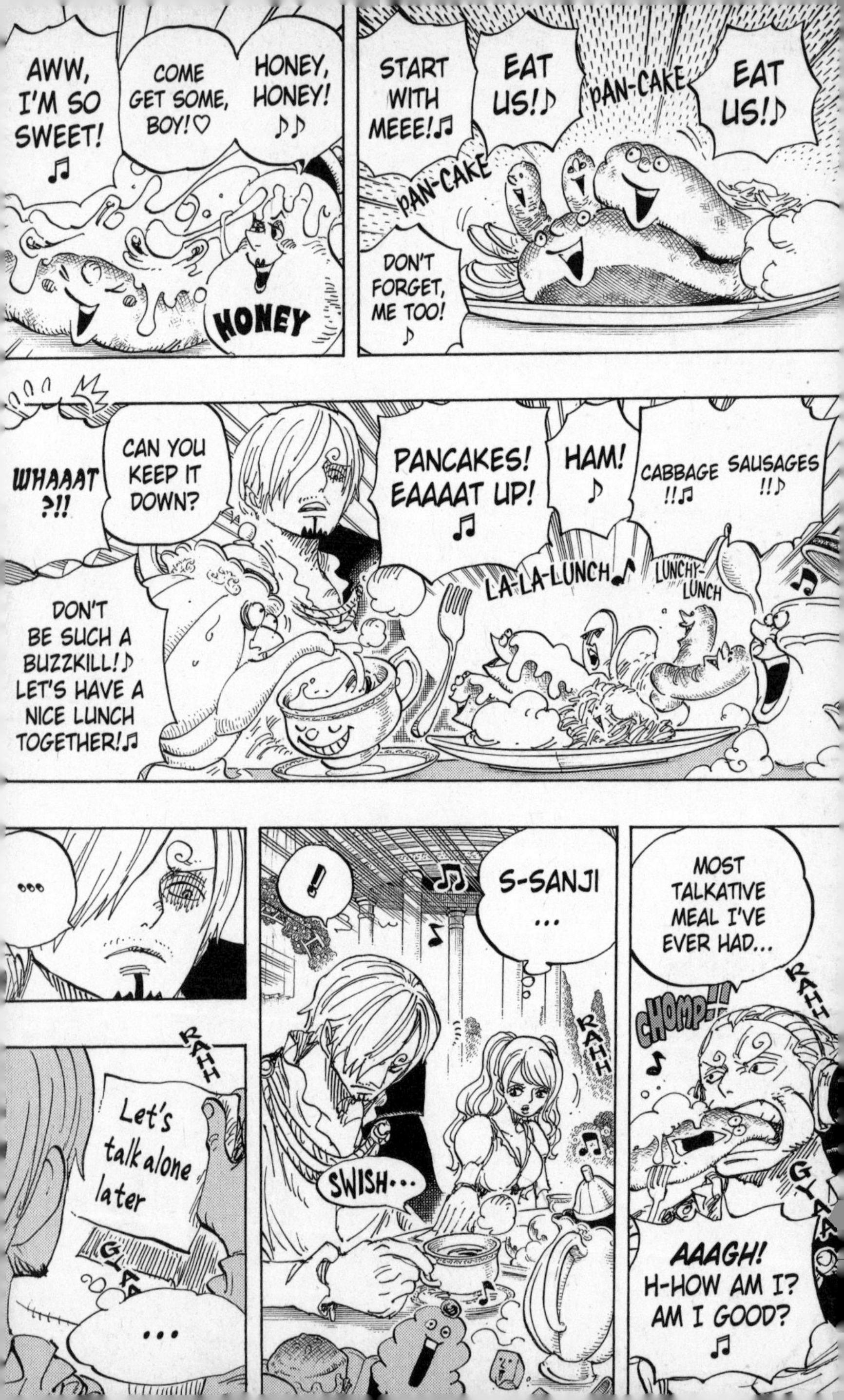
EAT US!♪
PAN-CAKE
EAT US!♪
START WITH MEEE!♬
PAN-CAKE
DON'T FORGET, ME TOO! ♪
HONEY, HONEY! ♪♪
COME GET SOME, BOY!♡
AWW, I'M SO SWEET! ♬
HONEY
SAUSAGES!!♪
CABBAGE!!♬
HAM!♪
PANCAKES! EAAAAT UP! ♬
LUNCHY-LUNCH
LA-LA-LUNCH♪
CAN YOU KEEP IT DOWN?
WHAAAT?!!
DON'T BE SUCH A BUZZKILL!♪ LET'S HAVE A NICE LUNCH TOGETHER!♬
MOST TALKATIVE MEAL I'VE EVER HAD...
RAHH
CHOMP!!
GIAAA
AAAGH! H-HOW AM I? AM I GOOD? ♬
S-SANJI...
!
RAHH
SWISH...
...
RAHH
Let's talk alone later
...

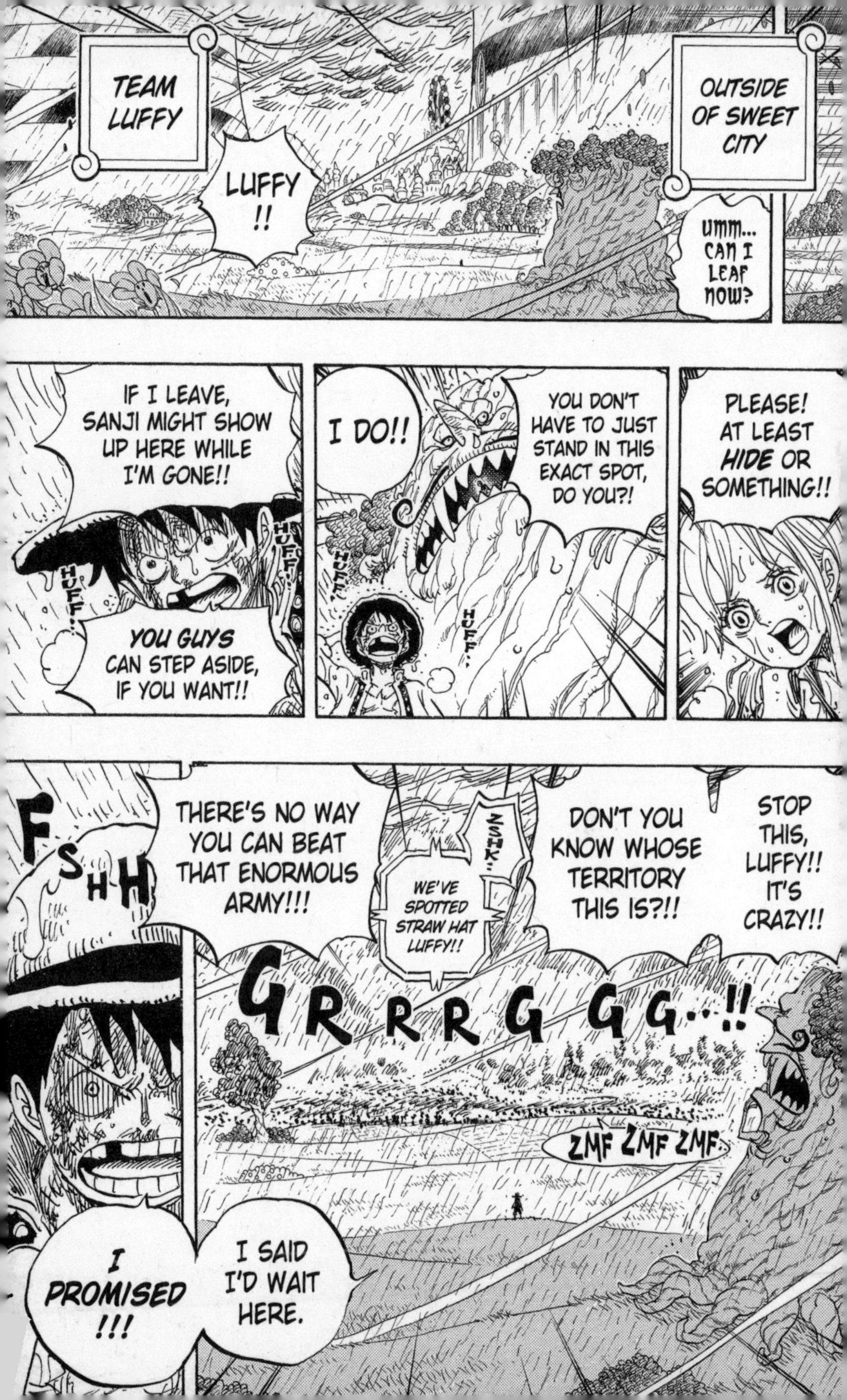
OUTSIDE OF SWEET CITY
TEAM LUFFY
LUFFY!!
umm... can I leaf now?
PLEASE! AT LEAST HIDE OR SOMETHING!!
YOU DON'T HAVE TO JUST STAND IN THIS EXACT SPOT, DO YOU?!
I DO!!
HUFF...
IF I LEAVE, SANJI MIGHT SHOW UP HERE WHILE I'M GONE!!
HUFF...
HUFF...
YOU GUYS CAN STEP ASIDE, IF YOU WANT!!
STOP THIS, LUFFY!! IT'S CRAZY!!
DON'T YOU KNOW WHOSE TERRITORY THIS IS?!!
ZSHK...
WE'VE SPOTTED STRAW HAT LUFFY!!
THERE'S NO WAY YOU CAN BEAT THAT ENORMOUS ARMY!!!
FSHH
GRRRGGG...!!
ZMF ZMF ZMF
I SAID I'D WAIT HERE.
I PROMISED!!!

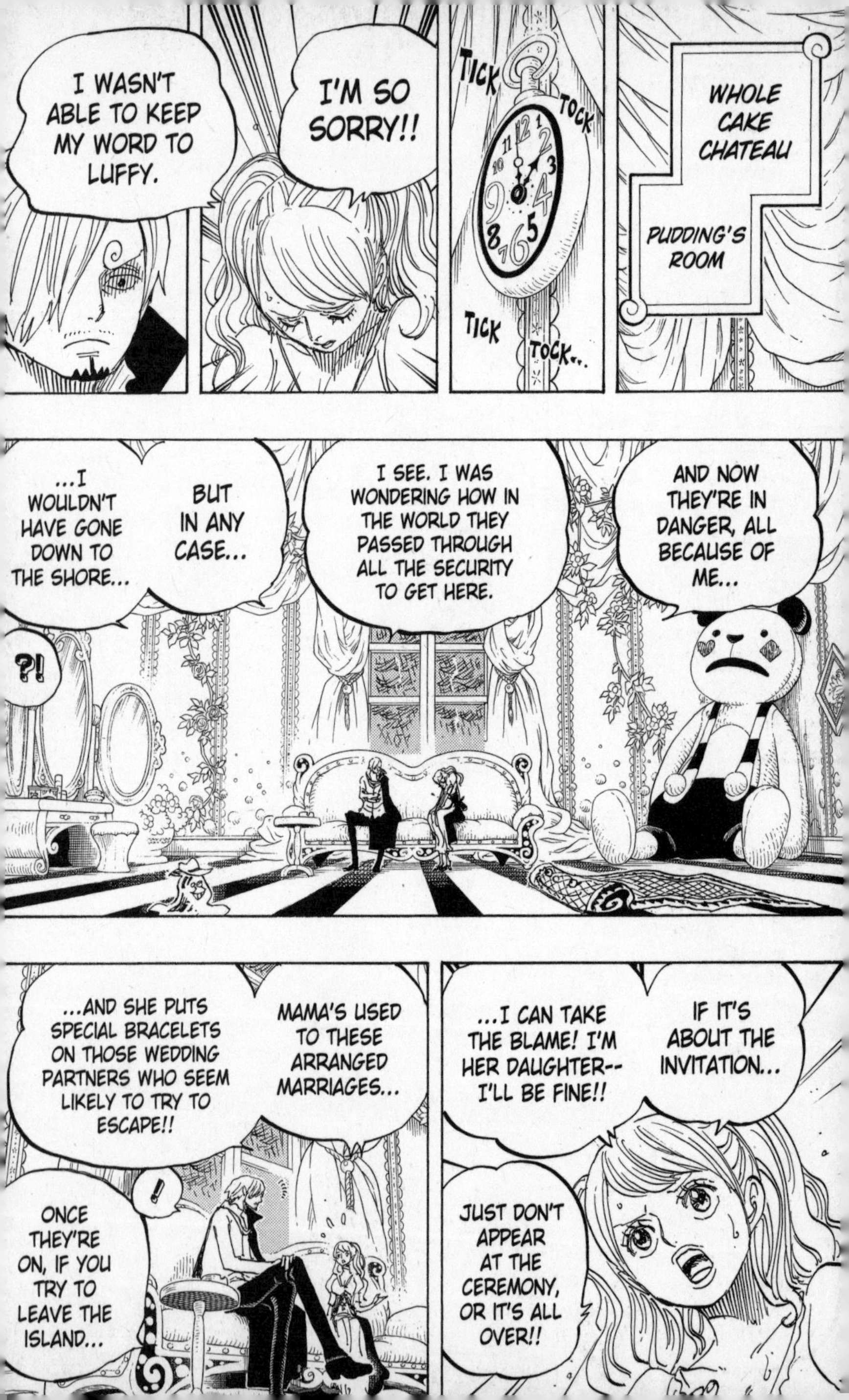
WHOLE CAKE CHATEAU
PUDDING'S ROOM
TICK
TOCK
TICK
TOCK...
I'M SO SORRY!!
I WASN'T ABLE TO KEEP MY WORD TO LUFFY.
AND NOW THEY'RE IN DANGER, ALL BECAUSE OF ME...
I SEE. I WAS WONDERING HOW IN THE WORLD THEY PASSED THROUGH ALL THE SECURITY TO GET HERE.
BUT IN ANY CASE...
...I WOULDN'T HAVE GONE DOWN TO THE SHORE...
?!
IF IT'S ABOUT THE INVITATION...
...I CAN TAKE THE BLAME! I'M HER DAUGHTER-- I'LL BE FINE!!
JUST DON'T APPEAR AT THE CEREMONY, OR IT'S ALL OVER!!
MAMA'S USED TO THESE ARRANGED MARRIAGES...
...AND SHE PUTS SPECIAL BRACELETS ON THOSE WEDDING PARTNERS WHO SEEM LIKELY TO TRY TO ESCAPE!!
!
ONCE THEY'RE ON, IF YOU TRY TO LEAVE THE ISLAND...

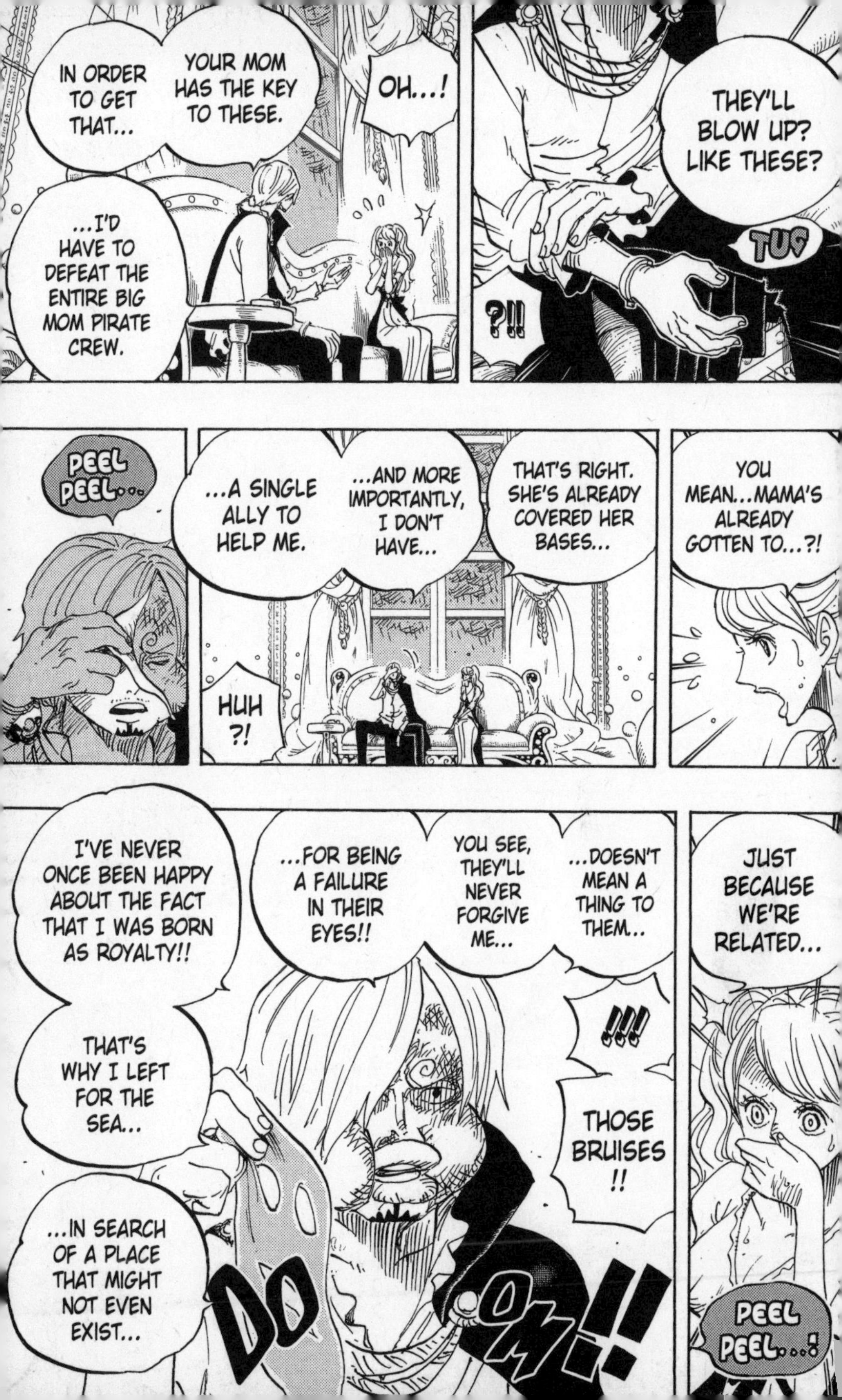
THEY'LL BLOW UP? LIKE THESE?
TUG
?!!
OH...!
YOUR MOM HAS THE KEY TO THESE.
IN ORDER TO GET THAT...
...I'D HAVE TO DEFEAT THE ENTIRE BIG MOM PIRATE CREW.
YOU MEAN...MAMA'S ALREADY GOTTEN TO...?!
THAT'S RIGHT. SHE'S ALREADY COVERED HER BASES...
...AND MORE IMPORTANTLY, I DON'T HAVE...
...A SINGLE ALLY TO HELP ME.
HUH?!
PEEL PEEL...
JUST BECAUSE WE'RE RELATED...
PEEL PEEL...!
...DOESN'T MEAN A THING TO THEM...
YOU SEE, THEY'LL NEVER FORGIVE ME...
...FOR BEING A FAILURE IN THEIR EYES!!
!!!
THOSE BRUISES!!
I'VE NEVER ONCE BEEN HAPPY ABOUT THE FACT THAT I WAS BORN AS ROYALTY!!
THAT'S WHY I LEFT FOR THE SEA...
...IN SEARCH OF A PLACE THAT MIGHT NOT EVEN EXIST...
DOOM!!

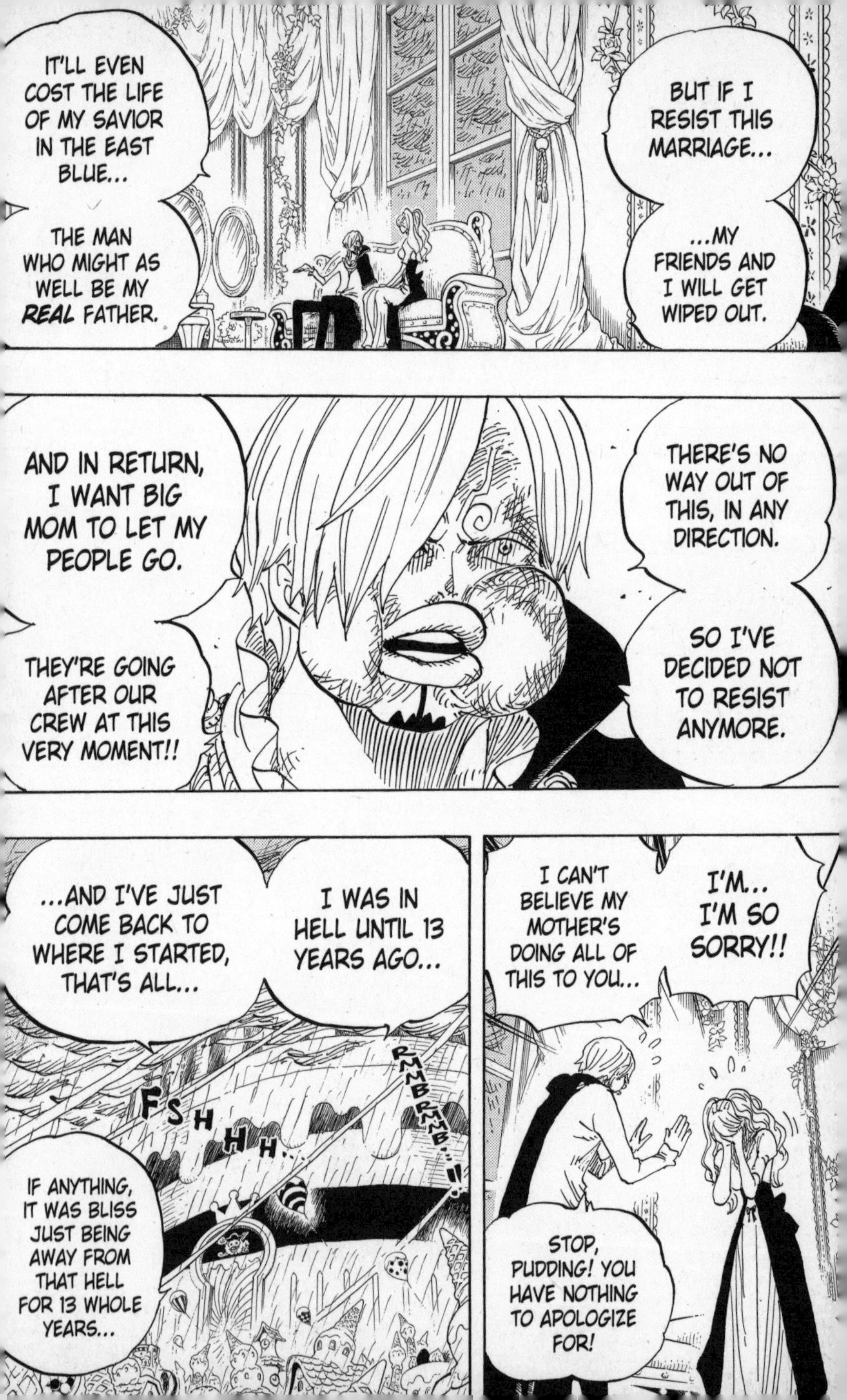
BUT IF I RESIST THIS MARRIAGE...
...MY FRIENDS AND I WILL GET WIPED OUT.
IT'LL EVEN COST THE LIFE OF MY SAVIOR IN THE EAST BLUE...
THE MAN WHO MIGHT AS WELL BE MY *REAL* FATHER.
THERE'S NO WAY OUT OF THIS, IN ANY DIRECTION.
SO I'VE DECIDED NOT TO RESIST ANYMORE.
AND IN RETURN, I WANT BIG MOM TO LET MY PEOPLE GO.
THEY'RE GOING AFTER OUR CREW AT THIS VERY MOMENT!!
I'M... I'M SO SORRY!!
I CAN'T BELIEVE MY MOTHER'S DOING ALL OF THIS TO YOU...
STOP, PUDDING! YOU HAVE NOTHING TO APOLOGIZE FOR!
I WAS IN HELL UNTIL 13 YEARS AGO...
...AND I'VE JUST COME BACK TO WHERE I STARTED, THAT'S ALL...
RMMB RMMB..!!
FSHHHH..
IF ANYTHING, IT WAS BLISS JUST BEING AWAY FROM THAT HELL FOR 13 WHOLE YEARS...

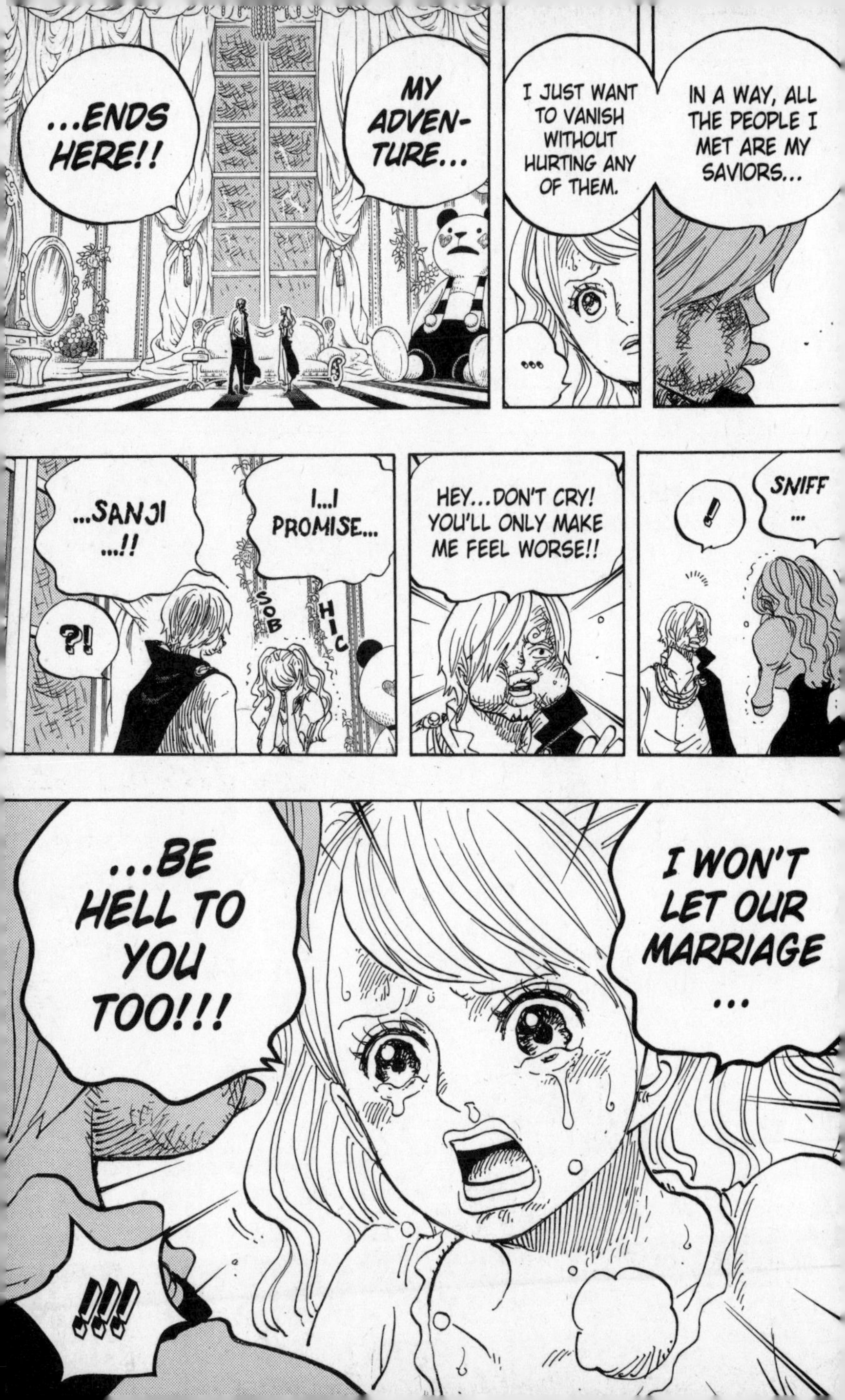
IN A WAY, ALL THE PEOPLE I MET ARE MY SAVIORS...
I JUST WANT TO VANISH WITHOUT HURTING ANY OF THEM.
...
MY ADVENTURE...
...ENDS HERE!!
SNIFF ...
!
HEY...DON'T CRY! YOU'LL ONLY MAKE ME FEEL WORSE!!
I...I PROMISE...
HIC
SOB
...SANJI ...!!
?!
I WON'T LET OUR MARRIAGE ...
...BE HELL TO YOU TOO!!!
!!!

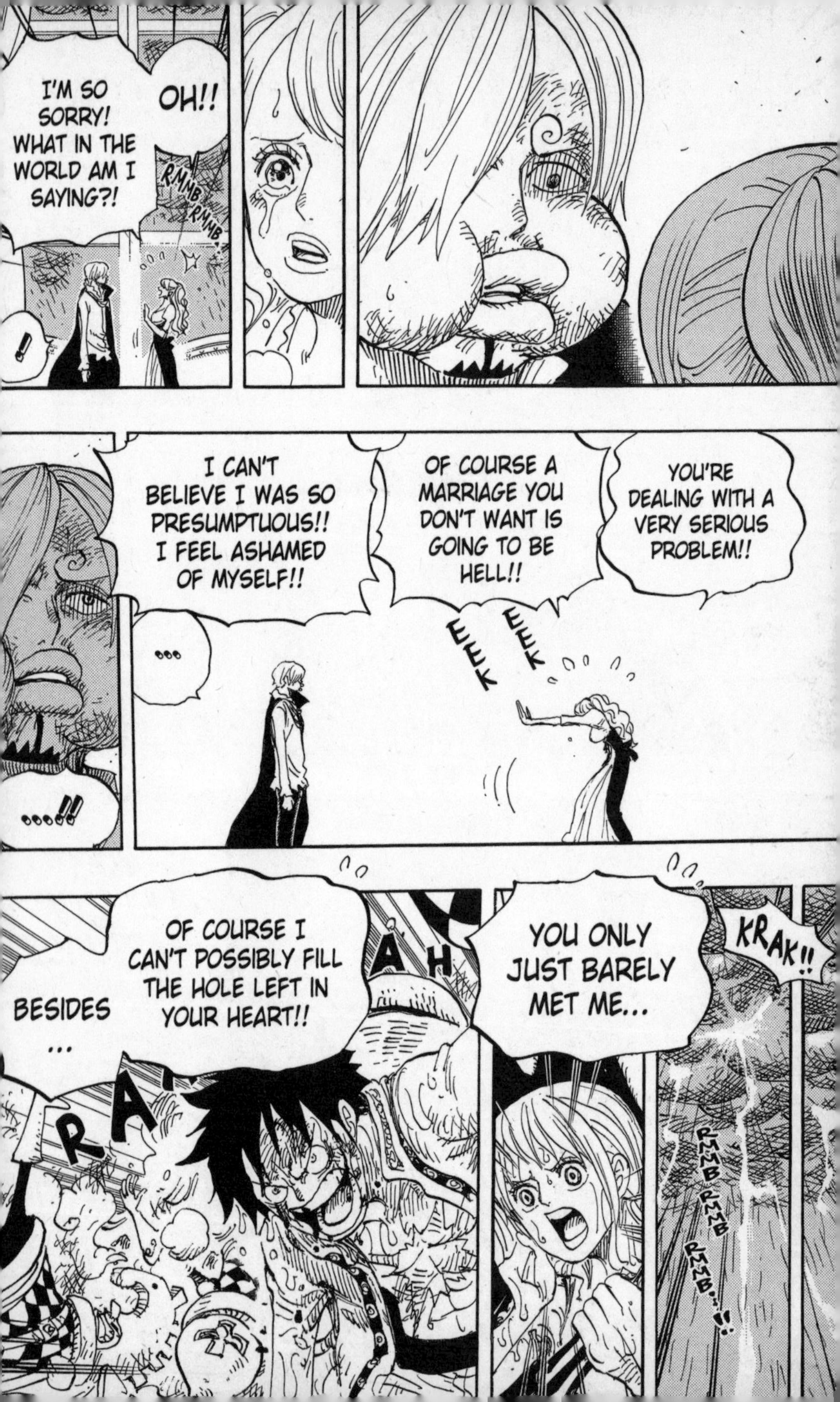
OH!!
I'M SO SORRY! WHAT IN THE WORLD AM I SAYING?!
RMMB RMMB
!
YOU'RE DEALING WITH A VERY SERIOUS PROBLEM!!
OF COURSE A MARRIAGE YOU DON'T WANT IS GOING TO BE HELL!!
I CAN'T BELIEVE I WAS SO PRESUMPTUOUS!! I FEEL ASHAMED OF MYSELF!!
EEEK EEEK
...
...!!
KRAK!!
RMMB RMMB RMMB...!!
YOU ONLY JUST BARELY MET ME...
AH
BESIDES ...
OF COURSE I CAN'T POSSIBLY FILL THE HOLE LEFT IN YOUR HEART!!
RA

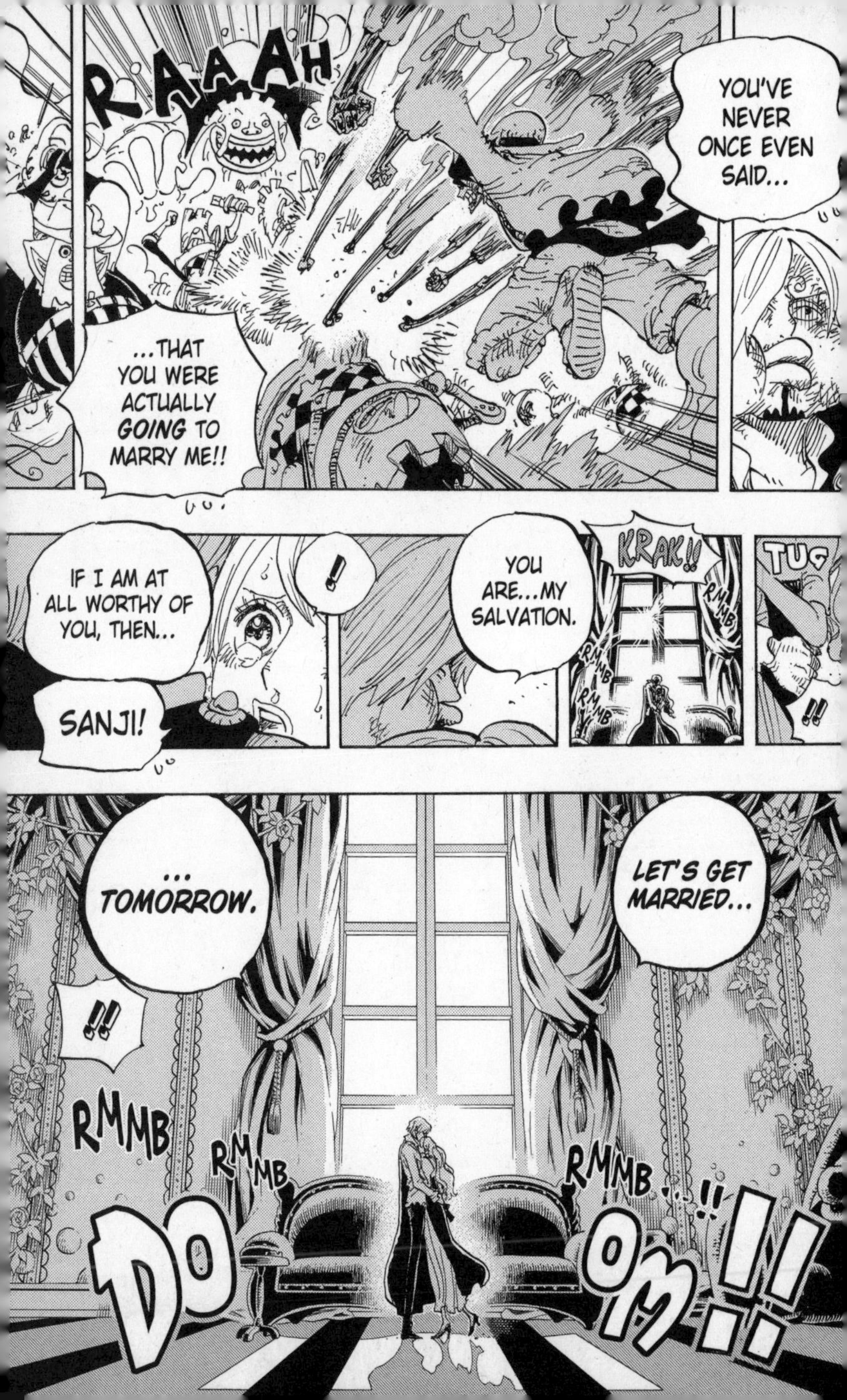
YOU'VE NEVER ONCE EVEN SAID...
RAAAAH
...THAT YOU WERE ACTUALLY *GOING* TO MARRY ME!!
TUG
!!
KRAK!!
RMMB
RMMB
RMMB
YOU ARE...MY SALVATION.
!
IF I AM AT ALL WORTHY OF YOU, THEN...
SANJI!
LET'S GET MARRIED...
...TOMORROW.
!!
RMMB
RMMB
RMMB
..!!
DOOM!!

SBS Question Corner

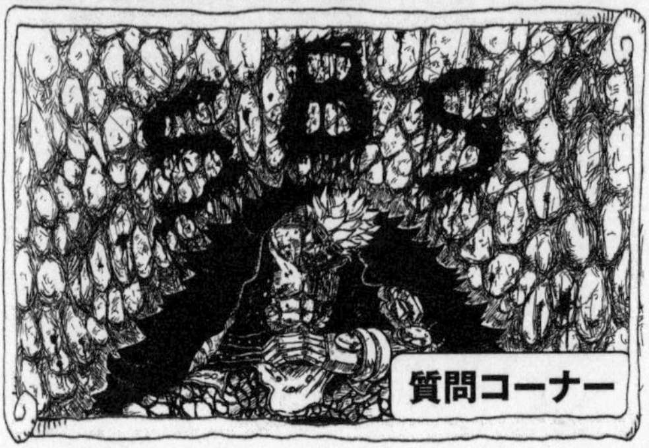
SBS
質問コーナー

(Sasaaki, Okinawa)

Q: Are those Reiju's bare legs? Are the 6 symbols drawn right on the skin? Isn't that kinda sexy?

--Takataka

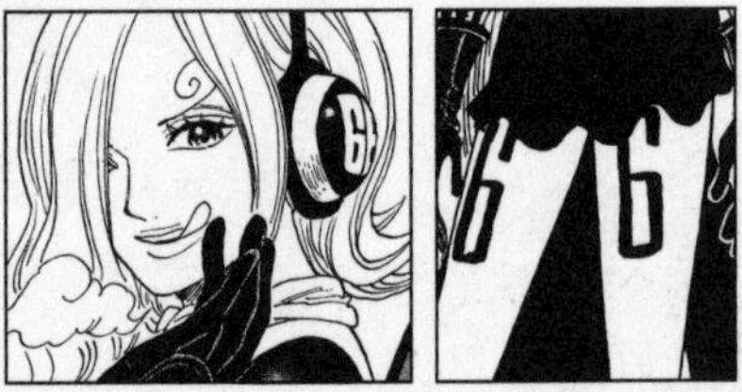

A: Ah, I see. You suspect she might be wearing tights. No worries!! Those are straight-up tattoos!!!

Q: According to Den's explanation on page 36 of volume 63, anyone in Fish-man Island can have any kind of child. What's the situation with the minks, then?

--OP Girl

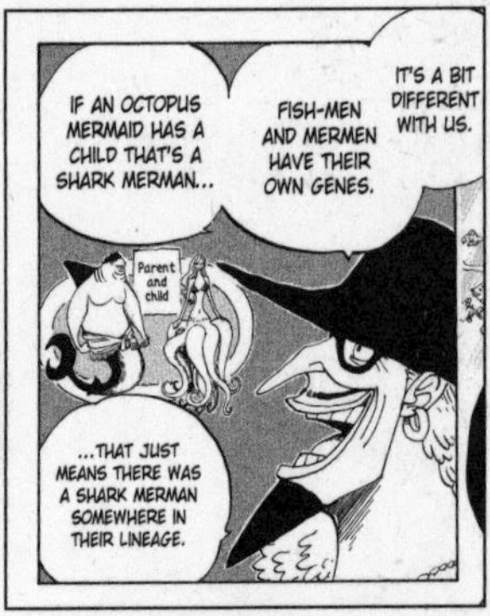
IT'S A BIT DIFFERENT WITH US.
FISH-MEN AND MERMEN HAVE THEIR OWN GENES.
IF AN OCTOPUS MERMAID HAS A CHILD THAT'S A SHARK MERMAN...
Parent and child
...THAT JUST MEANS THERE WAS A SHARK MERMAN SOMEWHERE IN THEIR LINEAGE.

A: Same property. There are all biological patterns on Zou: deer with a fox child, or pandas with a panda child, etc.

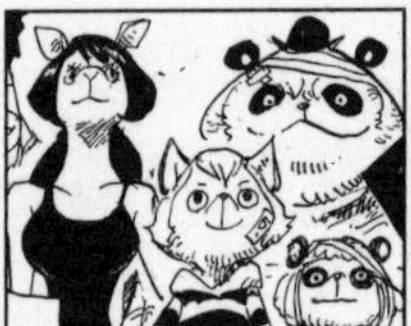

Q: Oda Sensei! I've come to ask a question! ＼(^∀^)／
So, I was reading volume 80 recently. And then Koala said, "What?! We're going to bring all those intense people here again?!!"
So it occurred to me… Can you tell Koala something?
Um, Koala…
Pretty much everyone in *One Piece* is intense!!
Welp, bye!

--Nodo

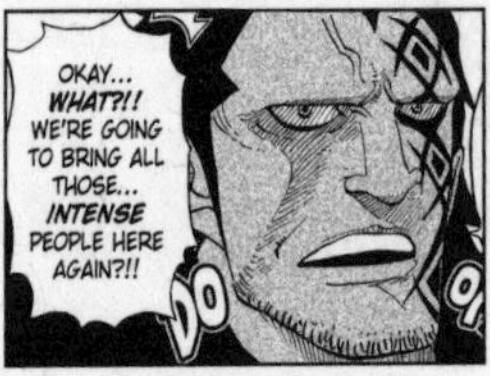
OKAY... WHAT?!! WE'RE GOING TO BRING ALL THOSE... INTENSE PEOPLE HERE AGAIN?!!

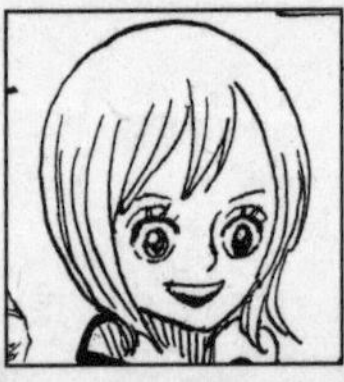

A: Very true!!!

Chapter 846:
TAMAGO SECURITY

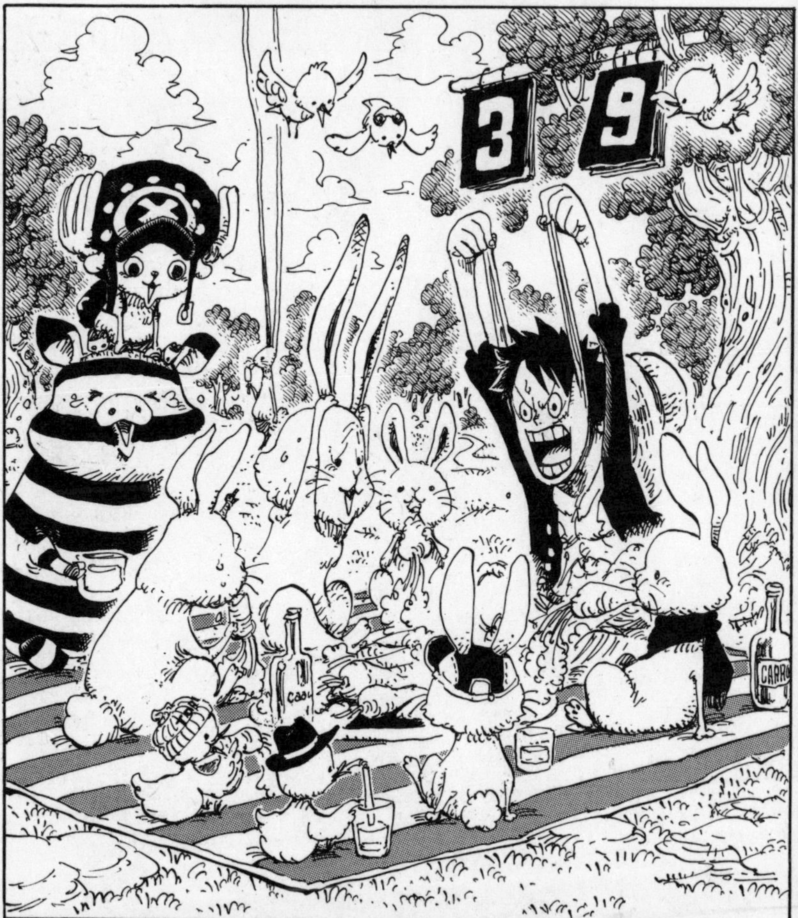
3 9
CARRO
CARRO

REQUEST: O: "WHAT'S YOUR FAVORITE ANIMAL?" S: "I LIKE RABBITS."
"PLEASE DRAW SOME RABBITS, M.S.'S FAVORITE ANIMAL"
BY EIICHIRO ODA FROM TOKYO

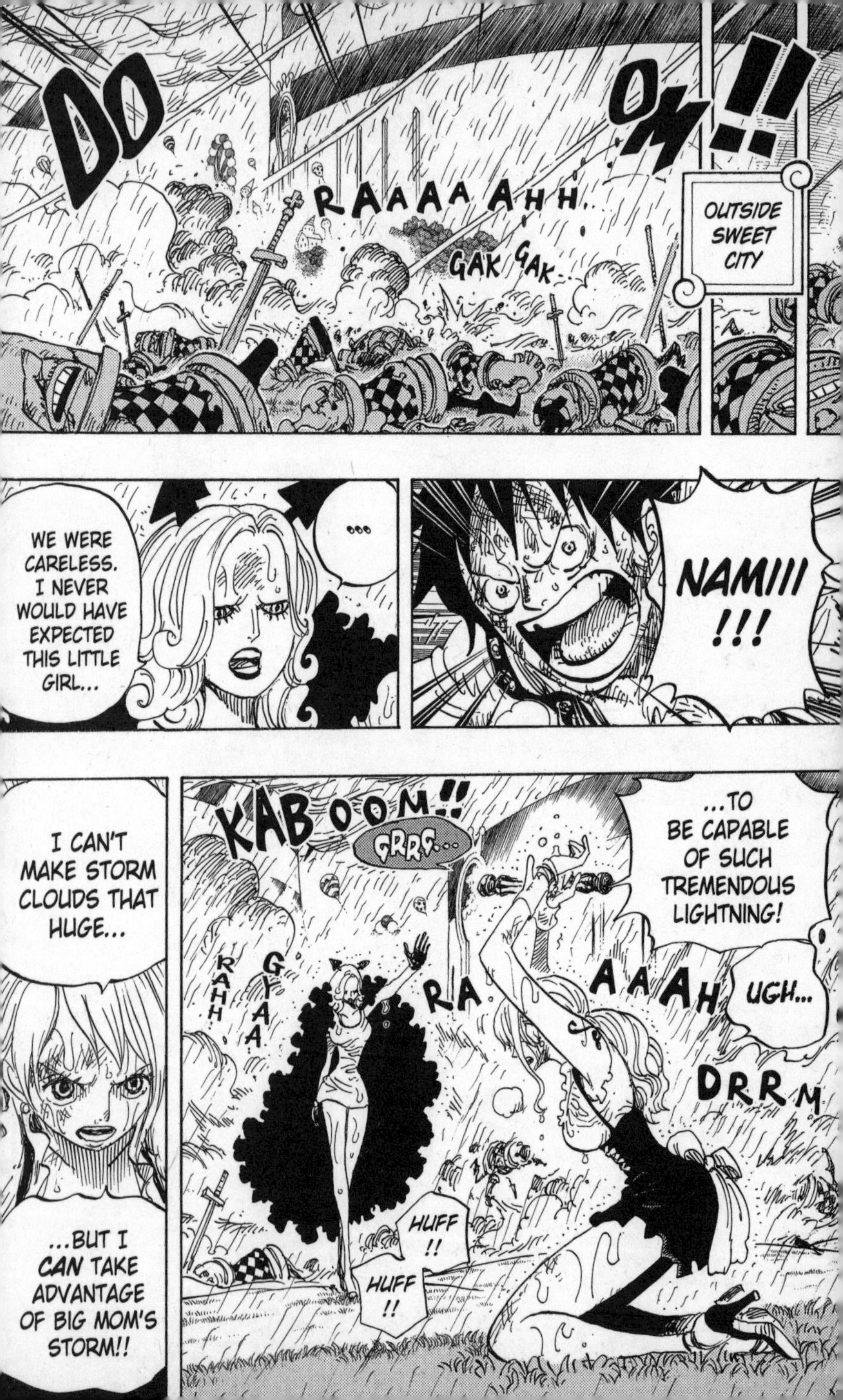
DO
OM!!
RAAAAAHH...
OUTSIDE SWEET CITY
GAK GAK
NAMIII!!!
...
WE WERE CARELESS. I NEVER WOULD HAVE EXPECTED THIS LITTLE GIRL...
...TO BE CAPABLE OF SUCH TREMENDOUS LIGHTNING!
KABOOM!!
GRRG...
UGH...
RAAAAH
GYAA
RAHH
DRRM
HUFF!!
HUFF!!
I CAN'T MAKE STORM CLOUDS THAT HUGE...
...BUT I CAN TAKE ADVANTAGE OF BIG MOM'S STORM!!

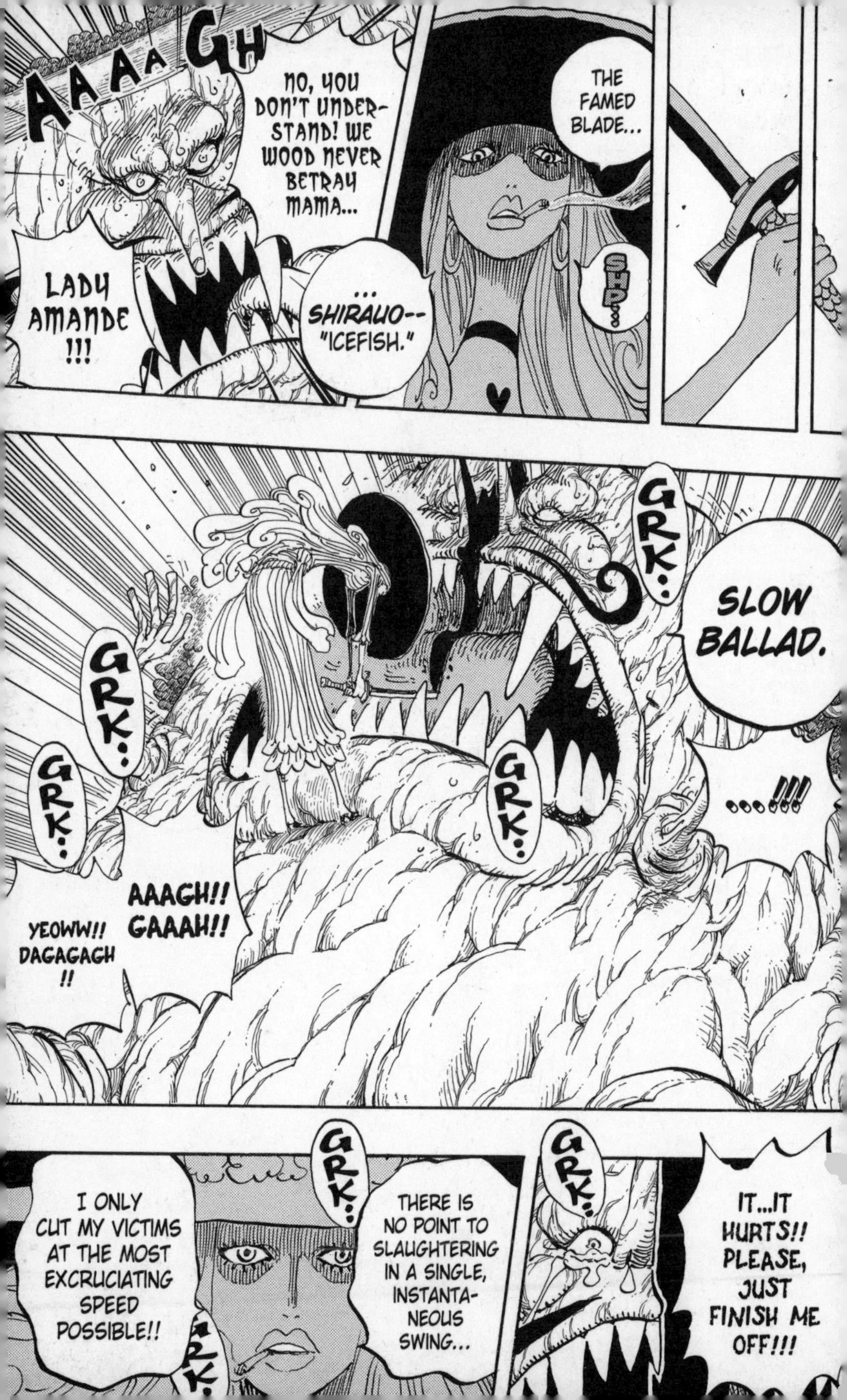

THE FAMED BLADE...
SHP
... SHIRAUO-- "ICEFISH."
AAAAGH
NO, YOU DON'T UNDER-STAND! WE WOOD NEVER BETRAY MAMA...
LADY AMANDE !!!
GRK..
SLOW BALLAD.
...!!!
GRK..
GRK..
GRK..
AAAGH!! GAAAH!!
YEOWW!! DAGAGAGH !!
IT...IT HURTS!! PLEASE, JUST FINISH ME OFF!!!
GRK..
GRK..
THERE IS NO POINT TO SLAUGHTERING IN A SINGLE, INSTANTA-NEOUS SWING...
I ONLY CUT MY VICTIMS AT THE MOST EXCRUCIATING SPEED POSSIBLE!!

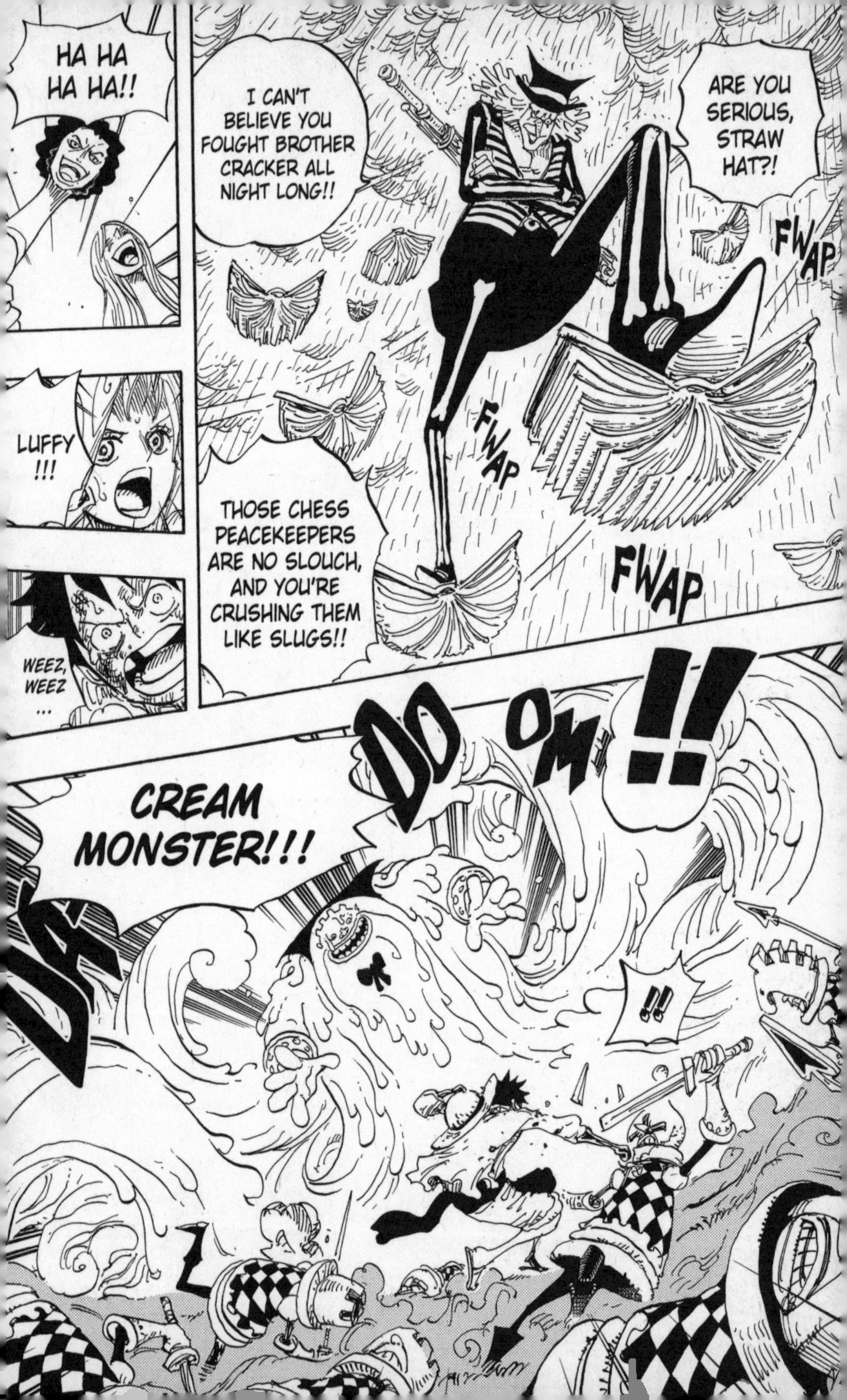
ARE YOU SERIOUS, STRAW HAT?!
I CAN'T BELIEVE YOU FOUGHT BROTHER CRACKER ALL NIGHT LONG!!
FWAP
FWAP
FWAP
THOSE CHESS PEACEKEEPERS ARE NO SLOUCH, AND YOU'RE CRUSHING THEM LIKE SLUGS!!
HA HA HA HA!!
LUFFY !!!
WEEZ, WEEZ ...
DOOM!!
CREAM MONSTER!!!
!!

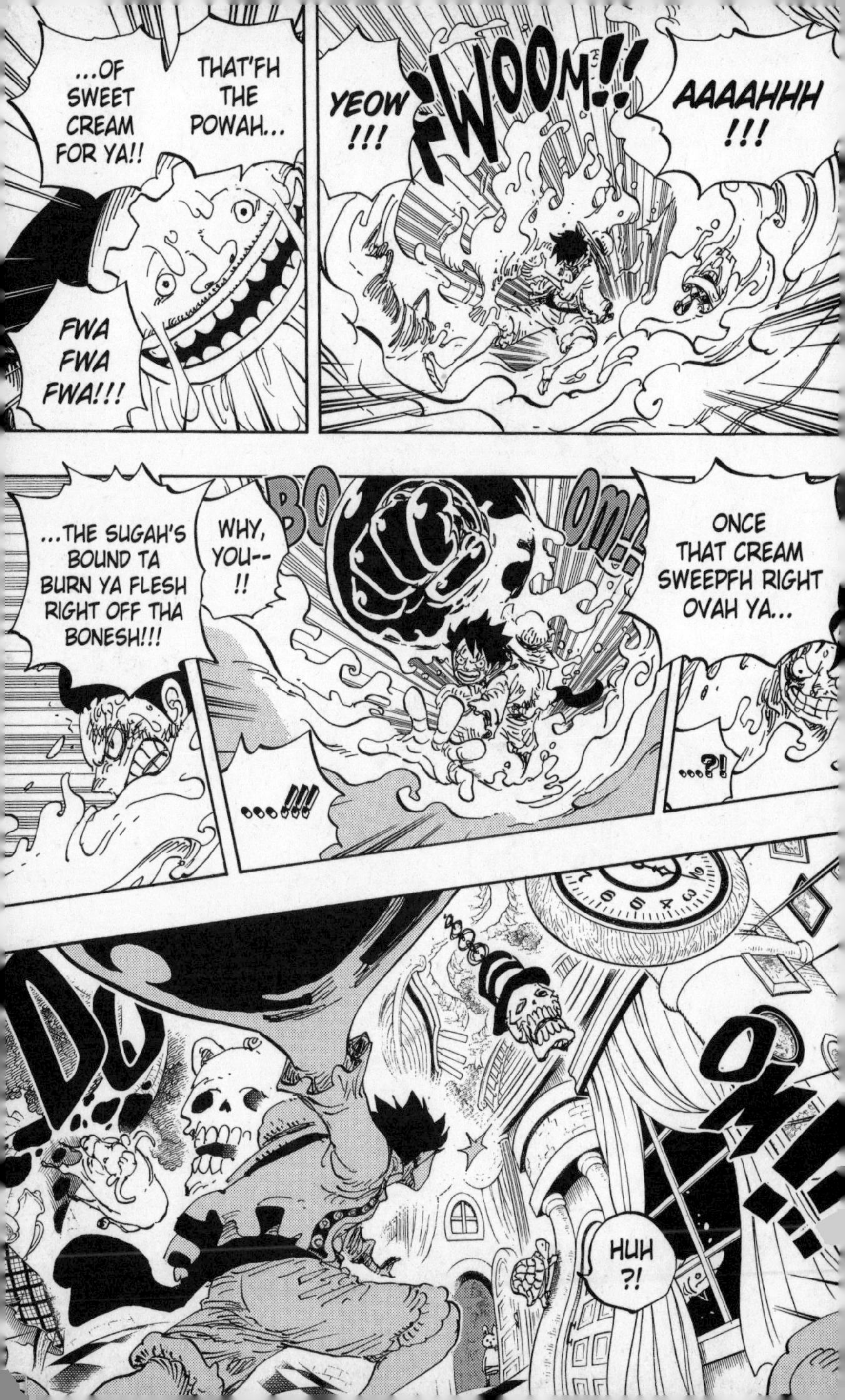
AAAAHHH!!!
FWOOM!!
YEOW!!!
THAT'FH THE POWAH...
...OF SWEET CREAM FOR YA!!
FWA FWA FWA!!!
ONCE THAT CREAM SWEEPFH RIGHT OVAH YA...
...?!
BOOM!!
WHY, YOU--!!
...!!!
...THE SUGAH'S BOUND TA BURN YA FLESH RIGHT OFF THA BONESH!!!
HUH?!

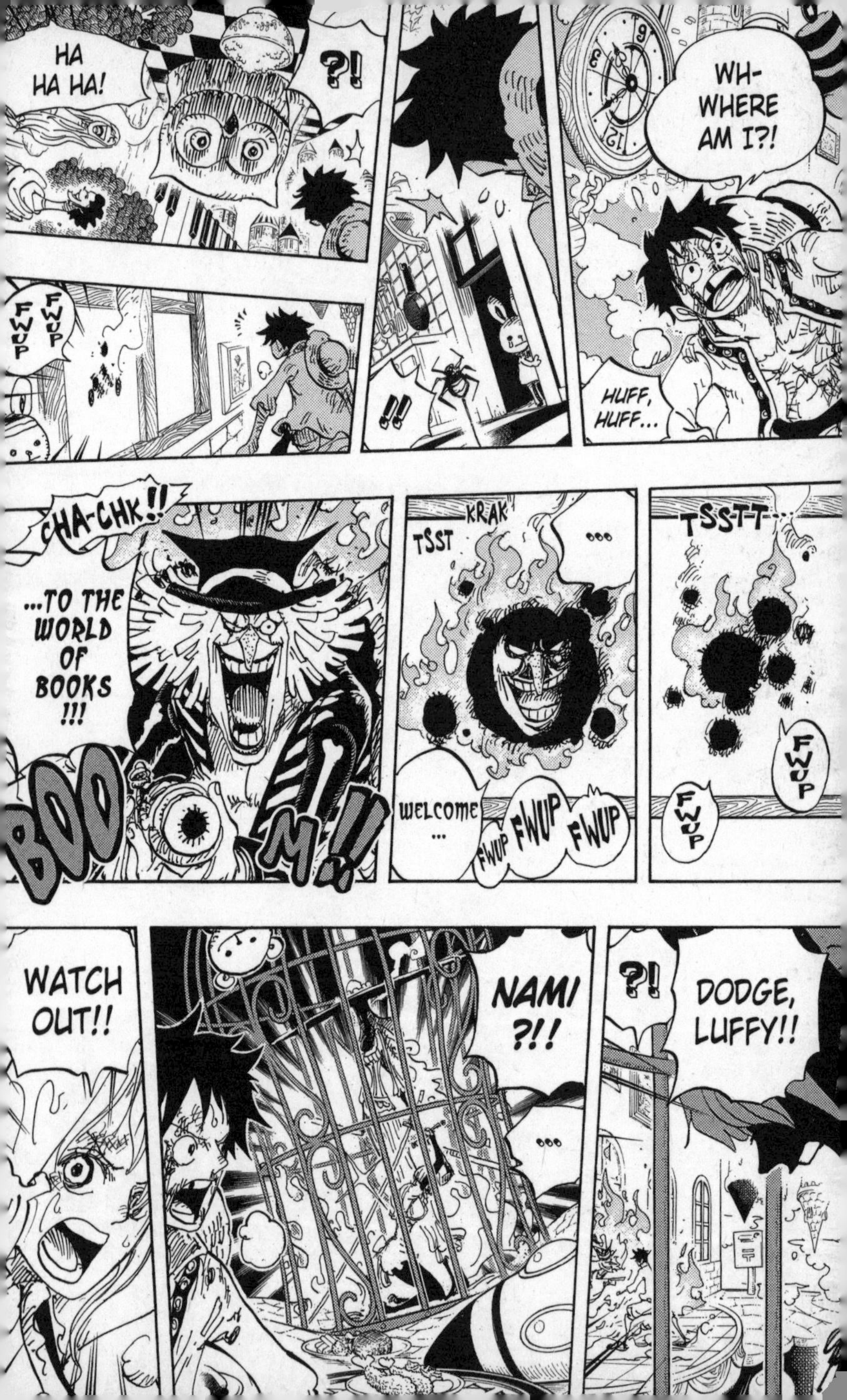
WH- WHERE AM I?!
HUFF, HUFF...
!!
HA HA HA!
?!
FWUP FWUP
TSSTT...
FWUP
FWUP
KRAK
TSST
...
WELCOME...
FWUP FWUP FWUP
CHA-CHK!!
...TO THE WORLD OF BOOKS!!!
BOOM!!
?!
DODGE, LUFFY!!
NAMI?!!
...
WATCH OUT!!

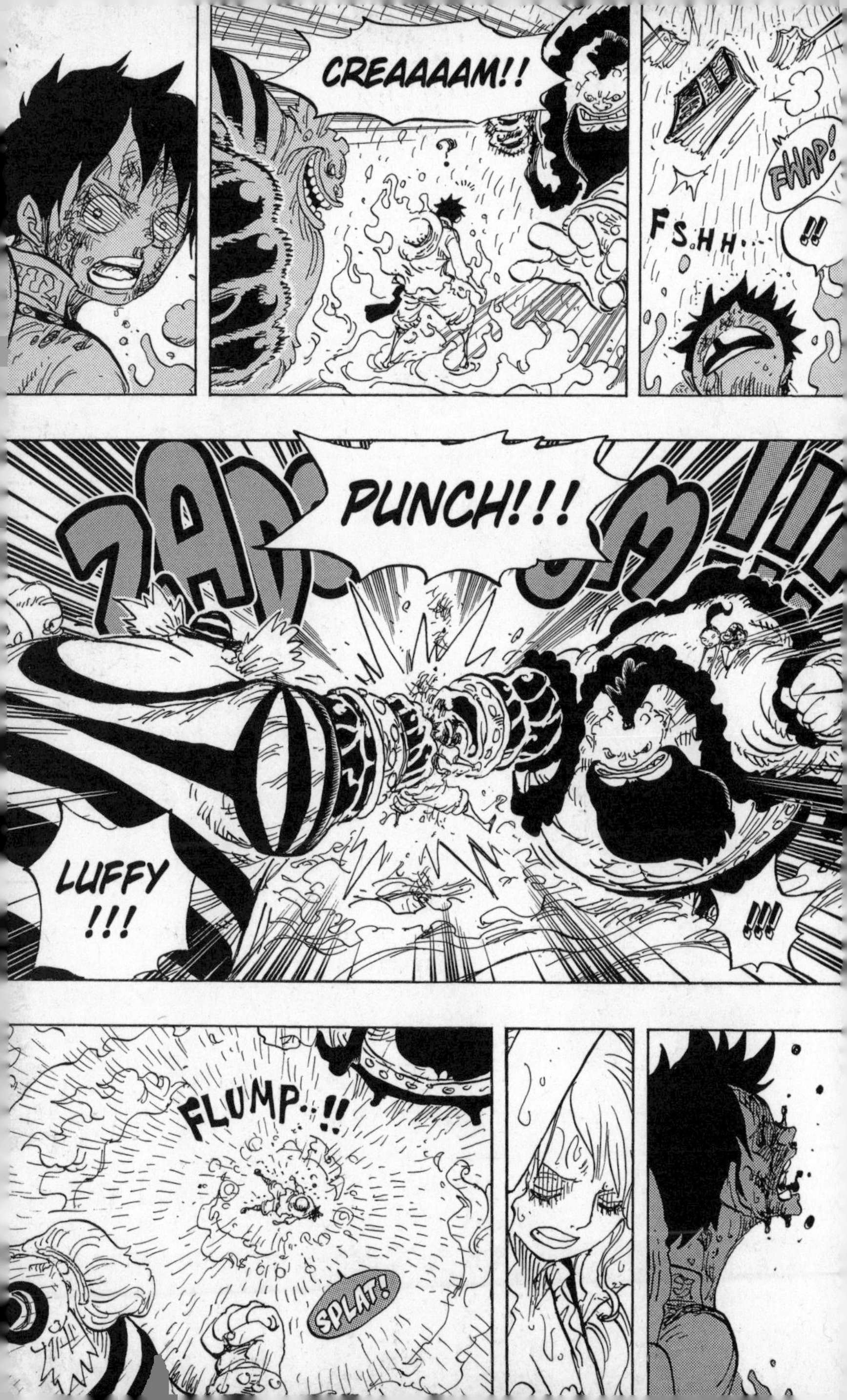
FWAP!
FSHH...
!!
CREAAAAM!!
?
PUNCH!!!
!!!
LUFFY !!!
FLUMP..!!
SPLAT!

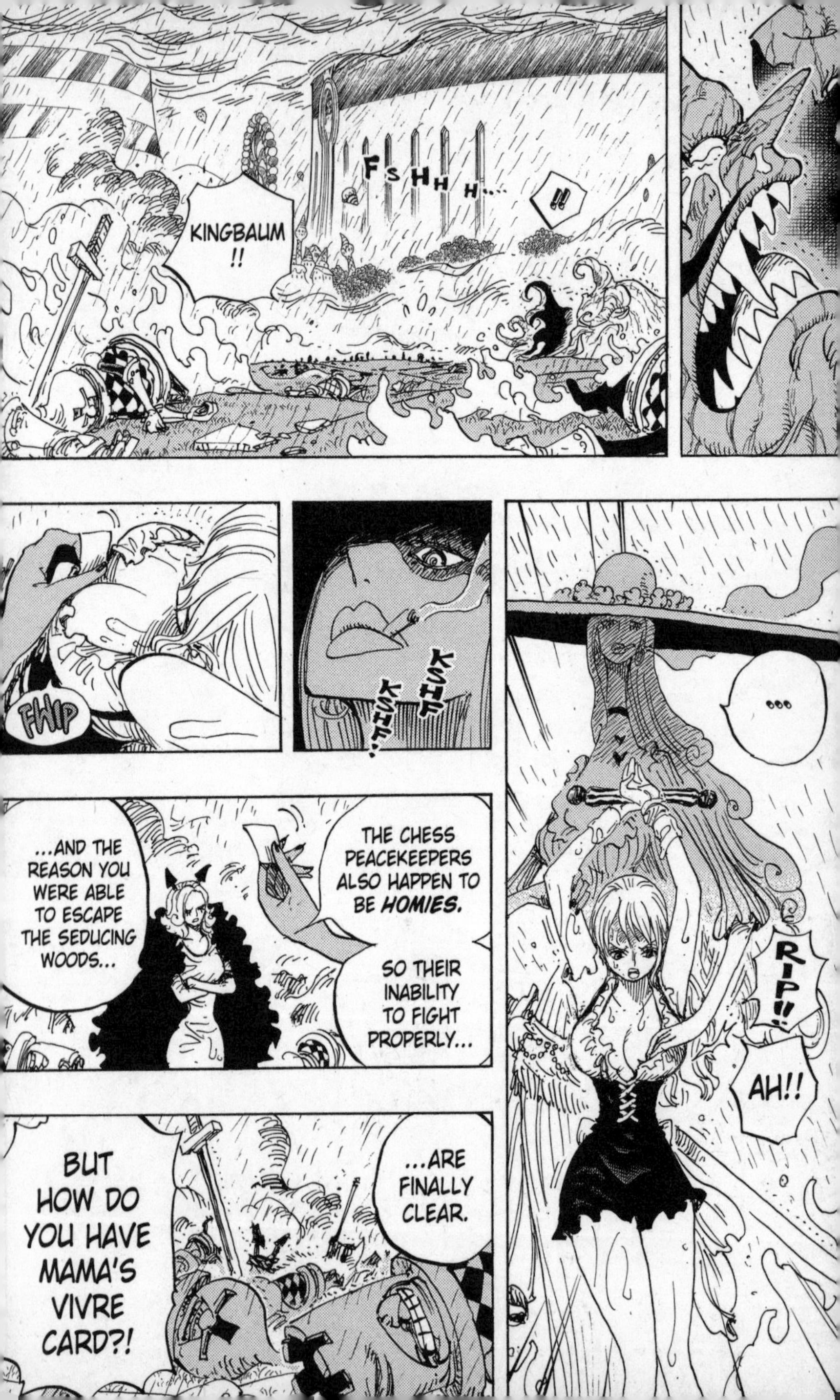
!!
FSHHH...
KINGBAUM !!
...
RIP!!
AH!!
KSHF KSHF
FWIP
THE CHESS PEACEKEEPERS ALSO HAPPEN TO BE *HOMIES.*
SO THEIR INABILITY TO FIGHT PROPERLY...
...AND THE REASON YOU WERE ABLE TO ESCAPE THE SEDUCING WOODS...
...ARE FINALLY CLEAR.
BUT HOW DO YOU HAVE MAMA'S VIVRE CARD?!

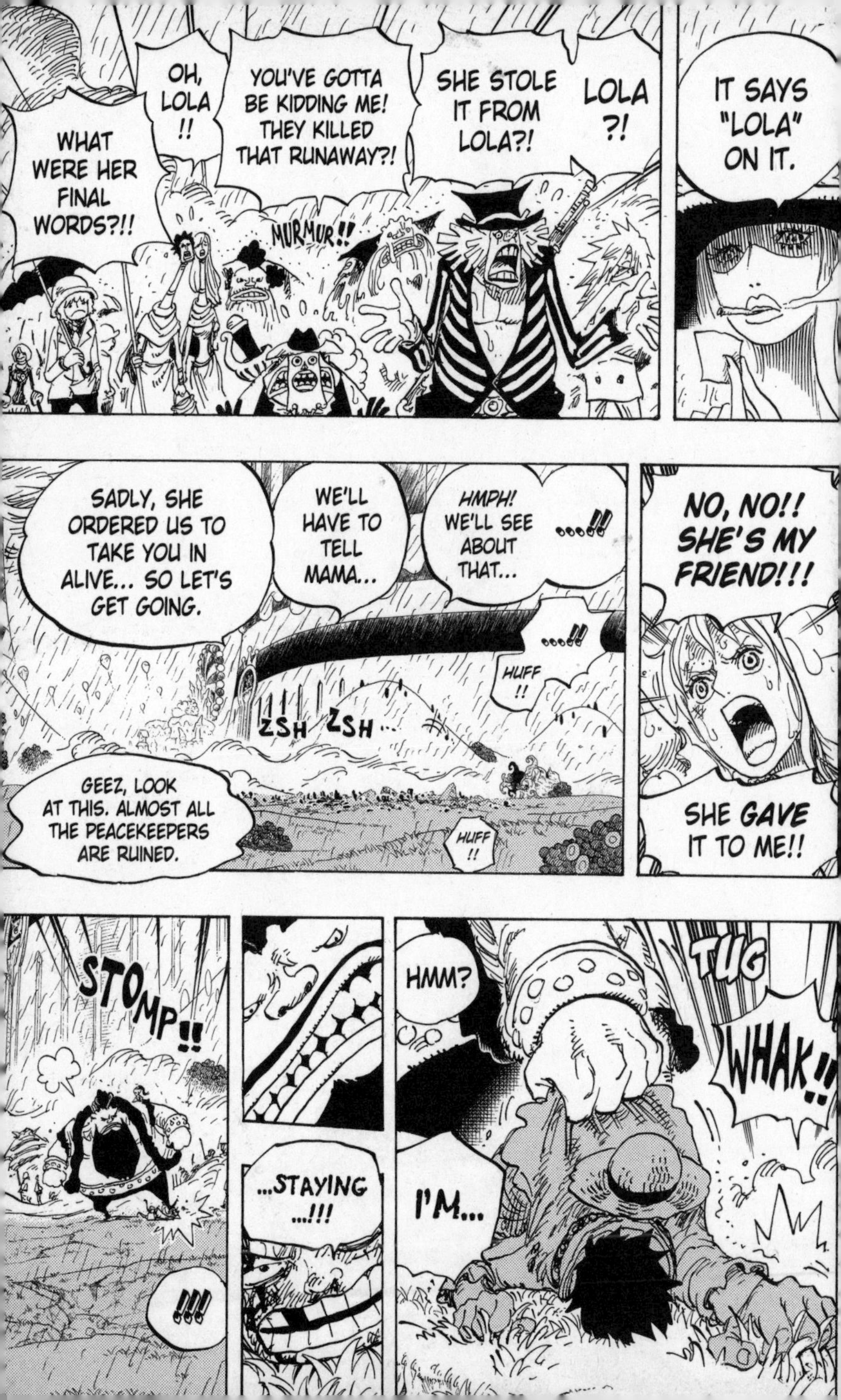
IT SAYS "LOLA" ON IT.
LOLA ?!
SHE STOLE IT FROM LOLA?!
YOU'VE GOTTA BE KIDDING ME! THEY KILLED THAT RUNAWAY?!
OH, LOLA !!
WHAT WERE HER FINAL WORDS?!!
MURMUR!!
NO, NO!! SHE'S MY FRIEND!!!
SHE GAVE IT TO ME!!
....!!
HMPH! WE'LL SEE ABOUT THAT...
WE'LL HAVE TO TELL MAMA...
SADLY, SHE ORDERED US TO TAKE YOU IN ALIVE... SO LET'S GET GOING.
....!!
HUFF !!
ZSH ZSH...
HUFF !!
GEEZ, LOOK AT THIS. ALMOST ALL THE PEACEKEEPERS ARE RUINED.
TUG
WHAK!!
HMM?
I'M...
...STAYING ...!!!
STOMP!!
!!!

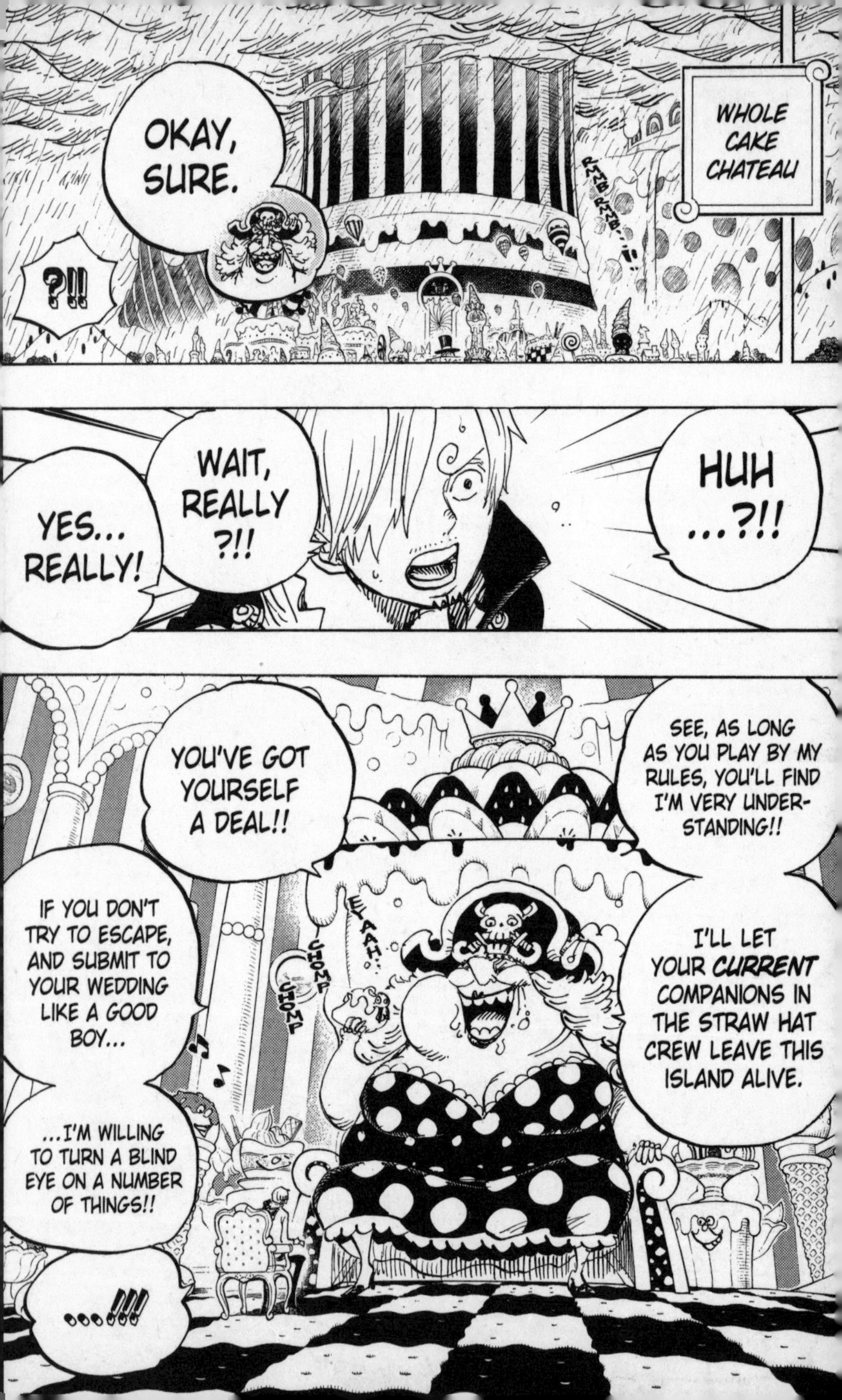
WHOLE CAKE CHATEAU
RMMB RMMB...!!
OKAY, SURE.
?!!
HUH ...?!!
WAIT, REALLY ?!!
YES... REALLY!
SEE, AS LONG AS YOU PLAY BY MY RULES, YOU'LL FIND I'M VERY UNDER-STANDING!!
YOU'VE GOT YOURSELF A DEAL!!
I'LL LET YOUR CURRENT COMPANIONS IN THE STRAW HAT CREW LEAVE THIS ISLAND ALIVE.
EYAAH...
CHOMP CHOMP
IF YOU DON'T TRY TO ESCAPE, AND SUBMIT TO YOUR WEDDING LIKE A GOOD BOY...
...I'M WILLING TO TURN A BLIND EYE ON A NUMBER OF THINGS!!
...!!!

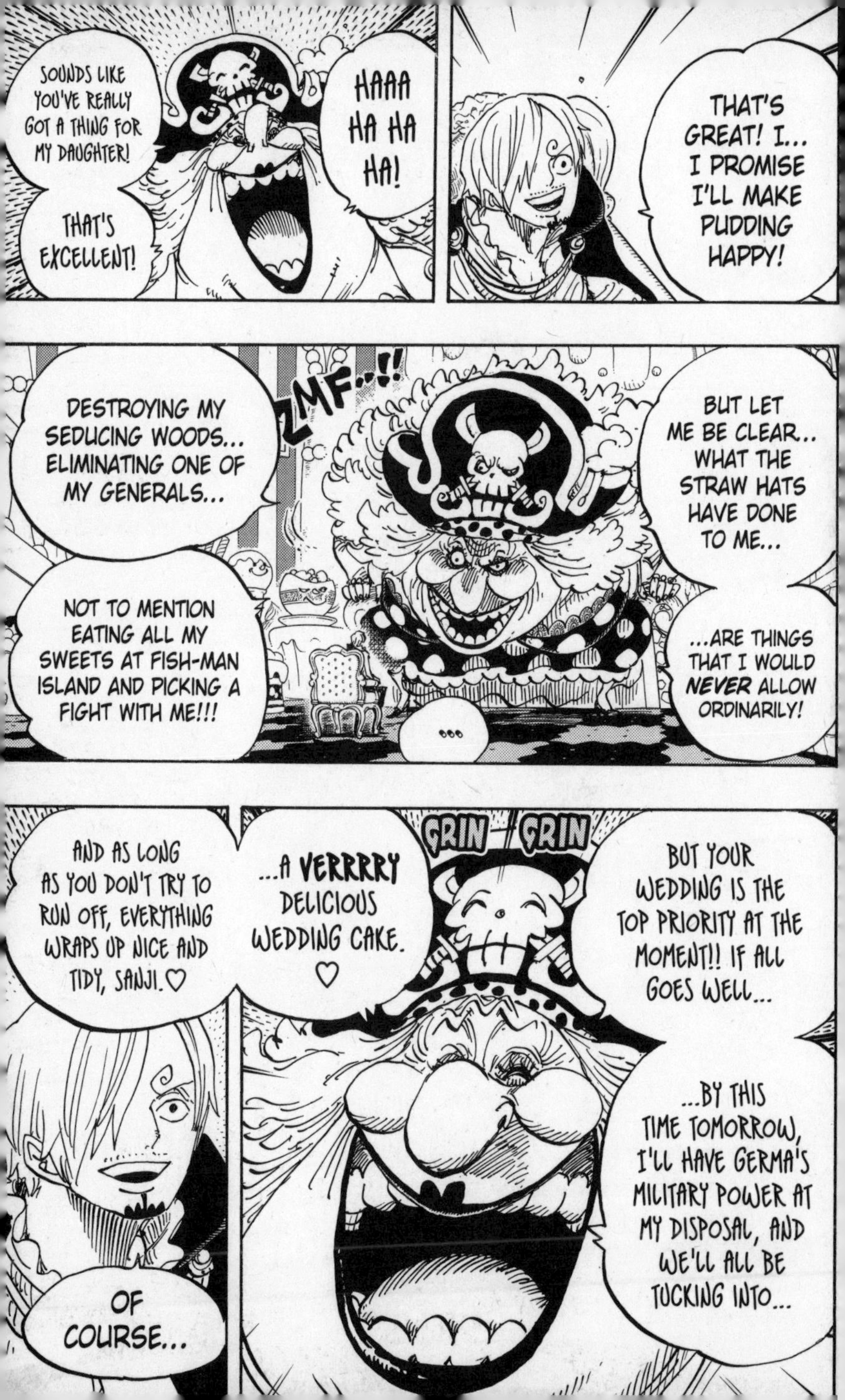
THAT'S GREAT! I... I PROMISE I'LL MAKE PUDDING HAPPY!
HAAA HA HA HA!
SOUNDS LIKE YOU'VE REALLY GOT A THING FOR MY DAUGHTER!
THAT'S EXCELLENT!
BUT LET ME BE CLEAR... WHAT THE STRAW HATS HAVE DONE TO ME...
ZMF..!!
DESTROYING MY SEDUCING WOODS... ELIMINATING ONE OF MY GENERALS...
NOT TO MENTION EATING ALL MY SWEETS AT FISH-MAN ISLAND AND PICKING A FIGHT WITH ME!!!
...ARE THINGS THAT I WOULD NEVER ALLOW ORDINARILY!
...
GRIN GRIN
BUT YOUR WEDDING IS THE TOP PRIORITY AT THE MOMENT!! IF ALL GOES WELL...
...BY THIS TIME TOMORROW, I'LL HAVE GERMA'S MILITARY POWER AT MY DISPOSAL, AND WE'LL ALL BE TUCKING INTO...
...A VERRRRY DELICIOUS WEDDING CAKE. ♡
AND AS LONG AS YOU DON'T TRY TO RUN OFF, EVERYTHING WRAPS UP NICE AND TIDY, SANJI. ♡
OF COURSE...

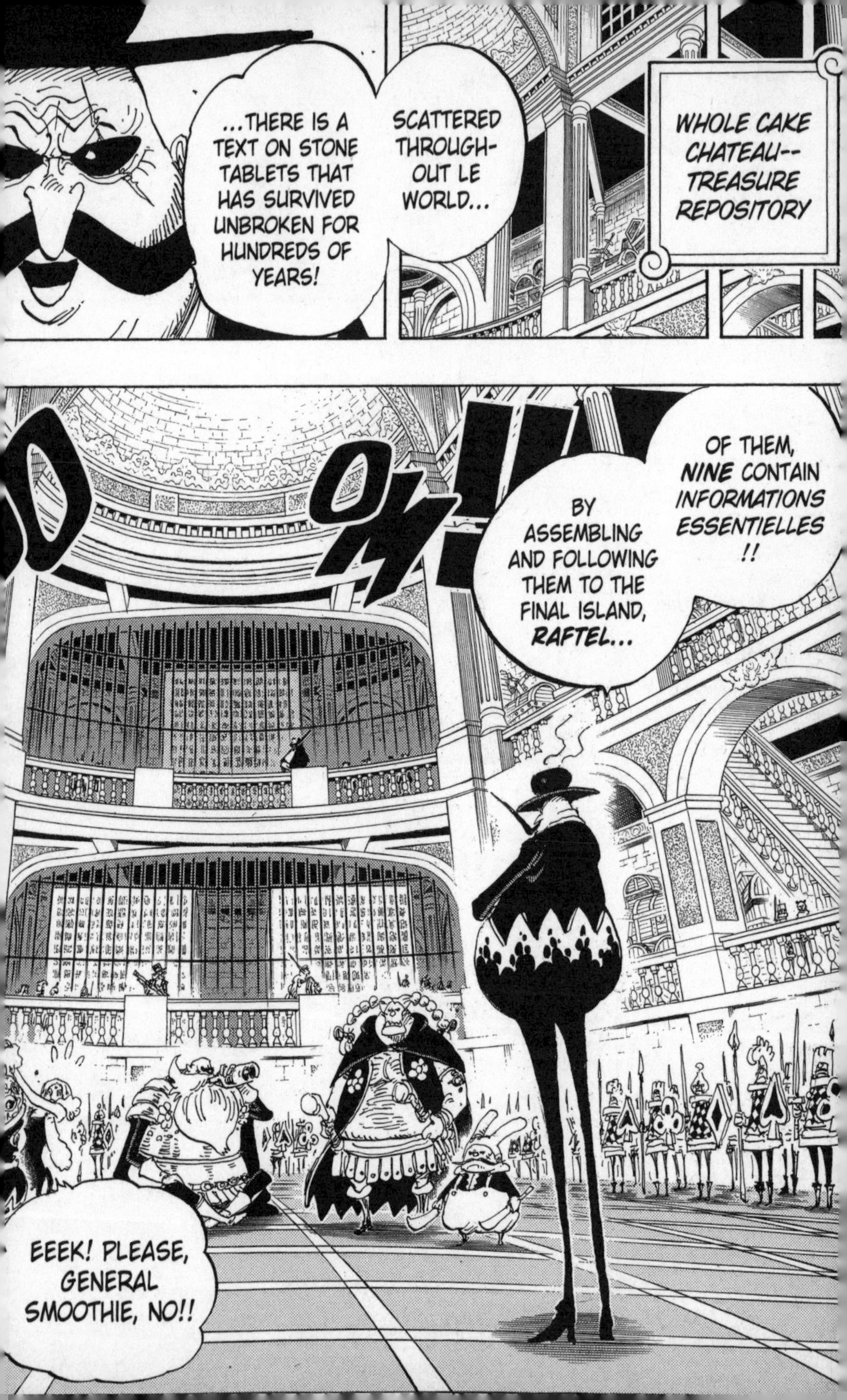
WHOLE CAKE CHATEAU-- TREASURE REPOSITORY
SCATTERED THROUGH-OUT LE WORLD...
...THERE IS A TEXT ON STONE TABLETS THAT HAS SURVIVED UNBROKEN FOR HUNDREDS OF YEARS!
OF THEM, NINE CONTAIN INFORMATIONS ESSENTIELLES !!
BY ASSEMBLING AND FOLLOWING THEM TO THE FINAL ISLAND, RAFTEL...
EEEK! PLEASE, GENERAL SMOOTHIE, NO!!

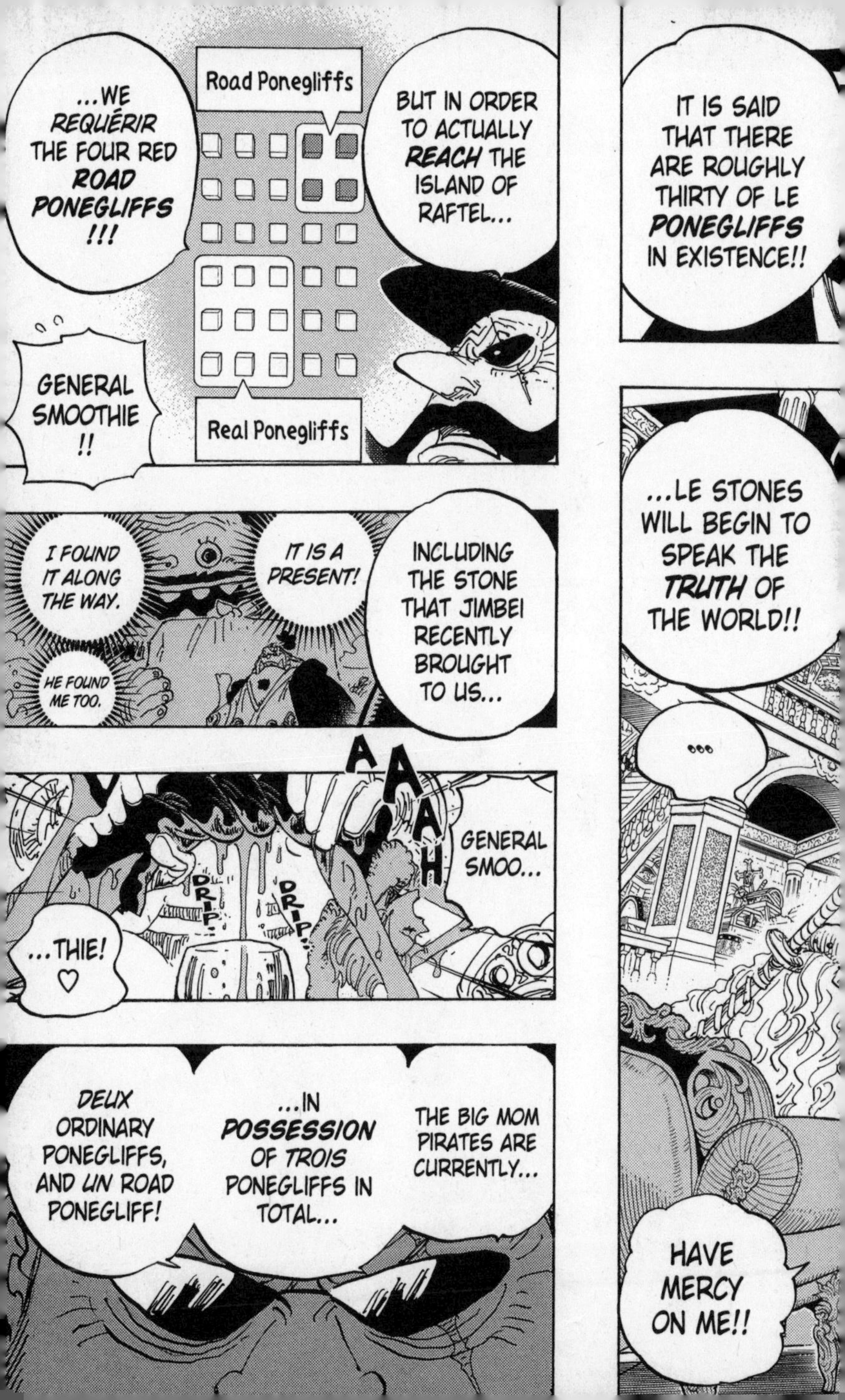
IT IS SAID THAT THERE ARE ROUGHLY THIRTY OF LE PONEGLIFFS IN EXISTENCE!!
...LE STONES WILL BEGIN TO SPEAK THE TRUTH OF THE WORLD!!
...
HAVE MERCY ON ME!!
BUT IN ORDER TO ACTUALLY REACH THE ISLAND OF RAFTEL...
Road Ponegliffs
Real Ponegliffs
...WE REQUÉRIR THE FOUR RED ROAD PONEGLIFFS!!!
GENERAL SMOOTHIE!!
INCLUDING THE STONE THAT JIMBEI RECENTLY BROUGHT TO US...
IT IS A PRESENT!
I FOUND IT ALONG THE WAY.
HE FOUND ME TOO.
AAAH
GENERAL SMOO...
DRIP
DRIP
...THIE! ♡
THE BIG MOM PIRATES ARE CURRENTLY...
...IN POSSESSION OF TROIS PONEGLIFFS IN TOTAL...
DEUX ORDINARY PONEGLIFFS, AND UN ROAD PONEGLIFF!

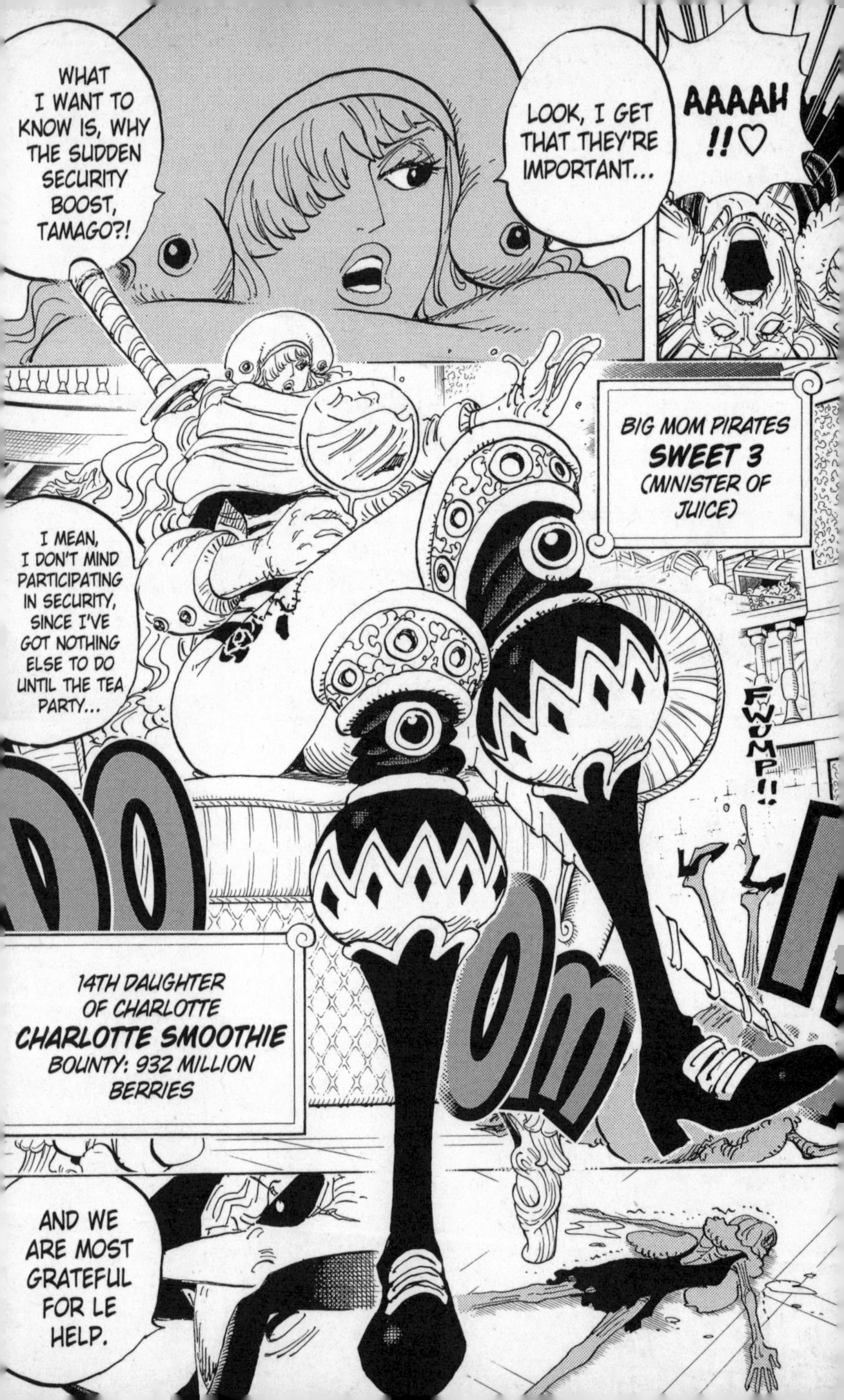
AAAAH!!♡
LOOK, I GET THAT THEY'RE IMPORTANT...
WHAT I WANT TO KNOW IS, WHY THE SUDDEN SECURITY BOOST, TAMAGO?!
BIG MOM PIRATES SWEET 3 (MINISTER OF JUICE)
FWUMP!!
I MEAN, I DON'T MIND PARTICIPATING IN SECURITY, SINCE I'VE GOT NOTHING ELSE TO DO UNTIL THE TEA PARTY...
14TH DAUGHTER OF CHARLOTTE CHARLOTTE SMOOTHIE BOUNTY: 932 MILLION BERRIES
AND WE ARE MOST GRATEFUL FOR LE HELP.

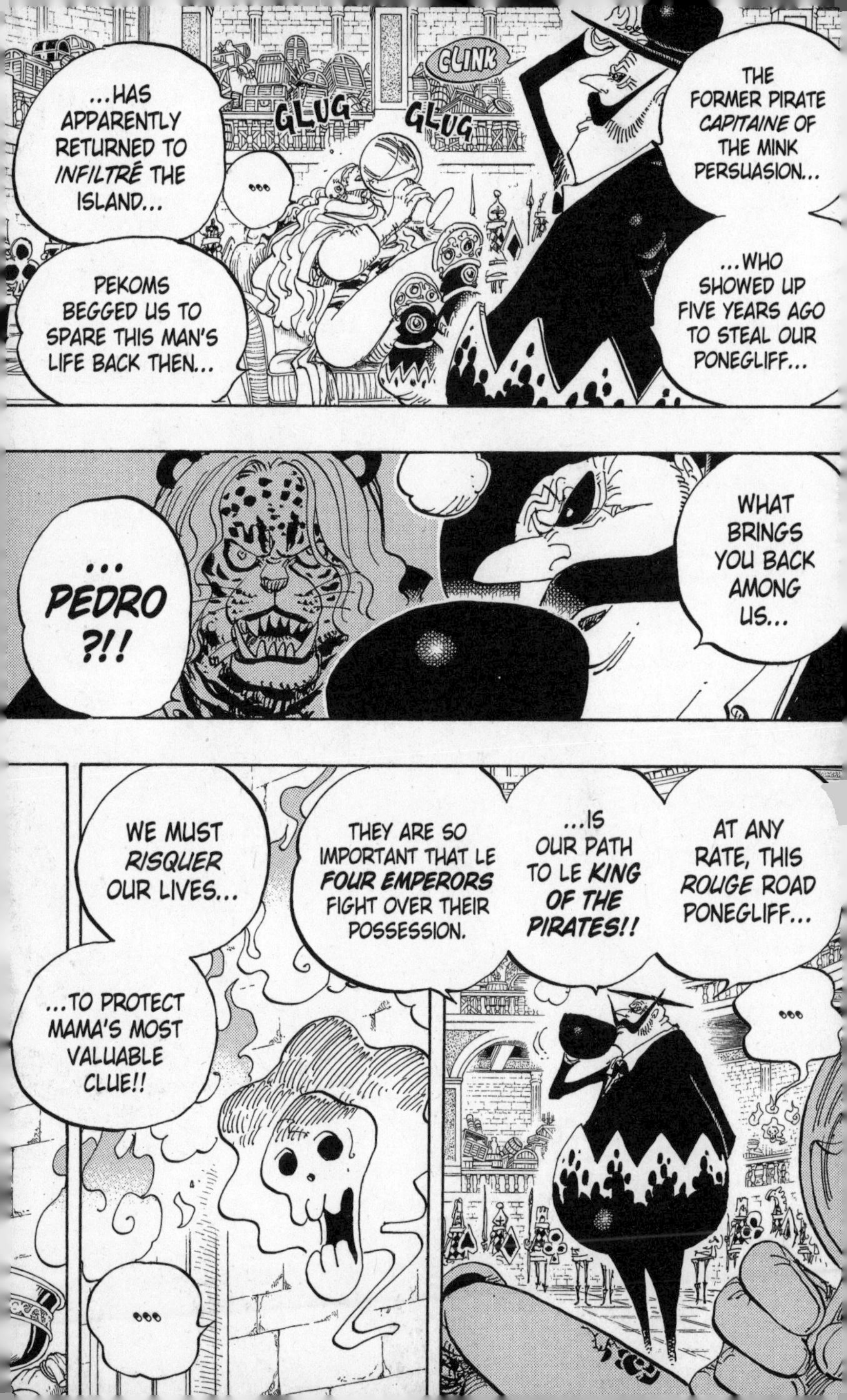
THE FORMER PIRATE CAPITAINE OF THE MINK PERSUASION...
...WHO SHOWED UP FIVE YEARS AGO TO STEAL OUR PONEGLIFF...
CLINK
GLUG GLUG
...
...HAS APPARENTLY RETURNED TO INFILTRÉ THE ISLAND...
PEKOMS BEGGED US TO SPARE THIS MAN'S LIFE BACK THEN...
WHAT BRINGS YOU BACK AMONG US...
... PEDRO ?!!
AT ANY RATE, THIS ROUGE ROAD PONEGLIFF...
...IS OUR PATH TO LE KING OF THE PIRATES!!
THEY ARE SO IMPORTANT THAT LE FOUR EMPERORS FIGHT OVER THEIR POSSESSION.
...
WE MUST RISQUER OUR LIVES...
...TO PROTECT MAMA'S MOST VALUABLE CLUE!!
...

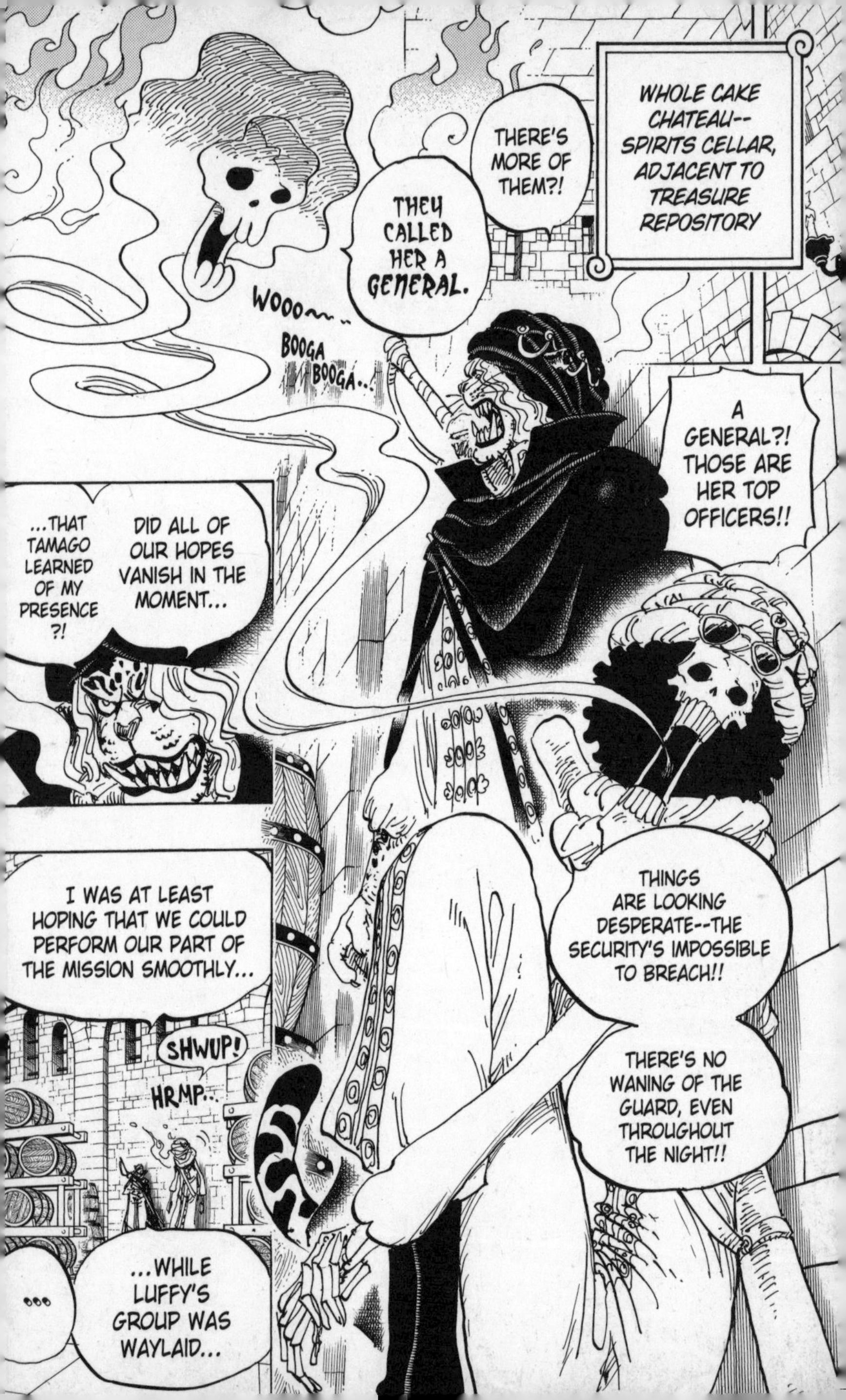
WHOLE CAKE CHATEAU-- SPIRITS CELLAR, ADJACENT TO TREASURE REPOSITORY
THERE'S MORE OF THEM?!
THEY CALLED HER A GENERAL.
WOOO~~
BOOGA BOOGA..!
A GENERAL?! THOSE ARE HER TOP OFFICERS!!
THINGS ARE LOOKING DESPERATE--THE SECURITY'S IMPOSSIBLE TO BREACH!!
THERE'S NO WANING OF THE GUARD, EVEN THROUGHOUT THE NIGHT!!
DID ALL OF OUR HOPES VANISH IN THE MOMENT...
...THAT TAMAGO LEARNED OF MY PRESENCE?!
I WAS AT LEAST HOPING THAT WE COULD PERFORM OUR PART OF THE MISSION SMOOTHLY...
SHWUP!
HRMP..
...WHILE LUFFY'S GROUP WAS WAYLAID...
...

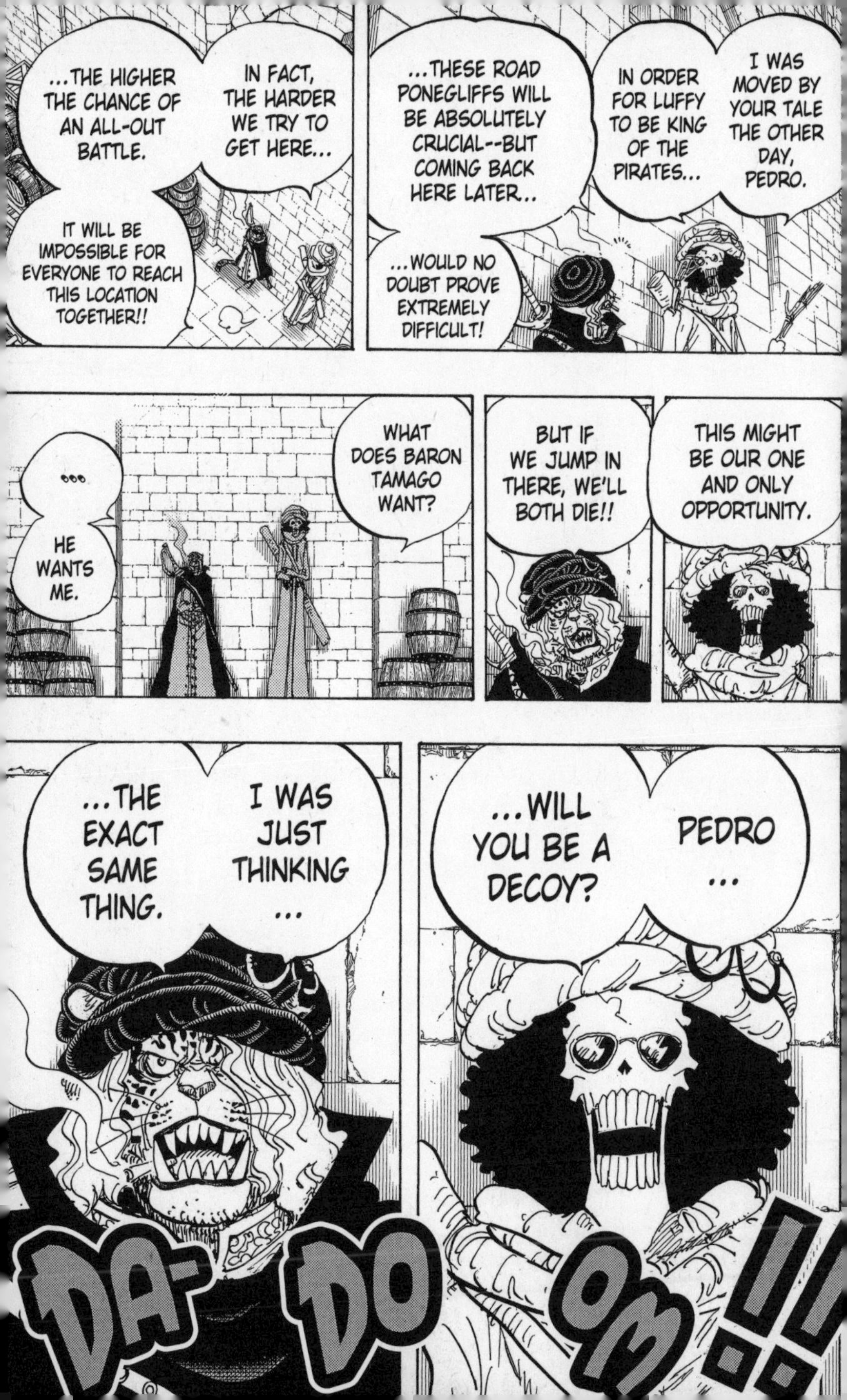
I WAS MOVED BY YOUR TALE THE OTHER DAY, PEDRO.
IN ORDER FOR LUFFY TO BE KING OF THE PIRATES...
...THESE ROAD PONEGLIFFS WILL BE ABSOLUTELY CRUCIAL--BUT COMING BACK HERE LATER...
...WOULD NO DOUBT PROVE EXTREMELY DIFFICULT!
IN FACT, THE HARDER WE TRY TO GET HERE...
...THE HIGHER THE CHANCE OF AN ALL-OUT BATTLE.
IT WILL BE IMPOSSIBLE FOR EVERYONE TO REACH THIS LOCATION TOGETHER!!
THIS MIGHT BE OUR ONE AND ONLY OPPORTUNITY.
BUT IF WE JUMP IN THERE, WE'LL BOTH DIE!!
WHAT DOES BARON TAMAGO WANT?
...
HE WANTS ME.
PEDRO ...
...WILL YOU BE A DECOY?
I WAS JUST THINKING ...
...THE EXACT SAME THING.
DA-DO-OM!!

SBS Question Corner

SBS

(Takahisa Fujimoto, Nara)

Q: Oda Sensei!! Please tell me which people in the Straw Hats like to chew their ice, and which don't.

--Goal and Gorilla Pupil No.19 Iona

A: Oh yeah, here we go. The really pointless questions! And I'm gonna answer it! Because the motto of the SBS is "You're not missing out if you don't read it"!!

Ice-Crunchers
Non-Crunchers

More people crunch their ice than I expected...

Q: Since in chapter 833, you said all four kids were born on the same day, does that mean that Ichiji, Niji, and Yonji are all 21 years old, born on March 2? How old is Reiju? Also, tell me the blood types and heights of the other Vinsmoke siblings.

--Katana★Roman

A: Okay. They're identical quadruplets. Reiju was born three years earlier, so she's 24 now. They're each slightly different in build, although it's not striking in number form. I wonder why Sanji turned out so different? It must have something to do with Germa's science.

F
5'8"
S-
6'1"
S-
6'
S-
5'11"
S-
6'4"

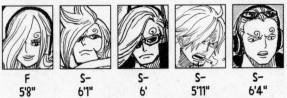

And that's the end of our time! See you in next volume's SBS!!

Chapter 847:
LUFFY AND
BIG MOM

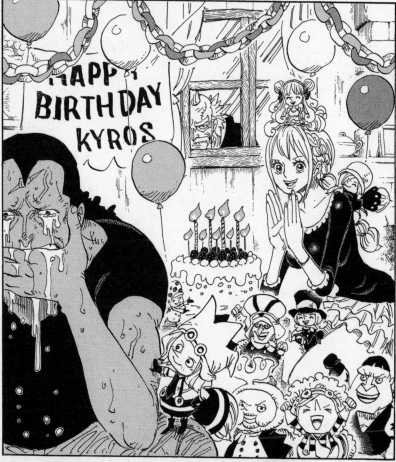

REQUEST: "REBECCA AND THE TONTATTAS CELEBRATING
KYROS'S BIRTHDAY" BY DAJI FROM TOCHIGI

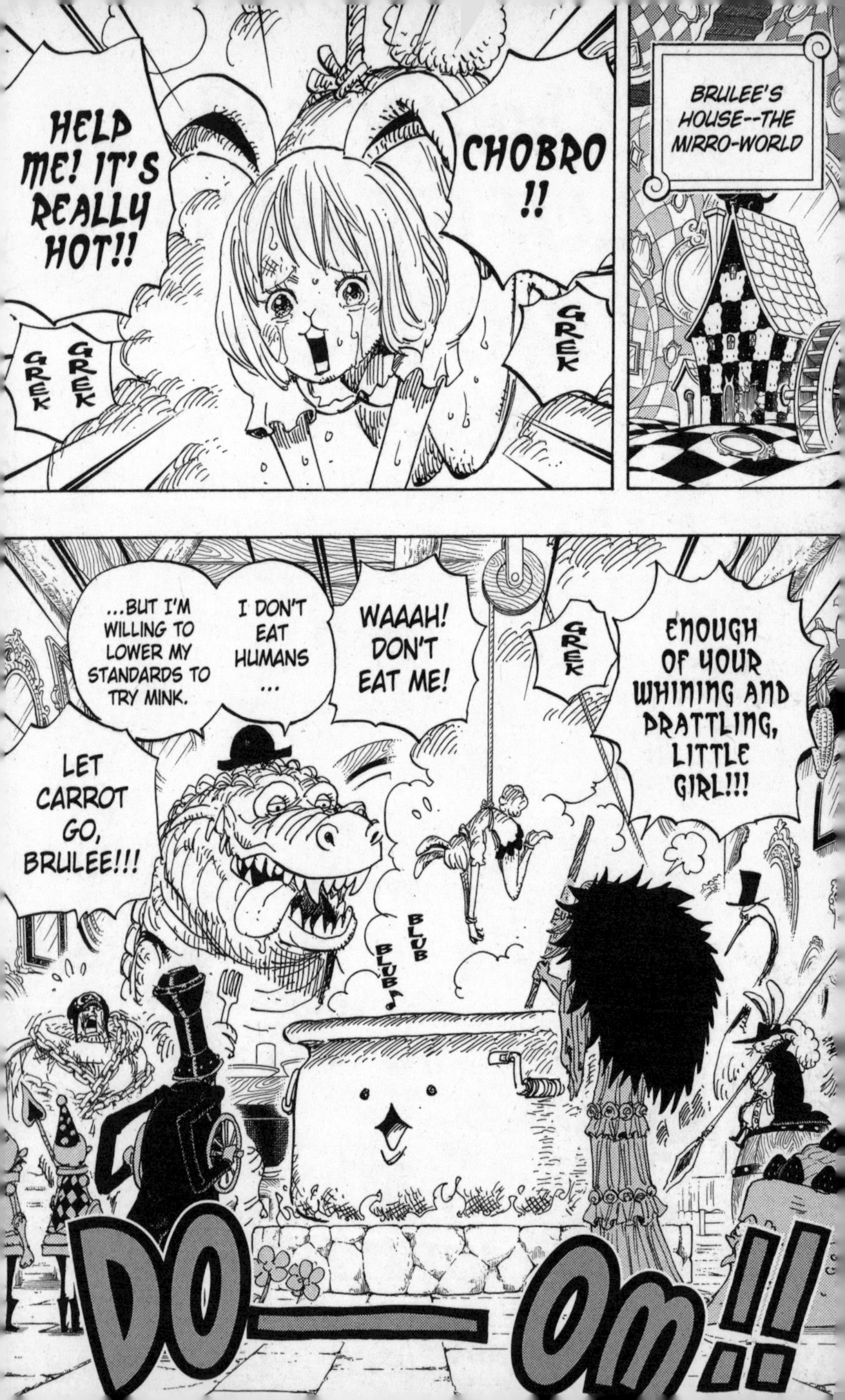
BRULEE'S HOUSE--THE MIRRO-WORLD
CHOBRO!!
HELP ME! IT'S REALLY HOT!!
GREK
GREK GREK
ENOUGH OF YOUR WHINING AND PRATTLING, LITTLE GIRL!!!
GREK
WAAAH! DON'T EAT ME!
I DON'T EAT HUMANS...
...BUT I'M WILLING TO LOWER MY STANDARDS TO TRY MINK.
LET CARROT GO, BRULEE!!!
BLUB BLUB
DO—OM!!

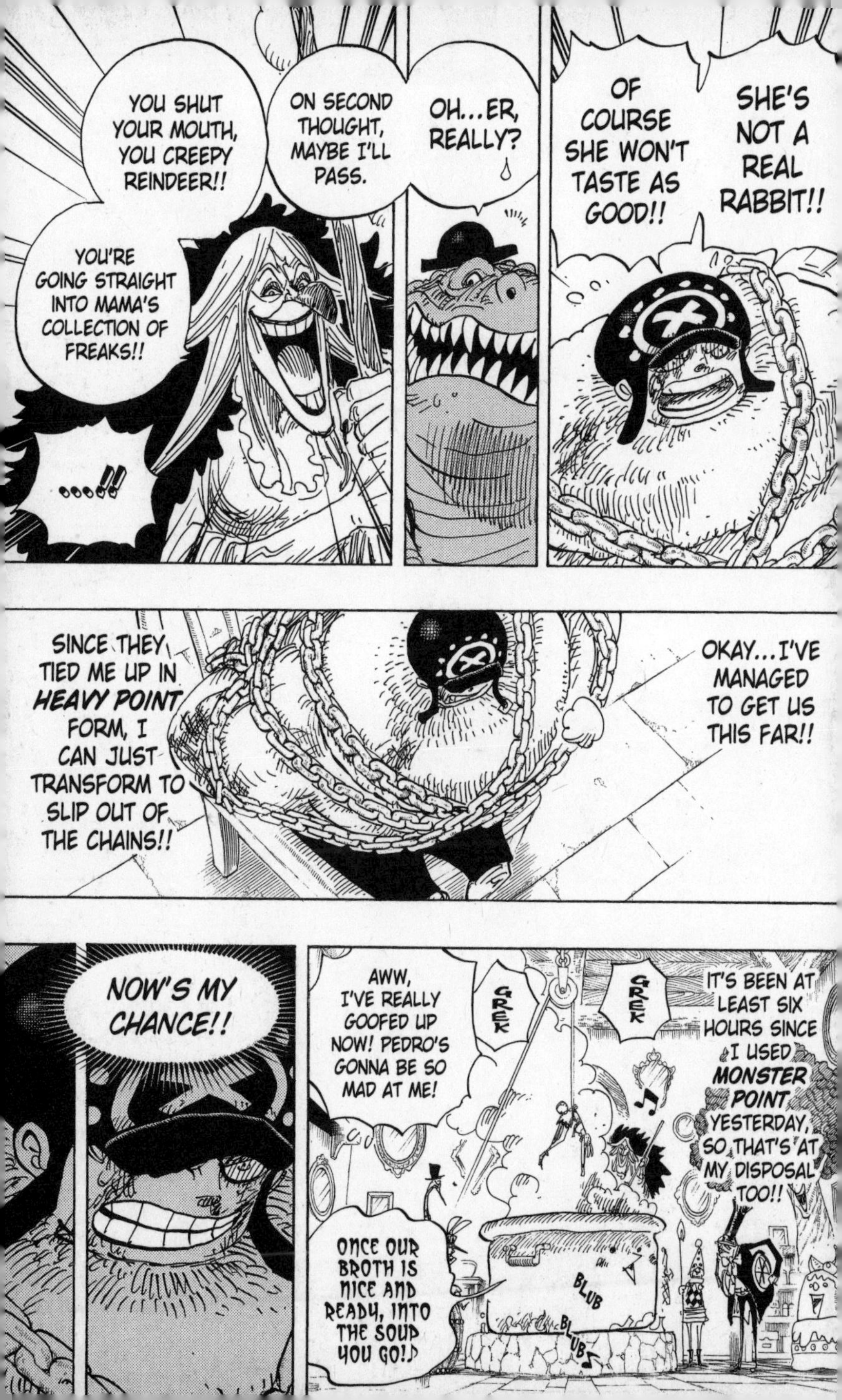

SHE'S NOT A REAL RABBIT!!
OF COURSE SHE WON'T TASTE AS GOOD!!
OH...ER, REALLY?
ON SECOND THOUGHT, MAYBE I'LL PASS.
YOU SHUT YOUR MOUTH, YOU CREEPY REINDEER!!
YOU'RE GOING STRAIGHT INTO MAMA'S COLLECTION OF FREAKS!!
.....!!
OKAY...I'VE MANAGED TO GET US THIS FAR!!
SINCE THEY TIED ME UP IN ***HEAVY POINT*** FORM, I CAN JUST TRANSFORM TO SLIP OUT OF THE CHAINS!!
IT'S BEEN AT LEAST SIX HOURS SINCE I USED ***MONSTER POINT*** YESTERDAY, SO THAT'S AT MY DISPOSAL TOO!!
GREK
GREK
AWW, I'VE REALLY GOOFED UP NOW! PEDRO'S GONNA BE SO MAD AT ME!
ONCE OUR BROTH IS NICE AND READY, INTO THE SOUP YOU GO!♪
BLUB
BLUB
NOW'S MY CHANCE!!

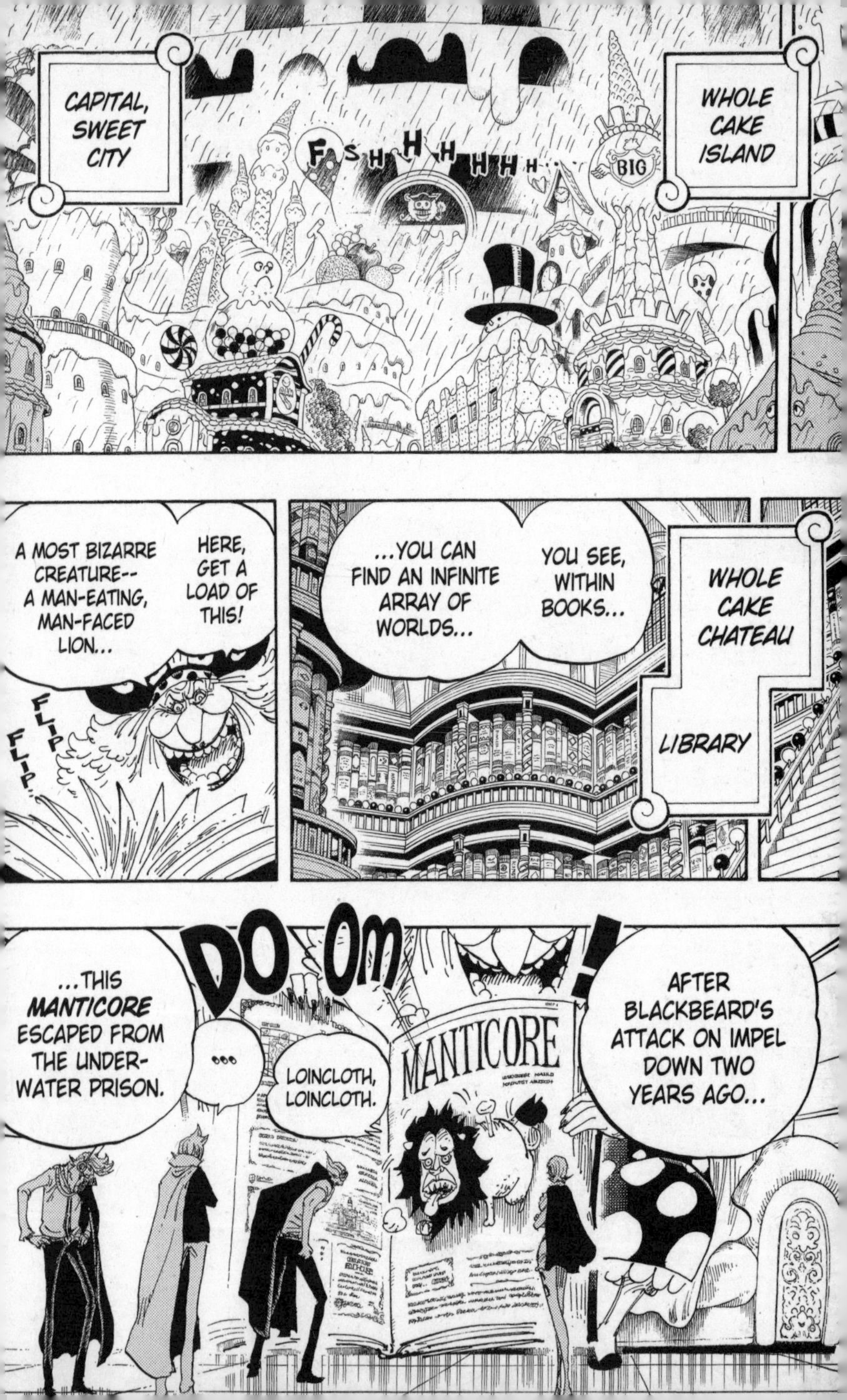
WHOLE CAKE ISLAND
CAPITAL, SWEET CITY
FSHHHHHH...
WHOLE CAKE CHATEAU
LIBRARY
YOU SEE, WITHIN BOOKS...
...YOU CAN FIND AN INFINITE ARRAY OF WORLDS...
HERE, GET A LOAD OF THIS!
A MOST BIZARRE CREATURE-- A MAN-EATING, MAN-FACED LION...
FLIP FLIP...
AFTER BLACKBEARD'S ATTACK ON IMPEL DOWN TWO YEARS AGO...
DOOOM!
MANTICORE
LOINCLOTH, LOINCLOTH.
...
...THIS MANTICORE ESCAPED FROM THE UNDER-WATER PRISON.

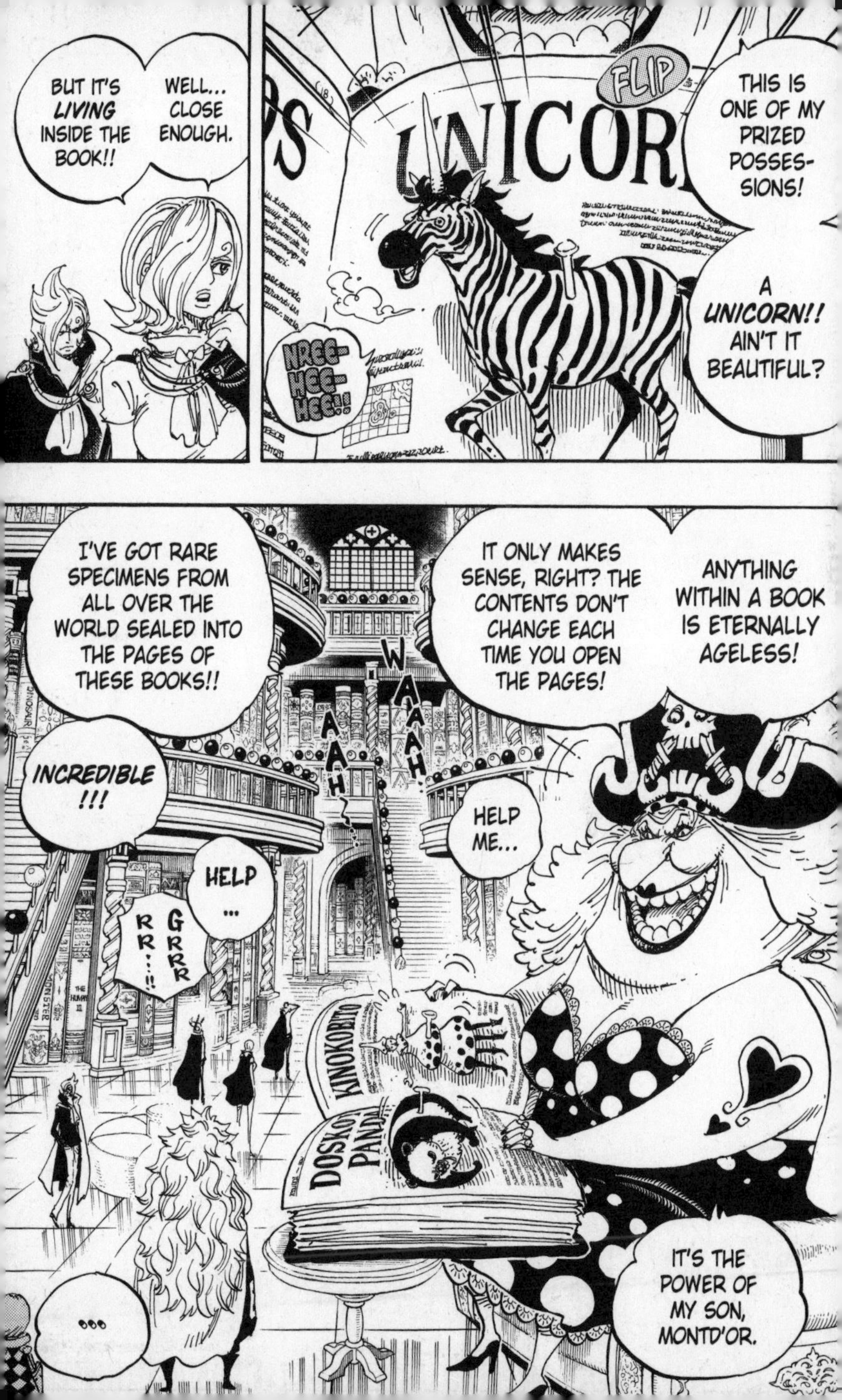
FLIP
UNICOR
THIS IS ONE OF MY PRIZED POSSES-SIONS!
A UNICORN!! AIN'T IT BEAUTIFUL?
NREE-HEE-HEE!!
WELL... CLOSE ENOUGH.
BUT IT'S LIVING INSIDE THE BOOK!!
ANYTHING WITHIN A BOOK IS ETERNALLY AGELESS!
IT ONLY MAKES SENSE, RIGHT? THE CONTENTS DON'T CHANGE EACH TIME YOU OPEN THE PAGES!
I'VE GOT RARE SPECIMENS FROM ALL OVER THE WORLD SEALED INTO THE PAGES OF THESE BOOKS!!
WAAAAH...
AAH...
HELP ME...
INCREDIBLE!!!
HELP...
GRRRRR...!!
KINOKOBITO
DOSKOI PANDA
IT'S THE POWER OF MY SON, MONTD'OR.
...

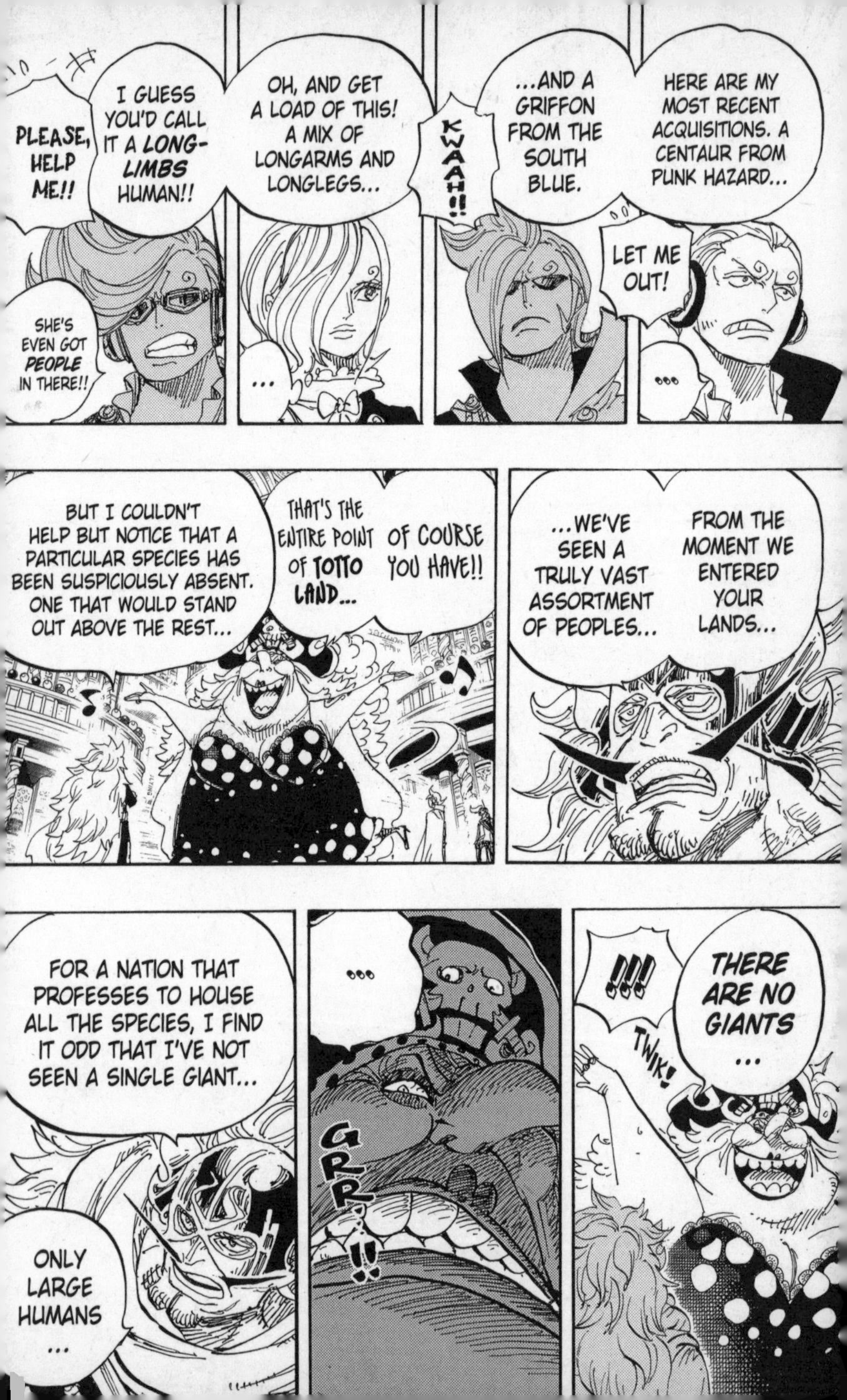
HERE ARE MY MOST RECENT ACQUISITIONS. A CENTAUR FROM PUNK HAZARD...
LET ME OUT!
...
...AND A GRIFFON FROM THE SOUTH BLUE.
KWAAH!!
OH, AND GET A LOAD OF THIS! A MIX OF LONGARMS AND LONGLEGS...
...
I GUESS YOU'D CALL IT A LONG-LIMBS HUMAN!!
PLEASE, HELP ME!!
SHE'S EVEN GOT PEOPLE IN THERE!!
FROM THE MOMENT WE ENTERED YOUR LANDS...
...WE'VE SEEN A TRULY VAST ASSORTMENT OF PEOPLES...
OF COURSE YOU HAVE!!
THAT'S THE ENTIRE POINT OF TOTTO LAND...
BUT I COULDN'T HELP BUT NOTICE THAT A PARTICULAR SPECIES HAS BEEN SUSPICIOUSLY ABSENT. ONE THAT WOULD STAND OUT ABOVE THE REST...
THERE ARE NO GIANTS...
!!!
TWIK!
...
GRR..!!
FOR A NATION THAT PROFESSES TO HOUSE ALL THE SPECIES, I FIND IT ODD THAT I'VE NOT SEEN A SINGLE GIANT...
ONLY LARGE HUMANS...

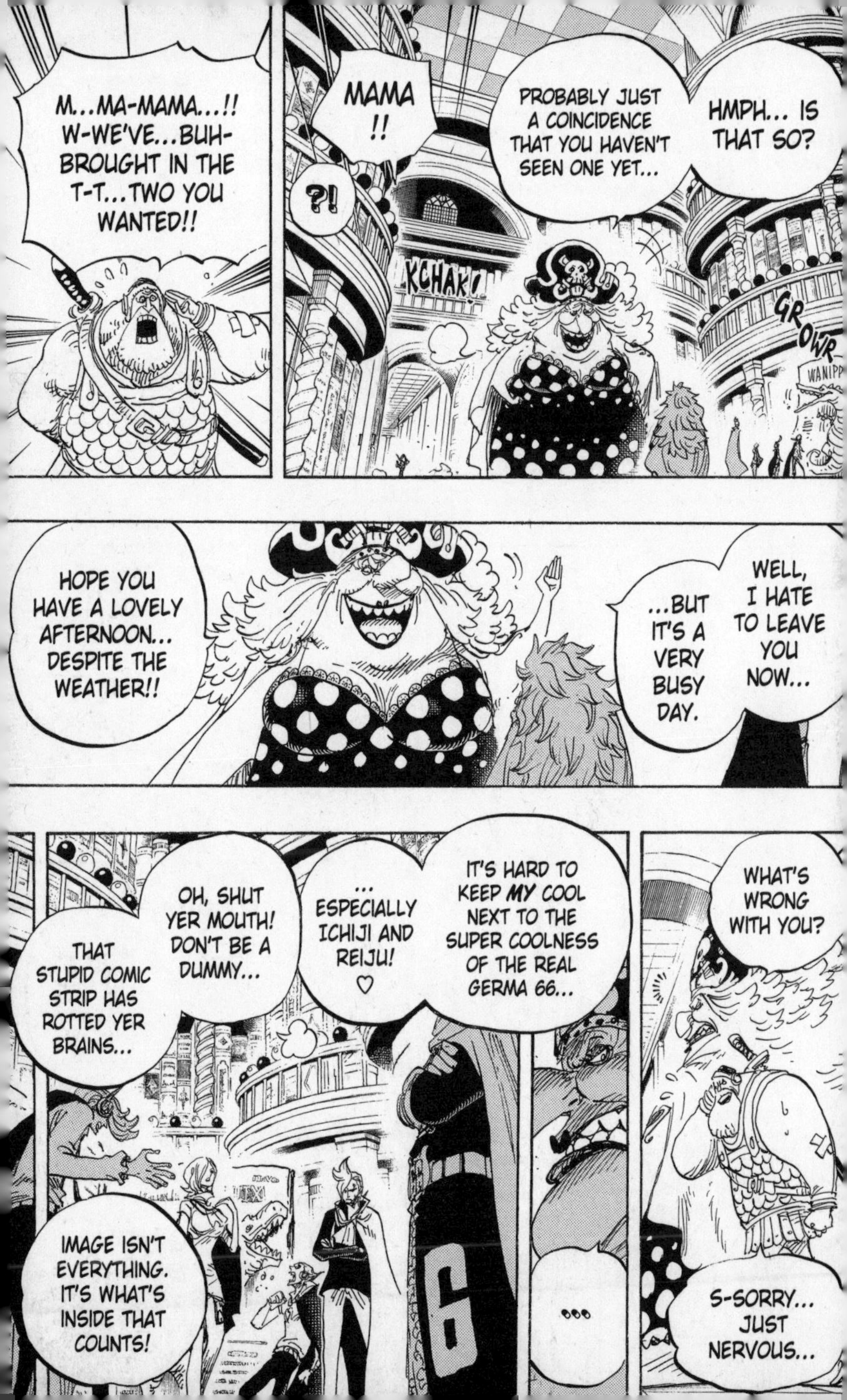
HMPH... IS THAT SO?
PROBABLY JUST A COINCIDENCE THAT YOU HAVEN'T SEEN ONE YET...
MAMA !!
?!
KCHAK!
GROWR
WANIPP
M...MA-MAMA...!! W-WE'VE...BUH-BROUGHT IN THE T-T...TWO YOU WANTED!!
WELL, I HATE TO LEAVE YOU NOW...
...BUT IT'S A VERY BUSY DAY.
HOPE YOU HAVE A LOVELY AFTERNOON... DESPITE THE WEATHER!!
WHAT'S WRONG WITH YOU?
S-SORRY... JUST NERVOUS...
IT'S HARD TO KEEP *MY* COOL NEXT TO THE SUPER COOLNESS OF THE REAL GERMA 66...
... ESPECIALLY ICHIJI AND REIJU! ♡
OH, SHUT YER MOUTH! DON'T BE A DUMMY...
THAT STUPID COMIC STRIP HAS ROTTED YER BRAINS...
...
IMAGE ISN'T EVERYTHING. IT'S WHAT'S INSIDE THAT COUNTS!

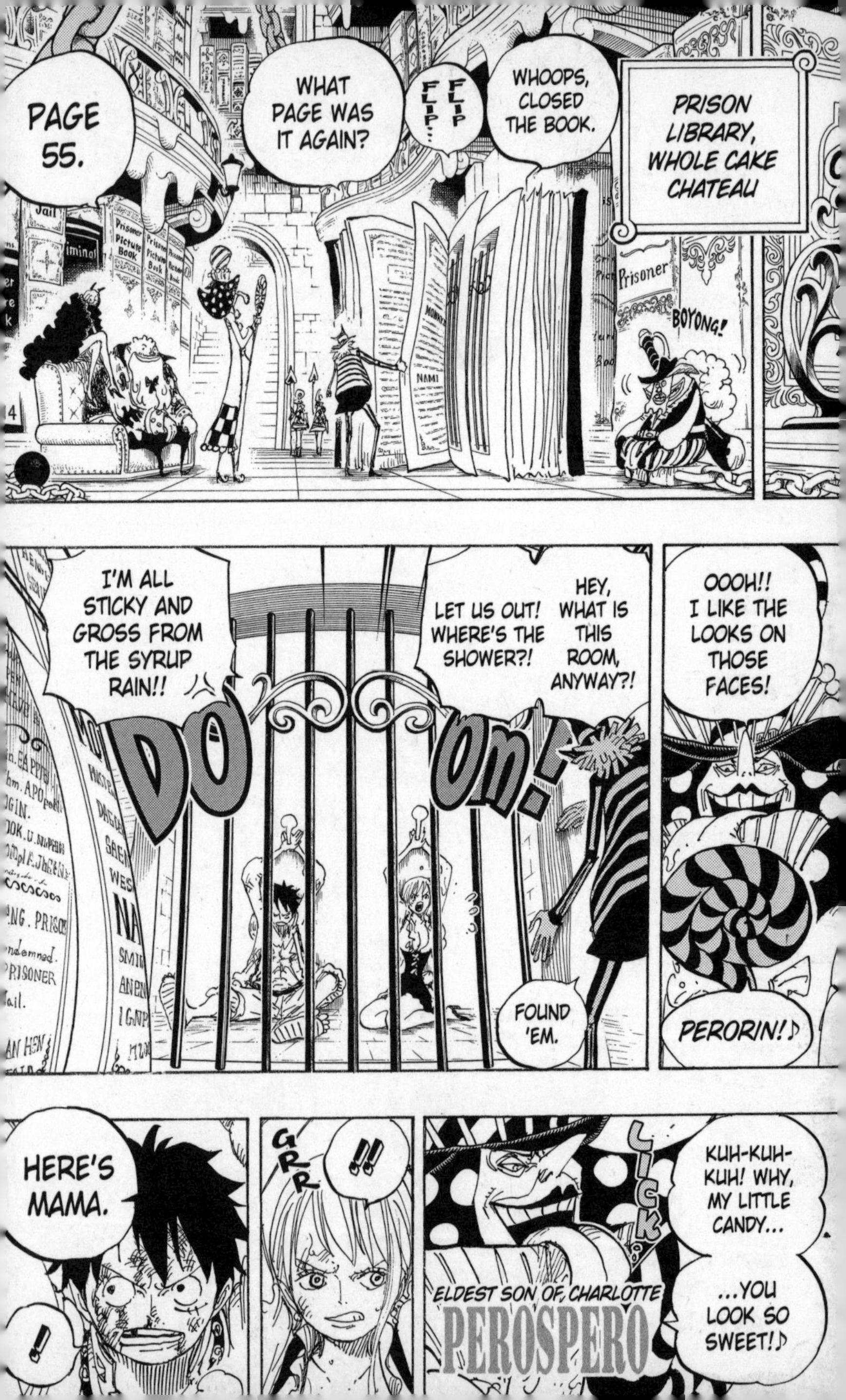
PRISON LIBRARY, WHOLE CAKE CHATEAU
WHOOPS, CLOSED THE BOOK.
FLIP FLIP...
WHAT PAGE WAS IT AGAIN?
PAGE 55.
BOYONG!
OOOH!! I LIKE THE LOOKS ON THOSE FACES!
PERORIN!♪
HEY, WHAT IS THIS ROOM, ANYWAY?!
LET US OUT! WHERE'S THE SHOWER?!
I'M ALL STICKY AND GROSS FROM THE SYRUP RAIN!!
DOOM!
FOUND 'EM.
LICK
KUH-KUH-KUH! WHY, MY LITTLE CANDY...
...YOU LOOK SO SWEET!♪
ELDEST SON OF CHARLOTTE
PEROSPERO
GRR
!!
HERE'S MAMA.
!

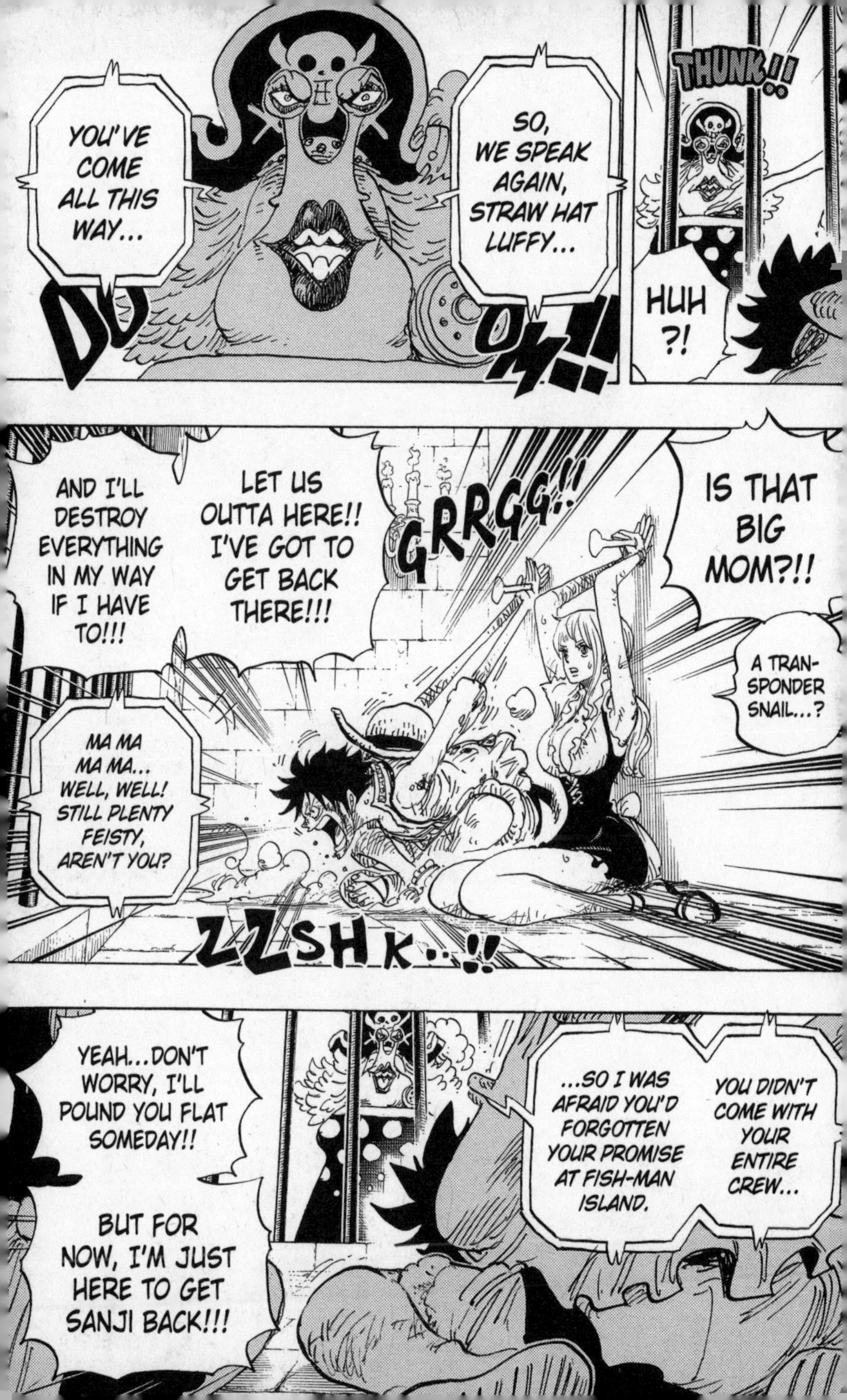
THUNK!!
HUH?!
SO, WE SPEAK AGAIN, STRAW HAT LUFFY...
YOU'VE COME ALL THIS WAY...
DO
OM!!
IS THAT BIG MOM?!!
GRRGG!!
LET US OUTTA HERE!! I'VE GOT TO GET BACK THERE!!!
AND I'LL DESTROY EVERYTHING IN MY WAY IF I HAVE TO!!!
A TRAN-SPONDER SNAIL...?
MA MA MA MA... WELL, WELL! STILL PLENTY FEISTY, AREN'T YOU?
ZZSHK..!!
YOU DIDN'T COME WITH YOUR ENTIRE CREW...
...SO I WAS AFRAID YOU'D FORGOTTEN YOUR PROMISE AT FISH-MAN ISLAND.
YEAH...DON'T WORRY, I'LL POUND YOU FLAT SOMEDAY!!
BUT FOR NOW, I'M JUST HERE TO GET SANJI BACK!!!

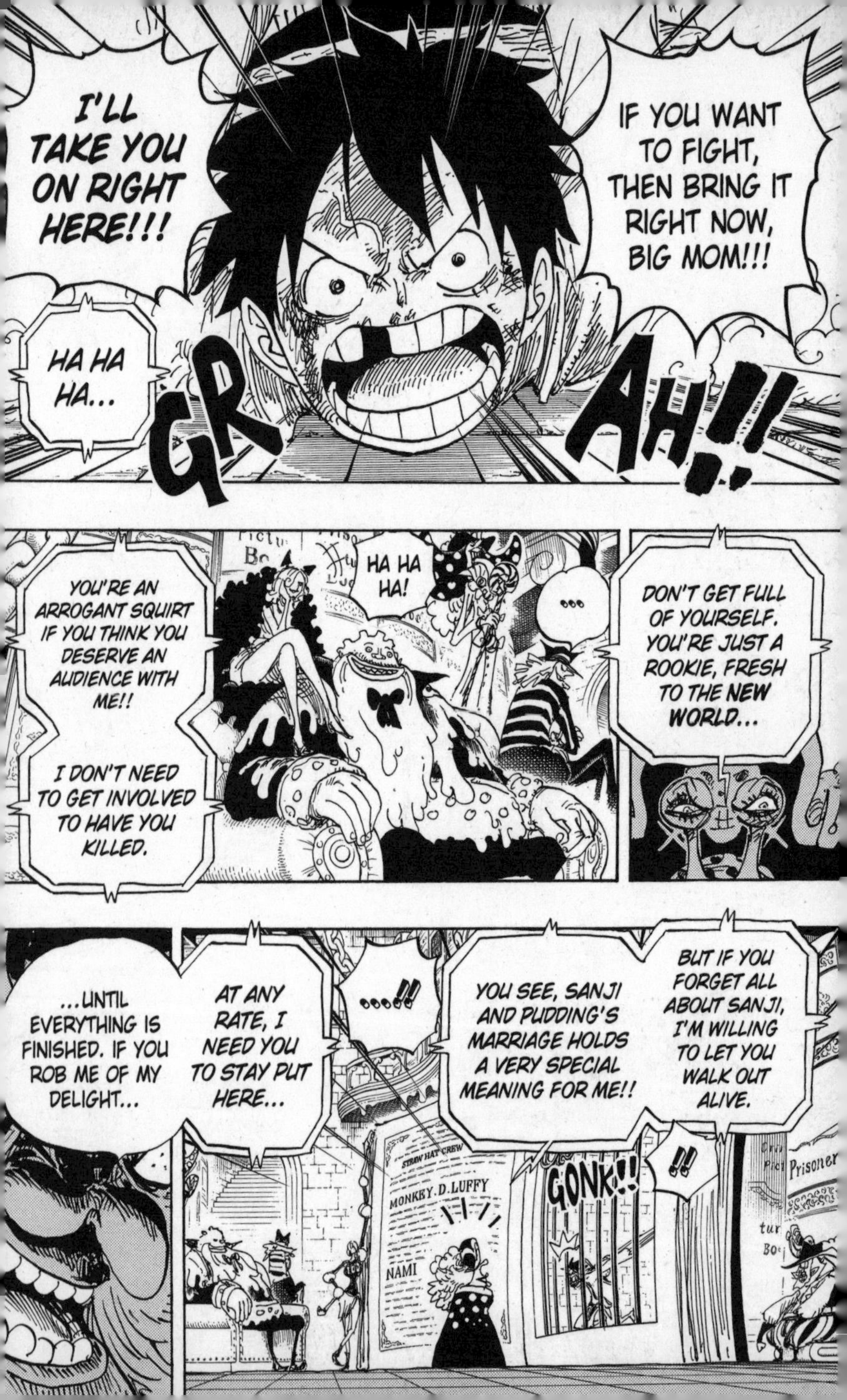
IF YOU WANT TO FIGHT, THEN BRING IT RIGHT NOW, BIG MOM!!!
I'LL TAKE YOU ON RIGHT HERE!!!
GRAH!!
HA HA HA...
DON'T GET FULL OF YOURSELF. YOU'RE JUST A ROOKIE, FRESH TO THE NEW WORLD...
...
HA HA HA!
YOU'RE AN ARROGANT SQUIRT IF YOU THINK YOU DESERVE AN AUDIENCE WITH ME!!
I DON'T NEED TO GET INVOLVED TO HAVE YOU KILLED.
BUT IF YOU FORGET ALL ABOUT SANJI, I'M WILLING TO LET YOU WALK OUT ALIVE.
Prisoner
!!
GONK!!
YOU SEE, SANJI AND PUDDING'S MARRIAGE HOLDS A VERY SPECIAL MEANING FOR ME!!
STRAW HAT CREW
MONKEY.D.LUFFY
NAMI
...!!
AT ANY RATE, I NEED YOU TO STAY PUT HERE...
...UNTIL EVERYTHING IS FINISHED. IF YOU ROB ME OF MY DELIGHT...

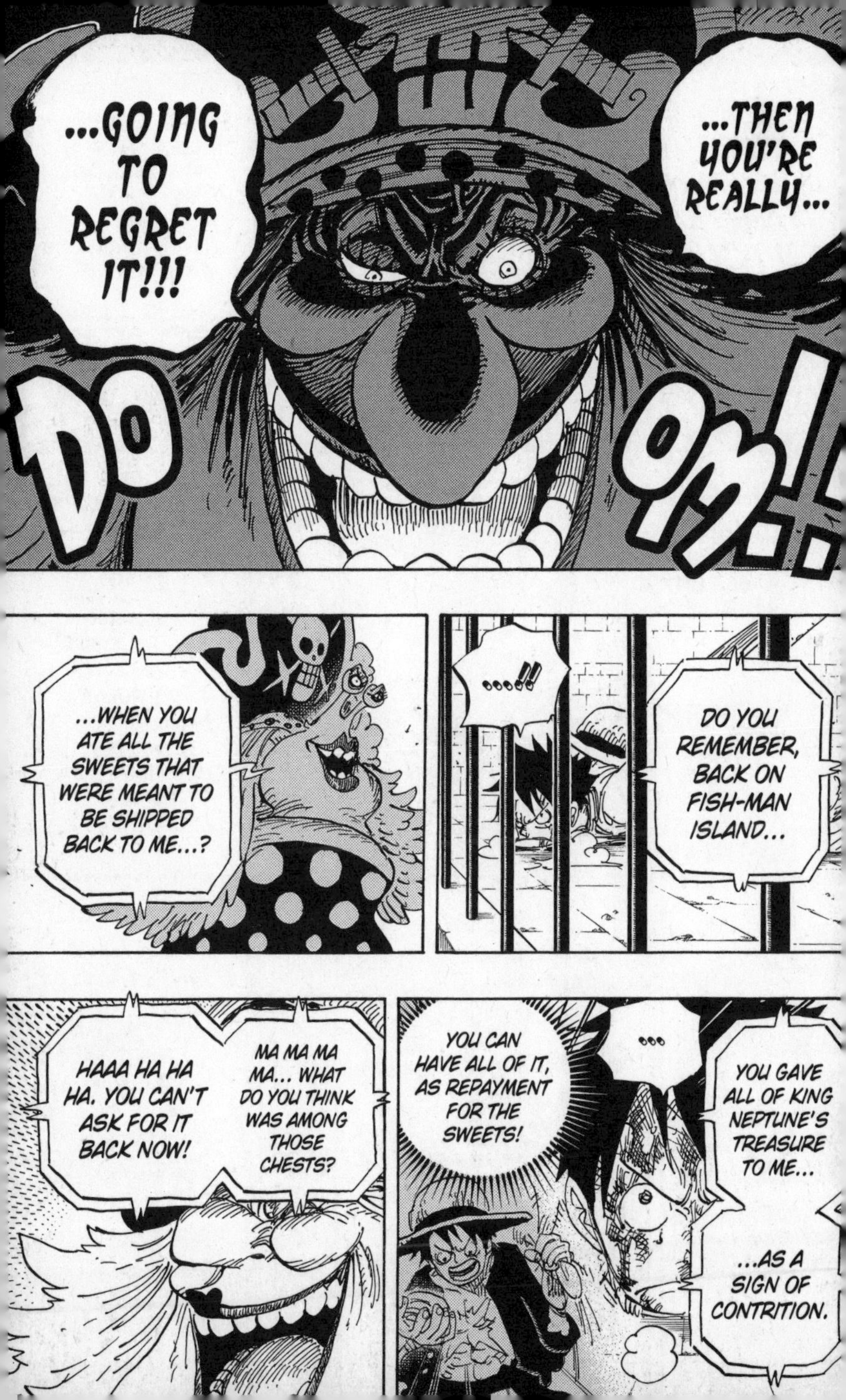
...THEN YOU'RE REALLY...
...GOING TO REGRET IT!!!
DOOM!!
DO YOU REMEMBER, BACK ON FISH-MAN ISLAND...
....!!
...WHEN YOU ATE ALL THE SWEETS THAT WERE MEANT TO BE SHIPPED BACK TO ME...?
YOU GAVE ALL OF KING NEPTUNE'S TREASURE TO ME...
...AS A SIGN OF CONTRITION.
...
YOU CAN HAVE ALL OF IT, AS REPAYMENT FOR THE SWEETS!
MA MA MA MA... WHAT DO YOU THINK WAS AMONG THOSE CHESTS?
HAAAA HA HA HA. YOU CAN'T ASK FOR IT BACK NOW!

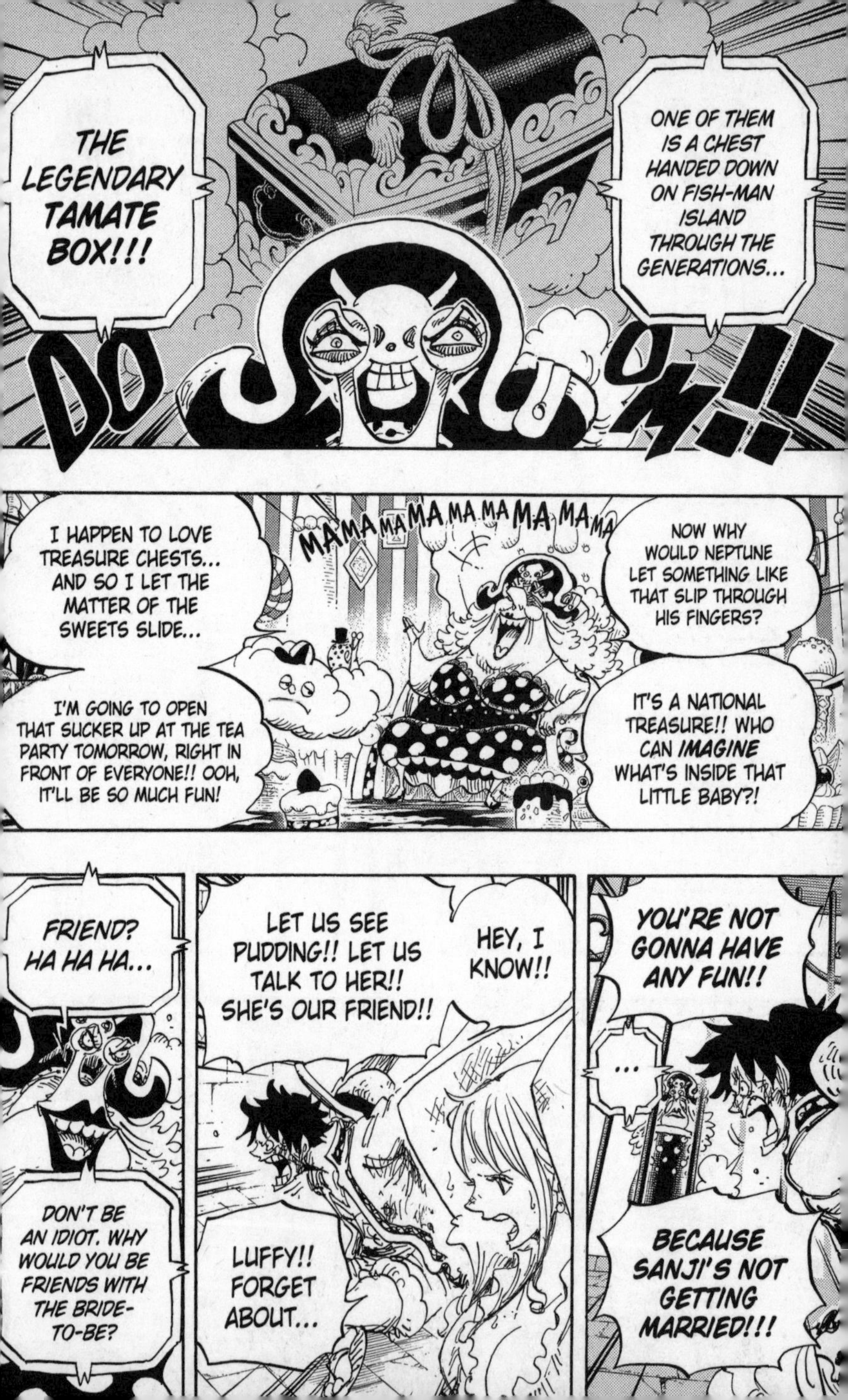
ONE OF THEM IS A CHEST HANDED DOWN ON FISH-MAN ISLAND THROUGH THE GENERATIONS...
THE LEGENDARY TAMATE BOX!!!
DOOM!!
MAMAMAMAMAMAMAMAMAMA
NOW WHY WOULD NEPTUNE LET SOMETHING LIKE THAT SLIP THROUGH HIS FINGERS?
IT'S A NATIONAL TREASURE!! WHO CAN IMAGINE WHAT'S INSIDE THAT LITTLE BABY?!
I HAPPEN TO LOVE TREASURE CHESTS... AND SO I LET THE MATTER OF THE SWEETS SLIDE...
I'M GOING TO OPEN THAT SUCKER UP AT THE TEA PARTY TOMORROW, RIGHT IN FRONT OF EVERYONE!! OOH, IT'LL BE SO MUCH FUN!
YOU'RE NOT GONNA HAVE ANY FUN!!
...
BECAUSE SANJI'S NOT GETTING MARRIED!!!
HEY, I KNOW!!
LET US SEE PUDDING!! LET US TALK TO HER!! SHE'S OUR FRIEND!!
LUFFY!! FORGET ABOUT...
FRIEND? HA HA HA...
DON'T BE AN IDIOT. WHY WOULD YOU BE FRIENDS WITH THE BRIDE-TO-BE?

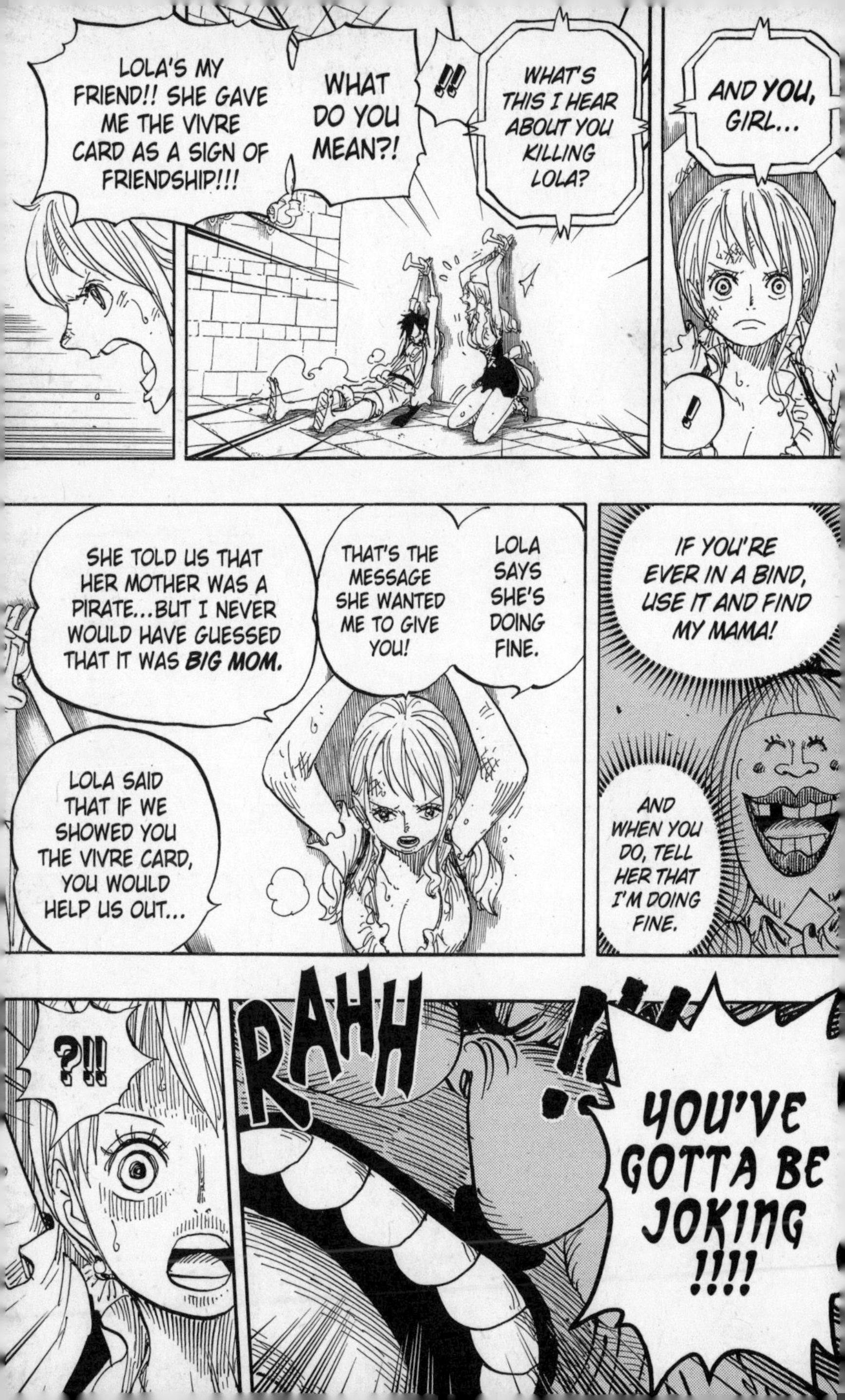
AND YOU, GIRL...
!
WHAT'S THIS I HEAR ABOUT YOU KILLING LOLA?
!!
WHAT DO YOU MEAN?!
LOLA'S MY FRIEND!! SHE GAVE ME THE VIVRE CARD AS A SIGN OF FRIENDSHIP!!!
IF YOU'RE EVER IN A BIND, USE IT AND FIND MY MAMA!
AND WHEN YOU DO, TELL HER THAT I'M DOING FINE.
LOLA SAYS SHE'S DOING FINE.
THAT'S THE MESSAGE SHE WANTED ME TO GIVE YOU!
SHE TOLD US THAT HER MOTHER WAS A PIRATE...BUT I NEVER WOULD HAVE GUESSED THAT IT WAS BIG MOM.
LOLA SAID THAT IF WE SHOWED YOU THE VIVRE CARD, YOU WOULD HELP US OUT...
YOU'VE GOTTA BE JOKING!!!!
RAHH
?!!

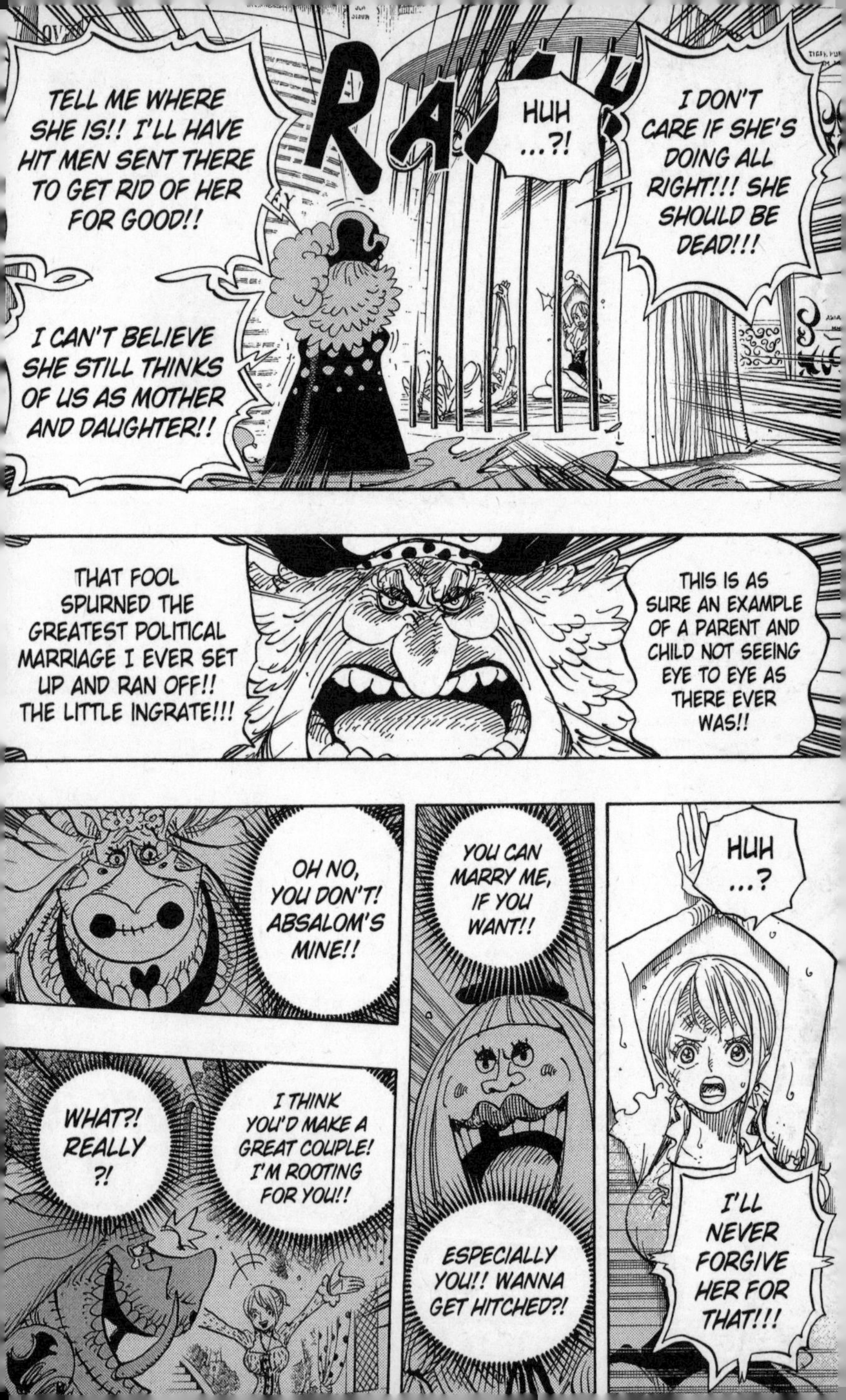
I DON'T CARE IF SHE'S DOING ALL RIGHT!!! SHE SHOULD BE DEAD!!!
HUH ...?!
TELL ME WHERE SHE IS!! I'LL HAVE HIT MEN SENT THERE TO GET RID OF HER FOR GOOD!!
I CAN'T BELIEVE SHE STILL THINKS OF US AS MOTHER AND DAUGHTER!!
THIS IS AS SURE AN EXAMPLE OF A PARENT AND CHILD NOT SEEING EYE TO EYE AS THERE EVER WAS!!
THAT FOOL SPURNED THE GREATEST POLITICAL MARRIAGE I EVER SET UP AND RAN OFF!! THE LITTLE INGRATE!!!
HUH ...?
I'LL NEVER FORGIVE HER FOR THAT!!!
YOU CAN MARRY ME, IF YOU WANT!!
ESPECIALLY YOU!! WANNA GET HITCHED?!
OH NO, YOU DON'T! ABSALOM'S MINE!!
I THINK YOU'D MAKE A GREAT COUPLE! I'M ROOTING FOR YOU!!
WHAT?! REALLY ?!

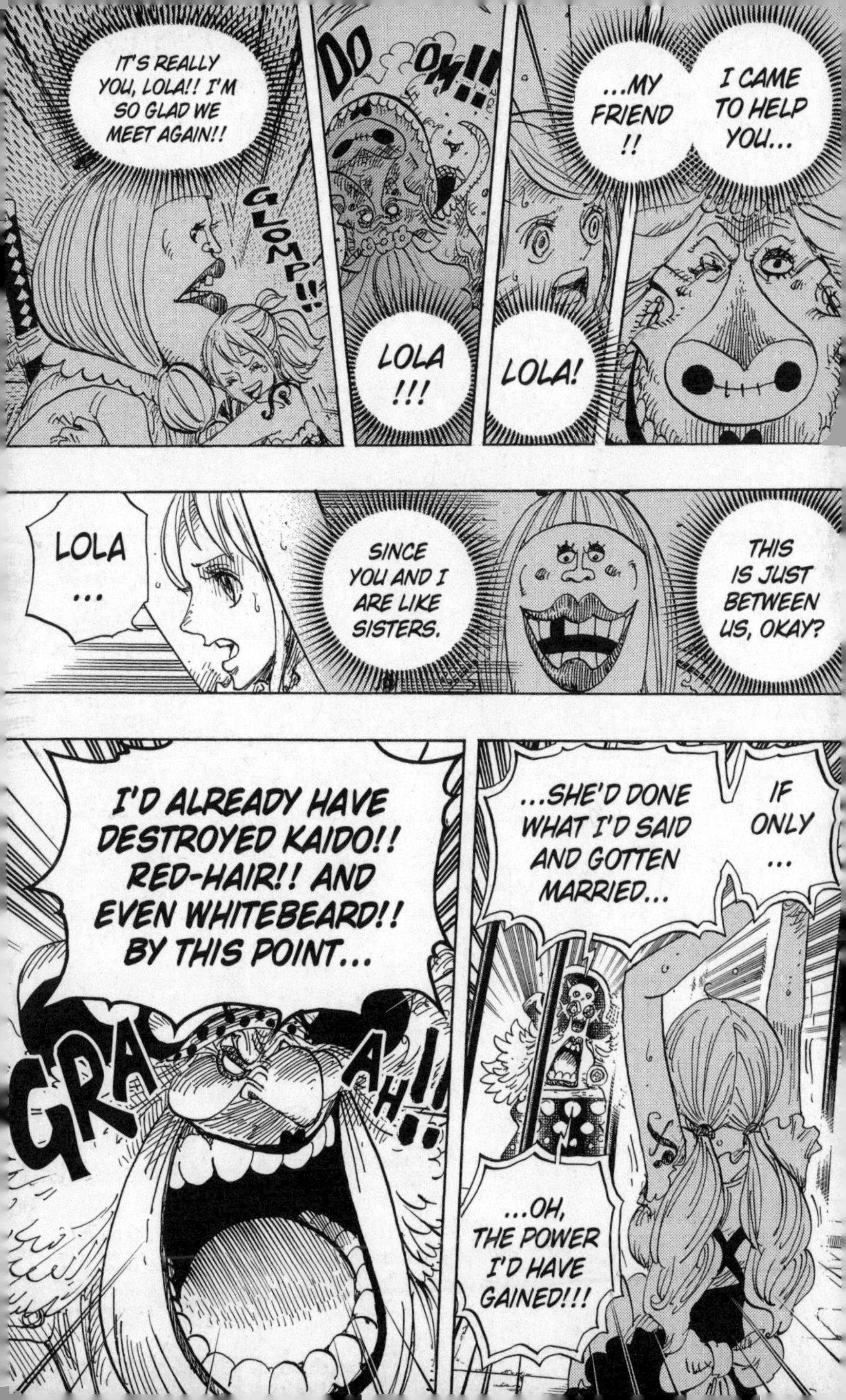
I CAME TO HELP YOU...
...MY FRIEND!!
LOLA!
DOOM!!
LOLA!!!
GLOMP!!
IT'S REALLY YOU, LOLA!! I'M SO GLAD WE MEET AGAIN!!
THIS IS JUST BETWEEN US, OKAY?
SINCE YOU AND I ARE LIKE SISTERS.
LOLA...
IF ONLY...
...SHE'D DONE WHAT I'D SAID AND GOTTEN MARRIED...
...OH, THE POWER I'D HAVE GAINED!!!
I'D ALREADY HAVE DESTROYED KAIDO!! RED-HAIR!! AND EVEN WHITEBEARD!! BY THIS POINT...
GRAAAH!!

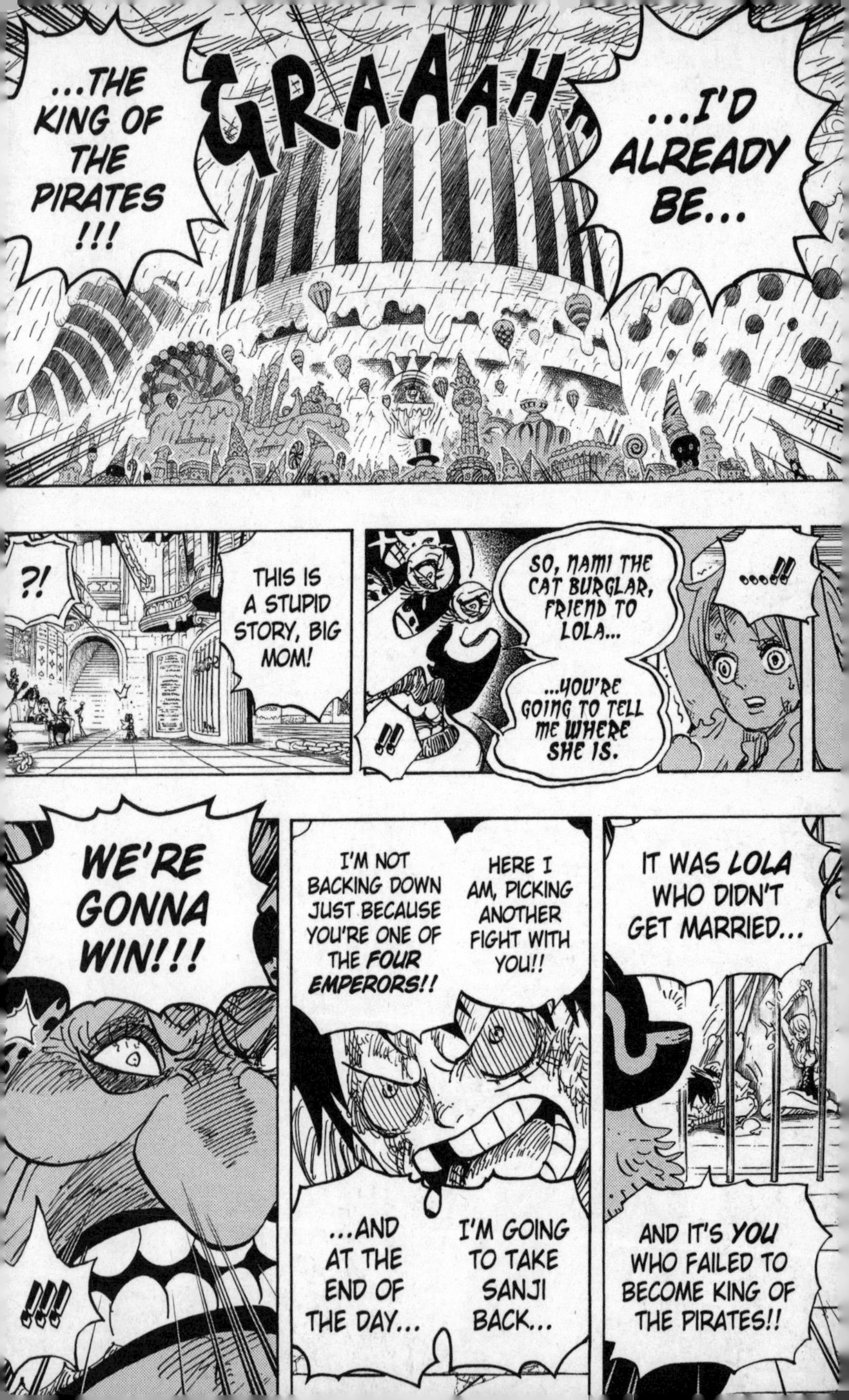

...I'D ALREADY BE...
GRAAAH
...THE KING OF THE PIRATES!!!
...!!
SO, NAMI THE CAT BURGLAR, FRIEND TO LOLA...
...YOU'RE GOING TO TELL ME WHERE SHE IS.
!!
THIS IS A STUPID STORY, BIG MOM!
?!
IT WAS LOLA WHO DIDN'T GET MARRIED...
AND IT'S YOU WHO FAILED TO BECOME KING OF THE PIRATES!!
HERE I AM, PICKING ANOTHER FIGHT WITH YOU!!
I'M NOT BACKING DOWN JUST BECAUSE YOU'RE ONE OF THE FOUR EMPERORS!!
I'M GOING TO TAKE SANJI BACK...
...AND AT THE END OF THE DAY...
WE'RE GONNA WIN!!!
!!!

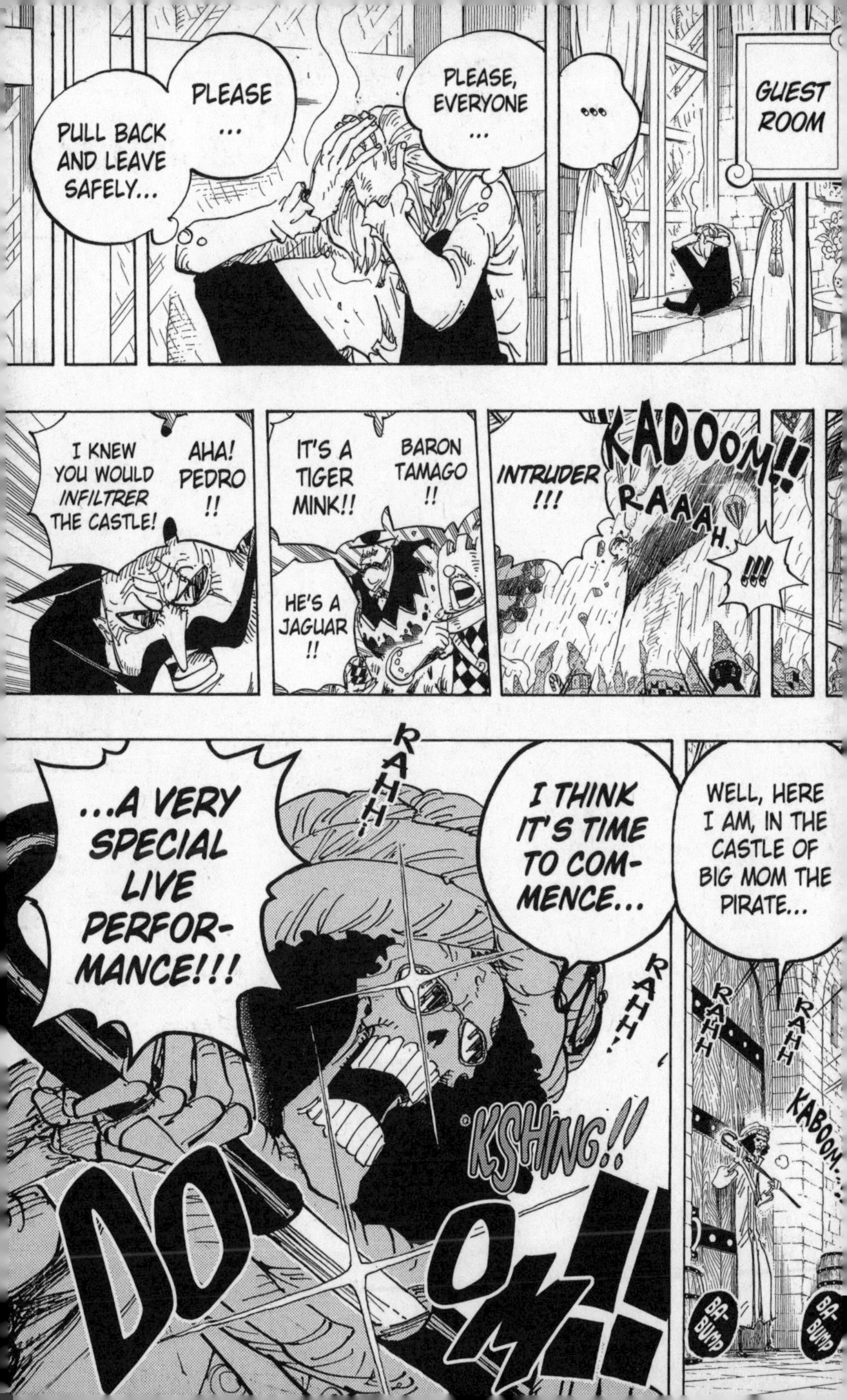
GUEST ROOM
...
PLEASE, EVERYONE ...
PLEASE ...
PULL BACK AND LEAVE SAFELY...
KADOOM!!
RAAAAH.
!!!
INTRUDER!!!
BARON TAMAGO!!
IT'S A TIGER MINK!!
HE'S A JAGUAR!!
AHA! PEDRO!!
I KNEW YOU WOULD INFILTRER THE CASTLE!
WELL, HERE I AM, IN THE CASTLE OF BIG MOM THE PIRATE...
RAHH
RAHH
KABOOM...
BA-BUMP
BA-BUMP
I THINK IT'S TIME TO COMMENCE...
RAHH
RAHH
...A VERY SPECIAL LIVE PERFORMANCE!!!
KSHING!!
DOOM!!

Chapter 848: GOODBYE

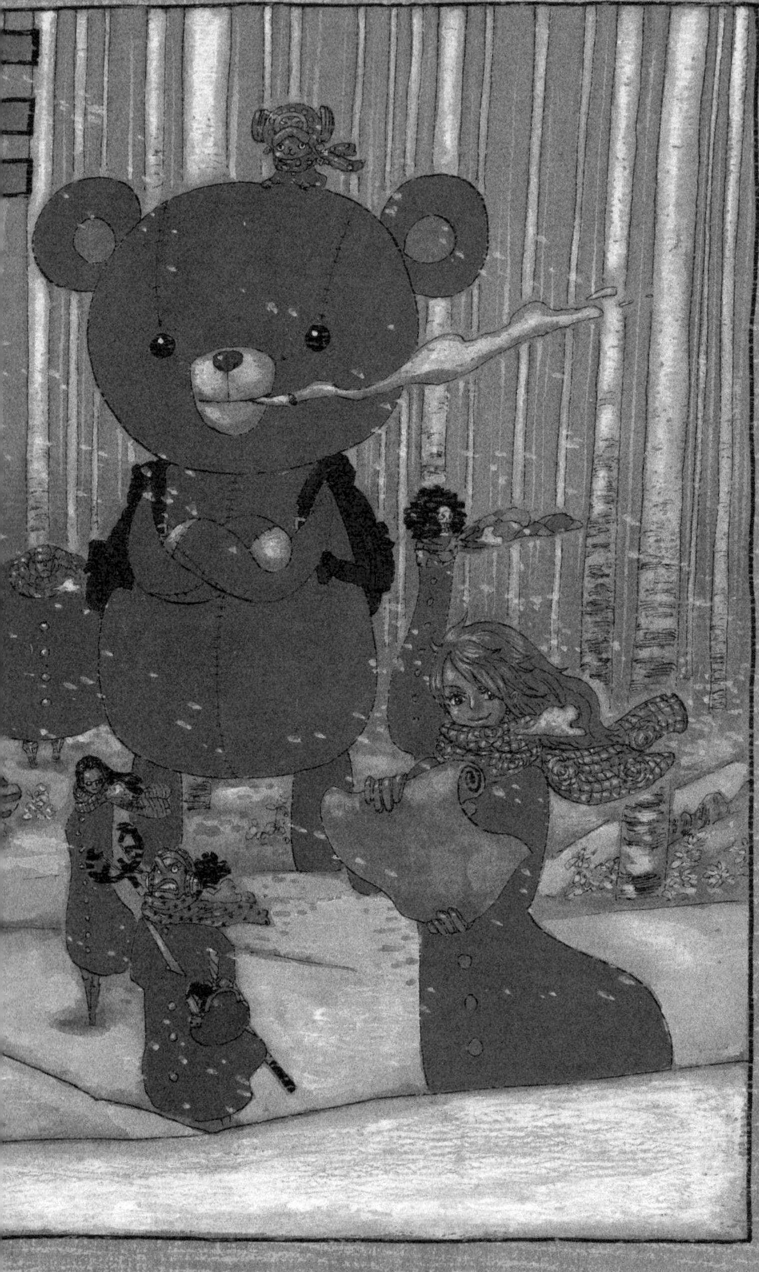

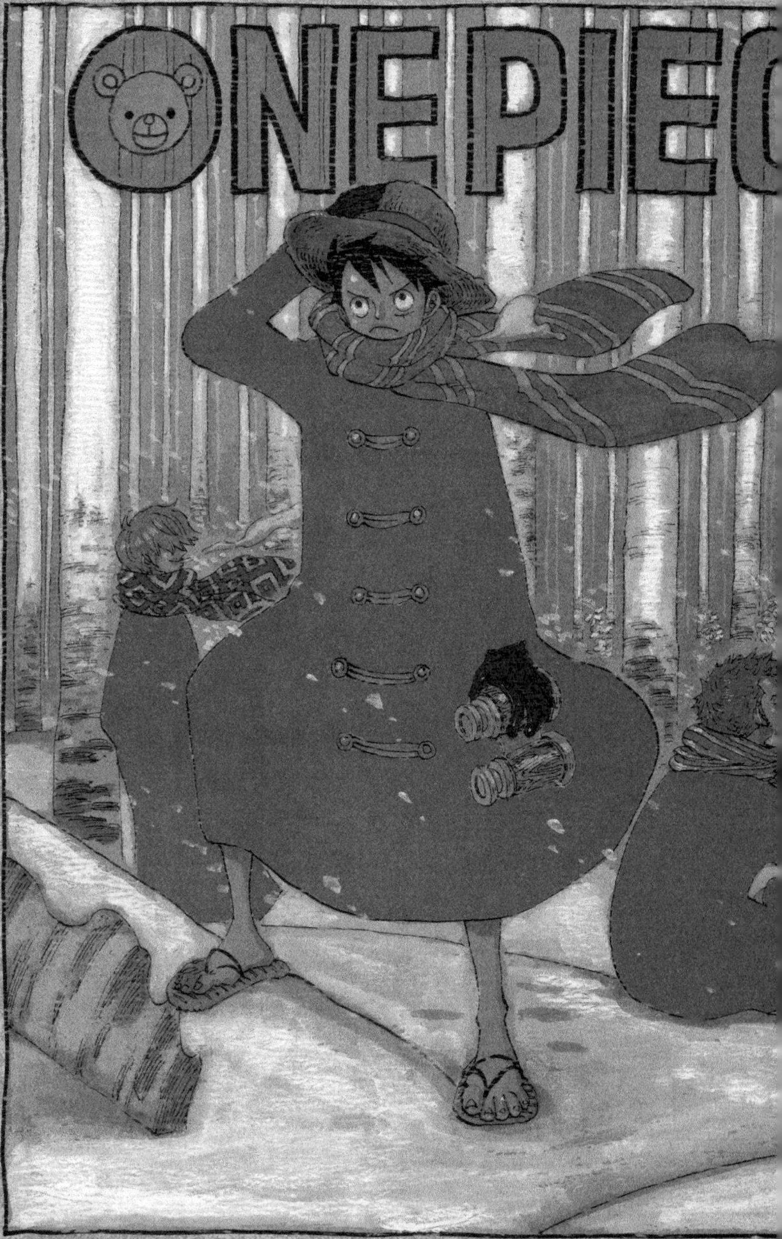
ONEPIEC

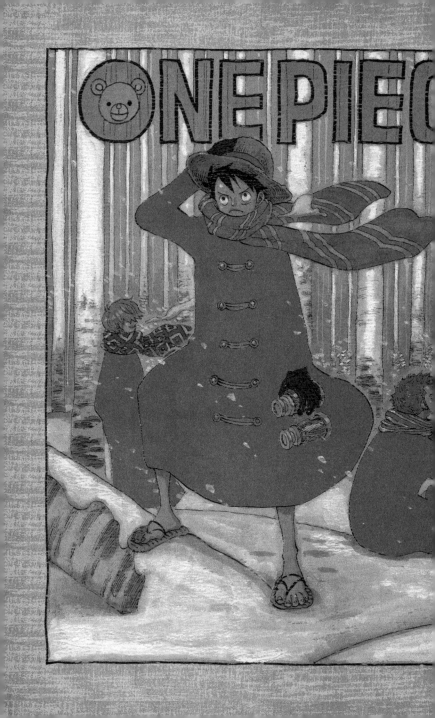

vol.84
ONE PIECE

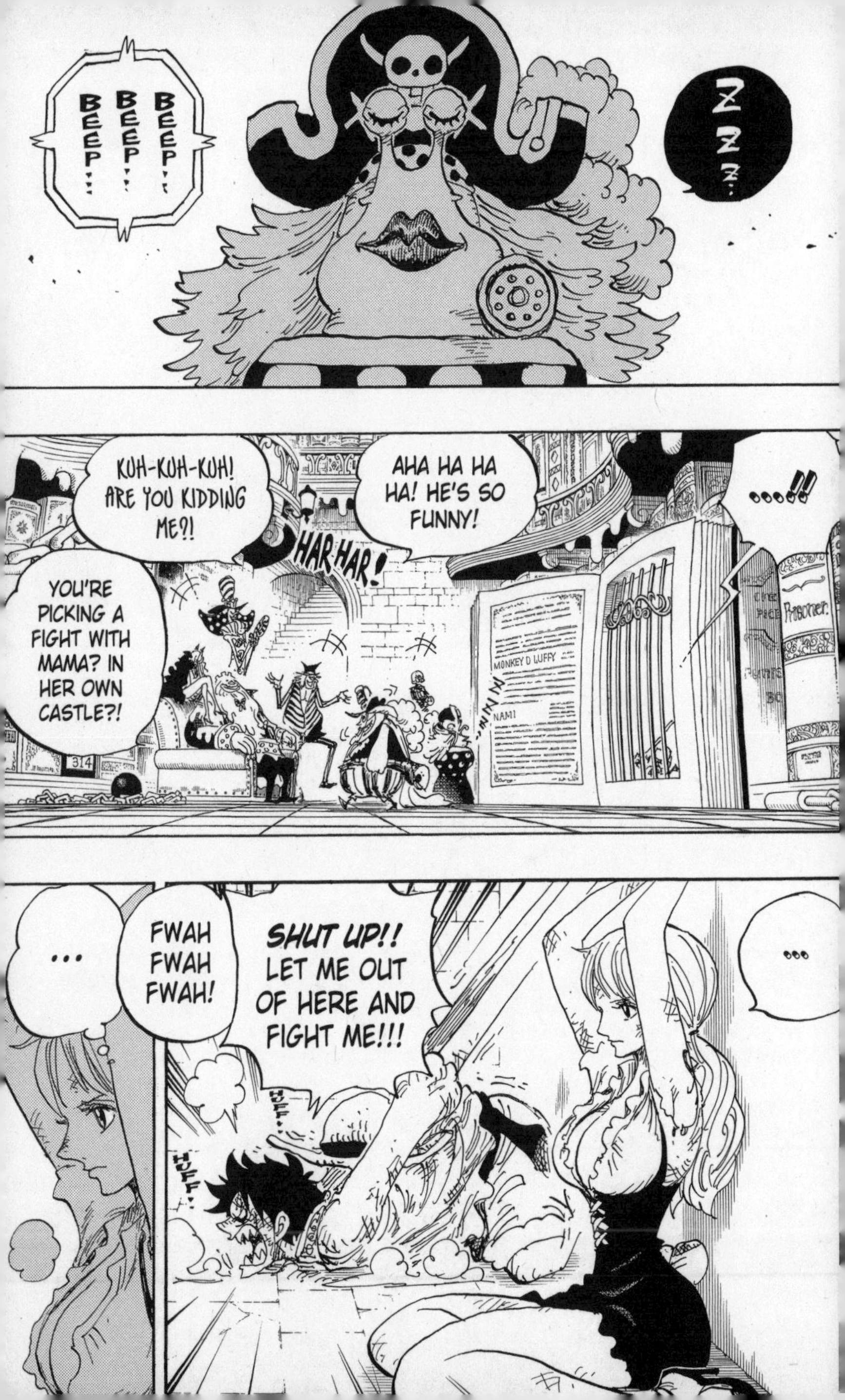
Z Z Z..
BEEP... BEEP... BEEP...
....!!
AHA HA HA HA! HE'S SO FUNNY!
HAR HAR!
KUH-KUH-KUH! ARE YOU KIDDING ME?!
YOU'RE PICKING A FIGHT WITH MAMA? IN HER OWN CASTLE?!
MONKEY D LUFFY
NAMI
Prisoner
314
...
SHUT UP!! LET ME OUT OF HERE AND FIGHT ME!!!
HUFF...
HUFF...
FWAH FWAH FWAH!
...

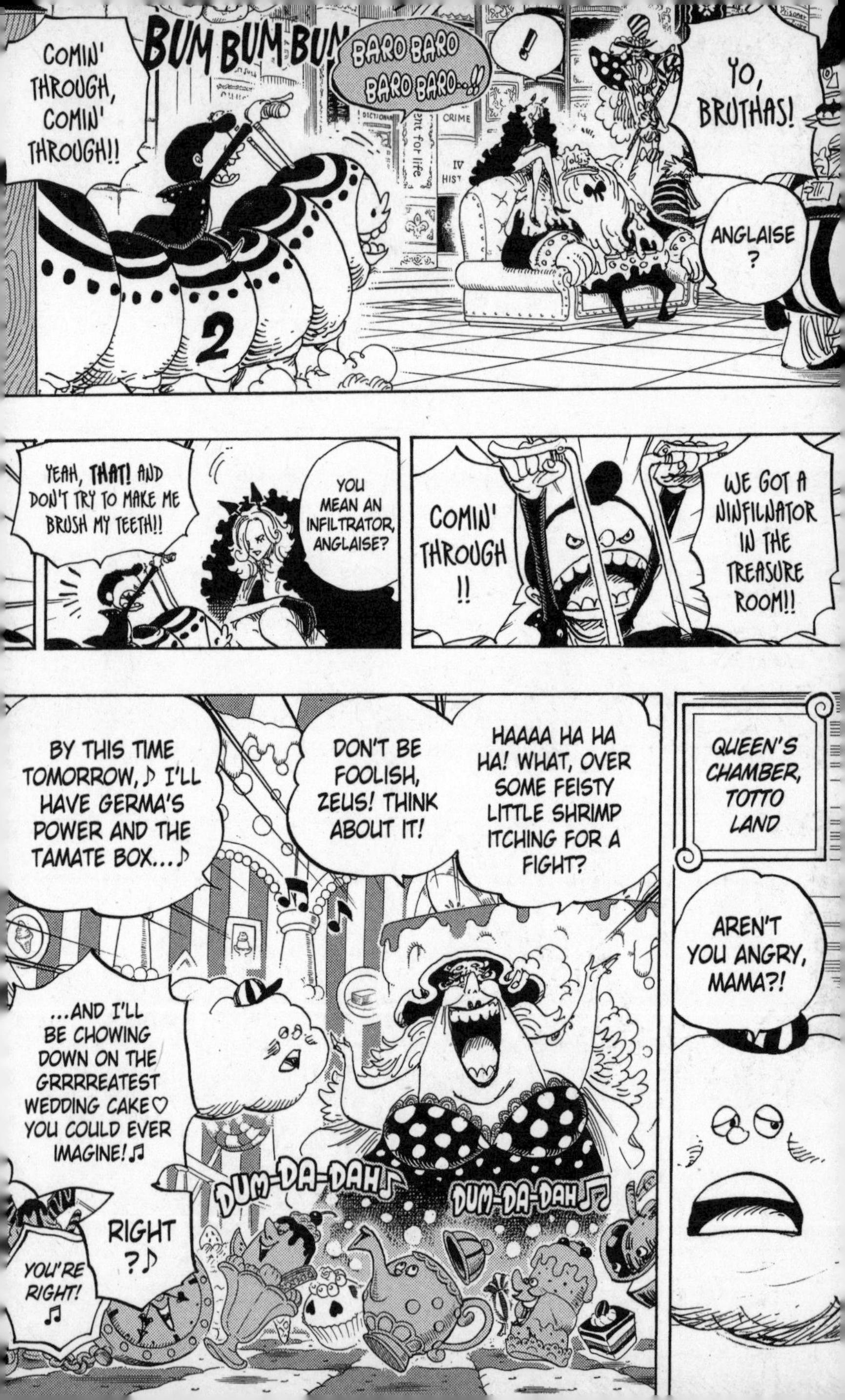
YO, BRUTHAS!
ANGLAISE ?
!
BARO BARO BARO BARO..!!
BUM BUM BUN
COMIN' THROUGH, COMIN' THROUGH!!
WE GOT A NINFILNATOR IN THE TREASURE ROOM!!
COMIN' THROUGH !!
YOU MEAN AN INFILTRATOR, ANGLAISE?
YEAH, **THAT!** AND DON'T TRY TO MAKE ME BRUSH MY TEETH!!
QUEEN'S CHAMBER, TOTTO LAND
AREN'T YOU ANGRY, MAMA?!
HAAAA HA HA HA! WHAT, OVER SOME FEISTY LITTLE SHRIMP ITCHING FOR A FIGHT?
DON'T BE FOOLISH, ZEUS! THINK ABOUT IT!
BY THIS TIME TOMORROW,♪ I'LL HAVE GERMA'S POWER AND THE TAMATE BOX...♪
...AND I'LL BE CHOWING DOWN ON THE GRRRREATEST WEDDING CAKE♡ YOU COULD EVER IMAGINE!♫
DUM-DA-DAH♫
DUM-DA-DAH♫
RIGHT ?♪
YOU'RE RIGHT! ♫

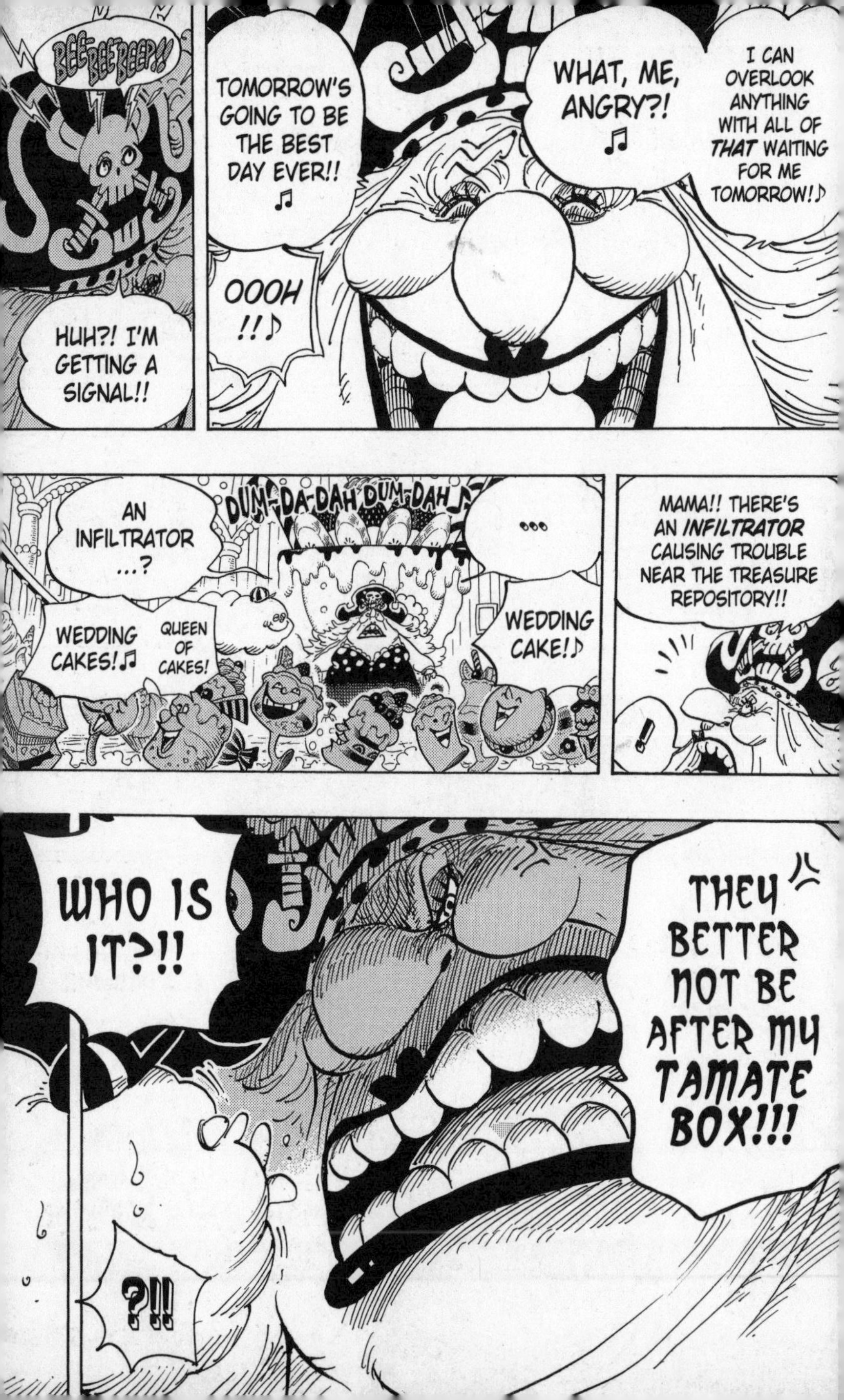
I CAN OVERLOOK ANYTHING WITH ALL OF THAT WAITING FOR ME TOMORROW!♪
WHAT, ME, ANGRY?! ♫
TOMORROW'S GOING TO BE THE BEST DAY EVER!! ♪
OOOH!!♪
BEE-BEE-BEEP!!
HUH?! I'M GETTING A SIGNAL!!
MAMA!! THERE'S AN INFILTRATOR CAUSING TROUBLE NEAR THE TREASURE REPOSITORY!!
!
...
DUM-DA-DAH DUM-DAH♪
AN INFILTRATOR ...?
WEDDING CAKE!♪
QUEEN OF CAKES!
WEDDING CAKES!♫
THEY BETTER NOT BE AFTER MY TAMATE BOX!!!
WHO IS IT?!!
?!!

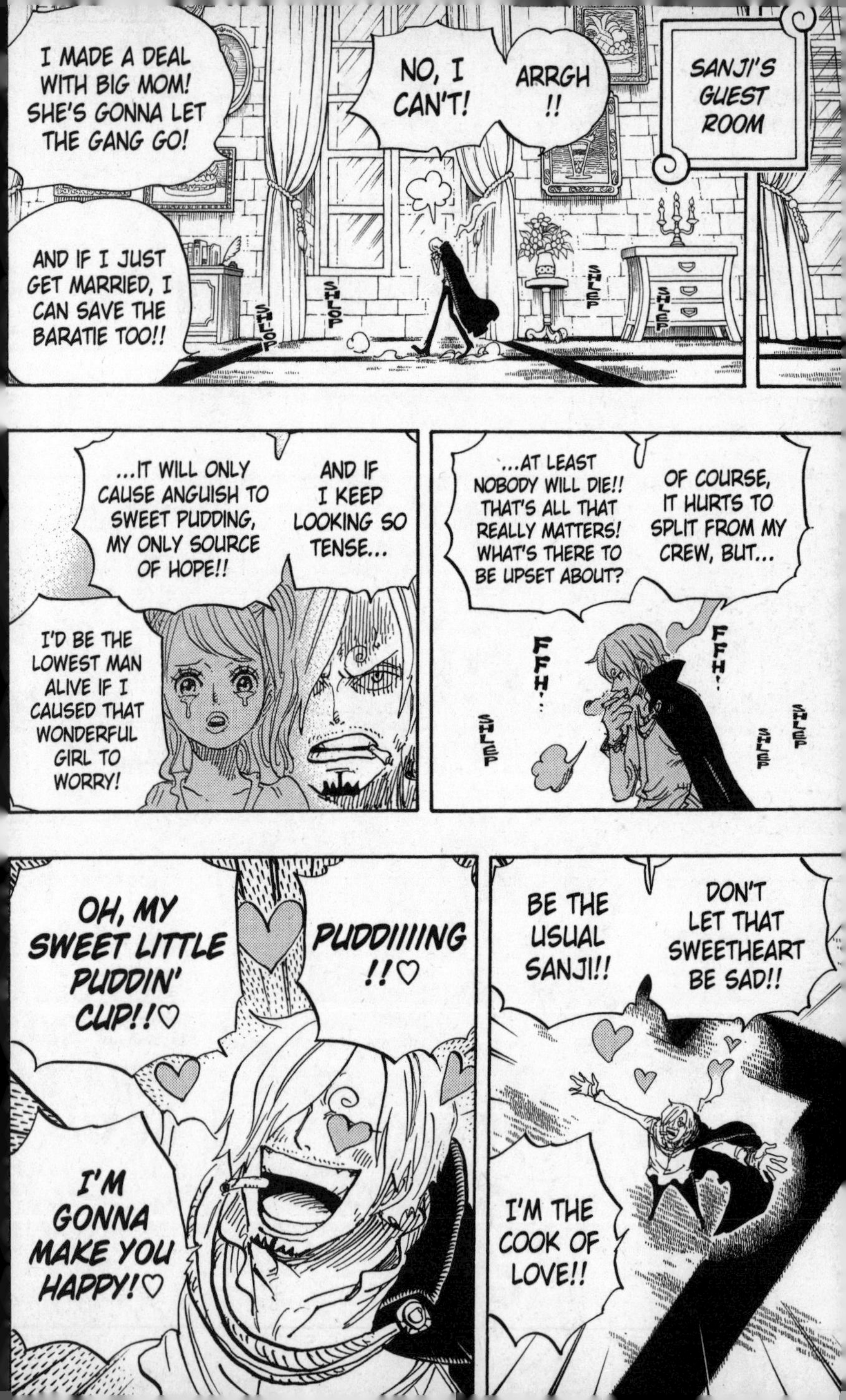
SANJI'S GUEST ROOM
ARRGH !!
NO, I CAN'T!
I MADE A DEAL WITH BIG MOM! SHE'S GONNA LET THE GANG GO!
AND IF I JUST GET MARRIED, I CAN SAVE THE BARATIE TOO!!
SHLEP
SHLEP
SHLOP
SHLOP
OF COURSE, IT HURTS TO SPLIT FROM MY CREW, BUT...
...AT LEAST NOBODY WILL DIE!! THAT'S ALL THAT REALLY MATTERS! WHAT'S THERE TO BE UPSET ABOUT?
FFH'
FFH'
SHLEP
SHLEP
SHLEP
AND IF I KEEP LOOKING SO TENSE...
...IT WILL ONLY CAUSE ANGUISH TO SWEET PUDDING, MY ONLY SOURCE OF HOPE!!
I'D BE THE LOWEST MAN ALIVE IF I CAUSED THAT WONDERFUL GIRL TO WORRY!
DON'T LET THAT SWEETHEART BE SAD!!
BE THE USUAL SANJI!!
I'M THE COOK OF LOVE!!
PUDDIIIING !!♡
OH, MY SWEET LITTLE PUDDIN' CUP!!♡
I'M GONNA MAKE YOU HAPPY!♡

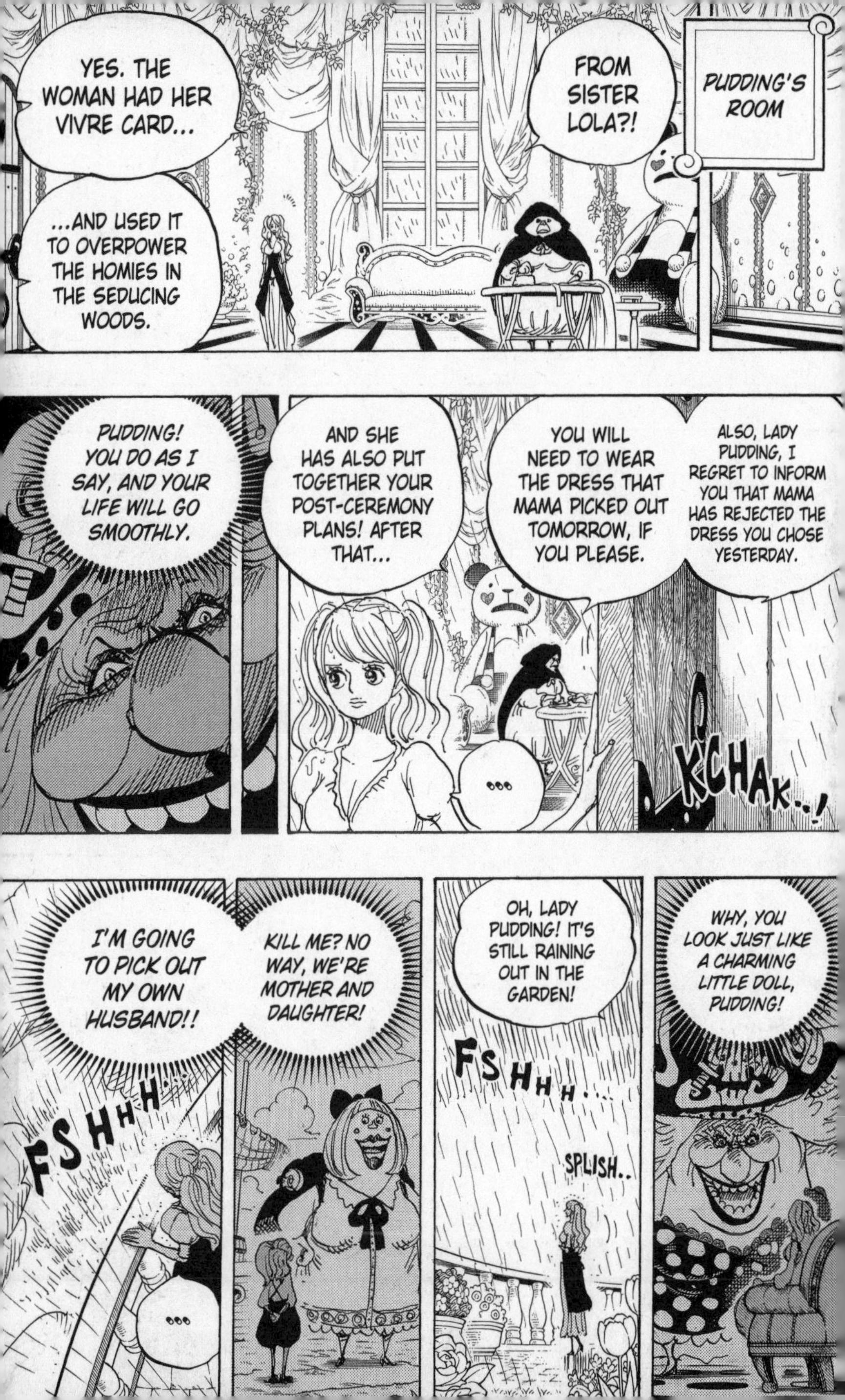
PUDDING'S ROOM
FROM SISTER LOLA?!
YES. THE WOMAN HAD HER VIVRE CARD...
...AND USED IT TO OVERPOWER THE HOMIES IN THE SEDUCING WOODS.
ALSO, LADY PUDDING, I REGRET TO INFORM YOU THAT MAMA HAS REJECTED THE DRESS YOU CHOSE YESTERDAY.
YOU WILL NEED TO WEAR THE DRESS THAT MAMA PICKED OUT TOMORROW, IF YOU PLEASE.
AND SHE HAS ALSO PUT TOGETHER YOUR POST-CEREMONY PLANS! AFTER THAT...
...
KCHAK..!
PUDDING! YOU DO AS I SAY, AND YOUR LIFE WILL GO SMOOTHLY.
WHY, YOU LOOK JUST LIKE A CHARMING LITTLE DOLL, PUDDING!
OH, LADY PUDDING! IT'S STILL RAINING OUT IN THE GARDEN!
FSHHH...
SPLISH..
KILL ME? NO WAY, WE'RE MOTHER AND DAUGHTER!
I'M GOING TO PICK OUT MY OWN HUSBAND!!
FSHHH...
...

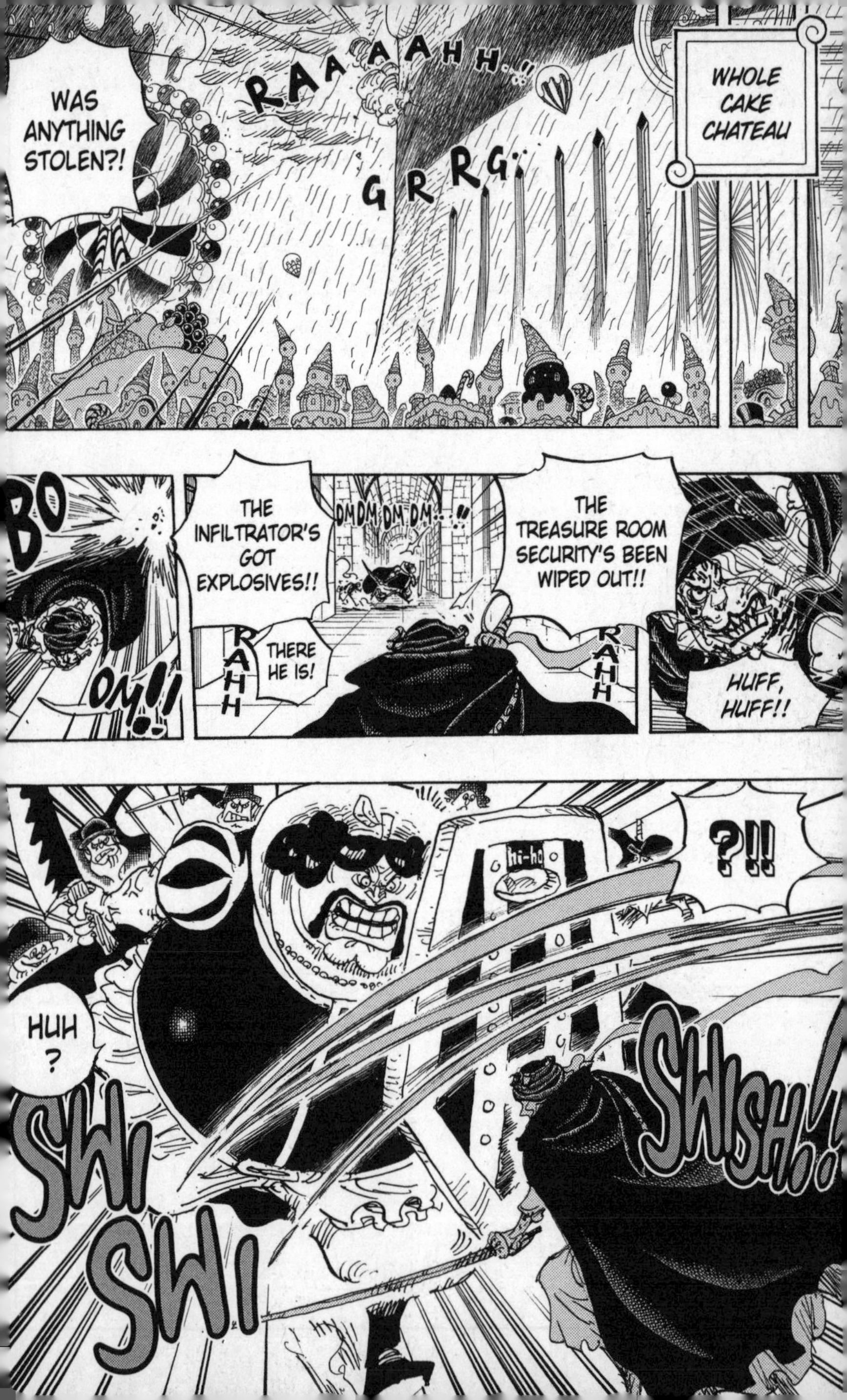
WHOLE CAKE CHATEAU
RAAAAHH..!!
GRRRG..
WAS ANYTHING STOLEN?!
THE TREASURE ROOM SECURITY'S BEEN WIPED OUT!!
RAHH
HUFF, HUFF!!
DMDM DM DM..!!
THE INFILTRATOR'S GOT EXPLOSIVES!!
THERE HE IS!
RAHH
BOOM!!
?!!
SWISH!!
hi-ho
HUH?
SHI SHI

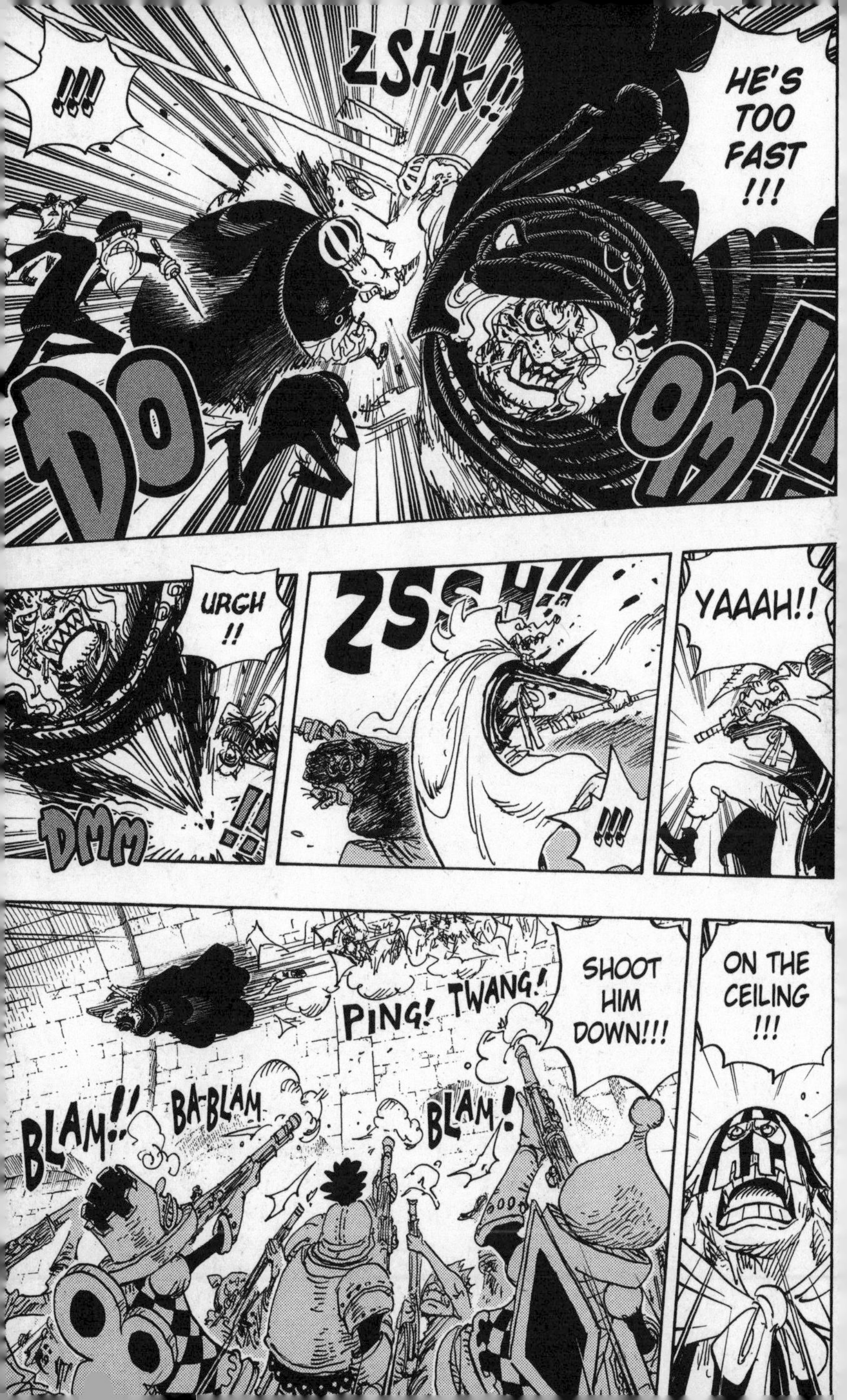
HE'S TOO FAST!!!
ZSHK!!
!!!
DOOM!!
YAAAH!!
ZSSH!!
!!!
URGH!!
DMM
!!
ON THE CEILING!!!
SHOOT HIM DOWN!!!
TWANG!
PING!
BLAM!
BA-BLAM
BLAM!!

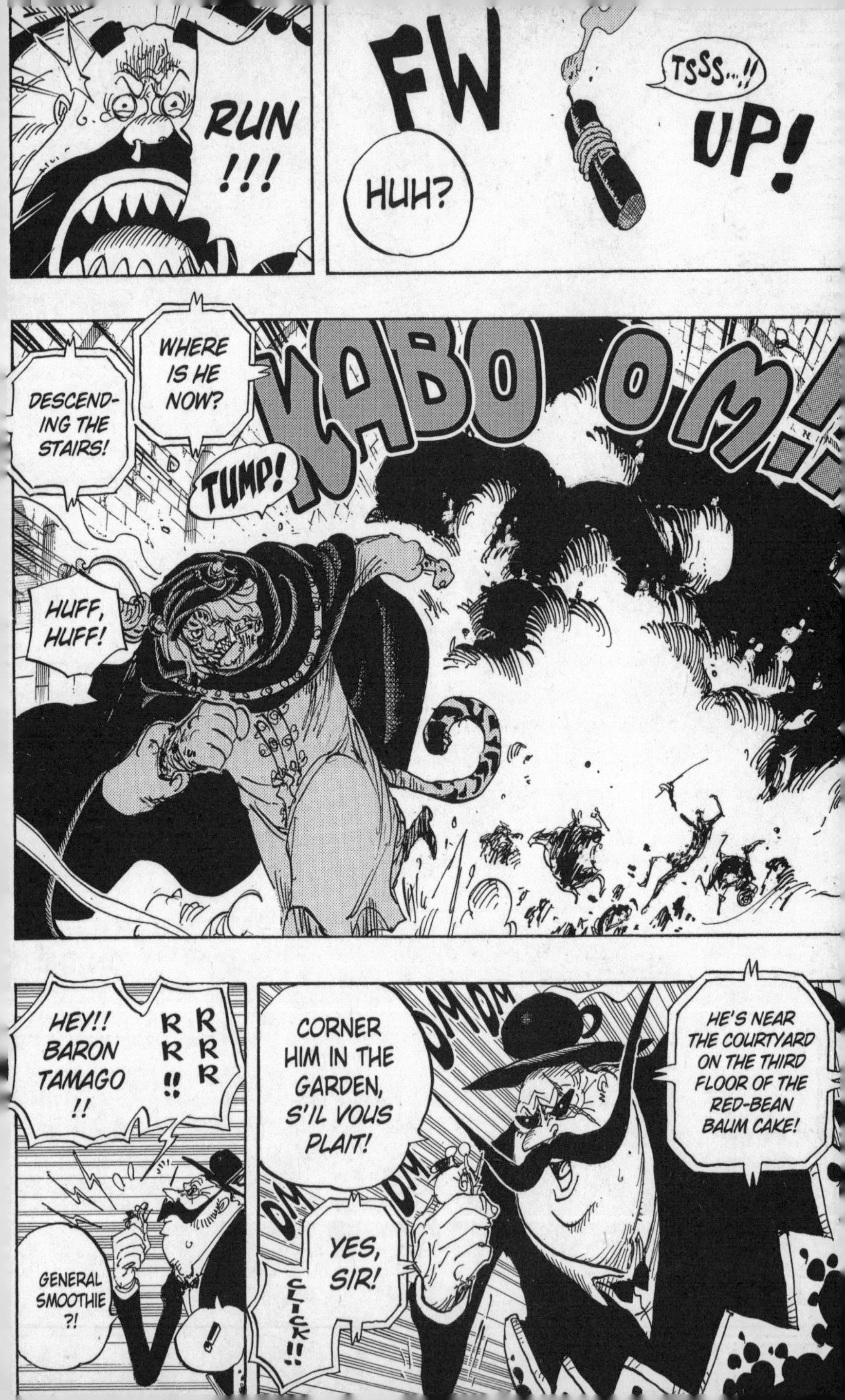
TSSS...!!
FW
UP!
HUH?
RUN!!!
KABOOM!!
WHERE IS HE NOW?
DESCENDING THE STAIRS!
TUMP!
HUFF, HUFF!
HE'S NEAR THE COURTYARD ON THE THIRD FLOOR OF THE RED-BEAN BAUM CAKE!
CORNER HIM IN THE GARDEN, S'IL VOUS PLAIT!
DM DM
DM DM
YES, SIR!
CLICK!!
RRR RR!!
HEY!! BARON TAMAGO!!
GENERAL SMOOTHIE?!
!

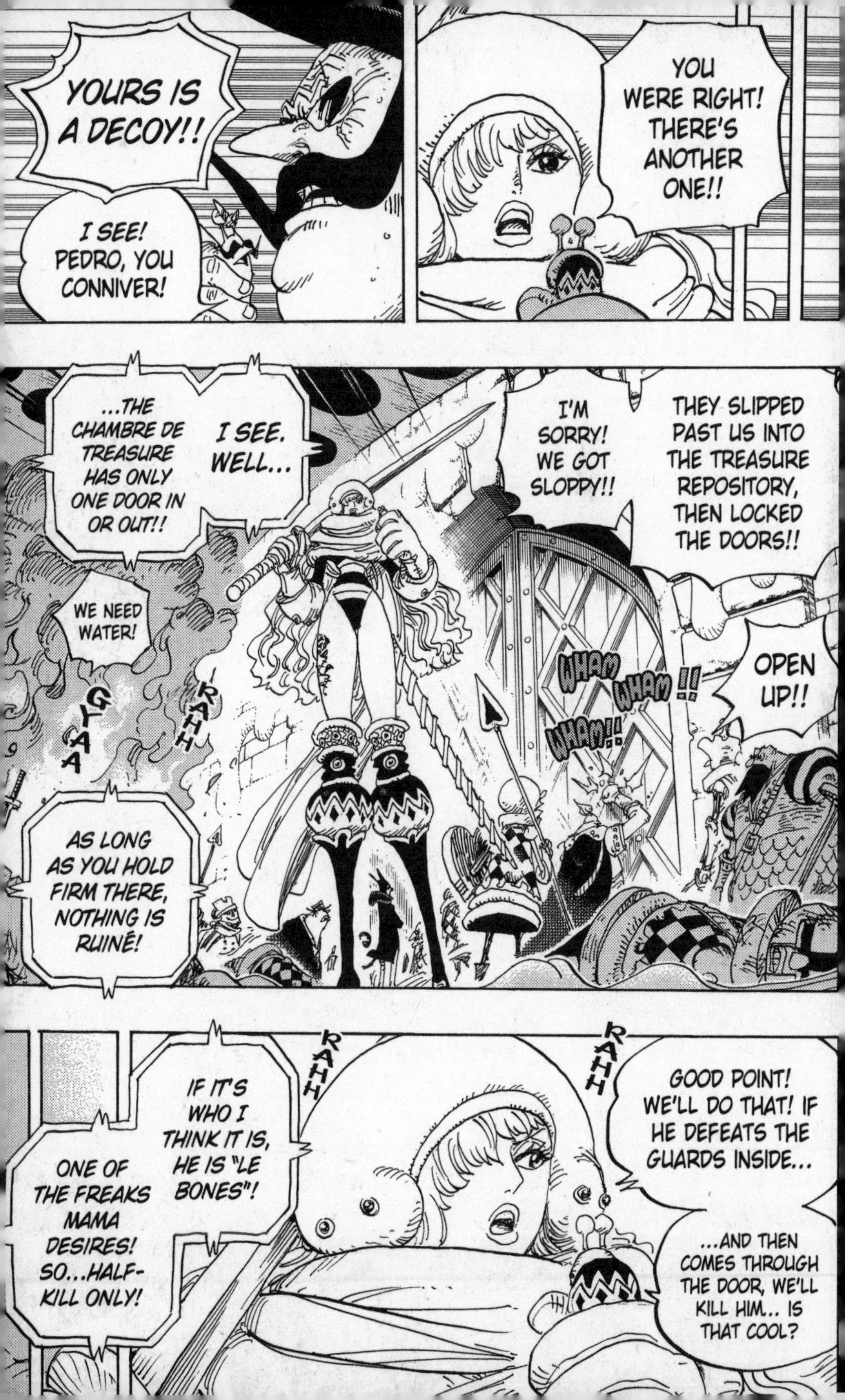
YOU WERE RIGHT! THERE'S ANOTHER ONE!!
YOURS IS A DECOY!!
I SEE! PEDRO, YOU CONNIVER!
THEY SLIPPED PAST US INTO THE TREASURE REPOSITORY, THEN LOCKED THE DOORS!!
I'M SORRY! WE GOT SLOPPY!!
OPEN UP!!
WHAM WHAM!!
WHAM!!
I SEE. WELL...
...THE CHAMBRE DE TREASURE HAS ONLY ONE DOOR IN OR OUT!!
RAHH
WE NEED WATER!
GYAA
AS LONG AS YOU HOLD FIRM THERE, NOTHING IS RUINÉ!
RAHH
RAHH
GOOD POINT! WE'LL DO THAT! IF HE DEFEATS THE GUARDS INSIDE...
...AND THEN COMES THROUGH THE DOOR, WE'LL KILL HIM... IS THAT COOL?
IF IT'S WHO I THINK IT IS, HE IS "LE BONES"!
ONE OF THE FREAKS MAMA DESIRES! SO...HALF-KILL ONLY!

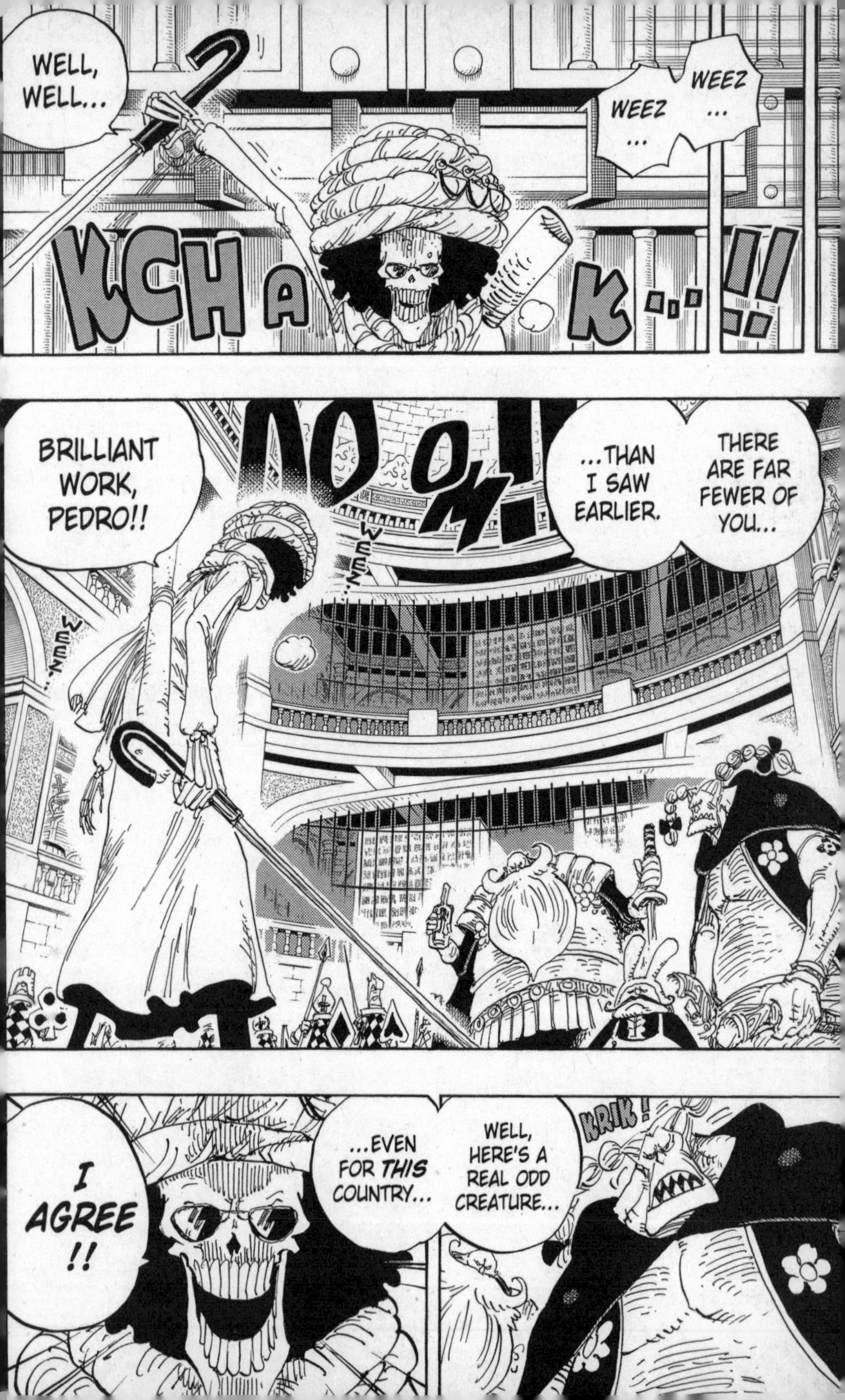
WEEZ ... WEEZ ...
WELL, WELL...
KCHAK...!!
THERE ARE FAR FEWER OF YOU...
...THAN I SAW EARLIER.
NOOM!
WEEZ...
BRILLIANT WORK, PEDRO!!
WEEZ...
KRIK!
WELL, HERE'S A REAL ODD CREATURE...
...EVEN FOR *THIS* COUNTRY...
I AGREE!!

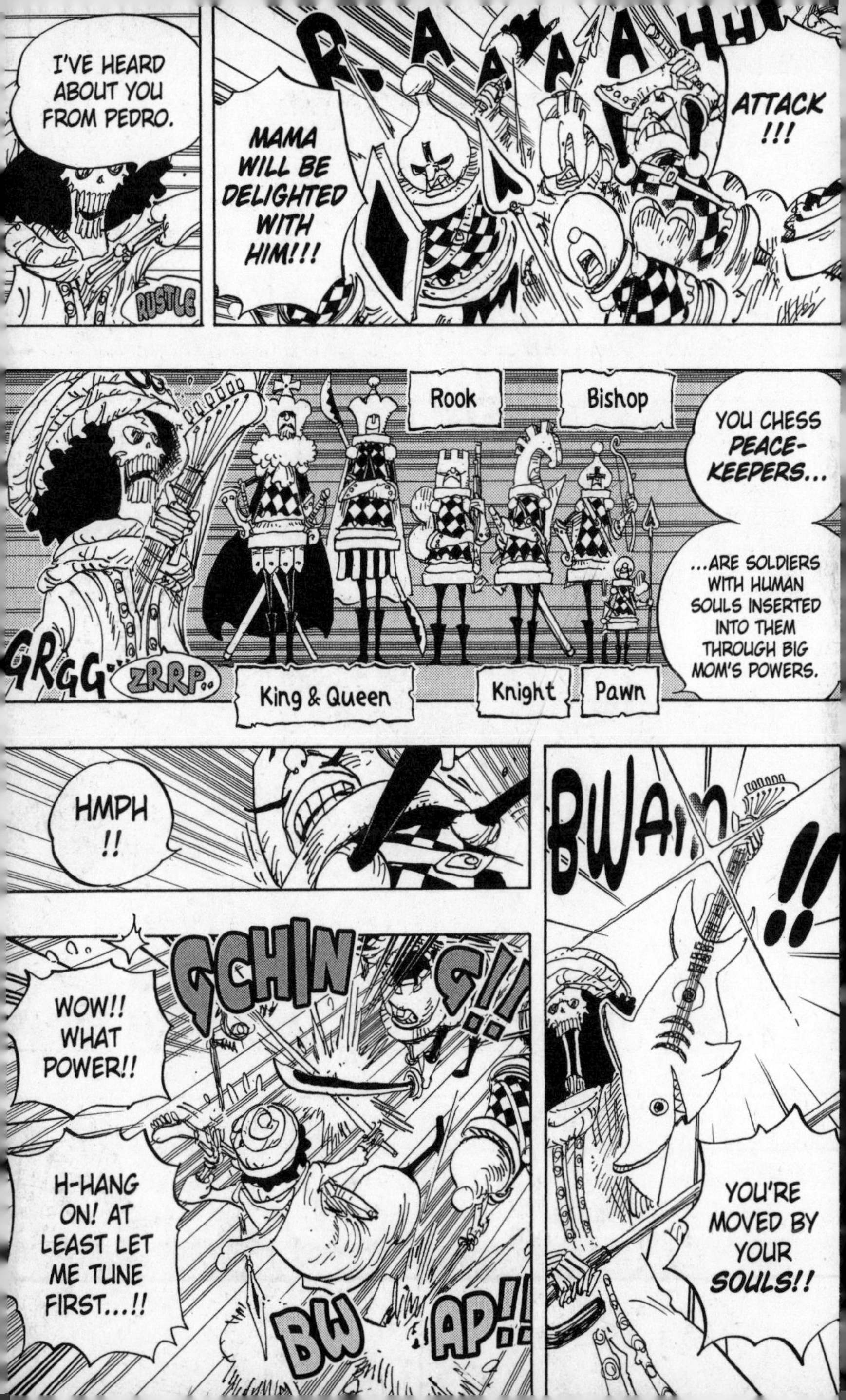
RAAAAHH
ATTACK !!!
MAMA WILL BE DELIGHTED WITH HIM!!!
I'VE HEARD ABOUT YOU FROM PEDRO.
RUSTLE
YOU CHESS PEACE-KEEPERS...
...ARE SOLDIERS WITH HUMAN SOULS INSERTED INTO THEM THROUGH BIG MOM'S POWERS.
Bishop
Rook
Pawn
Knight
King & Queen
ZRRP..
GRGG...
BWA
!!
YOU'RE MOVED BY YOUR SOULS!!
HMPH !!
GCHIN G!!
WOW!! WHAT POWER!!
H-HANG ON! AT LEAST LET ME TUNE FIRST...!!
BW AP!!

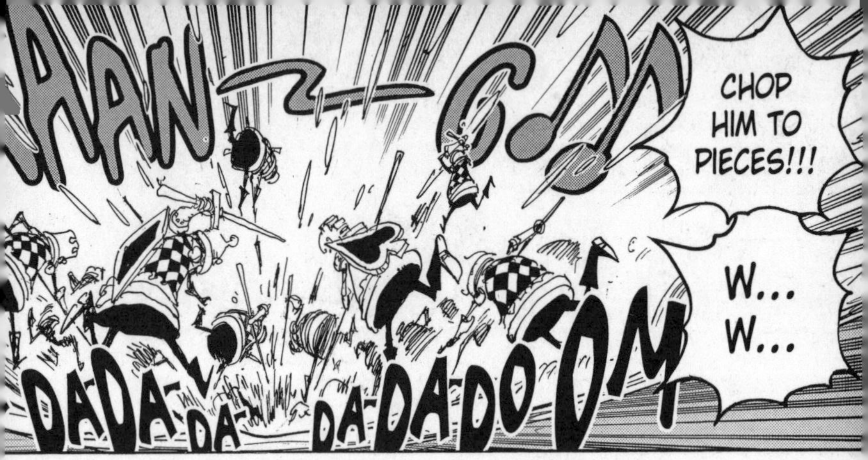
CHOP HIM TO PIECES!!!
W... W...
AAN
DADA-DA-DA-DADO-OM
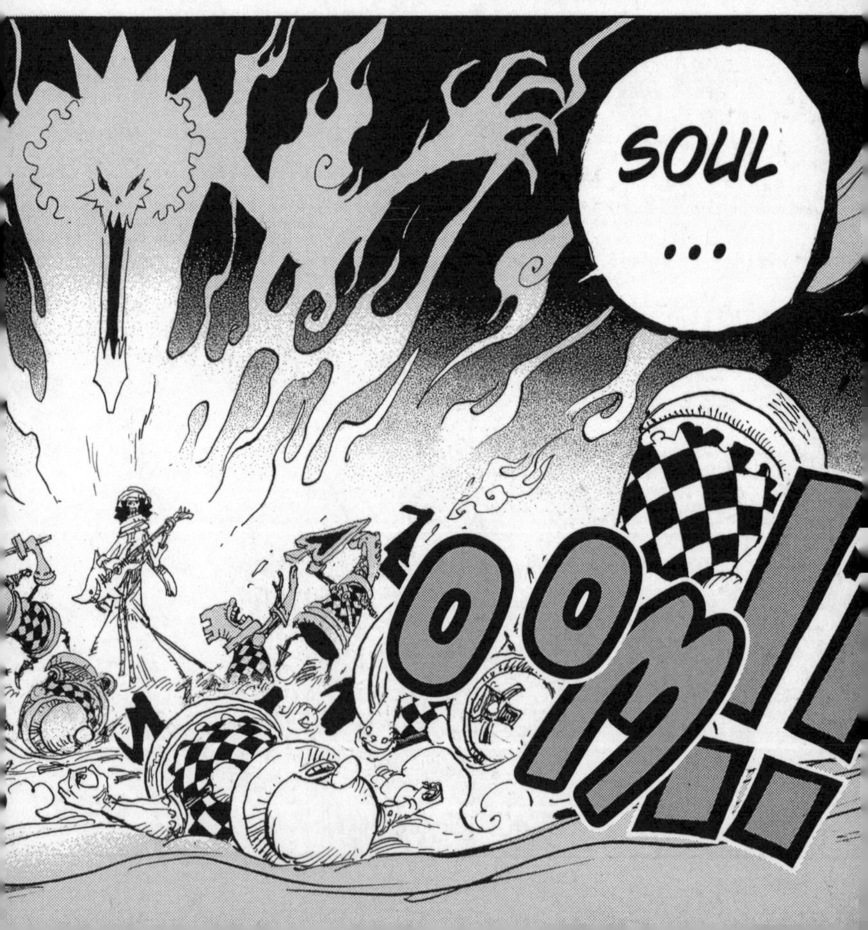
SOUL ...
OOM!!

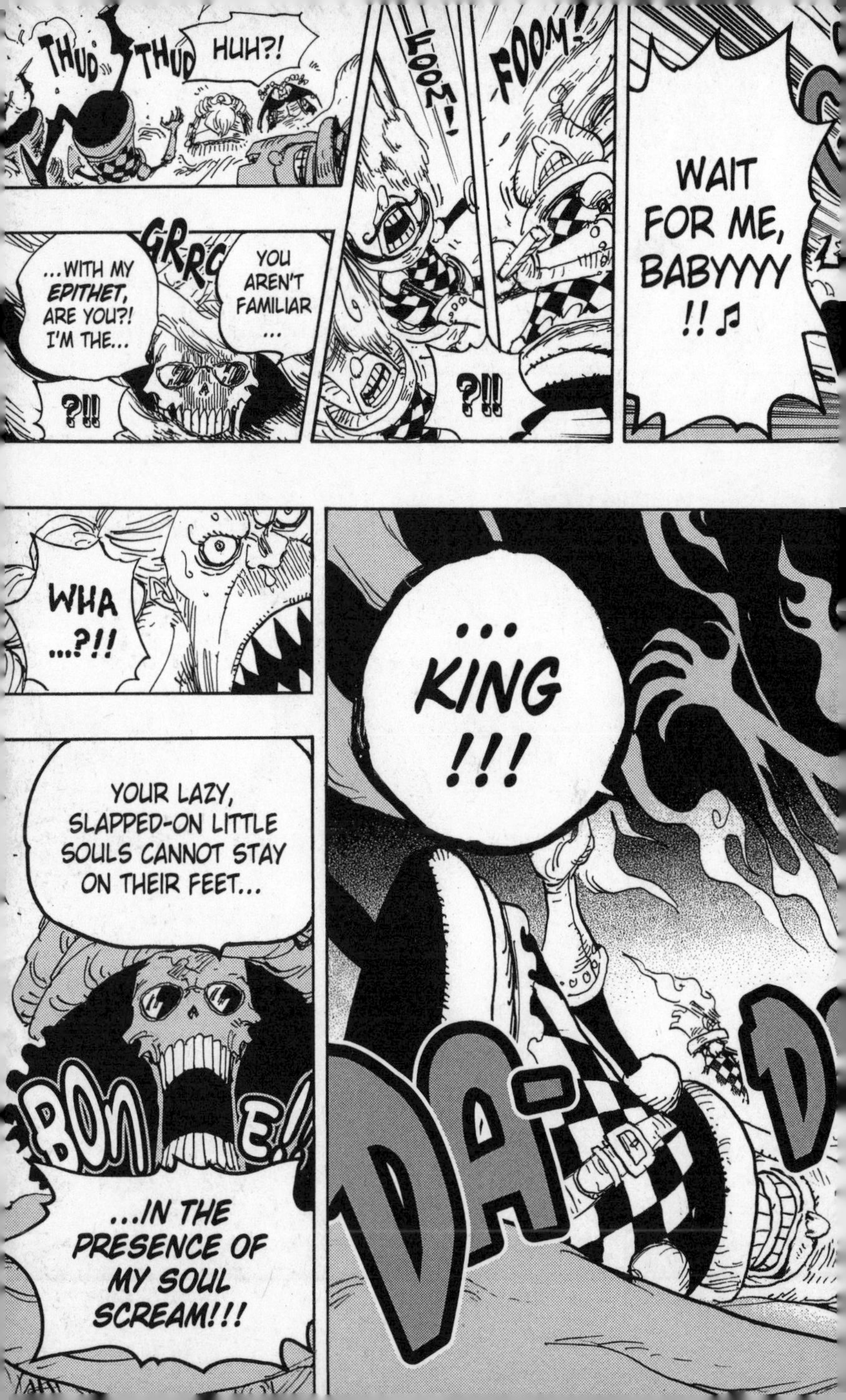
WAIT FOR ME, BABYYYY!! ♪
FOOM!
FOOM!
?!!
THUD
THUD
HUH?!
YOU AREN'T FAMILIAR...
...WITH MY EPITHET, ARE YOU?! I'M THE...
GRRG
?!!
...KING!!!
DA-D
WHA...?!!
YOUR LAZY, SLAPPED-ON LITTLE SOULS CANNOT STAY ON THEIR FEET...
BON
E!
...IN THE PRESENCE OF MY SOUL SCREAM!!!

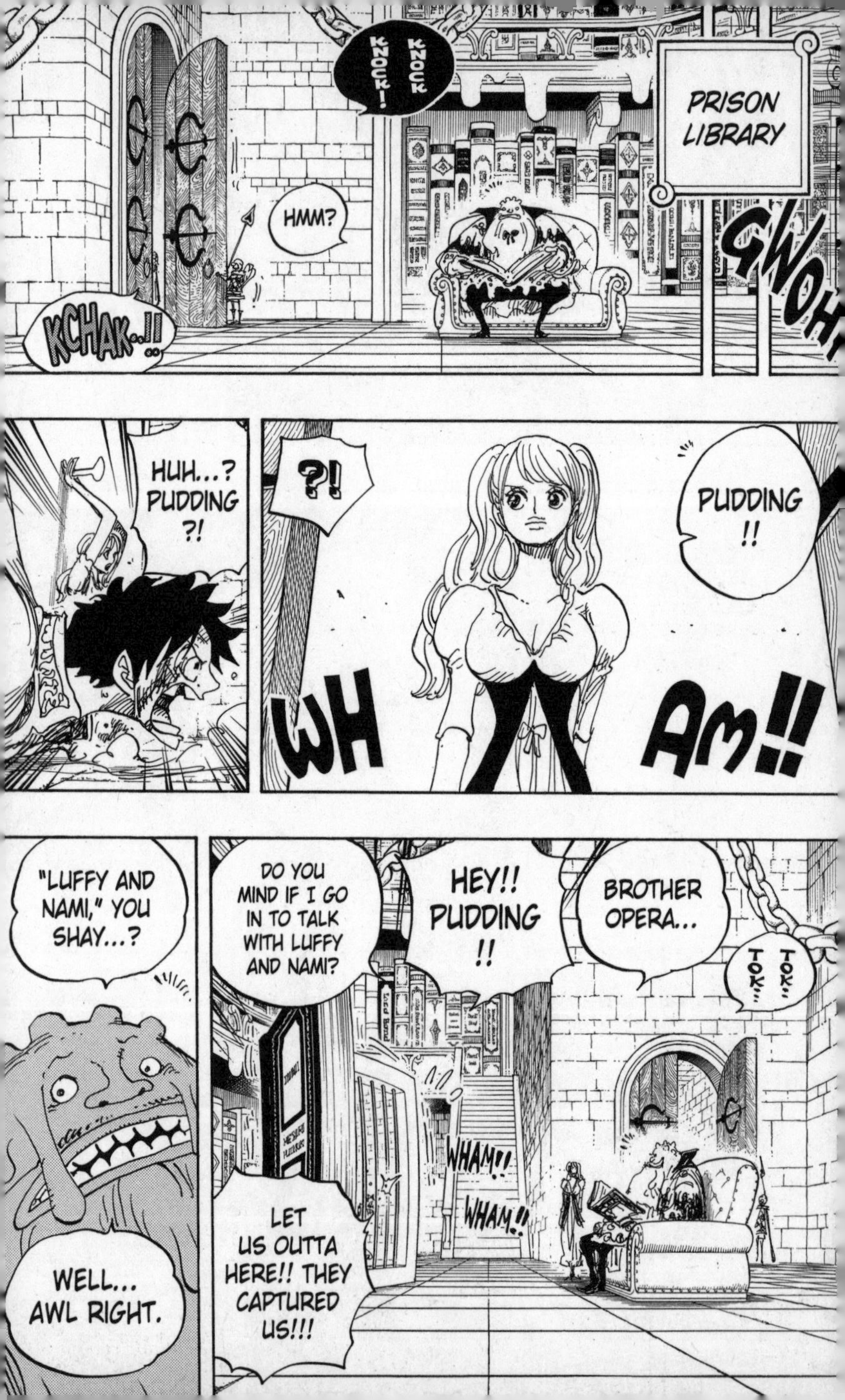
PRISON LIBRARY
GWOH
KNOCK KNOCK!
HMM?
KCHAK..!!
PUDDING!!
?!
WH AM!!
HUH...? PUDDING?!
BROTHER OPERA...
TOK TOK...
HEY!! PUDDING!!
DO YOU MIND IF I GO IN TO TALK WITH LUFFY AND NAMI?
WHAM!!
WHAM!!
LET US OUTTA HERE!! THEY CAPTURED US!!!
"LUFFY AND NAMI," YOU SHAY...?
WELL... AWL RIGHT.

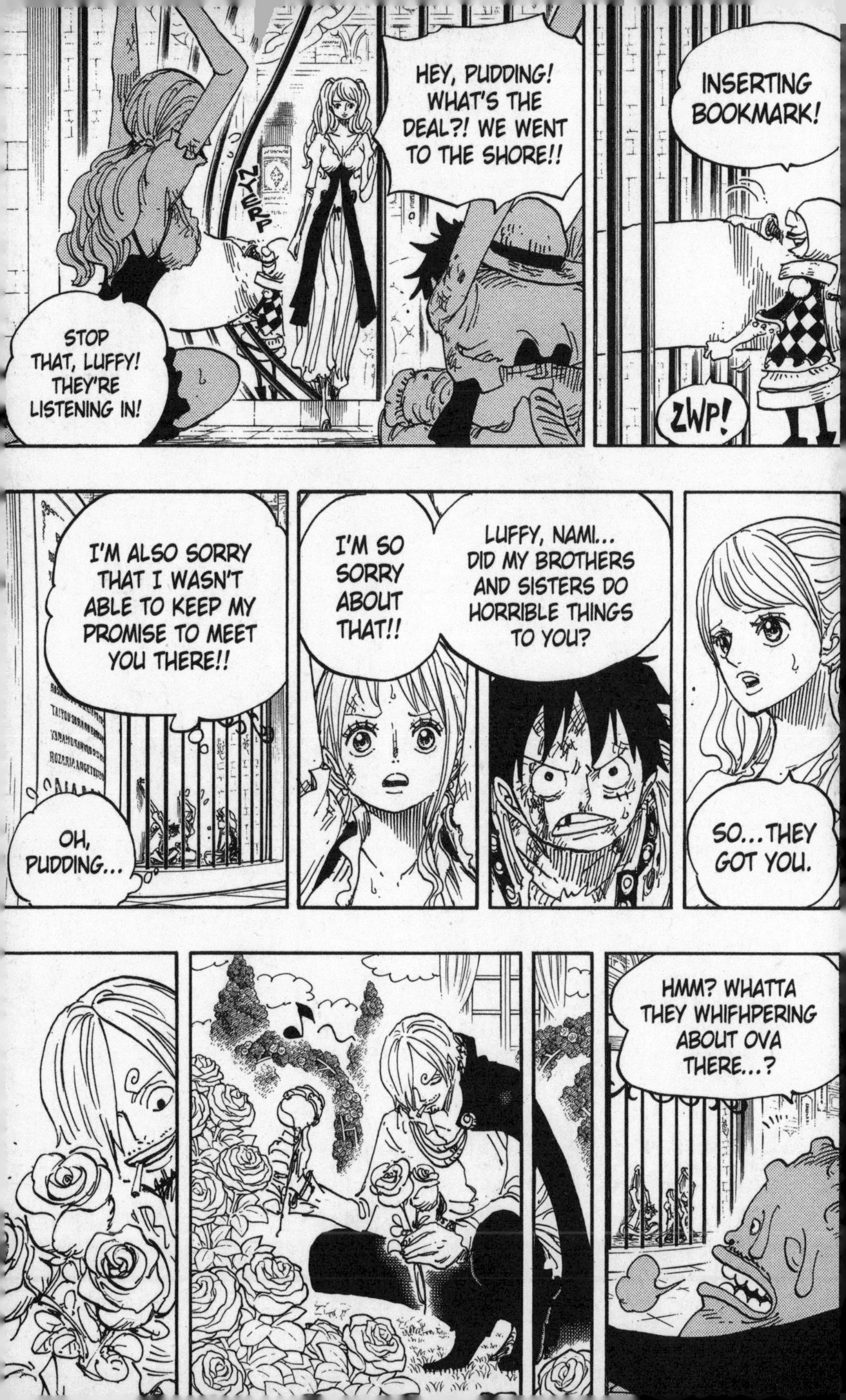
INSERTING BOOKMARK!
ZWP!
HEY, PUDDING! WHAT'S THE DEAL?! WE WENT TO THE SHORE!!
NYERP
STOP THAT, LUFFY! THEY'RE LISTENING IN!
SO...THEY GOT YOU.
LUFFY, NAMI... DID MY BROTHERS AND SISTERS DO HORRIBLE THINGS TO YOU?
I'M SO SORRY ABOUT THAT!!
I'M ALSO SORRY THAT I WASN'T ABLE TO KEEP MY PROMISE TO MEET YOU THERE!!
OH, PUDDING...
HMM? WHATTA THEY WHIFHPERING ABOUT OVA THERE...?

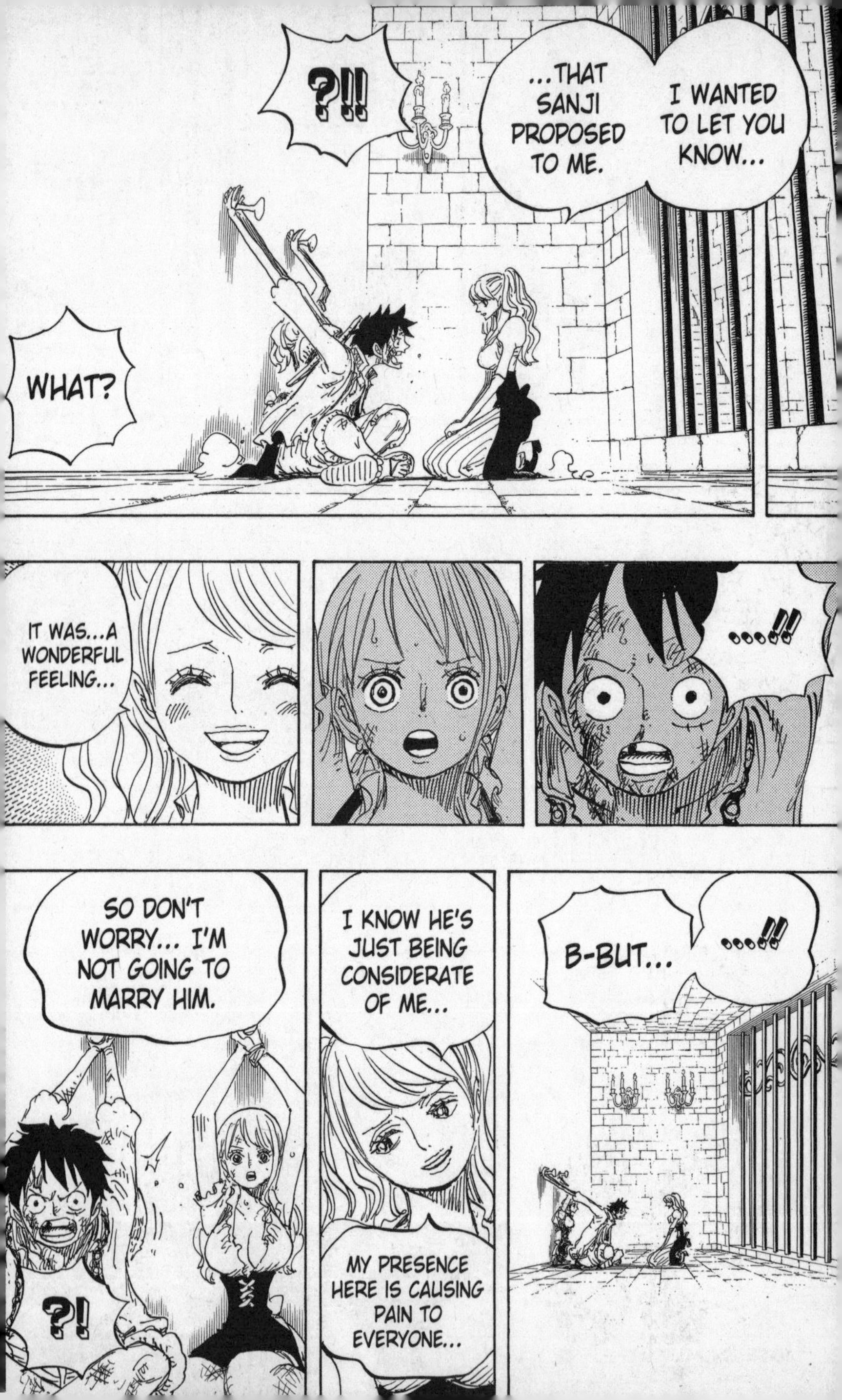
I WANTED TO LET YOU KNOW...
...THAT SANJI PROPOSED TO ME.
?!!
WHAT?
...!!
IT WAS...A WONDERFUL FEELING...
...!!
B-BUT...
I KNOW HE'S JUST BEING CONSIDERATE OF ME...
MY PRESENCE HERE IS CAUSING PAIN TO EVERYONE...
SO DON'T WORRY... I'M NOT GOING TO MARRY HIM.
?!

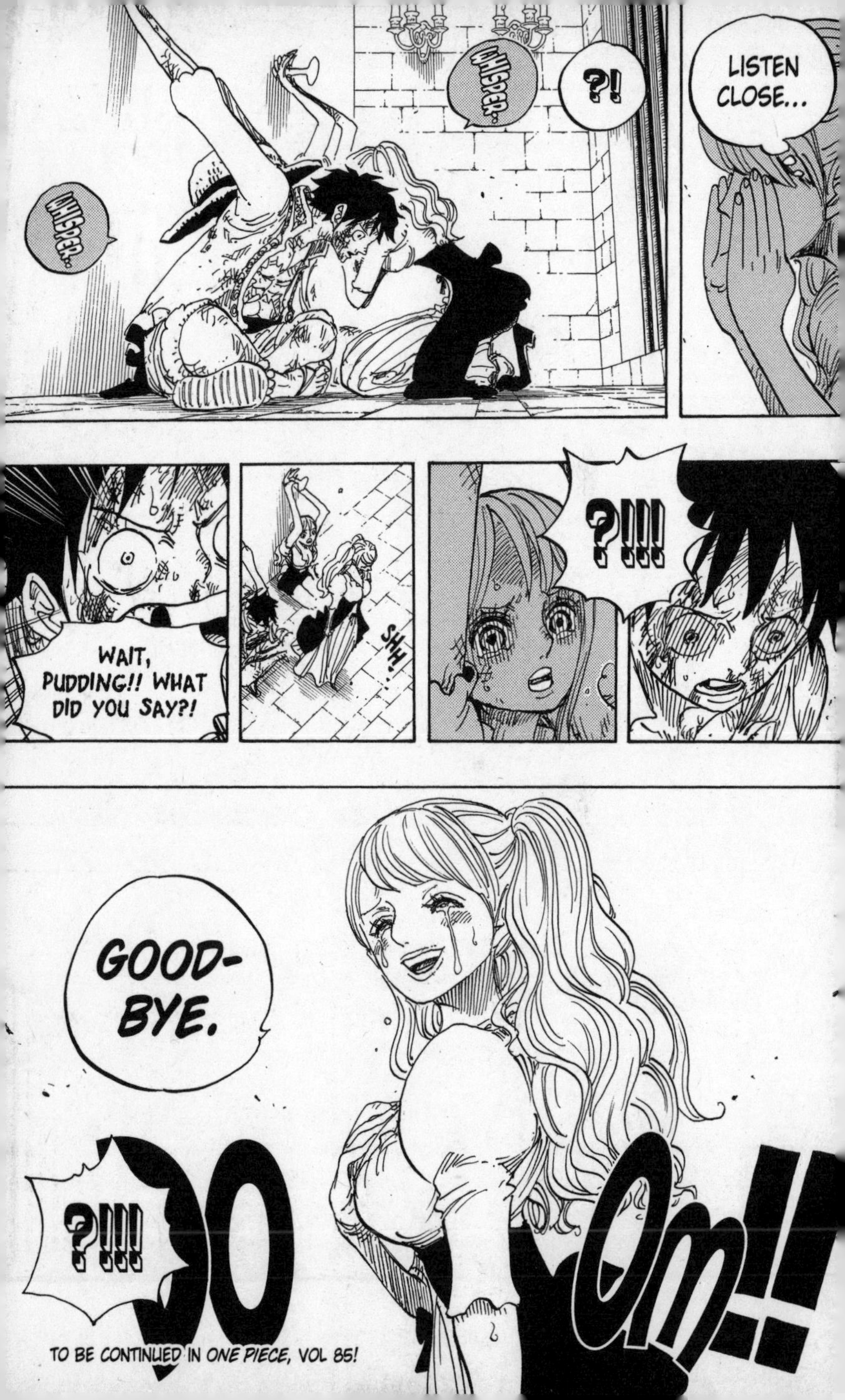
LISTEN CLOSE...
?!
WHISPER.
WHISPER..
?!!!
SHH...
WAIT, PUDDING!! WHAT DID YOU SAY?!
GOOD-BYE.
?!!!
DOOM!!
TO BE CONTINUED IN ONE PIECE, VOL 85!

COMING NEXT VOLUME:

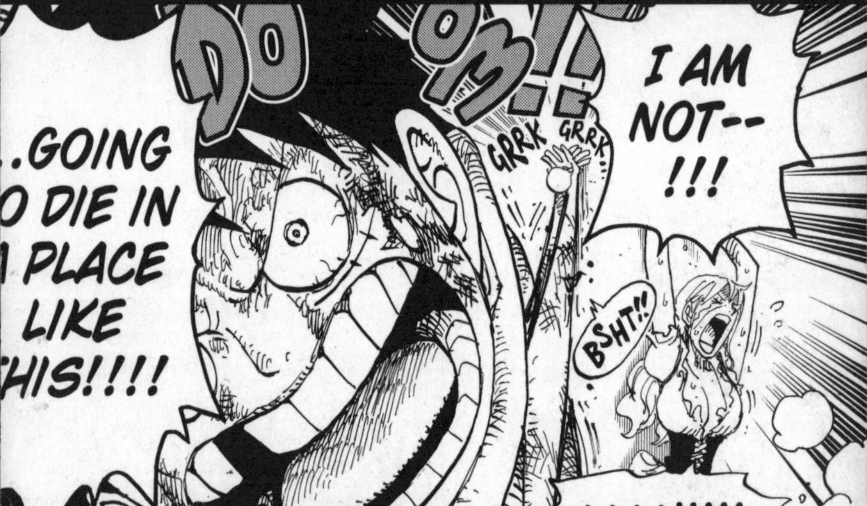

I AM NOT-- !!!
GRRK GRRK
DOOM!!
BSHT!!
AAAAH!!!
..GOING O DIE IN A PLACE LIKE THIS!!!!

With Luffy and Nami trapped in a book, Sanji's wedding is fast approaching. How will the Straw Hats stop it? And what is the dark secret that Pudding is hiding?

ON SALE FEBRUARY 2018!

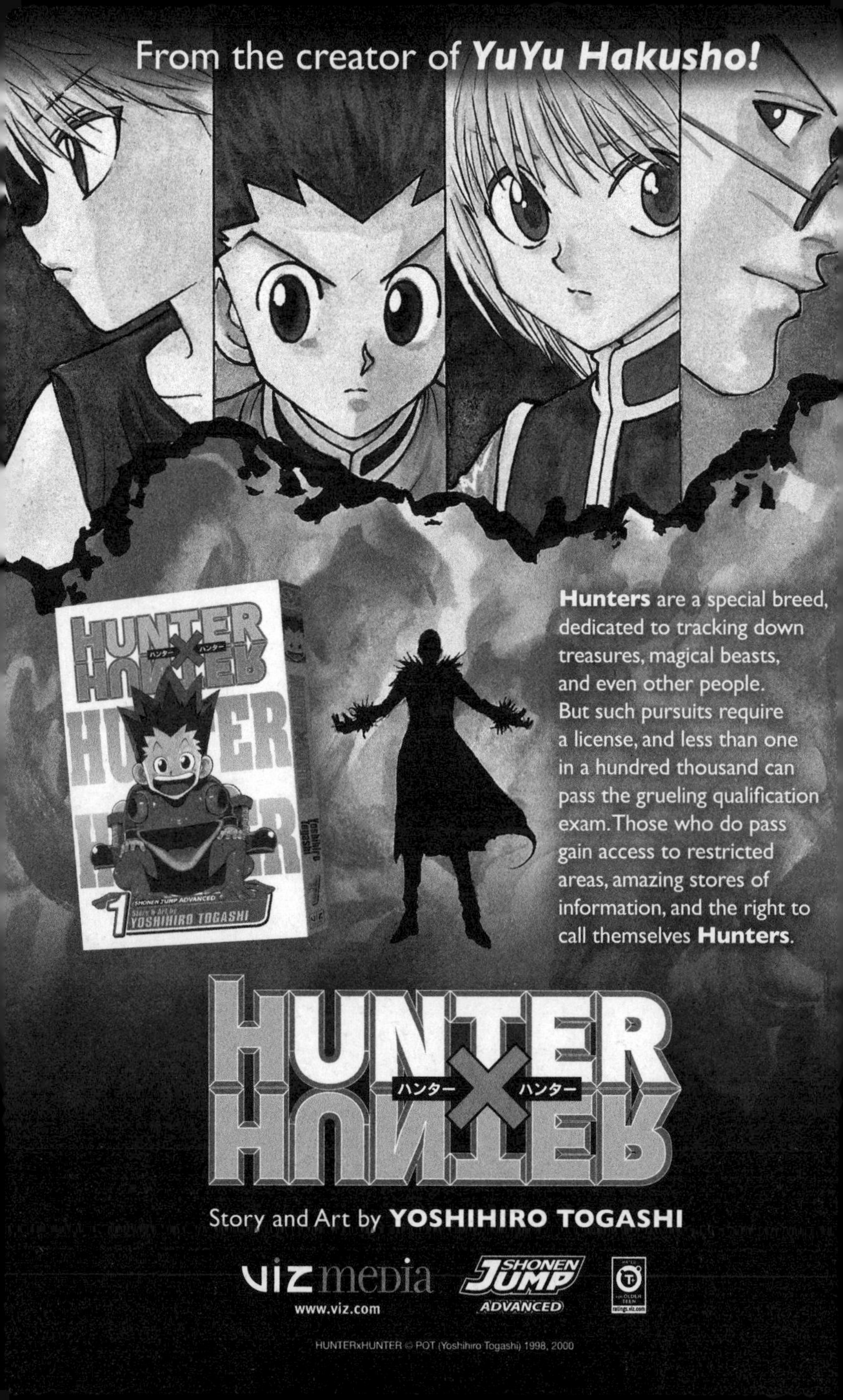
From the creator of *YuYu Hakusho!*
HUNTER × HUNTER
ハンター ハンター
SHONEN JUMP ADVANCED
Story & Art by YOSHIHIRO TOGASHI
Hunters are a special breed, dedicated to tracking down treasures, magical beasts, and even other people. But such pursuits require a license, and less than one in a hundred thousand can pass the grueling qualification exam. Those who do pass gain access to restricted areas, amazing stores of information, and the right to call themselves **Hunters**.
HUNTER × HUNTER
ハンター ハンター
Story and Art by **YOSHIHIRO TOGASHI**
VIZ media
www.viz.com
SHONEN JUMP ADVANCED
HUNTERxHUNTER © POT (Yoshihiro Togashi) 1998, 2000

Seraph of the End
VAMPIRE REIGN
1
STORY BY Takaya Kagami
ART BY Yamato Yamamoto
Daisuke Furuya

You're Reading in the Wrong Direction!!

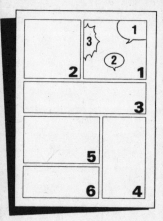

Whoops! Guess what? You're starting at the wrong end of the comic!

...It's true! In keeping with the original Japanese format, **One Piece** is meant to be read from right to left, starting in the upper-right corner.

Unlike English, which is read from left to right, Japanese is read from right to left, meaning that action, sound effects and word-balloon order are completely reversed...something which can make readers unfamiliar with Japanese feel pretty backwards themselves. For this reason, manga or Japanese comics published in the U.S. in English have sometimes been published "flopped"— that is, printed in exact reverse order, as though seen from the other side of a mirror.

By flopping pages, U.S. publishers can avoid confusing readers, but the compromise is not without its downside. For one thing, a character in a flopped manga series who once wore in the original Japanese version a T-shirt emblazoned with "M A Y" (as in "the merry month of") now wears one which reads "Y A M"! Additionally, many manga creators in Japan are themselves unhappy with the process, as some feel the mirror-imaging of their art skews their original intentions.

We are proud to bring you Eiichiro Oda's **One Piece** in the original unflopped format. For now, though, turn to the other side of the book and let the journey begin...!

—Editor